SANFORD GUIDE ®

The Sanford Guide To HIV/AIDS and Viral Hepatitis Therapy 2014

22nd Edition

THE SANFORD GUIDE TO HIV/AIDS AND VIRAL HEPATITIS THERAPY 2014
22ND EDITION

Editors

Michael S. Saag, M.D.
Director, UAB Center for AIDS Research,
Professor of Medicine
Jim Straley Chair in AIDS Research,
University of Alabama, Birmingham

Henry F. Chambers, M.D.
Professor of Medicine
Director, Clinical Research Services
UCSF Clinical and Translational Sciences Institute
University of California at San Francisco
San Francisco, California

George M. Eliopoulos, M.D.
Chief, James L. Tullis Firm,
Beth Israel Deaconess Hospital
Professor of Medicine
Harvard Medical School
Boston, Massachusetts

David N. Gilbert, M.D.
Chief of Infectious Diseases
Providence Portland Medical Center, Oregon

Contributing Editors

Andrew T. Pavia, M.D.
George and Esther Gross Presidential Professor
Chief, Division of Pediatric Infectious Diseases
University of Utah
Salt Lake City, Utah

Douglas Black, Pharm.D.
Associate Professor of Pharmacy
University of Washington
Seattle, Washington

David O. Freedman, M.D.
President, Gorgas Memorial Institute
of Tropical and Preventive Medicine
Professor of Medicine and Epidemiology,
University of Alabama, Birmingham

Brian S. Schwartz, M.D.
Assistant Professor of Medicine
University of California, San Francisco

Managing Editor
Jeb C. Sanford

Emeritus
Jay P. Sanford, M.D.
1928-1996

Merle A. Sande, M.D.
1935-2007

Publisher
Antimicrobial Therapy, Inc.

The Sanford Guides are published by

ANTIMICROBIAL THERAPY, INC.
P.O. Box 276, 11771 Lee Highway
Sperryville, VA 22740 USA
Tel 540-987-9480 Fax 540-987-9486
Email: info@sanfordguide.com   www.sanfordguide.com

Printed in the United States of America
ISBN 978-1-930808-81-2
Pocket Edition

The SANFORD GUIDE is available from a variety of sources. You may have purchased your copy at
a bookstore or directly from us. You may also have received your copy from a pharmaceutical
company representative. Regardless of the source, you can be assured that the SANFORD GUIDE
has been, and continues to be, independently prepared and published since its inception
in 1969. Decisions regarding the content of the SANFORD GUIDE are solely those of the editors
and the publisher. We welcome your questions, comments and feedback concerning the
SANFORD GUIDE. All of your feedback is reviewed and taken into account in preparing the next
edition. Digital editions content is updated monthly (Web Edition and Apps). Content-related
notices are posted at **www.sanfordguide.com**

Thanks to Ushuaia Solutions for its work on the manuscript design, to Alcom Printing
for printing and to Fox Bindery for finishing this edition.

IMPORTANT NOTE TO READER

— TABLE OF CONTENTS —

— LIST OF FIGURES —

— ABBREVIATIONS —

3TC = Lamivudine
ABC = abacavir
ABCC = ampho B cholesteryl complex
ABCD = ampho B colloidal dispersion
ABLC = ampho B lipid complex
ACIP = Advisory Committee on Immunization Practices
AD = after dialysis
ADC = AIDS dementia complex
ADV = adefovir
AFB = acid fast bacilli
AIDS = acquired immune deficiency syndrome
AM-CL = Amoxicillin-clavulanate
AM-SB = Ampicillin-sulbactam
AMK = amikacin
Ampho B = amphotericin B
Anidula = anidulafungin
AP = atovaquone proguanil
ART = antiretroviral therapy
ASA = aspirin
ATA = atazanavir
ATS = American Thoracic Society
AUC = area under curve
Azithro = azithromycin
bid = twice per day
BW = body weight
C&S = culture & sensitivity
CAPD = continuous ambulatory peritoneal dialysis
Caspo = caspofungin
CD4 = cluster differentiation antigen 4
CIP = ciprofloxacin
Cipro = Ciprofloxacin
Clinda = clindamycin
CLO = clofazamine
CMV = cytomegalovirus
Cobi = cobicistat
CQ = chloroquine phosphate
CrCl = creatinine clearance
CRF = circulating recombinant forms
CRRT = continuous renal replacement therapy
CSD = cat-scratch disease
CSF = cerebrospinal fluid
CXR = chest x-ray
d4T = stavudine
DAR = darunavir
DBPCT = double blind placebo-controlled trial
dc = discontinue
ddC = zalcitabine
ddI = didanosine
div = divided
DLV = delavirdine
DOT = directly observed therapy

DTG = dolutegravir
Doxy = doxycycline
DS = double strength
DSP = distal sensory symmetrical polyneuropathy
EBV = Epstein-Barr virus
EFV = efavirenz
EI = entry inhibitor
EIA = enzyme immunoassay
ELV = elvitegravir
ENF = enfuvirtide
ER = Extended release
Erythro = erythromycin
ESR = erythrocyte sedimentation rate
ETB = Ethambutol
ETR = etravirine
ETV = entecavir
FI = fusion inhibitor
Flu = fluconazole
Flucyt = flucytosine
FOS-APV = fosamprenavir
FQ = fluoroquinolone
FTC = emtricitabine
FUO = fever of unknown origin
G = generic
GC = gonorrhoea
Gent = gentamicin
gm = gram
HAD = HIV-associated dementia (HIV-D)
Hemo = hemodialysis
HHV = human herpes viruses
HIV = human immunodeficiency virus
HPV = human papilloma virus
HSV = herpes simplex virus
I = investigational
IA = injectable agent
IDP = inflammatory demyelinating polyneuropathy
IDSA = Infectious Diseases Society of America
IDV = indinavir
II = integrase inhibitor
IMP = Imipenem
INH = isoniazid
IP = intraperitoneal
IRIS = immune response inflammatory syndrome
IT = intrathecal
Itra = itraconazole
IVDU = intravenous drug user
IVIG = intravenous immune globulin
Keto = ketoconazole
KS = Kaposi's sarcoma
LAB = liposomal ampho B
LAM = lamivudine (3TC)

— ABBREVIATIONS (continued) —

LCM = lymphocytic choriomeningitis virus
LCR = ligase chain reaction
Levo = levofloxacin
LP/R = lopinavir/ritonavir
LPV = Lopinavir
M.TBc = mycobacterium tuberculosis
MAI = mycobacterium avium-intracellulare complex
mcg (or µg) = microgram
Metro = metronidazole
mg = milligram
Mica = micafungin
Mino = minocycline
mL = milliliter
Moxi = moxifloxacin
MQ = mefloquine
MVC = maraviroc
NAAT = nucleic acid amplification test
NB = name brand
NAI = not U.S. FDA approved indication
NFR = nelfinavir
NNRTI = non-nucleoside reverse transcriptase inhibitor
NRTI = nucleoside reverse transcriptase inhibitor
NSAIDs = non-steroidal anti-inflammatory drugs
NUS = not available in U.S.
NVP = nevirapine
Oflox = ofloxacin
OI = opportunistic infection
PJP = pneumocystis jiroveci pneumonia
PCR = polymerase chain reaction
Peg-INF = pegylated interferon
PEP = post-exposure prophylaxis
PI = protease inhibitor
PML = progressive multifocal leuko-encephalopathy
po = orally (by mouth)
Posa = posaconazole
PQ = primaquine
Pt = patient
Pyri = pyrimethamine
PZA = pyrazinamide
qam = in the morning
qpm = in the evening
qid = 4 times per day
qow = every other week
qhs = before sleep
QS = quinine sulfate
R = resistant
RAL = raltegravir
RFB = rifabutin
RFP = rifapentine
RIF = rifampin
RPV = rilpivirine
RTV = ritonavir
rx = treatment
S = potential synergy in combination with penicillin, ampicillin, vanco & teicoplanin
Sens = sensitive
SM = streptomycin
SQV = saquinavir
STD = sexually-transmitted disease
STII = Strand transfer integrase inhibitor
TBc = tuberculosis
TDF = tenofovir
TDM = therapeutic drug monitoring
tid = 3 times per day
TMP-SMX = trimethoprim sulfamethoxazole
TN = toxic neuropathy
Tobra = tobramycin
TPV = tipranavir
TST = tuberculin skin test
UTI = urinary tract infection

Vanco = vancomycin
VL = viral load
Vori = voriconazole
VZV = varicela zoster virus
WB = western blot
WHO = World Health Organization
XR = Extended release
ZDV = zidovudine

— JOURNALS AND OTHER REFERENCES —

AAC: Antimicrobial Agents & Chemotherapy
AIDS Res Hum Retrovir: AIDS Research & Human Retroviruses
AJG: American Journal of Gastroenterology
AJM: American Journal of Medicine
AJRCCM: American Journal of Respiratory Critical Care Medicine
AJTMH: American Journal of Tropical Medicine & Hygiene
AnIM: Annals of Internal Medicine
AnSurg: Annals of Surgery
ArDerm: Archives of Dermatology
Antivir Ther: Antiviral Therapy
ArIM: Archives of Internal Medicine
ARRD: American Review of Respiratory Disease
BMJ: British Medical Journal
Brit J Derm: British Journal of Dermatology
Can JID: Canadian Journal of Infectious Diseases
CCM: Critical Care Medicine
CDC: U.S. Centers for Disease Control
CID: Clinical Infectious Diseases
CROI: Conference on Retroviruses & Opportunistic Infections
DHHS: U.S. Dept of Health and Human Services
DMID: Diagnostic Microbiology and Infectious Disease
EID: Emerging Infectious Diseases
Gastro: Gastroenterology
Hpt: Hepatology
ICAAC: Interscience Conference on Antimicrobial Agents & Chemotherapy
ICHE: Infection Control and Hospital Epidemiology
IDC No Amer: Infectious Diseases Clinics of North America
JAIDS: Journal of Acquired Immune Deficiency Syndrome
J AIDS & HR: Journal of AIDS and Human Retrovirology
JCI: Journal of Clinical Investigation
J Clin Virol: Journal of Clinical Virology
J Hpt: Journal of Hepatology
J Med Micro: Journal of Medical Microbiology
J Ped: Journal of Pediatrics
JAC: Journal of Antimicrobial Chemotherapy
JAMA: Journal of the American Medical Association
JCM: Journal of Clinical Microbiology
JID: Journal of Infectious Diseases
JTMH: Journal of Tropical Medicine & Health
J Viral Hep: Journal of Viral Hepatitis
Ln: Lancet
Ln ID: Lancet Infectious Disease
Mayo Clin Proc: Mayo Clinic Proceedings
Med Lett: The Medical Letter
Med Myco: Medical Mycology
MMWR: Morbidity & Mortality Weekly Report
NEJM: New England Journal of Medicine
Peds: Pediatrics
PIDJ: Pediatric Infectious Diseases Journal
PLoS Med: PLoS Medicine Public Library of Medicine
QJM: Quarterly Journal of Medicine
Scand J Inf Dis: Scandinavian Journal of Infectious Diseases
SMJ: Southern Medical Journal

TABLE 1A: PROPHYLACTIC ANTIRETROVIRAL THERAPY REDUCES HIV TRANSMISSION RISK

Antiretroviral therapy (ART) prevents infection. Study compared rates of transmission among discordant heterosexual couples in Africa. HIV+ partners randomized to receive early ARV Rx (CD4 > 350 cells/ul) vs. Deferred ARV Rx (CD4 < 250 cells/ul). There were 27 transmissions in the deferred group (n=882) vs 1 in the immediate Rx group (n=880); a 96% reduction in transmission from early ARV Rx. First evidence of high level reduction in transmission from ARV Rx alone in a randomized trial (NEJM 365 (6): 493-505, 2011).

Antiretroviral therapy (ART) use and risk of HIV-1 transmission

	Follow-up during which HIV-1 infected partner had not initiated ART			Follow-up after HIV-1 infected partner initiated ART			Unadjusted Incidence rate ratio (95% CI; p value)*	Adjusted Incidence rate ratio (95% CI; p value)*
	Number of HIV-1 transmissions	Length of follow-up (person-years)	HIV-1 incidence per 100 person-years (95% CI)	Number of HIV-1 transmissions	Length of follow-up (person-years)	HIV-1 incidence per 100 person-years (95% CI)		
Overall	102	4558	2.24 (1.84-2.72)	1	273	0.37 (0.09-2.04)	0.17 (0.00-0.94; p=0.04)	0.08 (0.00-0.57; p=0.004)
By CD4 cell count†								
< 200 cells per µL	8	91	8.79 (4.40-17.58)	0	132	0.00 (0.00-2.80)	0.00 (0.00-0.40; p=0.002)	0.00 (0.00-0.38; p=0.001)
200-349 cells per µL	41	1467	2.79 (2.06-3.80)	1	90	1.11 (0.27-6.19)	0.40 (0.01-2.34; p=0.58)	0.65 (0.02-4.00; p=1.0)‡
350-499 cells per µL	24	1408	1.7 (1.14-2.54)	0	30	0.00 (0.00-12.30)	0.00 (0.00-8.16; p=1.0)	0.0 (0.0-15.3; p=1.0)‡
≥ 500 cells per µL	29	1592	1.82 (1.27-2.62)	0	21	0.00 (0.00-17.57)	0.00 (0.00-10.29; p=1.0)	0.0 (0.0-15.0; p=1.0)‡

* All analyses adjusted for time since study enrolment and, for the overall analysis, CD4 cell count (as ≥ 200 cells per µL vs < 200 cells per µL).

† For follow-up before ART initiation, CD4 cell count was lowest than previous value; for follow-up after ART initiation, CD4 cell count at the time of ART initiation was used.

‡ Adjusted incidence rate ratio for combined CD4 cell count strata of 200 cells per µL or more was 0.55 (95% CI 0.01-3.24; p=0.9).

Reference: Lancet. 2010 Jun 12;375:2092-8

TABLE 1B: ASSESSMENT OF HIV INFECTION RISKS & RECOMMENDATIONS FOR HIV TESTING

I. General

HIV risk assessment is an essential component of primary care for all patients. In talking to patients, avoid medical jargon (e.g., "intercourse"), vague terms ("sexually active"), group designations ("homosexual"), or judgmental terms ("promiscuous"). Learn the language & terminology understood & used by patients. Question responses to the depth necessary to elicit risky behavior & define extent of risk of acquisition & transmission. Eliciting risk is particularly difficult but equally important in resource-limited areas of the world, esp. when working through translators. It is essential that the clinician be knowledgeable about cultural sensitivities, customs & traditions relative to HIV risk behavior.

Risk-reduction counseling works to reduce high-risk behavior. (J Acquir Immune Defic Syndr 2005 Aug 1; 39:446-53; Ann Intern Med 2008 Oct 7; 149:497. U.S. Preventive Services Task Force.) It is time to include HIV counseling & testing as a critical component of health care maintenance [MMWR September 22, 2006 / 55(RR14); 1-17 http://www.cdc.gov/healthyyouth/sexualbehaviors/index.htm].

Poverty and HIV: Poverty accounts for a large portion of the observed racial and ethnic disparities in the prevalence of HIV in urban areas of the US. 2.8% of heterosexuals living in 23 urban areas with annual income < $10,000 are infected compared to 0.4% infected who earned more than $50,000/yr. 1.5% of those with income between $10,000 and $19,999 were infected with HIV while 1.2% of those earning $20,000 - $49,999 were infected. The overall (urban and non-urban) rate of infection nationally is 0.1% (MMWR 60 (31): 1045, 2011).

II. Specific Behaviors Associated With HIV Transmission

A. **Sexual Behaviors.** The CDC recommends ART post-exposure prophylaxis within 72 hrs after high risk sexual, injection-drug use, or other non-occupational exposure to HIV (MMWR Recom Rep 54:1, 2005) (See Table 7B). Not 100% effective: seroconversion still detected in 1% of 702 exposed individuals (CID 41:1507, 2005).

1. **High-Risk Sexual Partner(s)**
   - HIV-infected partners [especially those with ↑ HIV-RNA (NEJM 342:921, 2000, Sex Trans Dis 29:38, 2002)].
   - Partners who are at risk but have not been HIV tested or do not disclose their HIV status to their partners (MMWR 52:81, 2003).
   - Multiple partners: Unsafe sexual activity appears to be ↑ with MSM MMWR 53(38); 891-894, 2004; PLoS One 6(8): e17502, 2011.
   - Presence of mucosal ulceration or other STD in either partner (JID 178:1060, 1998).

2. **Sexual Practices**

   a. **High infection risk**
      - Unprotected anal receptive intercourse ("barebacking"): popular among gay males
      - Unprotected vaginal receptive intercourse

   b. **Infection risk documented**
      - Unprotected anal insertive intercourse
      - Unprotected vaginal insertive intercourse (risk may be higher during menses)
      - Unprotected oral receptive intercourse [HIV RNA levels in rectal secretions > serum with & without ART use (JID 190:156, 2004)]
      - Unprotected oral insertive intercourse rare (ArIM 159:303, 1999)

   c. **Lower infection risk**
      - Any of the above with latex/vinyl condom (vaginal or penile) protection. Male condoms are 80–95% effective in ↓ risk of HIV infection (AmFAR Issue Brief #1, Jan. 2005); female condoms 94–97% effective.
      - Cunnilingus, esp. with rubber dam, microwaveable plastic food wrap or other water-impervious barrier
      - Circumcision reduced HIV infection by 60% in a prospective randomized study (PLoS Med e298, 2005). Two other studies confirmed 50-60% reduction and were stopped early in 2007 (Ln 369:643, 657, 2007; PLoS Med 4 (7) e223, July 24, 2007).
      - Microbicides currently in development but data on effectiveness lacking (JID 193; 36, 2006). Nonoxynol-9 actually facilitated transmission (JAMA 287:1171, 2002).

   d. **Safer**
      - Deep kissing
      - Protected sex with HIV test negative partner
      - **Sex with HIV+ partner on successful ARV therapy (< 400 c/mL)** (The Lancet, Early Online Publication, 27 May 2010). See Table 1A, page 4.
      - Mutual monogamy
      - Mutual masturbation
      - Masturbation or massage

   e. **Safest**
      - Abstinence

Routes of Exposure and HIV

INFECTION ROUTE	RISK OF INFECTION
Sexual Transmission	
a. Female-to-male transmission	1 in 700 to 1 in 3,000
b. Male-to-female transmission	1 in 200 to 1 in 2,000
c. Male-to-male transmission	1 in 10 to 1 in 1,600
d. Fellatio??	0 (CDC) or 6% (SF)
Parenteral transmission	
a. Transfusion of infected blood	95 in 100
b. Needle sharing	1 in 150
c. Needle stick	1 in 300
d. Needle stick /AZT PEP	1 in 10,000
Transmission from mother to infant	
a. Without ARV treatment	1 in 4

Royce, Sena, Cates and Cohen, NEJM 336:1072-1078, 1997

TABLE 1B (2)

3. **Conditions That Facilitate HIV Sexual Transmission** *(J AIDS 30:73, 2002; JID 191:333, 2005)*

Male-to-Female Transmission | **Relative Risk Reported**

	Male-to-Female Transmission	Relative Risk Reported
(a)	Oral contraceptives	2.5–4.5
(b)	Gonococcal cervicitis	1.8–4.5
(c)	Candida vaginitis	3.3–3.6
(d)	Genital ulcers	2.0–4.0
(e)	Bacterial vaginosis	1.6 *(AIDS 22:1493, 2008)*
(f)	HSV-2	2.5
(g)	Vitamin A deficiency	2.6–12.9
(h)	CD4 count <200	6.1–17.6
(i)	Depomedroxyprogesterone acetate (DMPA) subdermal implant use as contraceptive	2.2 *(JID 178:1053, 1998)*
(j)	Sharing of HLA-B alleles in discordant couples	2.23 *(Ln 363:2137, 2004)*

Female-to-Male Transmission

(a)	Lack of circumcision	5.4–8.2 risk/coital act ↓ from 1/80 to 1/200 *(Ln 369:643, 2007; MMWR 53:523, 2004; AIDS 23:395, 2009)*
(b)	Genital ulcers	2.6–4.7
(c)	Sex during menses	3.4
(d)	Herpes simplex type 2 (genital herpes)	6–16.8 *(JID 187:1513, 2003 & 189:1209, 2004)*

↑ Titers of viral DNA in vaginal secretions *(JID 175:57, 1997)*

(a)	With low CD4 count	9.6 (<200 vs. >500)
(b)	Vitamin A deficiency	2.6
(c)	Presence of cervical mucopus	2.1
(d)	Acute primary HIV infection	↑↑ *(JID 189:1785, 2004; JID 198:687, 2008)*
(e)	With ↑ plasma HIV-RNA	↑ *(JID 177:1100, 1998)*
(f)	Cervicitis	↑ *(AIDS 15:105, 2001)*
(g)	Peak titer just prior to onset of menses	*(JID 189:2192, 2004)*

↑ Titers of viral DNA in semen (ejaculate) *(JID 172:1469, 1995; J AIDS & HR 18:277, 1998)*

(a)	Gonococcal urethritis	3.2
(b)	Acute primary HIV infection	↑↑ *(Curr Opin HIV AIDS. 5:277, 2010; PLoS One. 2011; 6(5): e19617)*

Not protective:

    (a) Nonoxynol-9 intravaginally *(Ln 360:971, 2002; AIDS 18:2191, 2004)*
    (b) IUD use

4. **Programs Aimed at Reducing Sexual Transmission**

The major route of HIV spread worldwide is via heterosexual vaginal intercourse. Efforts to change sexual behavior by reducing number of sexual partners & using safe sex techniques (condoms) have met with varying degrees of success. These are summarized here:

a. Voluntary counseling & testing (VCT): Prevention based on identifying infected persons & counseling them to prevent transmission to sexual partner(s) *(Am J Public Health. 96:114, 2006)*.

b. Counseling & controlling STD in female sex workers: ↓ seroincidence of HIV from 16.3 to 6.5/100 person yrs in 500 subjects in Cote d'Ivoire *(AIDS 15:1421, 2000)* & Benin *(AIDS 16:463, 2002; J AIDS 30:69, 2002)*, & U.S. *(JAMA 292:171, 2004)*

c. Condom distribution campaigns: Successfully ↓ HIV prevalence in Thailand from 17% in 1992 to 2% in 1999.

d. Prevention campaign focused on education about AIDS & promotion of safer sexual behavior *(J AIDS 25:77, 2000; JAMA 292:171, 2004)*.

e. Delivery of message complex. Examples of communication methods used:

    (1) Radio soap opera (Tanzania, *J Health Comm 5(Suppl.): 81, 2000*)
    (2) Combination of drama or video reached >85% in Uganda *(Health Educ Res 16:411, 2001)*
    (3) Traditional healers or theater in Sierra Leone *(J Assoc Nurs AIDS Care 12:48, 2001)*
    (4) Folk media in rural Ghana *(Am J Publ Health 91:1559, 2001)*
    (5) Religion has been shown to reduce protective behaviors toward AIDS & suggest a critical need to work with clergy to embrace the prevention message *(AIDS 14:2027, 2000)*

f. Circumcision programs for young men are being implemented widely across Africa and other countries with high incidence rates for HIV infection.

TABLE 1B (3)

g. Concern regarding increased transmission among older heterosexual adults (> 55 years old). Many older adults are sexually active *(NEJM 357: 762, 2007)*, and with increased use of erectile dysfunction drugs, higher rates of STDs, including HIV, expected.

h. **PREP (Pre-exposure Prophylaxis):** Use of ARV medication(s) in uninfected high-risk individuals. iPrEx Study showed a 44% reduction in transmission of HIV over one year among high-risk gay men randomized to receive Tenofovir-FTC daily compared to placebo recipients. For those randomized to receive TDF-FTC and who had detectable drug levels, the relative risk reduction was 92%. *(NEJM, 363, 2587, 2010.)* Using the overall rate of reduction, over 110 uninfected individuals would need to be treated to prevent one infection per year, at an estimated cost of > $1.8M / infection prevented / year. Cost effectiveness studies show, in selected very high risk populations of MSM, PrEP is borderline cost-effective (approx $60,000/QALY. *Ann Int Med 156: 541, 2012).*

B. **Injection (intravenous or "skin popping") Drug Use (IDU) or Smoking Crack Cocaine.** Assess injectable anabolic steroid use! Assess sexual behaviors in all drug users! In one study, infection rates in crack cocaine-smoking women are as high as in men who had sex with men (41% vs. 43%). Risk-reduction intervention can ↓ high risk sexual activity in crack cocaine users *(AIDS Edu Prev 15:15, 2003)* & IVDUs *(J AIDS 30:573, 2002).*
Drug Use Practices: (Drug abuse treatment & methadone use programs reduce HIV transmission: *AIDS 13:2151 & 1807, 1999)*

1. **Riskiest**
    *   Sharing uncleaned needles, syringes, other paraphernalia (works), especially in "shooting galleries." HIV DNA found on 85% of needles/syringes & 1/3–2/3 cottons, cookers, wash waters from shooting galleries.
    *   Practicing "registering," "booting," or "back loading"

2. **Less risky**
    *   Sharing cleaned needles, syringes, works. (Household bleach is effective, especially after washing & when contact time is greater than 5 minutes. It is important to rinse with water after bleach use)
    *   Drug paraphernalia used repeatedly but by single user

3. **Least risky**
    *   Single use needles, syringes, works (needle exchange programs reduce HIV transmission, *[see MMWR 54:673, 2005 for update of US programs])*
    *   Sterile needles, syringes, works (needle/syringe exchange appears effective & has not ↑drug use)

C. **Blood Product Infusion Recipient**
Blood Product Risks:

1. **Riskiest**
    *   Receipt of multiple units of blood products between **1978** and **1985**
    *   Receipt of blood products obtained from donors in countries where screening is unreliable or not done

2. **Less risky**
    *   Receipt of heterologous blood products in U.S. after 1985 (risk per unit 1:450,000 to 1:660,000 units or 1:28,000 after an average of 5.4 units). [This is because of a window (about 20 days) between infection & seroconversion (18–27 donations/yr are in this window). With widespread use of nucleic acid testing (NAT) procedures, transmission via blood transfusion in the US has been reduced to < 1: 2.2 Million transfusions *(MMWR 59:1335-39, 2010)*]. RhoGAM & hepatitis B vaccine (serum-derived) have never been reported to transmit HIV-1.
    *   Receipt of donor-selected blood products in U.S. after 1985 (but no safer than random donors)

3. **Safest**
    *   Receipt of autologous blood products
    *   Receipt of genetically engineered blood product substitutes

D. **Transplant Recipients:** Report of transmission of HIV from HIV infected donor to recipient via kidney transplant *(MMWR: 60: 297-301, 2011).*

E. **Perinatal Infection:** See Table 8B

F. **Occupational Exposure** *(See Table 7C) (CDC Guidelines, CDC Guidelines published: Inf Control Hosp Epi 34:875, 2013*
Relative Risk Determinants

1. Riskiest [risk may be decreased by glove use, which removes >50% blood from exposure site in some studies but HIV-size microbes can pass through 1/3 of latex gloves tested *(J All Clin Imm 97:575, 1996)*. With double-glove use, blood-hand contacts ↓ from 71 to 32/100 procedures.
    *   Deep parenteral inoculation (RR 16.8) via hollow needle of blood from source with high-titer viremia; seroconversion or advanced HIV disease (RR 7.8)
    *   Parenteral inoculation of materials containing high titer virus in research laboratory setting
    *   Failure to use ART after inoculation (RR 0.1 when used)

TABLE 1B (4)

2. **Less risky**
   - Small volume exposure via non-hollow needle
   - Mucosal exposure/non-intact skin exposure [risk is too low to be quantified in prospective studies; not zero but estimated to be at least a log (90%) lower than needlestick risk. Risk may be increased if large volume or prolonged contact occurs]

3. **Risk not identified**
   - **Cutaneous contact** (intact skin)
   - Exposure to urine, saliva, sweat, tears

G. **Donor Organ or Tissue Transplantation**
   1. Test potential donors for HIV (note window between infection & seroconversion *(C.2 above)*)
   2. Assess donors for risk factors
   3. Evaluate risk/benefits
      - Risk following artificial insemination with semen from HIV+ donor is 3.5% *(Ln 351: 728, 1998)*. HIV testing recommended but not legally required

III. Recommendations for HIV Testing

A. In Sept 2006, the CDC issued guidelines calling for routine universal testing of all Americans between ages 13 & 64 yrs (many experts suggest testing ALL sexually active persons regardless of age). Previously the recommendations had been to test people at risk *(see below)*, however, studies indicated that over 50% of new dx of HIV infection occurred within one yr of a dx of full blown AIDS and the incidence of new cases in the US has recently been estimated upward, now anticipating ~ 60,000 new cases per year (up from 40,000/yr). Universal HIV testing and linkage to care is a cornerstone of the US National AIDS Policy *(released July, 2010)*.

The CDC suggested that signed consent for HIV testing be eliminated and included in the general consent for medical care. [Pre-test counseling was not recommended unless pts were from high-risk groups.] Pts should be told verbally that they will be tested as part of their medical care and given the opportunity to opt out of testing. This discussion should include an explanation about HIV infection, how it is transmitted, and implications about a positive test. If pt declines, it should be recorded on his/her chart.

The implications of a positive test [screening & confirmatory *(See Table 2)*] can be profound and have the potential for physical & psychological harm, particularly for women. Counseling & referral services for partner notification should be made available.

While the new recommendations indicate a change in direction, they may conflict with established state laws. Clinicians need to be aware of local regulations regarding consent and counseling. See http://www.hret.org & Ln 369:243, 2007.

B. **Post-Test Counseling:**

Rapid HIV antibody tests, which can provide results within 20 minutes has improved the efficiency of point of care testing. However, a confirmatory test such as Western Blot is still required. It is critically important to offer counseling to those who test positive. Issues to be discussed should include:

1. Emphasize that HIV infection can now be can be managed successfully as a complicated disease like diabetes
2. Stigma & the fear of disclosure HIV status
3. Need to inform previous/current sexual partner
4. Testing of children & partners at potential risk
5. Strict adherence to safe-sex practices (especially consistent use of condoms)
6. Avoidance of drugs that may cause disinhibition (amphetamines, etc)

FIGURE 1   Natural History of HIV

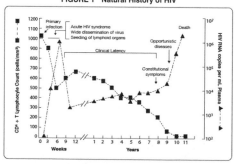

TABLE 2: INITIAL EVALUATION OF HIV-INFECTED ADULT PATIENT
(See CID 49:651, 2009; MMWR 58 (RR-4):1-207, 2009)

I. **Insist on documentation of a positive HIV antibody test: confirm with a 2nd antibody test, a Western blot, or positive plasma viral HIV RNA PCR quantitation**

II. **History, Review of Systems, & Past Medical History**
   A. **General health status**
      1. General well-being; constitutional symptoms
      2. Infectious diseases (TB, leishmaniasis, cocci, histo, etc.): childhood infections, infections in adult life, previous physician visits, hospitalizations (where, when)
      3. Immunization history, e.g., hepatitis A, B, BCG, pneumococcal
   B. **Drug history**
      1. Medications & dosages
         a. Prescription; non-prescription
         b. Alternative therapies
      2. "Recreational" drug use *(see Table 1B, above)*
         a. Intravenous/injection; crack cocaine
         b. Other
         c. Identify partners at risk
      3. Smoking & alcohol history
   C. **Sexual history**
      1. Sexual practices *(see Table 1B, page 5)*
      2. Past sexually transmitted diseases
      3. Obstetric/gynecologic history
      4. Contraceptive use
      5. Identify partners at risk
   D. **Past or present HIV-related illness, e.g., candidiasis**
   E. **Risks for opportunistic infections**
      1. Travel history
      2. Geographic location of current/prior residence, e.g., Southwest, Midwest of USA
      3. Occupational history, e.g., poultry worker
      4. Avocational activities
      5. Tuberculosis status: history of BCG vaccination, family members with &/or treated for tuberculosis, contacts (close) with patients with known tuberculosis, results of previous tuberculin tests &/or chest x-rays
      6. Pets, e.g., cats—Bartonella henselae; fish— M. marinum. Cat ownership not associated with toxoplasma antibody seroconversion
   F. **Past history of viral hepatitis, to include type if known, past history of herpes zoster**

III. **Comprehensive Physical Examination**
   A. Document weight & height
   B. Careful funduscopic & oral examination
   C. Complete dermatologic examination
   D. Exam of all lymph node areas: postoccipital, preauricular, cervical, submental, supraclavicular, axillary, epitrochlear, inguinal (measure & record size if palpable, record as negative if not palpable)
   E. Rectal/genital examination, to include pelvic exam with Pap smear in women, inspection for perianal/genital Herpes simplex. Repeat Pap smears every 12 months.
   F. Assess mental status for evidence of dementia.

IV. **Laboratory Evaluation**
   A. **Baseline**
      1. Complete blood cell count with differential
      2. Electrolytes, blood sugar, BUN, creatinine
      3. Liver enzyme tests: serum bilirubin, aspartate aminotransferase (AST, SGOT), alanine aminotransferase (ALT, SGPT), alkaline phosphatase (indinavir & atazanavir can elevate indirect bilirubin levels)
      4. Creatine kinase
      5. Fasting lipid profile
   B. **HIV staging** (Important for all future care decisions including when to initiate ART & prophylaxis)
      1. CD4 & CD8 T-lymphocyte count every 3-6 mos
      2. Quantitative measurement of plasma HIV RNA *(10)*—"viral load" or plasma "viral burden"
      3. Repeat every 3-6 months.
      4. Genotypic resistance testing
   C. **Additional studies**
      1. **PPD intermediate** (5TU), or blood assay for M. tbc infection (QuantiFERON-TB GOLD),
      2. Chest x-ray (baseline important for future care)
      3. VDRL or RPR (tests for syphilis); repeat annually.
      4. IgG antibody to toxoplasmosis (if + primary prophylaxis indicated when CD4<100
      5. Hepatitis B surface antigen (HBsAg), antibody to Hep B surface Ag (anti-HBsAg), antibody to Hep C; IgG antibody to Hepatitis A.
      6. CMV antibody, IgG
      7. G6PD Assay (African-Americans).
      8. Urine nucleic acid amplification test for C. trachomatis & N. gonorrhea.
      9. Type-specific Herpes simplex antibody.
      10. Perhaps serum testosterone level.
      11. Vitamin D serum level.

V. **Initial Health Care Maintenance**
   A. HIV risk reduction education *(see Table 1B)*
   B. Drug rehabilitation/safer needle use/needle exchange
   C. Smoking cessation
   D. Partner notification
   E. Reproductive counseling
   F. Psychosocial support
   G. Immunizations *(see Table 20)*. Immunizations transiently ↑ HIV viral load, clinical significance uncertain
      1. Pneumococcal vaccine (booster every 5 yrs)
      2. Influenza vaccine (annually)
      3. Hepatitis B vaccine, if sexually active or sharing needles; hepatitis A vaccine
   H. Preventive dentistry
   I. If CD4 count <100 cells/mm³, baseline ophthalmologic evaluation
   J. Cervical Pap smear females; anal Pap smear males

VI. **Primary Care of Patients Infected With HIV**
   Multiple studies demonstrate that patients cared for by physicians & other health care givers who care for large numbers of HIV-infected persons & who make delivery of this care a major focus of their practice have better outcomes. A team approach with integration of acute & long-term care is the most effective management.

TABLE 3A: LABORATORY DIAGNOSIS OF HIV INFECTION—ANTIBODY TESTS, WESTERN BLOT CONFIRMATION & HIV RNA QUANTITATION

See Figure 2 (page 13): Temporal relationships of circulating HIV RNA

I. **HIV enzyme immunoassay (EIA) Antibody Tests: Detectable within 6-8 wks of exposure**
   A. **Sensitivity/specificity:**
      - HIV-1: both 99.9%; detects all HIV-1 non-B subtypes.
      - HIV-2: variable; suspect if from West Africa; *see section VII, this Table.*
   B. **Confirmation of positive test results:**
      - Western Blot (identifies specific HIV proteins) and/or
      - HIV RNA quantitation by real-time polymerase chain reaction (RT-PCR)
   C. **False Positive EIA** antibody—**rare**—and due to:
      - Recent immunization (influenza, rabies, Hep B)
      - Autoimmune diseases: e.g., SLE
      - Pregnancy; infants with passive maternal antibody from HIV+ mother
      - Multiple myeloma
      - End-stage renal disease
      - DNA viral infection
      - Primary biliary cirrhosis
      - Alcoholic hepatitis
      - Malaria
      - Dengue
   D. **False Negative EIA** antibody can result from:
      - Window between infection and antibody response (3-6 wks)
      - Agammaglobulinemia
      - Immunosuppression from malignancy or medication
      - Infection by HIV genetic variants, e.g., HIV-2 or HIV-1 genetic forms other than main (M) group
      - For diagnosis of HIV-2, see section VII.B., below.
   E. **Classification of genetic forms of HIV-1**
      1. Three phylogenetic groups:
         - M = main/major: includes 10 subtypes (clades): A-J
            o Subtype B most common subtype in U.S & Europe; U.S.: only 2% are non-B subtypes
            o But, increasing prevalence of diverse non-B subtypes & recombinants in U.S.
         - O = outlier—Cameroon, Gabon, Equatorial Guinea
         - N, P = novel, non-M & non-O. Rare. Central Africa
      2. Circulating recombinant forms (CRF):
         - Definition: Intersubtype recombinant viruses that are identified in 3 or more epidemiologically unlinked people with full-length genome sequencing.
         - CRFs identified by a number (in order of discovery) followed by letters to identify parental subtypes. Complex recombinant from 3+ subtypes (abbreviated as CPX).
         - Examples of CRF identifiers: CRF01_AE, CRF06_CPX, CRF_14_BG.
      3. **Geographic distribution of HIV genetic forms:**
         - Constantly changing and expanding in number as of 03/12, 51 HIV-1 CRFs and 1 HIV-2 CRF.
         - For current details: *http://www.hiv.lanl.gov/content/sequence/HIV/CRFs/CRFs.html*

II. **Confirmation of positive EIA by Western Blot**
   A. **Western Blot:** agar gel electrophoresis of HIV proteins.
   B. **Positive** confirmation test for HIV-1 requires presence of bands to gp120/160 + either gp41 or p24 (as per CDC).
   C. **Negative** confirmation: No bands.
   D. **Indeterminate**: positive EIA antibody and single Western blot antibody (incidence is 1:5000).
      - Proceed to plasma HIV RNA quantitation
      - Causes of indeterminate Western Blot:
         I = infection (HIV-2, HTLV-1, schistosomiasis)
         N = neoplasms
         D = dialysis
         E = ethnicity—African
         T = thyroiditis
         E = elevated bilirubin
         R = rheumatologic diseases
         M = multiple pregnancies
         I = immunization
         N = nephrotic massive proteinuria
         E = error in lab testing

III. **Rapid HIV antibody screening tests**—results available within 30 minutes. See *CID 52:257, 2011* and *http://www.cdc.gov/hiv/topics/testing/rapid/index.htm* (for approved tests).
   - **Need confirmation of positive results with EIA & Western Blot.**
   - Clinical uses: a) Patient in labor, no prenatal HIV test; b) patient who is source of needlestick injury to health care worker; c) evaluation of acutely ill patient with possible PJP; d) patients who are unlikely to return for test results.

TABLE 3A (2)

Summary of FDA-Approved Rapid HIV Antibody Screening Tests

Test Name (Maker)	Specimen Type	CLIA* Category	Sensitivity (95% CI)	Specificity** (95% CI)	HIV-2 Detection
Oraquick Advance Rapid HIV-1/2 Antibody Test (Orasure Technologies, Inc) *www.orasure.com*	Oral fluid**	Waived	99.3% (98-100)	99.8% (99.6-99.9)	Yes
	Whole blood	Waived	99.6% (98.5-99.9)	100% (99.7-100)	
	Plasma	Moderate complexity	99.6% (98.9-99.8)	99.9% (99.6-99.9)	
Uni-Gold Recombigen HIV 1 (Trinity Biotech) *www.unigoldhiv.com*	Whole blood	Waived	100% (99.5-100)	99.7% (99-100)	No
	Serum or plasma	Moderate complexity	100% (99.5-100)	99.8% (99.3-100)	
Reveal G-3 Rapid HIV-1 Antibody Test (Med Mira, Inc) *www.medmira.com*	Serum or plasma	Moderate complexity	99.8% (99.7-100)	99.1% (98.8-99.4)	No
	Plasma or serum	Moderate complexity	99.8% (99-100)	99.9% (98.6-100)	
Multispot HIV-1/HIV-2 Rapid Test (Bio-Rad Laboratories)	Plasma or serum	Moderate complexity	100% (99.9-100)	99.9% (99.8-100)	Yes
Clearview HIV-1/2 Stat-Pak (Chembo Diagnostic Systems)	Whole blood	Waived	99.7% (98.9-100)	99.9% (98.6-100)	Yes
Vitros	Serum	Moderate complexity			Yes

* Clinical Laboratory Improvement Amendments (CLIA)
** Note: False positives reported on oral fluids *(MMWR 57:660, 2008)* and also when test kit close to expiration date.

IV. **Combined Antigen Antibody Tests**
   A. Detect both HIV antibody and HIV p24 antigen.
- Positive test is qualitative
- Does not distinguish between antigen positive & antibody positive.

   B. Abbott Labs Test (Architect HIV Ag/Ab Combo)
- **Detects HIV-1 and HIV-2 antibody** in adults and children age ≥ 2 yrs.
- Approved for pediatric use and in pregnancy
- Can use serum or plasma

   C. Alere Determine
- Detects HIV-1 & HIV-2 antibody
- Detects HIV-1 p24 antigen
- Can use serum, plasma, whole blood
- Sensitivity 100%, Specificity 99.2% (antibody) 99.7% (antigen)
- Results in 20 minutes

   D. Bio-Rad GS HIV Combo Ag/Ab Assay
- Detects HIV-1 & HIV-2 antibody
- Detects HIV-1 p24 antigen
- Sensitivity 100%, Specificity 99.9% for both antigen & antibody

V. **Home Antibody Tests**
   A   Available in pharmacies, online at *www.homeaccess.com* or by phone: 800-448-8378
   B.   Drop of blood on filter paper, mail to lab, tested by EIA (cost approx $44).
   C.   Sensitivity/specificity near 100% confirms positive result with Western Blot.
   D.   Second In-Home Test uses saliva. CLIA-waived. 92% sensitive and 98% specific. Wait 3 months after exposure to test.

VI. **Detection and quantitation ("viral load") of HIV-1 RNA**
   A.   HIV-1 RNA quantitation useful as:
- Predictor of rate of progression to AIDS;
- Benchmark for initiating ART;
- Monitoring response to ART;
- Establishing diagnosis of primary HIV infection.
- But not useful in quantitation of HIV-2

   B.   Not approved as a diagnostic test (use serology & Western Blot). Primary HIV *(see below)* is an exception.
   C.   Five FDA-approved assays to quantify HIV RNA copies/mL of plasma. Two are newer real-time HIV-1 RNA PCR (RT-PCR) assays which are less prone to contamination and more sensitive.
   D.   All use plasma (not serum) and are >98% sensitive. Separate plasma within 6 hrs; store at -20° C if not assayed promptly.
   E.   Important to use same assay when following HIV RNA levels over time; if assay method changes, must establish a new baseline.

TABLE 3A (3)

Summary of HIV RNA Detection & Quantitation Assay Tests				
Name (Maker)	**Method**	**Preferred Anticoagulant**	**HIV Subtype Detection**	**Range (RNA copies/mL)**
Versant HIV-1 RNA 3.0 (Bayer Diagnostics)	Branched DNA (bDNA)	EDTA	Group M (A-G)	75-500,000
NucliSens HIV RNA QT (bioMerieux)	Nucleic acid sequence based amplification (NASBA)	EDTA/ACD	Group M (may miss subtype G)	176-3,400,000
COBAS® AmpliPrep/ COBAS® TaqMan® HIV-1, v 2.0 (Roche Diagnostics)	RT-PCR	EDTA	Group M (A-M)	20-10,000,000
COBAS® TaqMan® HIV-1 Test v2.0 (For use with High Pure System) (Roche Diagnostics)	Manual extraction combined with PCR	EDTA	Group M (A-M)	34-10,000,000
RealTime HIV-1 (Abbott Molecular)	RT-PCR	EDTA	Groups M (all), N, O & recombinants	40-10,000,000

E. **Interpretation of Results**. Need change of ≥50% (3-fold or 0.5 log₁₀ copies/mL) to be significant.

1. **Guide to logarithmic changes** (for a person **starting with HIV RNA of 100,000 copies/mL**):

Log_{10} copies/mL	n-Fold Change	HIV RNA Copies Remaining
-0.3	2-fold	50,000
-0.5	3-fold	33,000
-1.0	10-fold	10,000
-1.5	30-fold	3,300
-2.0	100-fold	1,000

2. **Factors that increase viral load**:
   - Progressive uncontrolled HIV infection due to non-adherence with ART or ineffective regimen;
   - Active non-HIV infection, e.g., tuberculosis (5-160 fold ↑), pneumococcal pneumonia (3-5 fold ↑) and other acute illnesses;
   - Immunization, e.g., influenza, pneumococcal (return to baseline in 1-2 months).

3. **Falsely low viral loads**:
   - Non-B subtype of HIV-1 not detected by assay used;
   - HIV-2 infection.

VII. **Diagnosis in special populations**.

A. **Neonates and children**. See Table 8B, Table 8C.

B. **Diagnosis of HIV-2** (CID 52:780, 2011; MMWR 60:985, 2011)
   - No longer confined to West Africa. Dual infection with HIV-1 can occur.
   - Some, but not all, EIA antibody test kits have HIV-2 antigens; one FDA-approved HIV-2 EIA test has been used to screen blood donors since 1992.
   - HIV-1 Western Blot is usually weakly reactive in HIV-2 patients & produces indeterminate results.
   - Qualitative HIV-2 antibody testing available from Focus & Quest Laboratories.
   - Antibody tests:
     o Can screen with Bio-Rad multispot rapid test.
     o Need to confirm with Western Blot and/or RT-PCR specific for HIV-2 virus.
     o Western Blot has unusual indeterminate test band pattern: i.e., positive for gag (p55, p24, p17) + positive for POL (p66, p51, p32) and absence of env (gp160, gp120).
     o Qualitative HIV-2 RNA (viral load) testing available from Univ of Washington, Seattle: 1-800-713-5198 or commserv@u.washington.edu

C. **Diagnosis of primary HIV infection**. See Figure 5, page 24.
   - Patients with "mono-like" syndrome but HIV antibody negative.
   - Screen with rapid point of combination antigen/antibody test. If positive, test specifically for HIV-1 and HIV-2 antibody.
   - If antibody tests negative or indeterminate, do quantitative RNA PCR to diagnose primary HIV infection.

TABLE 3B: CD4/CD8 T-LYMPHOCYTE COUNTS IN HIV PATIENTS

I. **Introduction and Definitions**
   A. **T-lymphocytes of 2 types:**
   - 1) Helper T-lymphocytes—**CD4 cells;** 2) Cytotoxic T-lymphocytes—**CD8 cells.**
   - Unique surface antigens (cluster determinants) detected by flow cytometry.
   - HIV infects and destroys CD4 cells; CD8 cells cytotoxic for infected CD4 cells.
   B. **Clinical Use of CD4 counts in HIV patients:**
   - Marker of the stage of HIV infection
   - Assess risk for opportunistic infections
   - Benchmark for diagnosis of AIDS (<200 cells/mm³)
   - Benchmark for initiating antiretroviral therapy (ART)
   - Benchmark for instituting prophylaxis for opportunistic infections (OIs)
   - Indicator of response to antiretroviral therapy (ART); repeat every 6-12 months
   C. **CD4 count by flow cytometry:** perform within 18 hrs of cell collection*.

Method	Absolute CD4 Count (cells/mm³)*	Some Prefer % CD4 Cells*	Factors That Can ↑ or ↓ Absolute CD4 Count	Factors That Can Decrease CD4 Counts
Fluoresceniated CD4 antibody added; % CD4 cells counted. Total CD4 count = WBC x % lymphocytes x % CD4 cells	Mean: 800-1050	≥29% = absolute CD4 count >500	• Variability in test procedure: ↑/↓	• Acute infection other than HIV
	2SD: 500-1400	14-28% = absolute CD4 count of 200-500	• Time of day: ↑/↓	• Acute corticosteroids
	≤200 defined as AIDS	<14% = absolute CD4 count <200	• Season of year: ↑/↓	• Progression of HIV
	Note: cirrhotics have low absolute CD4 counts but normal % CD4 cells (CID 54:1798 & 1806, 2012).		• HTLV-1: ↑ • Splenectomy: ↑ • Alpha interferon: ↓	• Idiopathic CD4 lymphocytopenia

* *Significant change (2 SD) between 2 tests: 30% change in absolute count or 3% change in % CD4 cells.*

   D. **Course of CD4 counts (cells/mm³) in gay men:**
   - Mean count prior to seroconversion: 1000/mm³ (mean value)
   - One year after seroconversion: 670/mm³
   - Thereafter, average annual decline: 50/mm³/yr
   - Large variation between patients.
   E. **Discordant virologic (viral load) & immunologic responses (CD4 count) to ART:**

CD4 Count	Viral Load	Possible Explanations
Increases**	Decreases	Expected response if ART is effective.
Fails to ↑ or decreases (JID 199:1648, 2009; JID 204:1217, 2011)	Decreases	CD4 count failure to increase encountered most often in pts with lowest CD4 counts at time of starting ART. One theory: inadequate number of naïve T-cells. Role of different classes of antiretrovirals is controversial. CID 48:328, 350, 362, 370, 787, 795, 2009.
Increases	Remains high	Drug-induced defective virus with reduced replicative capacity (JID 191:1670, 2005; Pediatrics 114:e604, 2004).
Fails to increase	Increases	Non-adherence to ART or drug-resistant HIV.

** *Adequate response = increase of 50-150 cells/mm³/yr.*

   F. **Persistent elevation of CD8 counts during ART forecast treatment failure (JAIDS 57:396, 2011).**

FIGURE 2   Temporal Relationships of Circulating HIV RNA

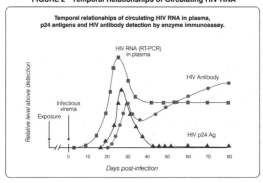

Temporal relationships of circulating HIV RNA in plasma, p24 antigens and HIV antibody detection by enzyme immunoassay.

TABLE 3C: ANTIRETROVIRAL DRUG RESISTANCE TESTING IN HIV INFECTION

I. **Genotype and Phenotype Resistance Testing Overview**
   (See DHHS Panel Recommendations March 2012; http://www.adisinfo.nih.gov; IAS-USA Resistance Guidelines CID 47:266-85, 2008)
   - **Genotypic testing is the preferred resistance testing method to guide therapy in treatment-naïve patients:**
     - Look for mutations in the reverse transcriptase and protease genes. If considering treatment with integrase inhibitor, look for integrase gene mutations.
     - Acute HIV infection: at time of diagnosis
     - Chronic HIV:
       - At time of initial evaluation; if ART is delayed, repeat testing prior to initiation of ART.
       - Patients who fail ART if HIV RNA > 1000 copies/mL.
       - Pregnancy (HIV+): test prior to initiating ART or when HIV RNA > 1000 copies/mL.
   - **Genotypic resistance testing is NOT recommended:**
     - If > 4 weeks after stopping ART.
     - Patients with HIV RNA < 500 copies/mL.
   - **Phenotypic resistance testing is recommended:**
     - In addition to genotypic testing if complex drug resistance mutation patterns are present, especially if genotypic resistance to protease inhibitors
   - **For resistance testing for integrase inhibitors and CCR5 antagonists,** see section III.F. of this Table.

II. **Genotypic vs. phenotypic resistance testing, in general:**

	Genotype Resistance Testing	Phenotype Resistance Testing
Identifies Specific Mutation:	Yes	No
Results Available:	1-2 weeks	2-3 weeks
Cost:	$300-500	$800-1500
Suggested Use:	Either pre-ART or to analyze failure on initial ART regimen	Known/complex resistance mutation patterns

III. **Genotype Resistance Testing**

A.

Anti-HIV Drug (by class)	Mechanism of Action	Mechanism of Resistance
Nucleoside Reverse Transcriptase Inhibitors (NRTIs):		
Abacavir Didanosine Emtricitabine/lamivudine Stavudine Zidovudine	• Analogues of nucleosides; • Active when triphosphorylated; • Incorporated into new viral DNA; • Prematurely terminate synthesis of HIV DNA	• Thymidine analogue (stavudine & zidovudine) mutations promote ATP- & pyrophosphate-mediated **excision** of incorporated chain terminator. • Other mutations **impair incorporation** of nucleoside analogues into new HIV DNA.
Nucleotide Reverse Transcriptase Inhibitor (Nucleotide RTI):		
Tenofovir	• Same as nucleosides	• Specific mutation impairs incorporation into HIV DNA
Non-nucleoside Reverse-transcriptase Inhibitors (NNRTIs):		
Delavirdine Efavirenz Etravirine (ETR) Nevirapine Rilpivirine (RPV)	• Binds to hydrophobic pocket of HIV, type 1 reverse transcriptase • HIV, type 2 resistant (ETR active vs. HIV-2) • Blocks polymerization of viral DNA	• Mutations decrease affinity for the enzyme; • Single mutation can lead to high-level resistance (except ETR and RPL— usually >1 mutation).
Protease Inhibitors (PIs):		
Atazanavir Darunavir Fosamprenavir Indinavir Lopinavir Nelfinavir Ritonavir Saquinavir Tipranavir	• Binds to, and interferes with, the active site of the protease	• Mutations reduce affinity of inhibitors for the protease; • High level resistance usually requires multiple mutations
Fusion Inhibitor:		
Enfuvirtide	• Interferes with glycoprotein 41-dependent membrane fusion	• Mutations in a portion of glycoprotein 41
CCR5 Inhibitor:		
Maraviroc	• Binds to and interferes with the attachment of HIV to CCR5 co receptor on CD4+ T-lymphocyte	• Unmasking of low-level Pre-existent population of dual-mixed trophic virus; • Mutations in V3 loop of gp120 not fully characterized yet
Integrase Inhibitor:		
Raltegravir Elvitegravir	• Interferes with integration of HIV into host genome at strand transfer step	• Unknown; likely a change in ability of enzyme to function

TABLE 3C (2)

B. **Low Frequency HIV Drug-Resistance Mutations** *(JAMA 305:1327, 2011)*
   - Standard PCR sequencing fails to detect low frequency drug resistance mutations.
   - With ultra-sensitive methods, low frequency resistance mutations in approximately 10% of patients with increased risk of treatment failure (Hazard Ratio 2.3)–especially to NNRTIs (Hazard Ratio 2.6).

C. **What do you need to know to interpret/understand HIV genotype results?**
   1. **For NRTIs:** need to know which drugs are analogs of the same nucleoside. Resistance to one thymidine analog forecasts resistance to all thymidine analogs as exemplified by the thymidine analog mutation (TAM) resistance pattern.

Drug:	Analog Of:
Abacavir	Guanosine
Didanosine	Deoxyadenosine
Emtricitabine	Cytidine
Lamivudine	Cytidine
Stavudine	Thymidine
Tenofovir	Adenosine
Zalcitabine	Cytidine
Zidovudine	Thymidine

   2. **How Are Resistance Mutations Reported?**
      - Gene (or codon) number is given plus the identified amino acid change.
      - Codon number is preceded by letter code indicating the amino acid encoded in wild-type virus.
      - M46I = codon (gene 41), isoleucine has replaced methionine.
      - Amino acid codes:

Code Letter	Amino Acid	Code Letter	Amino Acid
A (Ala)	Alanine	M (Met)	Methionine
C (Cys)	Cytosine	N (Asn)	Asparsgine
D (Asp)	Aspartic acid	P (Pro)	Proline
E (Glu)	Glutamic acid	Q (Glu)	Glutamine
F (Phe)	Phenylalanine	R (Arg)	Arginine
G (Gly)	Glycine	S (Ser)	Serine
H (His)	Histidine	T (Thr)	Threonine
I (Ile)	Isoleucine	V (Val)	Valine
K (Lys)	Lysine	W (Trp)	Tryptophan
L (Leu)	Leucine	Y (Tyr)	Tryosine

   Note: Specifics of amino acid substitutions have been deleted in some of the tables below.
   For full data, *see www.iasusa.org*

D. **Does resistance testing predict virologic response?** *(CID 47:266, 2008; AnIM 151:73, 2009).*
   - Using genotype & phenotype testing to guide treatment results in: 1) **extra 0.5-0.6 log$_{10}$ copies/mL** (approx. 30,000 copies/mL or 3-fold) **reduction in viral load;** 2) **extra 10-20% of patients with viral loads below 200-500 copies/mL.**
   - Improved long-term virologic outcome in treatment-experienced patients *(CID 38:723, 2004).*
   - Fair ability to predict phenotype from genotype *(CID 41:92, 2005).*

E. **Genotype resistance testing comments**—detects mutations in resistance-associated target proteins.
   1. - With "ultra-deep" sequencing, **increasing % of treatment-naïve patients harbor resistant virus** *(JAMA 305:1327, 2011).* Expert advice on interpretation of test results improves virologic response.
      - Use PCR to amplify HIV protease & reverse transcriptase genes; some labs do not detect mutations in the envelope gene or integrase gene. Sequence genes, report mutations found, mutations pattern used to predict response to antiretrovirals.
      See http://hivdb.stanford.edu for current mutation patterns. Selected mutations (or combinations) may ↓ replication capacity of HIV clinical isolates.
      - ○ **"Replication capacity"** means number of progeny produced per round of infection per unit of time.
      - ○ **"Fitness"** means relative reproductive success of various subtypes of HIV.
      - ○ **"Virulence"** means ability to destroy CD4 lymphocytes or impair immune system function.
   2. **Commercial genotype resistance testing assays:**

Name (Maker)	Contact	Minimum Viral Load Needed For Testing
Trugene (Visible Genetics)	*www.visgen.com* 877-786-8446	≥ 1000 copies/mL
Viro Seq (Applied Biosystems)	*www.appliedbiosystems.com* 800-327-3002	≥ 1000-2000 copies/mL
GeneSeq HIV (Monogram Biosciences)	*www.monogramhiv.com* 800-777-0177	≥ 500 copies/mL
Gen Chec (Virco)	*www.vircolab.com* 800-371-8302	≥ 200-400 copies/mL (combined geno- & phenotype)

TABLE 3C (3)

IV. **Genotype Resistance Mutations**
There are several data sources for HIV gene mutations associated with antiretroviral drugs. These include the HIV Drug Resistance Database at Stanford University, *http://hivdb.stanford.edu*; the International Antiviral Society-USA, *http://iasusa.org*; and numerous studies and reports in the published literature. The data shown in this table are derived from these sources and adapted for optimal display in the space available. As this data changes, see the Sanford Guide Web Edition, *webedition.sanfordguide.com* and the cited websites for the most current data.

A. **Selected genotype mutations that result in resistance to NRTIs NRTI resistance mutations**

Mutation*	Selected By	Mechanism	Effects On Other NRTIs	Comment
M184V	Lamivudine (3TC), Emtricitabine, (FTC), Abacavir	Impairs drug incorporation	Decreased susceptibility to 3TC & FTC. Increased susceptibility to ZDV, d4T & TDF.	Presence delays appearance of TAMs. TAMs + M184V decrease response to ABC.
Thymidine analogue associated mutations - (TAMs). M41L, D67N, K70R, L210W, T215Y/F, K219 Q/E	Zidovudine (ZDV), stavudine (d4T)	Mutation leads to excision of drug from DNA chain terminus	Decreased susceptibility to all NRTIs; the more TAMs, the more resistance.	TAM acquisition slowed by presence of M184V; **TAMs increase susceptibility to NNRTIs.**
Q151 M complex, T69 insertion	(ZDV)/didanosine (ddI) or (d4T/ddI)	Impairs drug incorporation	**Q151M complex**: resistance to all NRTIs except minimal activity of TDF; **T69 insertion**: resistance to all NRTIs.	
K65R	All NRTIs except zidovudine	Impairs drug incorporation	Variable decreased susceptibility to ABC, ddI, 3TC/FTC & especially TDF	Increases susceptibility to ZDV & d4T
L74V	ABC, ddI		Decreased susceptibility to ABC & ddI	Presented by presence of ZDV in treatment regimen

* *Shows amino acid encoded in wild type virus, number of mutated codons, then code for amino acid encoded in the mutated virus.*

1. **Major mutations that forecast resistance:**
   - **M184V** → Lamivudine, emtricitabine & partial abacavir resistance
   - **K65R** → All NRTIs except zidovudine
   - **Q151M** → All NRTIs except possibly tenofovir

2. Numerous nucleoside (or nucleotide) analog RTI mutations (e.g., M47L, L210W, T215Y) may increase susceptibility to NNRTIs in NNRTI-treatment-naïve patients.

B. **NNRTI resistance mutations.** Cross-resistance is the rule. Major mutations are **BOLD**.
Table Key: *Header* = letter code for amino acid encoded in wild type virus;
Number = mutated codon;
Letter = amino acid encoded in mutated virus.

	V	A	L	K	K	V	V	E	V	Y	Y	G	H	P	M	F
Delavirdine					103N*	106A				181C 181I	188L					
Efavirenz			100I	101P	103N* 103S	106M†	108I			181C 181I	188L	G190A G190S		225H	230L	
Etravirine	90I	98G	**100I***	**101E** **101H** **101P***		106I		138A 138G 138K,Q 138T	179D 179F 179T	**181C*** **181I*** **181V***		**190S** **190A**			**230L**	
Nevirapine			100I	101P	103N* 103S	106A 106M†	108I			181C 181I	188C 188L 188H	190A			230L	
Rilpivirine				101E 101P				138G 138A 138K 138Q 138R	179L 179I	181C 181I 181Y	188L		221Y		230I 230L	227C

* Indicated mutations are most common & usually occur first
† V106M: more common in HIV-1 subtype C; in U.S., most HIV-1 is subtype B

C. **PI resistance mutations.** Major mutations are **BOLD**. *See Figure 3, page 17.*
   - In general, multiple mutations are needed for high-level resistance.
   - Cross-resistance is common, e.g., mutations at codons 82, 84 & 90.
   - Exceptions: no cross-resistance for D30N nelfinavir & I50L atazanavir mutations.

TABLE 3C (4)

FIGURE 3 Protease Gene Mutations Associated With Resistance to Protease Inhibitors

Table Key: Header = letter code for amino acid encoded in wild type virus; Number = mutated codon; Letter = amino acid encoded in mutated virus.

	L10	V11	G16	K20	L24	D30	V32	L33	M36	K43	M46	I47	G48	I50	F53	I54	Q58	I62	L63	H69	A71	G73	T74	L76	V77	V82	N83	I84	I85	N88	L89	L90	I93
ATV+	10F 10I 10V 10G		16E	20T 20V 20R 20M 20I	24I		32I	33F	36I 36L 36V		46I 46L		48V	**50L**	53L 53Y	54L 54V 54M 54A		62V			71V 71I 71T 71L	73C 73S 73T 73A		76V		82A 82F 82S 82T		**84V**	85V	**88S**		**90M**	93L 93M
DRV+		11I					32I	33F				47V		**50V**		54M 54L							74P	76V				84V			89V		
FOS+	10F 10I 10R 10V						32I				46I 46L	47V		**50V**		54L 54V 54M								76V				84V				90M	
IDV+	10I 10R 10V			20M 20R	24I		32I		36I		46I 46L					54V		62V			71V 71T	73S 73A			77I	**82A 82F 82T**		**84V**				**90M**	
LPV+	10F 10I 10R 10V			20M 20R	24I		**32I**	33F			46I 46L	**47V 47A**		**50V**	53L	54V 54L 54A 54M 54T 54S			63P		71V 71T	73S		76V		**82A 82F 82T 82S**		84V				90M	
NFV	10F 10I					**30N**			36I		46I 46L										71V 71T				77I	82A 82F 82T 82S		84V		88D 88S		**90M**	
SQV+	10I 10R 10V				24I								**48V**			54V 54L		62V			71V 71T	73S			77I	82A 82F 82T 82S		84V				**90M**	
TPV+	10V							33F	36I 36L 36V	43T	46L	**47V**				54A 54M 54V 54T	58E			69K 69R			74P			**82L 82T**	**83D**	**84V**				**90M**	

BOLD means major mutations

ATV = atazanavir; DRV = darunavir; FOS = fosamprenavir; IDV = indinavir; LPV = lopinavir; NFV = nelfinavir; SQV = saquinavir; TPV = tipranavir; + means boosting with ritonavir

TABLE 3C (5)

D. **Entry inhibitor & CCR5 antagonist resistance mutations.**
   1. **Entry Inhibitor: Enfuvirtide Resistance Mutations**

	G	I	V	Q	Q	N	N
Enfuvirtide	36D 36S	37V	38A 38M 38E	39R	40H	42T	43D

   2. **CCR5 Antagonist: Maraviroc**
      • Activity requires presence of CCR5 co-receptor. HIV enters cells by attachment to CD4 receptor and then binding to either chemokine receptor 5 (CCR5) or chemokine receptor 4 (CXCR4) molecules. **CCR5 inhibitors bind to CCR5 & prevent viral entry.**
      • Frequency & rate of emergence of resistance mutations not yet known.
      • **Do co-receptor tropism assay prior to use of CCR5 antagonist** (Review: Ln ID 11:394, 2011):
         o Co-receptor assays are phenotypic; tropism assays use lab-generated pseudovirus that expresses gp120 & gp41.
         o **Enhanced Trofile™ assay available from Monogram Biosciences, www.trofileassay.com, 800-777-0177:** 1) 2-weeks required, need >1000 HIV RNA copies/mL; 2) detects X4 and dual-mixed (D/M) minor variants with 100% sensitivity down to frequency of 0.3% (CID 52:925, 2011); 3) results reported as: R5 (CCR5-tropic), X4 (CXCR4-tropic), D/M (dual/mixed) or nonphenotypable/non-reportable (NP/NR); 4) **expensive**. Percent positive for CCR5 receptor is only 50-58% in various studies, higher proportion in naïve pts and earlier stage of disease.
      • Tropism can be detected with **genotypic analysis** with outcomes similar to **phenotype**, especially with 454 (deep) sequencing technologies (JID 203:146 & 203, 2011).

E. **Integrase inhibitor resistance mutations.**

	T	L	E	T	E	G	Y	S	Q	N
DOL	66I*	92Q	143R 143H + 143C	148H 148K 148R	138A 138K	140S 140A			148H	
ELV	66I 66A 66K		92Q 92G	97A			147G	148H 148H 148K	155H	
RAL		74M	92Q	97A	138A 138K	140A 140S	143R 143H 143C	148H 148K 148R	155H	

DOL= doltegravir, ELV= elvitegravir, RAL= raltegravir

K. **Phenotype resistance testing**—measures ability of HIV to grow in presence of different concentrations of antiretroviral (ARV) drugs.
   1. **Indications for testing**: 1) multiple treatment failures; 2) multiple, complex mutation patterns on genotype test, especially resistance to PIs; 3) new drug susceptibility evaluation; 4) patient infected with non-subtype-B HIV.
   2. **General comments**: 1) methods & interpretation evolving; results reflect: accumulated genetic mutations, variables in assay system, end-point (cutoff) used (see below); **compared to genotyping, phenotype assays**:
      • Take longer (2-8 weeks), are easier to interpret, provide quantitative degree of resistance, cost more ($800-1500), need minimal viral load of 500-1000 copies/mL of plasma to test.
      • If circulating drug-resistant virus represents <10% of plasma viral load, resistant virus probably non-detectable; **only perform while on ART**.
      • Only detects resistance to single drug, not combinations.
   3. **Methods comments**:
      • Pertinent genes (reverse transcriptase, protease, integrase, envelope) from pts plasma HIV are inserted into lab strains of HIV. HIV replication in various drug concentrations is measured by expression of a reporter gene and the results are compared to replication of the lab strain of HIV.
      • Results are expressed as **fold increase** (or **fold resistance**). IC_{50} = drug concentration that inhibits viral replication by 50%. IC_{50} patient/virus/IC_{50} reference virus = fold increase (or fold resistance):

TABLE 3C (6)

FIGURE 4   Phenotypic Resistance Testing

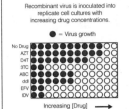

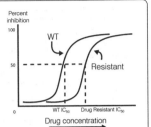

Recombinant virus is inoculated into replicate cell cultures with increasing drug concentrations.

● = Virus growth

No Drug
AZT
D4T
3TC
ABC
ddI
EFV
IDV

Increasing [Drug] ⟶

In this example, HIV-1 is sensitive to: 3TC, EFV and IDV
The recombinant virus is resistant to: AZT, D4T, ABC, ddI.

Percent inhibition plotted as function of drug concentration. The drug concentration that inhibits virus replication 50% is denoted IC_{50}. Fold increase on IC_{50} represents fold resistance.

4. **Defining phenotypic resistance (expert consultation recommended)**

   a. **Definition varies depending on cutoff value used.** "Cutoff" is dividing point between sensitive and resistant virus. There are 3 levels of cutoff in use: technical/reproducibility; biologic; clinical.

   b. **Technical/reproducibility cutoffs (though rarely used)**:
      • Defined as the lowest fold difference for which susceptible isolates are reliably separated from reference HIV strains.
      • **Sensitive** means <4-fold increase in IC_{50} patient/virus/IC_{50} reference virus in presence of test drug; **Intermediate** means 4-10-fold increase and **Resistant** means >10-fold increase.

   c. **Biologic cutoffs**:
      • Based on variability of wild-type virus from patients. Determined by study of IC_{50} concentration of test drug vs. HIV from wild-type virus (treatment naive patients). More relevant but still arbitrary; cutoffs vary depending on assay used.
      • Cutoff defined as IC_{50} above mean +250 (99th percentile).

   d. **Clinical cutoffs**:
      • Determined by correlation of in vitro IC_{50} with outcome data (virologic response) in clinical trial. Need large-scale trials. Does not measure influence of multi-drug ART regimens.
      • Provides the best definition of phenotypic resistance but is the most difficult to obtain. Some examples of validated clinical cutoffs:

Drug	Clinical Cutoff
Abacavir	4.5-fold increase means resistance (0.5-6.5, some pts may have at least 0.5 log ↓ in viral load) (*Antiviral Ther 9:37, 2004*).
Atazanavir	Decreased virologic response if >3-fold increase in IC_{50} (*AIDS 20:847, 2006*).
Didanosine/stavudine	1.7-fold increase means reduced susceptibility (*JID 195:392, 2007*).
Etravirine	Clinical cutoff for resistance estimated at >2.9-fold change (*CROI, Abst 687, 2009*).
Indinavir/ritonavir	>10-fold increase means reduced susceptibility.
Lopinavir	>10-fold increase means reduced susceptibility; >40-fold increase means resistance.
Tenofovir	1.4-fold increase means reduced susceptibility (*JID 189:837, 2004*).
Tipranavir	Decreased virologic response if >3-fold increase in IC_{50} (*AIDS 21:179, 2007*).

TABLE 3C (7)

5. **Commercial phenotype resistance tests:**

Name (Maker)	Contact	Minimum Viral Load Needed for Testing
Virco Type HIV-1 (Virco)	www.vircolab.com 800-325-7504	1000 copies/mL (combined pheno- & genotype; "Virtual Phenotype")
PhenoSense HIV (Monogram Biosciences)	www.monogrambio.com 800-777-0177	500 copies/mL (combined pheno- & genotype, also replication capacity)
Phenoscript (Specialty Labs & Viralliance)	www.specialtylabs.com 800-421-7110	500 copies/mL

L. **Discordance between genotype and phenotype susceptibility test results:**

Genotype Result	Phenotype Result	Cause	Interpretation
Resistant	Susceptible	Mixed HIV subtypes	Resistant
Resistant	Susceptible	Hyper-susceptibility	Resistance mutation, e.g., 184. Mutations in NRTIs increase susceptibility to NNRTIs
Not available	Susceptible or Resistant	New drug	Phenotype result invalid
Susceptible	Resistant	Novel drug	Resistant due to new mechanism of resistance

M. **Summary:** Failure to respond to ART depends on: percentage of viral population that is drug-resistant; plasma viral load; adherence to ART regimen; low drug potency; poor pharmacokinetics and high plasma protein binding.

TABLE 3D: DIAGNOSIS OF HUMAN T-LYMPHOTROPIC VIRUS (HTLV-1, HTLV-2)

I. **HTLV-1**
   - Worldwide retrovirus; causes illness in only 5% of infected persons.
   - Two associated diseases: 1) Adult T-cell leukemia/lymphoma; 2) HTLV-1-associated myelopathy (HAM), also known as tropical spastic paraparesis (TSP).
   - **Laboratory diagnosis–blood and CSF:**
     - Anti-HTLV antibodies and proviral DNA by PCR and sometimes abnormal lobulated lymphocytes.
     - Recent influenza vaccine can cause false-positive antibody elevation.
     - Confirm positives with Western Blot (Focus Diagnostics or Quest Diagnostics); may not differentiate HTLV-1 % HTLV-2.
   - HTLV-1 infection increases CD4 counts.
   - Blood donors screened for HTLV-1 antibody.
   - "Flower cells" in peripheral blood: sign of HTLV-1 infection; not a sign of leukemia or lymphoma

II. **HTLV-2**
   - No associated disease process as yet identified. Blood donors are not screened for HTLV-2. Based on antibody screening, HTLV-2 is endemic in Native Americans and injection drug users (IDU).

TABLE 4A: 1993 REVISED CDC HIV CLASSIFICATION SYSTEM & EXPANDED AIDS SURVEILLANCE DEFINITION FOR ADOLESCENTS & ADULTS

(MMWR 41:RR-17, Dec. 18, 1992)

The revised system emphasizes the importance of CD4 lymphocyte testing in clinical management of HIV infected persons. The system is based on 3 ranges of CD4 counts & 3 clinical categories giving a matrix of 9 exclusive categories. This system is less valuable in clinical decision-making today because of availability of measures of viral RNA.

CRITERIA FOR HIV INFECTION: Persons 13 years or older with repeatedly (2 or more) reactive screening tests (ELISA) + specific antibodies identified by a supplemental test, e.g., Western blot [reactive pattern = + vs any two of p24, gp41, or gp120/160 *(MMWR 40:681, 1991)*]. Other specific methods of diagnosis of HIV-1 include virus isolation, antigen detection, & detection of HIV genetic material by PCR or branched DNA assay (bDNA).

CLASSIFICATION SYSTEM

CD4 Cell[§] Category	Clinical Category A	Clinical Category B	Clinical Category C

CD4 Cell[§] Category	Clinical Category		
	A	**B**	**C**
(1) ≥500/mm³	A1	B1	C1
(2) 200–499/mm³	A2	B2	C2
(3) <200/mm³	A3	B3	C3

See table for clinical definitions. Shaded area indicates expansion of AIDS surveillance definition. Cats. A3, B3 & C require reporting as AIDS.

§ There is a diurnal variation in CD4 counts averaging 60/mm³ higher in the afternoon in HIV+ individuals. Blood for sequential CD4 counts should be drawn at about the same time of day each time (*J AIDS 3:144, 1990*). The equivalence between CD4 counts & CD4 % of total lymphocytes is ≥500 = ≥29%, 200–499 = 14–28%, <200 = <14%.

Clinical Category A

Asymptomatic HIV infection
Persistent generalized lymphadenopathy (PGL)[1]
Acute (primary) HIV illness

Clinical Category B

Symptomatic, not A or C conditions.
Examples include but not limited to:
- Bacillary angiomatosis
- Candidiasis, vulvovaginal: persistent >1 month, poorly responsive to rx
- Candidiasis, oropharyngeal
- Cervical dysplasia, severe or carcinoma in situ
- Constitutional sx, e.g., fever **(38.5°)** or **diarrhea >1 month**

The above must be attributed to HIV infection or have a clinical course or management complicated by HIV.

Clinical Category C

- Candidiasis: esophageal, trachea, bronchi
- Coccidioidomycosis, extrapulmonary
- Cryptococcosis, extrapulmonary
- Cervical cancer, invasive
- Cryptosporidiosis, chronic intestinal (>1 month)
- CMV retinitis, or CMV in other than liver, spleen, nodes
- HIV encephalopathy
- Herpes simplex with mucocutaneous ulcer >1 month, bronchitis, pneumonia
- Histoplasmosis: disseminated, extrapulmonary
- Isosporiasis, chronic, >1 month
- Kaposi's sarcoma
- Lymphoma: Burkitts, immunoblastic, primary in brain
- M. avium or M. kansasii, extrapulmonary
- M. tuberculosis, pulmonary or extrapulmonary
- Pneumocystis jiroveci pneumonia
- Pneumonia, recurrent (≥2 episodes in 1 year)
- Progressive multifocal leukoencephalopathy
- Salmonella bacteremia, recurrent
- Toxoplasmosis, cerebral
- Wasting syndrome due to HIV

These are the 1987 CDC case definitions *(MMWR 36:15, 1987)*. The 1993 *CDC Expanded Surveillance Case Definition* includes all conditions contained in the 1987 definition (above) plus persons with documented HIV infection & any of the following: (1) CD4 T-lymphocyte count <200/mm³ (or CD4 <14%), (2) pulmonary tuberculosis, (3) recurrent pneumonia (≥2 episodes within 1 year) or (4) invasive cervical carcinoma. There are no CDC definitions utilizing viral load available to date.

1 Nodes in 2 or more extrainguinal sites, at least 1 cm in diameter for ≥3 mos.

TABLE 4B: CORRELATION OF COMPLICATIONS WITH CD4 CELL COUNTS/WHO CLINICAL STAGING SYSTEM

	CORRELATION OF COMPLICATIONS WITH CD4 CELL COUNTS		WHO CLINICAL STAGING SYSTEM
CD4 Cell Count*	Infectious Complications	Noninfectious Complications	
>500/mm³	Acute retroviral syndrome Candidal vaginitis	Persistent generalized lymphadenopathy (PGL) Guillain-Barré syndrome Myopathy Aseptic meningitis	WHO Clinical Stage 1: No clinical symptoms May have persistent generalized lymphadenopathy (PGL) Performance scale 1 * Normal activity
200-500/mm³	Pneumococcal and other bacterial pneumonia Pulmonary tuberculosis Herpes zoster Oropharyngeal candidiasis (thrush) Cryptosporidiosis, self-limited Kaposi's sarcoma Oral hairy leukoplakia HPV: Cervical intraepithelial neoplasia/Cancer EBV: B-cell lymphoma; HHV-8: Kaposi's sarcoma/Castleman's Disease	Anemia Mononeuritis multiplex Idiopathic thrombocytopenic purpura Hodgkin's lymphoma Lymphocytic interstitial pneumonitis	WHO Clinical Stage 2: Weight loss <10% Minor skin rash Herpes zoster Recurrent oral ulcerations Angular cheilitis Fungal nail infections Recurrent upper respiratory infection Performance scale 2 * Symptomatic but normal activity
<200/mm³	Pneumocystis jiroveci pneumonia Disseminated histoplasmosis and coccidioidomycosis Miliary/extrapulmonary TB Progressive multifocal leukoencephalopathy (PML)	Peripheral neuropathy HIV-associated dementia Vacuolar myelopathy Progressive polyradiculopathy Non-Hodgkin's lymphoma	WHO Clinical Stage 3: Weight loss >10% Chronic diarrhea >1 month Recurrent fevers >1 month Oral thrush Oral hairy leukoplakia Severe presumed bacterial infections Acute necrotizing ulcerative stomatitis, gingivitis, or periodontitis Pulmonary tuberculosis Unexplained anemia (<8 gm/dl), neutropenia (<500 cells/ul), and/or Chronic thrombocytopenia (<50,000/ul) Performance scale 3 * Bedridden <50% of the day during the last month
<100/mm³	Disseminated herpes simplex Toxoplasmosis Cryptococcosis Cryptosporidiosis, chronic Microsporidiosis Candidal esophagitis	Wasting	WHO Clinical Stage 4: Cryptococcal meningitis Toxoplasmosis of the brain Pneumocystis pneumonia Chronic Herpes simplex infection Esophageal Candidiasis Disseminated non-TB mycobacterial disease Lymphoma Progressive Multifocal Leukoencephalopathy Isosporiasis	Cytomegalovirus disease Disseminated endemic mycoses (Histoplasmosis, Penicilliosis, Coccidiomycosis) Salmonellosis Invasive cervical carcinoma Visceral leishmaniasis Kaposi sarcoma Dementia Performance scale 4 * Bedridden >50% of the day during the last month
<50/mm³	Disseminated cytomegalovirus (CMV) Disseminated Mycobacterium avium complex	Central nervous system (CNS) lymphoma	NOTE that patients may move from a later stage to an earlier stage if the presenting opportunistic infection is treated.

* Most complications occur with increasing frequency at lower CD4 cell counts. Modified from Bartlett, 2003.

TABLE 5A: RAPID ORAL TMP/SMX DESENSITIZATION

HOUR	DOSE TMP/SMX (mg)	COMMENT
0	0.004/0.02	• Perform in hospital or clinic. Use oral suspension [40 mg TMP/200 mg SMX/5 mL (tsp.)].
1	0.04/0.2	• Take 6 oz. water after each dose. Corticosteroids, antihistamines NOT used.
2	0.4/2	• Refs: *CID* 20:849, 1995; *AIDS* 5:311, 1991.
3	4/20	
4	40/200	
5	160/800	

TABLE 5B: METHODS FOR PENICILLIN DESENSITIZATION
(CID 35:26, 2002; AJM 121:572, 2008)

Perform in ICU setting. Discontinue all β-adrenergic antagonists. Have IV line, ECG & spirometer (*Curr Clin Topics Int Dis 13:131, 1993*). Once desensitized, rx must not lapse or risk of allergic reactions ↑. Histories of Stevens-Johnson syndrome, exfoliative dermatitis, erythroderma are nearly absolute contraindications to desensitization (use only as an approach to IgE sensitivity).

Oral Route: If oral prep available & pt has functional GI tract, oral route is preferred. 1/3 pts will develop transient reaction during desensitization or treatment, usually mild.

Step*	1	2	3	4	5	6	7	8	9	10	11	12	13	14
Drug (mg/mL)	0.5	0.5	0.5	0.5	0.5	0.5	0.5	5	5	5	50	50	50	50
Amount (mL)	0.1	0.2	0.4	0.8	1.6	3.2	6.4	1.2	2.4	4.8	1.0	2.0	4.0	8.0

* Interval between doses: 15 min. After Step 14, observe for 30 minutes, then 1 gm IV.

Parenteral Route:

Step**	1	2	3	4	5	6	7	8	9	10	11	12	13	14	15	16	17
Drug (mg/mL)	0.1	0.1	0.1	0.1	1	1	1	10	10	10	100	100	100	100	1000	1000	1000
Amount (mL)	0.1	0.2	0.4	0.8	0.16	0.32	0.64	0.12	0.24	0.48	0.1	0.2	0.4	0.8	0.16	0.32	0.64

** Interval between doses: 15 min. After Step 17, observe for 30 minutes, then 1 gm IV.

Penicillin skin testing for evaluation of penicillin allergy: Testing with major determinant (benzyl penicillin polylysine) and minor determinants has negative predictive value of 97-99%. Risk of systemic reaction to skin testing < 1%. See *Ann Allergy Asthma Immunol* 106:1, 2011.

[Adapted from Sullivan, TJ, in Allergy: Principles & Practice, Middleton, E., et al. Eds. C.V. Mosby, 1993, p. 1726, with permission]

TABLE 6A: ANTIRETROVIRAL THERAPY (ART) IN TREATMENT-NAÏVE ADULTS (REGIMENS, DOSING)

The U.S. Dept of Health & Human Svcs (DHHS) provides updated guidelines on a regular basis. Current guidelines, as well as recommendations for anti-retroviral therapy (ART) in pregnant women and in children, are available at www.aidsinfo.nih.gov. These documents provide detailed recommendations and explanations, drug characteristics, explanations, and additional alternatives concerning the use of ART. The new Guidelines include: (1) recommendations to start therapy at any CD4 count for asymptomatic patients unless there is a reason to defer treatment; the strength of the recommendation increases with lower CD4 count values; (2) A simplified recommendation scheme for choice of initial therapy for naive patients (incorporated into 6A (2) below (3) Revised definitions for regimen failure (4) TB recommendations remain unchanged. For patients with CD4 counts <50 cells/mm³, ART should be initiated within 2 weeks of starting TB treatment **(AI)**.

- For patients with CD4 counts ≥50 cells/mm³ with clinical disease of major severity as indicated by clinical evaluation (including low Karnofsky score, low body mass index [BMI], low hemoglobin, low albumin, organ system dysfunction, or extent of disease), the Panel recommends initiation of ART within 2 to 4 weeks of starting TB treatment **(BI** for CD4 count 50-200 cells/mm³ and **BIII** for CD4 count >200 cells/mm³).

- For other patients with CD4 counts ≥50 cells/mm³, ART can be delayed beyond 2 to 4 weeks but should be initiated by 8 to 12 weeks of TB therapy **(AI** for CD4 count 50-500 cells/mm³, **BIII** for CD4 count >500 cells/mm³). Note that immune reconstitution syndromes (IRS or IRIS) may result from initiation of any ART, and may require medical intervention.

The following principles and concepts guide therapy:

- **The goal of rx is to inhibit maximally viral replication, allowing re-establishment & persistence of an effective immune response that will prevent or delay HIV-related morbidity.**
- **Fully undetectable levels of virus are the target of therapy for ALL patients, regardless of stage of disease or number/type of prior regimens.**
- **The lower the viral RNA can be driven, the lower the rate of accumulation of drug resistance mutations & the longer the therapeutic effect will last.**
- **To achieve maximal & durable suppression of viral RNA, combinations of potent antiretroviral agents are required, as is a high degree of adherence to the chosen regimens.**
- **Virologic failure is defined as confirmed virus > 200 c/mL.**
- **Treatment regimens must be tailored to the individual as well as to the virus. Antiretroviral drug toxicities can compromise adherence in the short term & can cause significant negative health effects over time. Carefully check for specific risks to the individual, for interactions between the antiretrovirals selected & between those & concurrent drugs, & adjust doses as necessary for body weight, for renal or hepatic dysfunction, & for possible pharmacokinetic interactions.**

A. When to start therapy? (www.aidsinfo.nih.gov)

Guidelines	Any symptoms or CD4 <200/μL	CD4 200-350/μL	CD4 350-500/μL	CD4 > 500/μL
IAS-USA: *JAMA 308: 387, 2012*	Treat	Treat	Treat	Consider Treatment* * No Apparent Harm in treating earlier
DHHS: www.aidsinfo.nih.gov	Treat	Treat	Treat	Treat* * Strength of rating increases as CD4 count decreases

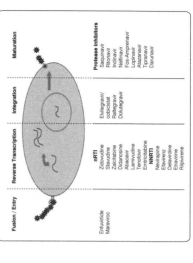

FIGURE 5   Life Cycle of HIV With Sites of Action of Antiretrovirals

Fusion / Entry	Reverse Transcription	Integration	Maturation
Enfuvirtide Maraviroc	**nRTI** Zidovudine Stavudine Zalcitabine Didanosine Abacavir Tenofovir Emtricitabine **NNRTI** Nevirapine Efavirenz Delavirdine Etravirine Rilpivirine	Elvitegravir/ cobicistat Raltegravir Dolutegravir	**Protease Inhibitors** Saquinavir Ritonavir Indinavir Nelfinavir Fos-Amprenavir Lopinavir Atazanavir Tipranavir Darunavir

TABLE 6A (2)

B. Recommended Antiretroviral Regimen Options for Antiretroviral Therapy-Naive Patients *(modified from DHHS Guidelines, www.AIDSinfo.gov)*

Combination antiretroviral therapy (ART) regimens typically consist of two NRTIs plus one active 'anchor' drug. Anchor drugs are either an NNRTI, a PI (usually boosted with RTV), an INSTI, or a CCR5 antagonist. Refer to *section E (Table 6A)* below for characteristics of each drug and their usual doses, and *Table 6B* for common adverse events and safety discussion. The regimens in each category are listed in **alphabetical order.**

Recommended Initial ART Regimens for All Patients, regardless of Pre-ART Viral Load

NNRTI-Based Regimen
- EFV/TDF/FTC[a]

PI-Based Regimens
- ATV/r + TDF/FTC[a] **(AI)**
- DRV/r + TDF/FTC[a] **(AI)**

INSTI-Based Regimen
- DTG + ABC/3TC[a] – **only** for patients who are HLA-B*5701 negative
- DTG + TDF/FTC
- EVG/COB/TDF/FTC – **only** for patients with pre-treatment estimated CrCl > 70 mL/min
- RAL + ABC/3TC[a] – **only** for patients who are HLA-B*5701 negative
- RAL + TDF/FTC[a]

Recommended Initial ART Regimens patients with pre-ART plasma HIV RNA < 100,000 copies/mL *(in addition to the regimens listed above for all patients regardless of Pre-ART VL)*

NNRTI-Based Regimen
- EFV + ABC/3TC[a] – **only** for patients with HIV RNA < 100,000 copies/mL **and** who are HLA-B*5701 negative
- RPV/TDF/FTC[a] – **only** for patients with pre-treatment HIV RNA < 100,000 copies/mL **and** CD4 cell count > 200 cells/mm³

PI-Based Regimen
- ATV/r + ABC/3TC[a] – **only** for patients with HIV RNA < 100,000 copies/mL **and** who are HLA-B*5701 negative

Alternative Initial ART Regimen Options Regimens that are effective and tolerable, but have potential disadvantages when compared with the recommended regimens listed above or for which there is limited data from randomized clinical trials. An alternative regimen may be the preferred regimen for some patients.

NNRTI-Based Regimens
- RPV + ABC/3TC[a] – **only** for patients who are HLA-B*5701 negative, **and** with pre-ART HIV RNA < 100,000 copies/mL, **and** CD4 count > 200 cells/mm³

PI-Based Regimens
- DRV/r + ABC/3TC[a] – **only** for patients who are HLA-B*5701 negative
- LPV/r (once or twice daily) + ABC/3TC[a] – **only** for patients who are HLA-B*5701 negative
- LPV/r (once or twice daily) + TDF/FTC[a]

TABLE 6A (3)

Regimens that may be selected for some patients but are less satisfactory than recommended or alternative regimens

NNRTI-Based Regimen

- EFV + ZDV/3TC[a]
- NVP + (TDF/FTC[a] or ZDV/3TC) – **only** for ART-naive women with pre-ART CD4 count < 250 cells/mm3 or males with pre-ART CD4 count < 400 cells/mm³
- NVP + ABC/3TC[a] – **only** for ART-naive women with pre-ART CD4 count < 250 cells/mm³ or males with pre-ART CD4 count < 400 cells/mm³, who are HLA-B*5701 negative, and with pre-ART HIV RNA < 100,000 copies/mL
- RPV + ZDV/3TC[a] – **only** for patients with pre-ART HIV RNA < 100,000 copies/mL

PI-Based Regimens

- (ATV or ATV/r or DRV/r or FPV/r or LPV/r or SQV/r) + ZDV/3TC[a]
- ATV + ABC/3TC[a] – **only** for patients who are HLA-B*5701 negative and with pre-ART HIV RNA < 100,000 copies/mL
- FPV/r + ABC/3TC[a] – **only** for patients who are HLA-B*5701 negative and with pre-ART HIV RNA < 100,000 copies/mL
- FPV + TDF/FTC[a]
- SQV/r + ABC/3TC[a] – **only** for patients who are HLA-B*5701 negative, with pre-ART HIV RNA < 100,000 copies/mL, and pretreatment QT interval < 450 msec
- SQV/r + TDF/FTC[a] – **only** for patients with pretreatment QT interval < 450 msec

INSTI-Based Regimen

- RAL + ZDV/3TC[a]
- DTG + ZDV/3TC[a]

CCR5 Antagonist-Based Regimens

- MVC + (TDF/FTC or ZDV/3TC[a]) – **only** for patients with CCR5 tropic HIV
- MVC + ABC/3TC[a] – **only** for patients with CCR5 tropic HIV, who are HLA-B*5701 negative, and with pre-ART HIV RNA < 100,000 copies/mL.

[a] 3TC may substitute for FTC or vice versa. The following combinations in the recommended list above are available as coformulated fixed-dose combinations: ABC/3TC, EFV/TDF/FTC, EVG/COBI/TDF/FTC, LPV/r, RPV/TDF/FTC, TDF/FTC, and ZDV/3TC.

Key to Abbreviations: 3TC = lamivudine, ABC = abacavir, ART = antiretroviral therapy, ARV = antiretroviral, ATV/r = atazanavir/ritonavir, COBI = cobicistat, CrCl = creatinine clearance, DTG = dolutegravir, DRV/r = darunavir/ritonavir, EFV = efavirenz, EVG = elvitegravir, FDA = Food and Drug Administration, FPV/r = fosamprenavir/ritonavir, FTC = emtricitabine, INSTI = integrase strand transfer inhibitor, LPV/r = lopinavir/ritonavir, NNRTI = non-nucleoside reverse transcriptase inhibitor, NRTI = nucleoside reverse transcriptase inhibitor, PI = protease inhibitor, PPI = proton pump inhibitor, RAL = raltegravir, RPV = rilpivirine, RTV = ritonavir, TDF = tenofovir disoproxil fumarate.

TABLE 6A (4)

C. **During pregnancy.** Expert consultation mandatory. Timing of rx initiation & drug choice must be individualized. Viral resistance testing should be strongly considered. Long-term effects of agents unknown. Certain drugs hazardous or contraindicated. *(See Table 17).* For additional information & alternative options, *see www.aidsinfo.nih.gov.* For regimens to prevent perinatal transmission, *see Table 6A. See JID 193:1191, 2006 re pre-term delivery with PIs.*

D. **Antiretroviral Therapies That Should NOT Be Offered** *(Modified from www.aidsinfo.nih.gov)*

1. Regimens not recommended

	Regimen	Logic	Exception
a.	Monotherapy with NRTI	Rapid development of resistance & inferior antiviral activity	Perhaps ZDV to reduce peripartum mother-to-child transmission. *See Perinatal Guidelines at www.aidsinfo.nih.gov and Table 6B*
b.	Dual NRTI combinations	Resistance and inferior antiretroviral activity compared with standard drug combinations	Perhaps ZDV to reduce peripartum mother-to-child transmission. *See Perinatal Guidelines at www.aidsinfo.nih.gov and Table 6B*
c.	Triple-NRTI combinations	Triple-NRTI regimens have shown inferior virologic efficacy in clinical trials: (tenofovir + lamivudine + abacavir) & (didanosine + lamivudine + tenofovir) & others	(Zidovudine + lamivudine + abacavir) or (zidovudine + lamivudine + tenofovir) might be used if no alternative exists.
d.	Double Boosted PIs	Using 2 or more PI agents boosted with ritonavir adds nothing in terms of anti-HIV activity but can add extra toxicity	No exceptions
e.	2 NNRTI agents	Increased rate of side effects. Drug-drug interaction between etravirine and nevirapine and etravirine and efavirenz	No exceptions

2. Drug, or drugs, not recommended as part of antiretroviral regimen

		Logic	Exception
a.	Saquinavir hard gel cap or tab (Invirase), darunavir, or tipranavir as single (unboosted) PI	Bioavailability only 4%; inferior antiretroviral activity	No exceptions
b.	Stavudine + didanosine	High frequency of toxicity: peripheral neuropathy, pancreatitis & mitochondrial toxicity (lactic acidosis). In pregnancy: lactic acid acidosis, hepatic steatosis, ± pancreatitis	Toxicity partially offset by potent antiretroviral activity of the combination. Use only when potential benefits outweigh the sizeable risks
c.	Stavudine + zidovudine	Antagonistic	No exceptions
d.	Atazanavir + indinavir	Additive risk of hyperbilirubinemia	No exceptions
e.	Emtricitabine + lamivudine	Same target and resistance profile	No exceptions
f.	Abacavir + tenofovir	Rapid development of K65R mutation; loss of effect	Can avoid if zidovudine also used in the regimen; might be an option for salvage therapy but not earlier lines of therapy.
g.	Tenofovir + didanosine	Reduced CD4 cell count increase; concern of K 65R development	Use with caution. Likely increases ddI concentrations and serious ddI toxicities
h.	Abacavir + didanosine	Insufficient data in naive patients	Use with caution

E.

TABLE 6A (5)

1. **Selected Characteristics of Antiretroviral Drugs** (CPE = CSF penetration effectiveness)

Selected Characteristics of Nucleoside or Nucleotide Reverse Transcriptase Inhibitors (NRTIs)

All agents have Black Box warning: Risk of lactic acidosis/hepatic steatosis. Also, labels note risk of fat redistribution/accumulation with ARV therapy. For combinations, see warnings for component agents.

* **CPE (CNS Penetration Effectiveness) value:** 1 = Low Penetration; 2 - 3 = Intermediate Penetration; 4 = Highest Penetration into CNS (Letendre, et al, CROI 2010, abs #430)

Generic/ Trade Name	Pharmaceutical Prep.	Usual Adult Dosage & Food Effect	% Absorbed, po	Serum T½, hrs	Intracellular T½, hrs	CPE*	Elimination	Major Adverse Events/Comments (See Table 6B)
Abacavir (ABC, Ziagen)	300 mg tabs or 20 mg/mL oral solution	300 mg po bid or 600 mg po q24h. Food OK	83	1.5	20	1	Liver metab., renal excretion of metabolites, 82%	**Hypersensitivity reaction:** fever, rash, N/V, malaise, diarrhea, abdominal pain, respiratory symptoms. (Severe reactions may be ↑ with 600 mg dose.) **Do not rechallenge!** Report to 800-270-0425. **Test HLA-B*5701 before use. See Comment Table 6B.** Studies raise concerns re ABC/3TC regimens in pts with VL ≥ 100,000 (www.niaid.nih.gov/news/newsreleases/2008/acctg5202bulletin.htm). Controversy re increased CV events with use of ABC. Large meta-analysis shows no increased risk (JAIDS 61, 441, 2012)
Abacavir (ABC)/lamivudine (3TC) (Epzicom or Kivexa)	Film coated tabs ABC 600 mg + 3TC 300 mg	1 tab once daily (not recommended)						(See Comments for individual components) Note: **Black Box warnings** for ABC hypersensitivity reaction & others. Should only be used for regimens intended to include these 3 agents. Black Box warning— limited data for VL >100,000 copies/mL. Not recommended as initial therapy because of inferior virologic efficacy.
Abacavir (ABC)/ lamivudine (3TC)/ zidovudine (AZT) (Trizivir)	Film-coated tabs: ABC 300 mg + 3TC 150 mg + ZDV 300 mg	1 tab po bid (not recommended for wt <40 kg or CrCl <50 mL/min or impaired hepatic function)						(See individual components)
Didanosine (ddI; Videx or Videx EC)	125, 200, 250, 400 enteric-coated caps; 100, 167, 250 mg powder for oral solution;	≥60 kg Usually 400 mg enteric-coated po q24h 0.5 hr before or 2 hrs after meal. Do not crush. <60 kg 250 mg EC po q24h; Food ↓ levels. See Comment	30–40	1.6	25–40	2	Renal excretion, 50%	**Pancreatitis**, peripheral neuropathy, lactic acidosis & hepatic steatosis (rare but life-threatening, esp. combined with stavudine in pregnancy). Retinal, optic nerve changes. **The combination ddI + TDF is generally avoided, but if used, reduce dose of ddI-EC from 400 mg to 250 mg EC q24h (or from 250 mg EC to 200 mg EC for adults <60 kg). Monitor for ↑ toxicity & possible ↓ in efficacy of this combination; may result in ↓ CD4.** Possibly associated with noncirrhotic portal hypertension.

TABLE 6A (6)

E. **Selected Characteristics of Antiretroviral Drugs** (CPE = CSF penetration effectiveness)

1. **Selected Characteristics of Nucleoside or Nucleotide Reverse Transcriptase Inhibitors (NRTIs)** *(continued)*

Generic/ Trade Name	Pharmaceutical Prep.	Usual Adult Dosage & Food Effect	% Absorbed, po	Serum T½, hrs	Intracellular T½, hrs	CPE*	Elimination	Major Adverse Events/Comments *(See Table 6B)*
Emtricitabine (FTC, Emtriva)	200 mg caps; 10 mg per mL oral solution.	200 mg po q24h. Food OK	93 (caps), 75 (oral sol'n	Approx. 10	39	3	Renal excretion 86%, minor bio-transforma-tion, 14% excretion in feces	Well tolerated; headache, nausea, vomiting & diarrhea occasionally, skin rash rarely. Skin hyperpigmentation. Differs only slightly in structure from lamivudine (5-fluoro substitution). **Exacerbation of Hep B reported in pts after stopping FTC.** Monitor at least several months after stopping FTC in Hep B pts; some may need anti-HBV therapy.
Emtricitabine/ tenofovir disoproxil fumarate (Truvada)	Film-coated tabs: FTC 200 mg + TDF 300 mg	1 tab po q24h for CrCl ≥50 mL/min. Food OK	92/25	10/17	—	*(See individual compo-nents)*	Primarily renal/renal	See *Comments for individual agents* **Black Box warning—Exacerbation of HepB after stopping FTC;** but preferred therapy for those with Hep B.
Emtricitabine/ tenofovir/efavirenz (Atripla)	Film-coated tabs: FTC 200 mg + TDF 300 mg + efavirenz 600 mg	1 tab po q24h on an empty stomach, preferably at bedtime. Do not use if CrCl <50 mL/min		*(See individual components)*				Not recommended for pts <18 yrs. *(See warnings for individual components).* **Exacerbation of Hep B** reported in pts discontinuing component drugs; some may need anti-HBV therapy (preferred anti-HBV therapy). **Pregnancy category D-** may cause fetal harm. Avoid in pregnancy or in women who may become pregnant.
Emtricitabine/rilpivirine (Complera/ Eviplera)	Film-coated tabs: FTC 200 mg + RPL 25 mg	1 tab po q24h with food		*(See individual components)*				See *individual components.* Preferred use in pts with HIV RNA level <100,000 c/mL. Should not be used with PPI agents.
Lamivudine (3TC; Epivir)	150, 300 mg tabs; 10 mg/mL oral solution	150 mg po bid or 300 mg po q24h. Food OK	86	5–7	18	2	Renal excretion, minimal metabolism	**Use HIV dose, not Hep B dose.** Usually well-tolerated. **Risk of exacerbation of Hep B after stopping 3TC.** Monitor at least several months after stopping 3TC in Hep B pts; some may need anti-HIV therapy.
Lamivudine/ abacavir (Epzicom)	Film-coated tabs: 3TC 300 mg + abacavir 600 mg	1 tab po q24h. Food OK Not recommended for CrCl <50 mL/min or impaired hepatic function	86/83	5–7/1.5	16/20	*(See individual compo-nents)*	Primarily renal/ metabolism	See *Comments for individual agents.* **Note abacavir hypersensitivity Black Box warnings** (severe reactions may be somewhat more frequent with 600 mg dose) and 3TC Hep B warnings. Test HLA-B*5701 before use.
Lamivudine/ zidovudine (Combivir)	Film-coated tabs: 3TC 150 mg + ZDV 300 mg	1 tab po bid. Not recommended for CrCl <50 mL/min or impaired hepatic function Food OK	86/64	5–7/ 0.5–3	—	*(See individual compo-nents)*	Primarily renal/ metabolism with renal excretion of glucuronide	See *Comments for individual agents* **Black Box warning**—exacerbation of Hep B in pts stopping 3TC

TABLE 6A (7)

E. Selected Characteristics of Antiretroviral Drugs (CPE = CSF penetration effectiveness)

1. Selected Characteristics of Nucleoside or Nucleotide Reverse Transcriptase Inhibitors (NRTIs) (continued)

Generic/Trade Name	Pharmaceutical Prep.	Usual Adult Dosage & Food Effect	% Absorbed, po	Serum T½, hrs	Intracellular T½, hrs	CPE*	Elimination	Major Adverse Events/Comments (See Table 6B)
Stavudine (d4T, Zerit)	15, 20, 30, 40 mg capsules; 1 mg per mL oral solution	≥60 kg: 40 mg po bid <60 kg: 30 mg po bid Food OK	86	1.2–1.6	3.5	2	Renal excretion. 40%	Not recommended by DHHS as initial therapy because of adverse reactions. **Highest incidence of lipoatrophy, hyperlipidemia, & lactic acidosis of all NRTIs.** Pancreatitis. Peripheral neuropathy. (See didanosine comments.)
Tenofovir disoproxil fumarate (TDF; Viread)—a nucleotide	300 mg tabs	CrCl ≥50 mL/min: 300 mg po q24h. Food OK; high-fat meal ↑ absorption	39 (with food) 25 (fasted)	17	>60	1	Renal excretion	Headache. N/V. **Cases of renal dysfunction reported:** check renal function before using (dose reductions necessary if CrCl <50 cc/min); avoid concomitant nephrotoxic agents. One study found ↑ renal function at 48-wk in pts receiving TDF with a PI (mostly lopinavir/ritonavir) than with a NNRTI (JID 197:102, 2008). Must adjust dose of ddI (↓) if used concomitantly but best to avoid this combination (see ddI Comments). Atazanavir & lopinavir/ritonavir ↑ tenofovir concentrations; monitor for adverse effects. **Black Box warning—exacerbations of Hep B reported after stopping tenofovir.** Monitor several months after stopping TDF in Hep B pts; some may need anti-HBV Rx.
Zidovudine (ZDV, AZT; Retrovir)	100 mg caps, 300 mg tabs: 10 mg per mL IV solution; 10 mg/mL oral syrup	300 mg po q12h. Food OK	64	1.1	11	4	Metabolized to glucuronide & excreted in urine	Bone marrow suppression. GI intolerance, headache, insomnia, malaise, myopathy.

2. Selected Characteristics of Non-Nucleoside Reverse Transcriptase Inhibitors (NNRTIs)

Generic/Trade Name	Pharmaceutical Prep.	Usual Adult Dosage & Food Effect	% Absorbed, po	Serum T½, hrs	Intracellular T½, hrs	CPE*	Elimination	Major Adverse Events/Comments (See Table 6B)
Delavirdine (Rescriptor)	100, 200 mg tabs	400 mg po three times daily. Food OK	85	5.8	3		Cytochrome P450 (3A inhibitor). 51% excreted in urine (<5% unchanged), 44% in feces	Rash severe enough to stop drug in 4.3%. ↑ AST/ALT, headaches. **Use of this agent is not recommended.**

TABLE 6A (8)

E. **Selected Characteristics of Antiretroviral Drugs** (CPE = CSF penetration effectiveness)

2. **Selected Characteristics of Non-Nucleoside Reverse Transcriptase Inhibitors (NNRTIs)** (continued)

Generic/ Trade Name	Pharmaceutical Prep.	Usual Adult Dosage & Food Effect	% Absorbed, po	Serum T½, hrs	Intracellular T½, hrs	CPE*	Elimination	Major Adverse Events/Comments (See Table 6B)
Efavirenz (Sustiva)	50, 100, 200 mg capsules; 600 mg tablet	600 mg po q24h at bedtime, without food. Food may ↑ serum conc., which can lead to ↑ in risk of adverse events.	42	40–55 See Comment	3		Cytochrome P450 286 (3A mixed inducer/ inhibitor). 14–34% of dose excreted in urine as glucuronidated metabolites, 16–61% in feces	Rash severe enough to dc use of drug in 1.7%. High frequency of diverse CNS AEs: somnolence, dreams, confusion, agitation. Serious psychiatric symptoms. Certain CYP2B6 polymorphisms may predict exceptionally high plasma levels with standard doses (CID 45:1230, 2007). False-pos. cannabinoid screen. **New Guidelines indicate is OK to use in pregnant women (WHO Guidelines) or continue EFV in women identified as pregnant (HHS Guidelines).** Very long tissue T½. **If rx to be discontinued, stop efavirenz 1–2 wks before stopping companion drugs.** Otherwise, risk of developing efavirenz resistance, as after 1–2 days only efavirenz in blood &/or tissue. Some authorities bridge this gap by adding a PI to the NRTI backbone if feasible after efavirenz is discontinued. (CID 42:401, 2006)
Etravirine (Intelence)	100 mg tabs 200 mg tabs	200 mg twice daily after a meal. May also be given as 400 mg once daily	Unknown (↓ systemic exposure if taken fasting)	41	2		Metabolized by CYP 3A4 (inducer) & 2C9, 2C19 (inhibitor). Excreted into feces (>90%), mostly unchanged drug	For pts with HIV-1 resistant to NNRTIs & others. Active in vitro against most such isolates. Rash common, but rarely can be severe. Potential for multiple drug interactions. Generally, multiple mutations are required for high-level resistance. See Table 3C, page 16 for specific mutations and effects. Because of interactions, do not use with boosted atazanavir, boosted tipranavir, unboosted PIs, or other NNRTIs.
Nevirapine (Viramune) Viramune XR	200 mg tabs; 50 mg per 5 mL, oral suspension; XR 400 mg tabs	200 mg po q24h x 14 days & then 200 mg po bid (see comments & *Black Box warning*). Food OK. **If using Viramune XR, Still need the lead in dosing of 200 mg q24h prior to using 400 mg/d**	>90	25–30	4		Cytochrome P450 (3A4, 2B6) inducer. 80% of dose excreted in urine as glucuronidated metabolites, 10% in feces	**Black Box warning—fatal hepatotoxicity.** Women with CD4 >250 esp. vulnerable, inc. pregnant women. Avoid in this group unless benefits clearly > risks (www.fda.gov/cder/drug/advisory/nevirapine.htm). If used, intensive monitoring required. Men with CD4 >400 also at ↑ risk. Rash severe enough to stop drug in 7%. **severe or life-threatening skin reactions** in 2%. Do not restart if any suspicion of such reactions. 2 wk dose escalation period may ↓ skin reactions. As with efavirenz, because of long T½, consider continuing companion agents for several days if nevirapine is discontinued.

TABLE 6A (9)

(CPE = CSF penetration effectiveness)

2. Selected Characteristics of Non-Nucleoside Reverse Transcriptase Inhibitors (NNRTIs) (continued)

Generic/ Trade Name	Pharmaceutical Prep.	Usual Adult Dosage & Food Effect	% Absorbed, po	Serum T½, hrs	Intracellular T½, hrs	CPE*	Elimination	Major Adverse Events/Comments (See Table 6B)
Rilpivirine (Edurant)	25 mg tabs	25 mg daily with food	absolute bio-availability unknown; 40% lower Cmax in fasted state	50	unknown		Metabolized by Cyp3A4 majority of drug metabolized by liver; 25% of dose excreted unchanged in feces	QTc prolongation with doses higher than 50 mg per day. Most common side effects are depression, insomnia, headache, and rash. Rilpivirine should not be co-administered with carbamazepine, phenobarbital, phenytoin, rifabutin, rifampin, rifapentine, proton pump inhibitors, or multiple doses of dexamethasone. A fixed dose combination of rilpivirine + TDF-FTC (Complera/Eviplera) is approved. **Needs stomach acid for absorption. Do not administer with PPI.**

3. Selected Characteristics of Protease Inhibitors (PIs).

All PIs: Glucose metabolism: new diabetes mellitus or deterioration of glucose control; fat redistribution; possible hemophilia bleeding; hypertriglyceridemia or hypercholesterolemia. Exercise caution re: potential drug interactions & contraindications. QTc prolongation has been reported in a few pts taking PIs; some PIs can block hERG channels in vitro (Lancet 365:682, 2005).

Generic/ Trade Name	Pharmaceutical Prep.	Usual Adult Dosage & Food Effect	% Absorbed, po	Serum T½, hrs		CPE*	Elimination	Major Adverse Events/Comments (See Table 6B)
Atazanavir (Reyataz)	100, 150, 200, 300 mg capsules	400 mg po q24h with food. Ritonavir-boosted dose (atazanavir 300 mg po q24h + ritonavir 100 mg po q24h), with food, is recommended for ART-experienced pts. The boosted dose is also used when combined with either efavirenz 600 mg po q24h or TDF 300 mg po q24h. If used with buffered ddI, take with food 2 hrs pre or 1 hr post ddI.	Good oral bioavailability; food enhances bioavailability & ↓ pharmacokinetic variability. Absorption ↓ by antacids, H₂-blockers, proton pump inhibitors. Avoid unboosted drug with PPIs/H2-blockers. Boosted drug can be used with or >10 hr after H2-blockers or >12 hr after a PPI, as long as limited doses of the acid agents are used (see 2008 drug label changes).	Approx. 7		2	Cytochrome P450 (3A4, 1A2 & 2C9 inhibitor) & UGT1A1 inhibitor. 13% excreted in urine (7% unchanged), 79% excreted in feces (20% unchanged)	Lower potential for ↑ lipids. Asymptomatic unconjugated hyperbilirubinemia common; jaundice especially likely in Gilbert's syndrome (JID 192:1381, 2005). Headache, rash, GI symptoms. Prolongation of PR interval (1st degree AV block) reported. Caution in pre-existing conduction system disease. Efavirenz ↓ tenofovir ↓ atazanavir exposure: use atazanavir/ritonavir regimen; also, atazanavir ↑ tenofovir concentrations—watch for adverse events. In experienced pts taking TDF and needing H2-blockers, atazanavir 400 mg with ritonavir 100 mg can be given; do not use PPIs. Rare reports of renal stones.
Darunavir (Prezista)	400 mg, 600 mg, 800 mg tablets	[600 mg darunavir + 100 mg ritonavir] po bid, with food **or** [800 mg darunavir (two 400 mg tabs or one 800 mg tab) + 100 mg ritonavir] po once daily with food (Preferred regimen in ART naive pts)	82% absorbed (taken with ritonavir). Food ↑ absorption.	Approx 15 hr (with ritonavir)		3	Metabolized by CYP3A and is a CYP3A inhibitor	Once daily dosing regimen mostly in 1st line therapy. Contains sulfa moiety. Rash, nausea, headaches seen. Coadmin of certain drugs cleared by CYP3A is contraindicated (see label). Use with caution in pts with hepatic dysfunction. (Recent FDA warning about occasional hepatic dysfunction early in the course of treatment). Monitor carefully, esp. first several months and with pre-existing liver disease. May cause hormonal contraception failure.

TABLE 6A (10)

E. Selected Characteristics of Antiretroviral Drugs (CPE = CSF penetration effectiveness)
3. Selected Characteristics of Protease Inhibitors (PIs). *(continued)*

Generic/ Trade Name	Pharmaceutical Prep.	Usual Adult Dosage & Food Effect	% Absorbed, po	Serum T½, hrs	CPE*	Elimination	Major Adverse Events/Comments *(See Table 6B)*
Fosamprenavir (Lexiva)	700 mg tablet; 50 mg/mL oral suspension	1400 mg (two 700 mg tabs) po bid **OR** with ritonavir: [1400 mg fosamprenavir (2 tabs) + ritonavir 200 mg] po q24h **OR** [1400 mg fosamprenavir (2 tabs) + ritonavir 100 mg] po q24h **OR** [700 mg fosamprenavir (1 tab) + ritonavir 100 mg] po bid	Bioavailability not established. Food OK	7.7 Ampre-navir	3	Hydrolyzed to amprenavir, then acts as cytochrome P450 (3A4 sub-strate, inhibitor, inducer)	Amprenavir prodrug. Contains sulfa moiety. Potential for serious drug interactions *(see label)*. Rash, including Stevens-Johnson syndrome. Once daily regimens: (1) not recommended for PI-experienced pts, (2) additional ritonavir needed if given with efavirenz *(see label)*. Boosted twice daily regimen is recommended for PI-experienced pts. Potential for PI cross-resistance with darunavir.
Indinavir (Crixivan)	100, 200, 400 mg capsules Store in original container with desiccant	Two 400 mg caps (800 mg) po q8h, without food or with light meal. Can take with enteric-coated Videx. *[If taken with ritonavir (e.g., 800 mg indinavir + 100 mg ritonavir po q12h), no food restrictions]*	65	1.2–2	4	Cytochrome P450 (3A4 inhibitor)	**Maintain hydration. Nephrolithiasis**, nausea, inconsequential ↑ of indirect bilirubin (jaundice in Gilbert syndrome), ↑ AST/ALT, headache, asthenia, blurred vision, metallic taste, hemolysis, ↑ urine WBC (>100/hpf) has been assoc. with nephritis/ medullary calcification, cortical atrophy.
Lopinavir + ritonavir (Kaletra)	200 mg lopinavir + 50 mg ritonavir) and (100 mg lopinavir + 25 mg ritonavir) tablets. Tabs do not need refrigeration. Oral solution. (80 mg lopinavir + 20 mg ritonavir) per mL. Refrigerate, but can be kept at room temp. (≤77 °F) x 2 mos.	(400 mg lopinavir + 100 mg ritonavir)—2 tabs po bid Higher dose may be needed in non-rx-naïve pts when used with efavirenz, nevirapine, or unboosted fosamprenavir. [Dose adjustment in con-comitant drugs may be necessary; see Table 16A]	No food effect with tablets.	5–6	3	Cytochrome P450 (3A4 inhibitor)	Nausea/vomiting/diarrhea (worse when administered with zidovudine). ↑ AST/ ALT, pancreatitis. Oral solution 42% alcohol Lopinavir + ritonavir can be taken as a single daily dose of 4 tabs (total 800 mg lopinavir + 200 mg ritonavir), except in treatment-experienced pts or those taking concomitant efavirenz, nevirapine, amprenavir, or nelfinavir. Possible PR and QT prolongation. Use with caution in those with cardiac conduction abnormalities or when used with drugs with similar effects
Nelfinavir (Viracept)	625, 250 mg tabs; 50 mg/gm oral powder	Two 625 mg tabs (1250 mg) po bid, with food	20–80 Food ↑ exposure & ↓ variability	3.5–5	1	Cytochrome P450 (3A4 inhibitor)	Diarrhea. Coadministration of drugs with life-threatening toxicities & which are cleared by CYP3A4 is contraindicated. Not recommended in initial regimens because of inferior efficacy; prior concerns about EMS now resolved. **Acceptable choice in pregnant women although it has inferior virologic efficacy than most other ARV anchor drugs.**

TABLE 6A (11)

E. Selected Characteristics of Antiretroviral Drugs (CPE = CSF penetration effectiveness)

3. Selected Characteristics of Protease Inhibitors (PIs). *(contd)*

Generic/ Trade Name	Pharmaceutical Prep.	Usual Adult Dosage & Food Effect	% Absorbed, po	Serum T½, hrs	CPE*	Elimination	Major Adverse Events/Comments *(See Table 6B)*
Ritonavir (Norvir)	100 mg capsules; 600 mg per 7.5 mL solution. Refrigerate caps but not solution. Room temperature for 1 mo. is OK.	Full dose not recommended (see comments). **With rare exceptions, used exclusively to enhance pharmacokinetics of other PIs, using lower ritonavir doses.**	Food ↑ absorption	3–5	1	Cytochrome P450. Potent 3A4 & 2 d6 inhibitor	Nausea/vomiting/diarrhea, extremity & circumoral paresthesias, hepatitis, pancreatitis, taste perversion, ↑ CPK & uric acid. **Black Box warning**—potentially fatal drug interactions. Many drug interactions—see Table 16A–Table 16B.
Saquinavir (Invirase—hard gel caps or tabs) + ritonavir	Saquinavir 200 mg caps, 500 mg film-coated tabs; ritonavir 100 mg caps	[2 tabs saquinavir (1000 mg) + 1 cap ritonavir (100 mg)] po bid with food	Erratic, 4 (saquinavir alone). Much more reliably absorbed when boosted with ritonavir.	1–2	1	Cytochrome P450 (3A4 inhibitor)	Nausea, diarrhea, headache, ↑ AST/ALT. Avoid rifampin with saquinavir + ritonavir: ↑ hepatitis risk. **Black Box warning**—Invirase to be used only with ritonavir. Possible QT prolongation. Use with caution in those with cardiac conduction abnormalities or when used with drugs with similar effects.
Tipranavir (Aptivus)	250 mg caps. Refrigerate unopened bottles. Use opened bottles within 2 mo. 100 mg/mL solution	[500 mg (two 250 mg caps) + ritonavir 200 mg] po bid with food.	Absorption low. ↑ with high fat meal, ↓ with Al⁺⁺⁺ & Mg⁺⁺ antacids.	5.5-6	1	Cytochrome 3A4 but with ritonavir, most of drug is eliminated in feces.	Contains sulfa moiety. **Black Box warning—reports of fatal/nonfatal intracranial hemorrhage, hepatitis, fatal hepatic failure.** Use cautiously in liver disease, esp. hepB, hepC. Contraindicated in Child-Pugh class B–C. Monitor LFTs. Coadministration of certain drugs contraindicated (see label). **For highly ART-experienced pts or for multiple-PI resistant virus.** Do not use tipranavir and etravirine together owing to 76% reduction in etravirine levels.

4. Selected Characteristics of Fusion Inhibitors

Generic/ Trade Name	Pharmaceutical Prep.	Usual Adult Dosage	% Absorbed	Serum T½, hrs	CPE*	Elimination	Major Adverse Events/Comments *(See Table 6B)*
Enfuvirtide (T20, Fuzeon)	Single-use vials of 90 mg/ml when reconstituted. Vials should be stored at room temperature. Reconstituted vials can be refrigerated for 24 hrs only.	90 mg (1 mL) subcut. bid. Rotate injection sites, avoiding those currently inflamed.	84	3.8	1	Catabolism to its constituent amino acids with subsequent recycling of the amino acids in the body pool. Elimination pathway(s) have not been performed in humans. Does not alter the metabolism of CYP3A4, CYP2 d6, CYP1A2, CYP2C19 or CYP2E1 substrates.	Local reaction site reactions 98%, 4% discontinue, erythema/induration ~80–90%, nodules/cysts ~80%, chills, N/V, ↓ BP & fever. **Hypersensitivity reactions reported** (fever, rash, chills, N/V, ↓ BP & ↑ AST/ALT)—do not restart if occur, including back/ground (re)pneumonia; peripheral neuropathy 8.9%, insomnia 11.3%, ↓ appetite 6.3%, myalgia 5%, lymphadenopathy 2.3%, eosinophilia ~10%. ↑ incidence of bacterial pneumonias. Alone offers little benefit to a failing regimen (*NEJM 348:2249, 2003*).

35

TABLE 6A (12)

E. Selected Characteristics of Antiretroviral Drugs (CPE = CSF penetration effectiveness) *(continued)*

5. Selected Characteristics of CCR-5 Co-receptor Antagonists

Generic/ Trade Name	Pharmaceutical Prep.	Usual Adult Dosage	% Absorbed	Serum T½, hrs	CPE*	Elimination	Major Adverse Events/Comments *(See Table 6B)*
Maraviroc (Selzentry)	150 mg, 300 mg film-coated tabs	Without regard to food: - 150 mg bid if concomitant meds include CYP3A inhibitors including PIs (except tipranavir/ritonavir) and delavirdine (with/without CYP3A inducers) - 300 mg bid without significantly interacting meds including NRTIs, tipranavir/ritonavir, nevirapine - 600 mg bid if concomitant meds include CYP3A inducers, including efavirenz (without strong CYP3A inhibitors)	Est. 33% with 300 mg dosage	14-18	3	CYP3A and P-glycoprotein substrate. Metabolites (via CYP3A) excreted feces > urine	**Black Box Warning-Hepatotoxicity,** may be preceded by rash; ↑ eos or IgE. NB: no hepatotoxicity was noted in MVC trials. Black box inserted owing to concern about potential CCR5 class effect. Data lacking in hepatic/renal insufficiency; ↑ concern with either could ↑ risk of ↓BP. Currently for treatment-experienced patients with multi-resistant strains. **Document CCR-5-tropic virus before use, as treatment failures assoc. with appearance of CXCR-4 or mixed-tropic virus.**

6. Selected Characteristics of Integrase Inhibitors

Generic/ Trade Name	Pharmaceutical Prep.	Usual Adult Dosage	% Absorbed	Serum T½, hrs	CPE*	Elimination	Major Adverse Events/Comments
Raltegravir (Isentress)	400 mg film-coated tabs	400 mg po bid, without regard to food	Unknown	~ 9	3	Glucuronidation via UGT1A1, with excretion into feces and urine. (Therefore does NOT require ritonavir boosting)	For naive patients and treatment experienced pts with multiply-resistant virus. Well-tolerated. Nausea, diarrhea, headache, fever similar to placebo. CK↑ & rhabdomyolysis reported: unclear relationship. Increased depression in those with a history of depression. Low genetic barrier to resistance. Increase in CPK, myositis, rhabdomyolysis have been reported. Rare Stevens Johnson Syndrome. Better oral absorption if chewed (CID 57:480, 2013).
Elvitegravir/ cobicistat (Stribild)	150 mg - 150 mg	150 mg-150 mg once daily with or without food	<10%	12.9 (Cobi), 3.5 (ELV)	Unknown	The majority of **elvitegravir** metabolism is mediated by CYP3A enzymes. Elvitegravir also undergoes glucuronidation via UGT1A1/3 enzymes. **Cobicistat** is metabolized by CYP3A and to a minor extent by CYP2D6	For both treatment naive patients and treatment experienced pts with multiply-resistant virus. Generally well-tolerated. Use of cobicistat increases serum creatinine by ~ 0.1 mg/d via inhibition of proximal tubular enzyme; this does not result in reduction in true GFR but will result in erroneous apparent reduction in eGFR by MDRD or Cockcroft Gault calculations. Usual AEs are similar to those observed with ritonavir (cobi) and tenofovir/FTC.
Dolutegravir (Tivicay)	50 mg	50 mg po once daily 50 mg po BID (if STI resistance present or if co-admin with EFV, FOS, TIP or Rif)	Unknown	14	4	Glucuronidation via UGT1A1 (therefore does not require ritonavir or cobicistat boosting)	Hypersensitivity (rare). Most common: insomnia (3%), headache (2%). N/V (1%), rash (<1%). Watch for IRIS; Watch for elevated LFTs in those with HCV (Letendre, et al, CROI 2010, abs #430)

* **CPE (CNS Penetration Effectiveness) value:** 1 = Low Penetration; 2 -3 = Intermediate Penetration; 4 = Highest Penetration into CNS *(Letendre, et al, CROI 2010, abs #430)*

TABLE 6A (13)

F. **Other Considerations in Selection of Therapy**
Caution: Initiation of ART may result in immune reconstitution syndrome with significant clinical consequences. See *TABLE 11B, page 128 (AIDS Reader 16:199, 2006)*.

1. Resistance testing: Given current rates of resistance, resistance testing is
    recommended in all patients prior to initiation of therapy, including those with acute
    infection syndrome (may initiate therapy while waiting for test results and adjusting Rx
    once results return), at time of change of therapy owing to antiretroviral failure, when
    suboptimal virologic response is observed, and in pregnant women. **Resistance testing**
    NOT recommended if pt is off ART for > 4 weeks or if HIV RNA is < 1000 c/mL.
    See Table 6F, page 47.

2. Drug-induced disturbances of glucose & lipid metabolism *(see Table 6C)*

3. Drug-induced lactic acidosis & other FDA "box warnings" *(see Table 6C)*

4. Drug-drug interactions *(see Table 16A)*

5. Risk in pregnancy *(see Table 17)*

6. Use in women & children *(see Table 8A)*

7. Dosing in patients with renal or hepatic dysfunction *(see Table 15A & Table 15B)*

TABLE 6B: ANTIRETROVIRAL DRUGS & ADVERSE EFFECTS
(See also www.aidsinfo.nih.gov; for combinations, see individual components)

DRUG NAME(S): GENERIC (TRADE)	MOST COMMON ADVERSE EFFECTS	MOST SIGNIFICANT ADVERSE EFFECTS
Nucleoside Reverse Transcriptase Inhibitors (NRTI) Black Box warning for all nucleoside/nucleotide RTIs: lactic acidosis/hepatic steatosis, potentially fatal. Also carry Warnings that fat redistribution and immune reconstitution syndromes (including autoimmune syndromes with delayed onset) have been observed		
Abacavir (Ziagen)	Headache 7–13%, nausea 7–19%, diarrhea 7%, malaise 7–12%	**Black Box warning–Hypersensitivity reaction (HR)** in 8% with malaise, fever, GI upset, rash, lethargy & respiratory symptoms most commonly reported; myalgia, arthralgia, edema, paresthesia less common. **Discontinue immediately if HR suspected. Rechallenge contraindicated; may be life-threatening.** Severe HR may be more common with once-daily dosing. **HLA-B*5701 allele** predicts ↑ risk of HR in Caucasian pop.; excluding pts with B*5701 markedly ↓ HR incidence (NEJM 358:568, 2008; CID 46:1111-1118, 2008). DHHS guidelines recommend testing for B*5701 and use of abacavir-containing regimens only if HLA-B*5701 negative. Vigilance essential in all groups. Possible increased risk of MI with use of abacavir had been suggested (JID 201:318, 2010). Other studies found no increased risk of MI (CID 52: 929, 2011). A meta-analysis of randomized trials by FDA also did not show increased risk of MI (www.fda.gov/drugs/drugsafety/ucm245164.htm). Nevertheless, care is advised to optimize potentially modifiable risk factors when abacavir is used.
Didanosine (ddI) (Videx)	Diarrhea 28%, nausea 6%, rash 9%, headache 7%, fever 12%, hyperuricemia 2%	**Pancreatitis 1–9%, Black Box warning—Cases of fatal & nonfatal pancreatitis** have occurred in pts receiving ddI, especially when used in combination with d4T or ddI + hydroxyurea. Fatal lactic acidosis in pregnancy with ddI + d4T. Peripheral neuropathy in 20%, 12% required dose reduction. ↑ toxicity if used with ribavirin. Use with TDF generally avoided (but would require dose reduction of ddI) because of ↑ toxicity and possible ↓ efficacy; may result in ↓ CD4. Rarely, retinal changes or optic neuropathy. Diabetes mellitus and rhabdomyolysis reported in post-marketing surveillance. Possible increased risk of MI under study (www.fda.gov/CDER. JID 201:318, 2010). Non-cirrhotic portal hypertension with ascites, varices, splenomegaly reported in post-marketing surveillance. See also Clin Infect Dis 49:626, 2009; Amer J Gastroenterol 104:1707, 2009. This entity has been associated with SNPs in 5'-nucleotidase and xanthine oxidase genes (CID 56:1117, 2013).
Emtricitabine (FTC) (Emtriva)	Well tolerated. Headache, diarrhea, nausea, rash, skin hyperpigmentation	Potential for lactic acidosis (as with other NRTIs). Also in Black Box—**severe exacerbation of hepatitis B on stopping drug reported—monitor clinical/labs for several months after stopping in pts with hepB.** Anti-HBV rx may be warranted if FTC stopped.
Lamivudine (3TC) (Epivir)	Well tolerated. Headache 35%, nausea 33%, diarrhea 18%, abdominal pain 9%, insomnia 11% (all in combination with ZDV). Pancreatitis more common in pediatrics.	**Black Box warning.** Make sure to use HIV dosage, not Hep B dosage. **Exacerbation of hepatitis B on stopping drug. Patients with hepB who stop lamivudine require close clinical/lab monitoring for several months.** Anti-HBV rx may be warranted if 3TC stopped.
Stavudine (d4T) (Zerit)	Diarrhea, nausea, vomiting, headache	**Peripheral neuropathy** 15–20%. Pancreatitis 1%. Appears to produce lactic acidosis, hepatic steatosis and lipoatrophy/lipodystrophy more commonly than other NRTIs. **Black Box warning—Fatal & nonfatal pancreatitis with d4T + ddI.** Use with TDF generally avoided (but would require dose reduction of ddI) because of ↑ toxicity and possible ↓ efficacy; may result in ↓ CD4. Rarely, retinal changes or optic neuropathy. Diabetes mellitus and rhabdomyolysis reported in post-marketing surveillance. **Fatal lactic acidosis/steatosis in pregnant women receiving d4T + ddI.** Fatal and non-fatal lactic acidosis and severe hepatic steatosis can occur in others receiving d4T. Use with particular caution in patients with risk factors for liver disease, but lactic acidosis can occur even in those without known risk factors. Possible ↑ toxicity if used with ribavirin. Motor weakness in the setting of lactic acidosis mimicking the clinical presentation of Guillain-Barré syndrome (including respiratory failure) (rare).
Zidovudine (ZDV, AZT) (Retrovir)	Nausea 50%, anorexia 20%, vomiting 17%, **headache 62%**. Also reported: asthenia, insomnia, myalgias, nail pigmentation. Macrocytosis expected with all dosage regimens.	**Black Box warning—hematologic toxicity, myopathy. Anemia** (<8 gm, 1%) granulocytopenia (<750, 1.8%). Anemia may respond to epoetin alfa if endogenous serum erythropoietin levels are ≤500 milliUnits/mL. Possible ↑ toxicity if used with ribavirin. Co-administration with Ribavirin not advised. Hepatic decompensation may occur in HIV/HCV co-infected patients receiving zidovudine with interferon alfa ± ribavirin.

TABLE 6B (2)

DRUG NAME(S): GENERIC (TRADE)	MOST COMMON ADVERSE EFFECTS	MOST SIGNIFICANT ADVERSE EFFECTS
Nucleotide Reverse Transcriptase Inhibitor (NRTI): Black Box warning for all nucleoside/nucleotide RTIs: lactic acidosis/hepatic steatosis, potentially fatal. Also carry Warnings that fat redistribution and immune reconstitution syndromes (including autoimmune syndromes with delayed onset) have been observed *(continued)*		
Tenofovir disoproxil fumarate (TDF) (Viread)	Diarrhea 11%, nausea 8%, vomiting 5%, flatulence 4% (generally well tolerated)	**Black Box Warning—Severe exacerbations of hepatitis B reported in pts who stop tenofovir.** Monitor carefully if drug is stopped; anti-HBV rx may be warranted if TDF stopped. Reports of renal injury from TDF, including Fanconi syndrome *(CID 37:e174, 2003; J AIDS 35:269,204; CID 42:283, 2006)*. Fanconi syndrome and diabetes insipidus reported with TDF + cdi *(AIDS Reader 19:114, 2009)*. Modest decline in renal function appears greater with TDF than with NRTIs *(CID 51:296, 2010)* and may be greater in those receiving TDF with a PI instead of an NNRTI *(JID 197:102, 2008; AIDS 26:567, 2012)*. In a VA study that followed >10,000 HIV-infected individuals, TDF exposure was significantly, associated with increased risk of proteinuria, a more rapid decline in renal function and chronic kidney disease *(AIDS 26:867, 2012)*. Monitor Ccr, serum phosphate and urinalysis, especially carefully in those with pre-existing renal dysfunction or nephrotoxic medications. TDF also appears to be associated with increased risk of bone loss. In a substudy of an ACTG comparative treatment trial, those randomized to TDF-FTC experienced greater decreases in spine and hip bone mineral density (BMD) at 96 weeks compared with those treated with ABC-3TC *(JID 203:1791, 2011)*. Consider monitoring BMD in those with history of pathologic fractures, or who have risks for osteoporosis or bone loss. **Black Box warning**—before using TDF-FTC as pre-exposure prophylaxis (PrEP), confirm HIV-1 negative status immediately before start and at least Q3Months; do not start PrEP in presence of any symptoms suggesting acute HIV infection until this is excluded.
Non-Nucleoside Reverse Transcriptase Inhibitors (NNRTI). Labels caution that fat redistribution and immune reconstitution can occur with ART.		
Delavirdine (Rescriptor)	Nausea, diarrhea, vomiting, headache	**Skin rash** has occurred in 18%; can continue or restart therapy in most cases. Stevens-Johnson syndrome & erythema multiforme have been reported rarely, 1 in liver enzymes in <5% of patients.
Efavirenz (Sustiva)	**CNS side effects 52%**; symptoms include dizziness, insomnia, somnolence, impaired concentration, psychiatric sx. & abnormal dreams; symptoms are worse after 1st or 2nd dose & improve over 2-4 weeks; discontinuation rate 2.6%. Rash 26% (vs. 17% in comparators); often improves with oral antihistamines; discontinuation rate 1.7%. Can cause false-positive urine test results for cannabinoid with CEDIA DAU multi-level THC assay. Metabolite can cause false-positive urine screening test for benzodiazepines *(CID 48:1787, 2009)*.	**Caution:** CNS effects may impair driving and other hazardous activities. Serious neuropsychiatric symptoms reported, including severe depression (2.4%) & suicidal ideation (0.7%). Elevation in liver enzymes. Fulminant hepatic failure has been reported *(see FDA label)*. **Teratogenicity reported in primates; pregnancy category D—may cause fetal harm, avoid in pregnant women or those who might become pregnant** *(see Table 8A)*. NOTE: No single method of contraception is 100% reliable. Barrier + 2nd method of contraception advised, continued 12 weeks after stopping efavirenz. Contraindicated with certain drugs metabolized by CYP3A4. Slow metabolism in those homozygous for the CYP-286 G516T allele can result in exaggerated toxicity and intolerance. This allele much more common in blacks and women *(CID 42:408, 2006)*. Stevens-Johnson syndrome and erythema multiforme reported in post-marketing surveillance.
Etravirine (Intelence)	Rash 9%, generally mild to moderate and spontaneously resolving; 2% dc clinical trials for rash. More common in women. Nausea 5%.	Severe rash (erythema multiforme, toxic epidermal necrolysis, Stevens-Johnson syndrome') has been reported. Hypersensitivity reactions can occur with rash, constitutional symptoms and organ dysfunction, including hepatic failure *(see FDA label)*. Potential for CYP450-mediated drug interactions. Rhabdomyolysis has been reported in post-marketing surveillance.

TABLE 6B (3)

DRUG NAME(S): GENERIC (TRADE)	MOST COMMON ADVERSE EFFECTS	MOST SIGNIFICANT ADVERSE EFFECTS
Non-Nucleoside Reverse Transcriptase Inhibitors (NNRTI) *(continued)*		
Nevirapine (Viramune)	**Rash 37%:** usually occurs during 1° 6 wks of therapy. Follow recommendations for 14-day lead-in period to ↓ risk of rash (see *Table 6A*, Women experience 7-fold ↑ in risk of severe rash (*CID 32:124, 2001*). 50% resolve within 2 wks of drug & 80% by 1 month. 6.7% discontinuation rate. In a Malawi cohort, HLA-C*04:01 was a risk factor for nevirapine-related Stevens-Johnson syndrome or TEN (*CID 56:1330, 2013*).	**Black Box warning—Severe life-threatening skin reactions reported:** Stevens-Johnson syndrome, toxic epidermal necrolysis, & hypersensitivity reaction or drug rash with eosinophilia & systemic symptoms (DRESS) (*AJM 161:2501, 2001*). For severe rashes, dc drug immediately & do not restart. In a clinical trial, the use of prednisone ↑ the risk of rash. **Black Box warning—Life-threatening hepatotoxicity reported,** 2/3 during the first 12 wks of rx. Overall 1% develops hepatitis. Monitor carefully (↑ in ALT or AST &/or history of chronic Hep B or C ↑ susceptible (*Hepatol 35:182, 2002*). Women with CD4 >250, including pregnant women, at ↑ risk. Avoid in this group unless no other option. Men with CD4 >400 also at ↑ risk. Monitor pts intensively (clinical & LFTs), esp. during the first 12 wks of rx. If clinical hepatotoxicity, severe skin or hypersensitivity reactions occur, dc drug & never rechallenge.
Rilpivirine (Edurant)	Headache (3%), rash (3% led to discontinuation in 0.1%), insomnia (3%), depressive disorders (8%). Psychiatric disorders led to discontinuation in 1%. Increased liver enzymes observed.	Drugs that induce CYP3A or increase gastric pH may decrease plasma concentration of rilpivirine and co-administration with rilpivirine should be avoided. Among these are certain anticonvulsants, rifamycins, PPIs, dexamethasone and St. John's wort. At supra-therapeutic doses, rilpivirine can increase QTc interval: use with caution with other drugs known to increase QTc. May cause depressive disorder, including suicide attempts or suicidal ideation. Overall, appears to cause fewer neuropsychiatric side effects than efavirenz (*JAIDS 60:33, 2012*). Hepatitis especially with pre-existing liver disease, including HBV and HCV: monitor LFTs. Nephrolithiasis and nephrotic syndrome reported
Protease inhibitors (PI)		
Abnormalities in glucose metabolism, dyslipidemias, fat redistribution syndromes (*see Table 6C, page 45*) are potential problems. Pts taking PI may be at increased risk for developing osteopenia/osteoporosis. (*See Table 6C, page 45*). Spontaneous bleeding episodes have been reported in HIV+ pts with hemophilia (being treated with PI. Rheumatoid complications have been reported with use of PIs (*Ann Rheum Dis 61:82, 2002*). Potential of some PIs for QTc prolongation has been suggested (*Lancet 365:682, 2005*). **Caution for all PIs**—Coadministration with certain drugs dependent on CYP3A or other enzymes for elimination & for which ↑ levels can cause serious toxicity may be contraindicated. As with other classes, rx may result in immune reconstitution syndromes, which may include early or late presentations of autoimmune syndromes. Taking into account both spontaneous and induced deliveries, a French cohort study demonstrated increased premature births among women receiving ritonavir-boosted PIs as compared with those receiving other antiretroviral therapy, even after accounting for other potential risk factors (*CID 54: 1348, 2012*).		
Atazanavir (Reyataz)	Asymptomatic unconjugated hyperbilirubinemia in up to 60% of pts, jaundice in 7–9% [especially with Gilbert syndrome (*JID 192: 1381, 2005*)]. Moderate to severe events: Diarrhea 1–3%, nausea 6–14%, abdominal pain 4%, headache 6%, rash 20%.	Prolongation of PR interval (1° degree AV block in 5–6%) reported; rarely 2° AV block: QTc increase and torsades reported (*CID 44:e67, 2007*). Acute interstitial nephritis (*Am J Kid Dis 44:E81, 2004*) and urolithiasis (atazanavir stones) reported (*AIDS 20:2131, 2006; NEJM 355:2158, 2006*). 10-fold increased risk of renal stones compared with pts receiving other PIs (*CID 55: 1262, 2012*). D:A:D study found atazanavir/ritonavir to be an independent risk factor for eGFR ≤ 70 in those with normal baseline renal function (*JID 207:1359, 2013*). Potential ↑ transaminases in pts co-infected with HBV or HCV. Severe skin eruptions (Stevens-Johnson syndrome, erythema multiforme, and toxic eruptions, or DRESS syndrome) have been reported.
Darunavir (Prezista)	With background regimens, headache 15%, nausea 18%, diarrhea 20%, amylase 17%. Rash in 10% of treated, 0.5% discontinuation.	Hepatitis in 0.5%, some with fatal outcome. Use caution in pts with HBV or HCV co-infections or other hepatic dysfunction. Monitor for clinical symptoms and LFTs. Stevens-Johnson syndrome, toxic epidermal necrolysis, erythema multiforme. May cause failure of hormonal contraceptives. Contains sulfa moiety. Potential for major drug interactions.
Fosamprenavir (Lexiva)	Skin rash ~ 20% (moderate or worse in 3–8%), nausea, headache, diarrhea.	Rarely Stevens-Johnson syndrome, hemolytic anemia. Pro-drug of amprenavir. Contains sulfa moiety. Angioedema and nephrolithiasis reported in post-marketing experience. Potential increased risk of MI (*see FDA label*). Angioedema, oral paresthesias, myocardial infarction and nephrolithiasis reported in post-marketing experience. Elevated LFTs seen with higher than recommended doses; increased risk in those with pre-existing liver abnormalities. Acute hemolytic anemia reported with amprenavir.

TABLE 6B (4)

DRUG NAME(S): GENERIC (TRADE)	MOST COMMON ADVERSE EFFECTS	MOST SIGNIFICANT ADVERSE EFFECTS
Protease Inhibitors (PI) *(continued)*		
Indinavir (Crixivan)	↑ in indirect bilirubin 10–15% (≥2.5 mg/dl), with overt jaundice especially likely in those with Gilbert syndrome (*JID* 192: 1381, 2005). Nausea 12%, vomiting 4%, diarrhea 5%. Metallic taste. Paronychia and ingrown toenails reported (*CID* 32:140, 2001).	**Kidney stones.** Due to indinavir crystals in collecting system. Nephrolithiasis in 12% of adults, higher in pediatrics. Minimize risk with good hydration (at least 48 oz. water/day) (*AAC* 42:332, 1998). Tubulointerstitial nephritis/renal cortical atrophy reported in association with asymptomatic ↑ urine WBC. Severe hepatitis reported in 3 cases (*Ln* 349:924, 1997). Hemolytic anemia reported.
Lopinavir/Ritonavir (Kaletra)	GI: **diarrhea** 14–24%, nausea 2–16%. More diarrhea with q24h dosing.	Lipid abnormalities in up to 20–40%. Possible increased risk of MI with cumulative exposure (*JID* 201:318, 2010). ↑ PR interval, 2° or 3° heart block described. Post-marketing reports of ↑ QTc and torsades: avoid use in congenital QTc prolongation or in other circumstances that prolong QTc or increase susceptibility to torsades. Hepatitis, with hepatic decompensation; caution especially in pts with pre-existing liver disease. Pancreatitis. Inflammatory edema of legs (*AIDS* 16:673, 2002). Stevens-Johnson syndrome & erythema multiforme reported. Note high drug concentration in oral solution (contains ethanol and propylene glycol) in neonates.
Nelfinavir (Viracept)	Mild to moderate **diarrhea** 20%. Oat bran tabs, calcium, or oral anti-diarrheal agents (e.g., loperamide, diphenoxylate/atropine sulfate) can be used to manage diarrhea.	Potential for drug interactions. Powder contains phenylalanine.
Ritonavir (Norvir) (Currently, primary use is to enhance levels of other anti-retrovirals, because of ↑toxicity/interactions with full-dose ritonavir)	GI: bitter aftertaste ↓ by taking with chocolate milk, Ensure, or Advera; nausea 23%, ↓ by initial dose esc. (titration) regimen; vomiting 13%, diarrhea 15%. Circumoral paresthesias 5–6%. Dose >100 mg bid assoc. with ↑ GI side effects & ↑ in lipid abnormalities.	Black Box warning relates to many important drug-drug interactions—inhibits P450 CYP3A & CYP2 D6 system— may be life-threatening (see Table 16A). Several cases of iatrogenic Cushing's syndrome reported with concomitant use of ritonavir and corticosteroids, including dosing of the latter by inhalation, epidural injection or a single IM injection. Rarely Stevens-Johnson syndrome, toxic epidermal necrolysis and anaphylaxis. Primary A-V block (and higher degrees) reported. Hepatic reactions, including fatalities. Monitor LFTs carefully during therapy, especially in those with pre-existing liver disease, including HBV and HCV. Small % pts with ritonavir-induced diarrhea may benefit from crofelemer 125 mg po bid (*Med Lett* 55:59, 2013).
Saquinavir (Invirase: hard cap, tablet)	**Diarrhea,** abdominal discomfort, nausea, headache.	**Warning—Use Invirase only with ritonavir.** Avoid garlic capsules (may reduce SQV levels) and use cautiously with proton-pump inhibitors (increased SQV levels significant). Use of saquinavir/ritonavir can prolong QTc interval or may rarely cause 2° or 3° heart block; torsades reported. Contraindicated in patients with prolonged QTc or those taking drugs or who have other conditions (e.g., low K+ or Mg++) that pose a risk with prolonged QTc (*http://www.fda.gov/drugs/DrugSafety/ucm230096.htm*, accessed May 25, 2011). Contraindicated in patients with complete AV block, or those at risk, who do not have a pacemaker. Hepatic toxicity encountered in patients with pre-existing liver disease or in individuals receiving concomitant rifampin. Rarely, Stevens Johnson syndrome.
Tipranavir (Aptivus)	Nausea & vomiting, diarrhea, abdominal pain. Rash in 8–14%, more common in women, & 33% in women taking ethinyl estradiol. Major lipid effects.	Black Box **Warning—associated with hepatitis & fatal hepatic failure.** Risk of hepatotoxicity increased in HBV or HCV co-infection. Possible photosensitivity skin reactions. Contraindicated in Child-Pugh Class B or C hepatic impairment. **Associated with fatal/nonfatal intracranial hemorrhage (can inhibit platelet aggregation).** Caution in those with bleeding risks. Potential for major drug interactions. Contains sulfa moiety and vitamin E.
Fusion Inhibitor		
Enfuvirtide (T20, Fuzeon)	Local injection site reactions (98%, at least 1 local ISR, 4% dc because of ISR) (pain & discomfort, induration, erythema, nodules & cysts, pruritus, & ecchymosis). Diarrhea 32%, nausea 23%, fatigue 20%.	↑ Rate of bacterial pneumonia (3.2 pneumonia events/100 pt yrs). **hypersensitivity reactions** ≤1% (rash, fever, nausea & vomiting, chills, rigors, hypotension, & ↑ serum liver transaminases); can occur with reexposure. Cutaneous amyloid deposits containing enfuvirtide peptide persisting after discontinuation of drug (*J Cutan Pathol* 39:220, 2012).

TABLE 6B (5)

DRUG NAME(S): GENERIC (TRADE)	MOST COMMON ADVERSE EFFECTS	MOST SIGNIFICANT ADVERSE EFFECTS
CCR5 Co-receptor Antagonists		
Maraviroc (Selzentry)	With ARV background: cough 13%; fever 12%, rash 10%, abdominal pain 8%. Also, dizziness, myalgia, arthralgias. ↑ Risk of URI, HSV infection.	**Black box warning-Hepatotoxicity.** May be preceded by allergic features (rash, ↑eosinophils or ↑IgE levels). Use with caution in pt with HepB or C. Cardiac ischemia/infarction in 1.3%. May cause ↓BP, orthostatic syncope, especially in patients with renal dysfunction. Significant interactions with CYP3A inducers/inhibitors. Long-term risk of malignancy unknown. Stevens-Johnson syndrome reported post-marketing. Generally favorable safety profile during trial of ART-naive individuals (*JID 201: 803, 2010*). Immune reconstitution syndrome, including autoimmune manifestations, may occur in those receiving ART, including maraviroc.
Integrase Inhibitors		
Raltegravir (Isentress)	Diarrhea, headache, insomnia, nausea. LFT ↑ may be more common in pts co-infected with HBV or HCV.	Hypersensitivity reactions can occur. Rash, Stevens-Johnson syndrome, toxic epidermal necrolysis reported. Hepatic failure reported. ↑CK, myopathy and rhabdomyolysis reported (*AIDS 22:1382, 2008*). 1 of preexisting depression reported in 4 pts; all could continue raltegravir after adjustment of psych. meds (*AIDS 22:1890, 2008*). Chewable tablets contain phenylalanine. Immune reconstitution syndrome, including autoimmune manifestations, may occur in those receiving ART, including raltegravir.
Elvitegravir (Stribild)	Nausea and diarrhea are the two most common AEs. An increase in serum creatinine of 0.1 - 0.15 mg/dl with use of cobicistat (related to inhibition of prox. tubular enzymes, not a true reduction in GFR).	Same Black box warnings as ritonavir and tenofovir. Rare lactic acidosis syndrome. Owing to renal toxicity, should not initiate Rx when pre-Rx eGFR is < 70 cc/min. Follow serial serum creatinine and urinary protein and glucose. Discontinue drug if serum Cr rises > 0.4 mg/dl above baseline value. Immune reconstitution syndrome, including autoimmune manifestations, may occur in those receiving ART. Fat redistribution may occur.
Dolutegravir (Tivicay)	Insomnia, headache. Diarrhea uncommon. Small increase in serum creatinine due to inhibition of tubular secretion of creatinine; no change in GFR. Increases in ALT/AST, cholesterol, glucose.	Hypersensitivity reactions, which may include fever, rash, fatigue/malaise, myalgia/arthralgia, angioedema, hepatitis, eosinophilia; stop immediately and do not rechallenge. Elevation of transaminases in HBV, HCV. Neutropenia (1%). Fat redistribution and immune reconstitution syndrome, including autoimmune manifestations, may occur.
Other		
Cobicistat Boosts serum levels of ARVs by blocking CYP3A	Nausea 17.7%, vomiting 7.3%, diarrhea, 15.4%. All of mild severity	Competes with creatinine for tubular secretion; can increase serum creatinine ≤ 0.4 mg/dL. Compared to ritonavir, less impact on function of fat cells & better solubility.

TABLE 6C: DRUG ADVERSE EFFECTS BY CLINICAL PRESENTATION[1]

Clinical Presentation	Implicated Drug Class or Drug(s)	Onset; Clinical Signs & Symptoms (S&S)	Estimated Frequency	Risk Factors	Prevention/ Monitoring	Clinical Management
LIFE THREATENING ADVERSE EFFECTS (in alphabetical order)						
Drug-induced hepatitis: Nevirapine	Nevirapine (Viramune) hypersensitivity reaction most important	Onset: 1st 6-18 weeks of rx. S&S: nausea/vomiting/icterus. Skin rash in 50%	2.5–11% in clinical trials	Females with CD4 >250; men with CD4 >400.	Monitor ALT/AST q2 wks x 1 mo., then every month x 3, then q3 mos.	DC all antiretrovirals + other potential hepatotoxic drugs.
Lactic acidosis/ hepatic steatosis ± pancreatitis (Mitochondrial toxicity: *JAC* 61:8, 2008)	Nucleoside reverse transcriptase inhibitors: stavudine (Zerit), didanosine (Videx), zidovudine (Retrovir)	Onset: Months after starting therapy. S&S: Nausea, vomiting, fatigue, dyspnea, icterus. Lab: Metabolic acidosis with anion gap & elevated lactate	Rare: 0.85 cases/1000 pt yrs, mortality up to 50%	Didanosine + stavudine. Female gender, pregnancy, obesity.	Lactic acid levels if suggestive symptoms and low serum HCO₃ and/or high anion gap. Routine lactate levels **not** recommended	DC all antiretrovirals. IV thiamine &/or riboflavin reported helpful. If needed, use NRTIs[2] with low potential for mitochondrial toxicity; i.e., abacavir, tenofovir, lamivudine, emtricitabine.
Lactic acidosis/rapid progressive ascending neuromuscular weakness	Stavudine (Zerit) & other nucleoside analogues, esp. ddI & ZDV	Onset: After months S&S: Rapid progressive ascending polyneuropathy that mimics Guillain-Barré. Lab: Metabolic acidosis with anion gap & elevated lactate + high CPK	Rare	Prolonged stavudine use; female gender, obesity.	Early recognition	DC all antiretrovirals, mechanical ventilation. Unclear benefit from plasmapheresis, IVIG, corticosteroids, carnitine. **Do not rechallenge with stavudine.**
Stevens-Johnson syndrome/toxic epidermal necrosis (see *drug-induced hepatitis* above)	Non-nucleoside reverse transcriptase inhibitors. Rare case reports with other classes of ARVs. TMP-SMX	Onset: 1st few days to weeks S&S: Skin eruption with mucosal ulcers ± epidermal detachment	Nevirapine (Viramune) 0.3–1% Efavirenz (Sustiva) & delavirdine (Rescriptor) 0.1%	Nevirapine— female, black, Asian, Hispanic.	Educate pts for early recognition	DC all antiretrovirals + other possible drug etiology; e.g., TMP/SMX. Usually requires ICU care.
Systemic hyper-sensitivity reaction	Abacavir (Ziagen) **DO NOT rechallenge** with abacavir.	Onset: Median 9 days; 90% within 1st 6 wks. S&S: Fever, diffuse rash, nausea/ vomiting/diarrhea/arthralgia, dyspnea, cough, or pharyngitis.	8% in clinical trials (range 2-9%)	HLA-B 5701, HLA-DR7 or HLA-B*5701 positive.	Screen for HLA-B*5701	DC all antiretrovirals; Resolution within 48 hrs.; do not rechallenge.
	Nevirapine (Viramune)	Severe skin reactions	2%		Do not restart	See *drug-induced Hepatitis.*
SERIOUS ADVERSE EFFECTS (in alphabetical order)						
Bleeding events: CD8 Encephalitis	ART	Cognitive impairment, confusion, seizure	Rare	CNS IRIS, ART interruption	Gadolinium enhanced MRI for Dx	Glucocorticoids (*CID* 57::101, 2013)

[1] Adapted from *Table 18, Guidelines for use of antiretroviral agents in HIV-1 infected adults and adolescents, DHHS, 01/29/2008*

[2] **NRTI** = nucleoside reverse transcriptase inhibitor

TABLE 6C (2)

Clinical Presentation	Implicated Drug Class or Drug(s)	Onset; Clinical Signs & Symptoms (S&S)	Estimated Frequency	Risk Factors	Prevention/ Monitoring	Clinical Management
SERIOUS ADVERSE EFFECTS (in alphabetical order) (continued)						
Hemophiliac patients	Protease inhibitors	Spontaneous bleeding	Unknown	Protease inhibitor use	Try to avoid PIs	Increased use of Factor VIII.
Intracranial hemorrhage	Ritonavir boosted tipranavir (TPV/r)	Median time to hemorrhage: 525 days of TPV/r therapy	24 cases with TPV/r; 2 deaths	CNS disease, injury or surgery, anti-coagulants, Vitamin E	Avoid vitamin E supplements.	Discontinue TPV/r.
Bone marrow suppression	Zidovudine (Retrovir)	Onset: Weeks to months S&S: Fatigue Lab: Anemia &/or neutropenia	Severe anemia 1.1–4% Severe neutropenia 1.8–8%	AIDS; high dose concomitant marrow-suppressive drug(s)	Avoid marrow suppressive drugs. CBC & differential at least q3 mos.	If severe, could use G-CSF &/or erythropoietin.
Hepatotoxicity; steatosis to NASH (see drug-induced hepatitis, page 40)	All NNRTIs, all PIs, most NRTIs, maraviroc. **Steatosis:** most common with ZDV, d4T, ddI	PIs: clinical hepatitis reported with TPV/r Onset: variable NRTI: Asym ↑ed AST/ALT + lactic acidosis (ZDV, ddI, d4T)	Variable with different drugs	Co-infection: Hep B. Hep C, alcoholism, other hepatotoxic drugs	Nevirapine: monitor LFTs frequently, especially females. TPV/r: avoid in pts with hepatic insufficiency.	Test for Hep B&C. If symptomatic, discontinue all retroviral drugs. **Vitamin E** may improve steatosis. **L-carnitine** (2 gm/day) may help (Dig Dis Sci 53:114, 2008).
Nephrolithiasis; urolithiasis/ crystalluria	Indinavir (Crixivan) most often, rarely atazanavir	Onset: Any time S&S: Flank pain & dysuria Lab: Hematuria, crystalluria, pyuria	Range in clinical trials: 4.7–34.4%	Dehydration; history of nephrolithiasis	Intake of 1.5–2 liters water/day.	Hydration
Nephrotoxicity—tenofovir Based on meta-analysis, severity of toxicity is modest (CID 51:496, 2010).	Indinavir (Crixivan) crystalluria (see above) & **tenofovir (Viread)** tubular injury. Cobicistat inhibits proximal tubular creatinine excretion leading to 0.1–0.15 mg/dl increase in serum creatinine	Onset: Tenofovir—weeks to months. Cobi impact of serum creatinine is immediate. S&S: Tenofovir—nephrogenic diabetes insipidus, **Fanconi syndrome.** Lab: Non-anion gap metabolic acidosis, glycosuria, hypokalemia, hypophosphatemia.	Unknown but severe toxicity is rare	Other nephrotoxic drugs; other anti-HIV drugs handled by proximal tubular cells; predisposing human genetic variant (JID 194:1471 & 1481, 2006)	Monitor serum creatinine. Theoretic drug-drug interactions with ritonavir, didanosine & atazanavir. Decrease dosing frequency of tenofovir if est. CrCl < 50 cc/min. Discontinue Cobi if serum Cr increases > 0.4 mg/dl or eGFR drops to < 60 cc/min.	**Stop offending drug if possible.** Renal injury is reversible. Tenofovir (TDF): Fall in CrCl greater with TDF + PIs vs. TDF + NNRTI (JID 197:102, 2008). Risk with tenofovir offset by potent antiretroviral effect (JAC 63:374, 2009).
Pancreatitis	Didanosine (Videx); didanosine + stavudine (Zerit); ddI + ribavirin or tenofovir.	Onset: Weeks to months S&S: Abd./back pain nausea/vomiting Lab: ↑ amylase/lipase	Didanosine alone 1–7%. Increased frequency if ddI with d4T, TDF or ribavirin.	High serum/cell didanosine levels; alcoholism; hypertriglyceridemia. Failure to ↓ dose of didanosine if given with tenofovir	No advisory in history of pancreatitis. Adjust dose of didanosine if tenofovir used. Avoid use of ddI with d4T, tenofovir or ribavirin.	Discontinue antiretrovirals.
Polyneuropathy	**D4T (Stavudine) > ddI** and ddC	d4T-induced: Rapidly progressive ascending polyneuropathy mimics Guillain-Barré syndrome.	Rare	Prolonged use of d4T	Early recognition	DC all ARVs. Variable success with plasmapheresis, steroids, IVIG, carnitine.

TABLE 6C (3)

Clinical Presentation	Implicated Drug Class or Drug(s)	Onset; Clinical Signs & Symptoms (S&S)	Estimated Frequency	Risk Factors	Prevention/ Monitoring	Clinical Management
ADVERSE EFFECTS WITH LONG-TERM COMPLICATIONS (in alphabetical order) Ref: *HIV & Aging. JAIDS 60 (Suppl 1):S1, 2012.*						
Atherosclerotic MIs & CVAs. May be driven by chronic infection & immune reactivation *(JID 205 (Suppl 3): S355 & 375, 2012)*	Traditional risk factors and uncontrolled HIV infection most important. Selected HIV drugs suspected but unproven risk factors. Abacavir considered then rejected as risk factor *(CID 52:929, 2011; CID 53:84 & 92, 2011).*	Onset: Months to years S&S: Premature or accelerated atherosclerotic vascular disease (e.g. MI, stroke).	Data controversial.	Tobacco use, age, hyperlipidemia, hypertension, diabetes, obesity, HIV infection + low CD4 *(CID 51:435, 2010).* Undetectable VL, but falling CD4 *(CID 57:314, 2013).*	Address risk factors; suppress HIV viremia.	Manage risk factors: control HIV viremia. Review: *Topics in HIV Med 18:164, 2010.* Check Vitamin D level; correlation with silent coronary artery disease *(CID 54:1747, 2012).*
Hyperlipidemia *(JID 205 (Suppl 3): S383, 2012; CID 52:387, 2011)*	All protease inhibitors (PIs) except atazanavir; **stavudine; efavirenz.** Ritonavir boosting elevates triglyceride levels.	Associated elevation of TG, LDL, HDL. • Stavudine > ZDV > ABC • Efavirenz • All RTV-boosted PIs (LPV/r > DRV/r > ATV/r)	1.7–2.3 fold increase with PIs other than atazanavir.	PIs: ritonavir boosted lopinavir NNRTI: Efavirenz NRTI: Stavudine	ART causes modest increase in serum lipids. Check with statins. Check fasting lipid panel at baseline at 3–6 months, then annually.	Check for drug-drug interactions; statins and PIs. In general, prefer treatment with atorvastatin or rosuvastatin *(AIDS 24:77, 2010; CID 52:387, 2011).*
Insulin resistance/ diabetes mellitus *(JID 205 (Suppl 3): S383, 2012)*	ZDV, Stavudine, ddI. Relation to PIs unclear.	Onset: Weeks to months S&S: Polydipsia, polyuria, polyphagia	Diabetes in 3–5%	Obesity, genetics, dyslipidemia.	Avoid ZDV & Stavudine	Diet & exercise, metformin, "glitazones," sulfonylureas, insulin.
Osteonecrosis *CID 51:937, 2010* (See Osteoporosis, page 45)	HIV itself, tenofovir *(CID 51:963, 2010),* **boosted atazanavir & efavirenz suspect.**	Onset: Insidious S&S: Periarticular pain. 85% involve one or both femoral heads	Symptomatic 0.08–1.3% Asymptomatic by MRI 4%	Diabetes, prior steroid use, alcohol use, Vitamin D deficiency.	No steroids. Periodic MRIs to assess disease progression. Check Vitamin D levels.	Remove risk factors; less weight-bearing; eventually total joint arthroplasty. Vitamin D supplement if levels low.
ADVERSE EFFECTS THAT INFLUENCE QUALITY OF LIFE						
Fat Maldistribution: Association with elevated intracellular concentration of stavudine *(CID 50:1033, 2010)*						
Lipoatrophy *(JID 205 (Suppl 3):S383, 2012)*	PI or NRTI combined with d4T or ZDV. **NRTIs, especially Stavudine > zidovudine.** > TDF, ABC, 3TC, FTC, esp. when combined with EFV *(CID 51:591, 2010).*	Loss of subcutaneous fat on face, buttocks & extremities. Note: HLA-B*4001 presence risk factor for stavudine-associated lipodystrophy *(CID 50:597, 2010).*	Precise frequency unknown	Low nadir CD4 count, older age. Low baseline body mass index (BMI).	If possible, avoid stavudine and zidovudine.	**What makes it worse?** Exercise, testosterone, metformin, recombinant human growth hormone. **What helps?** Pravastatin, drug switch. Dermal fillers (poly-L-lactic acid) of limited help.
Fat Accumulation: Lipodystrophy (Lipohypertrophy)	PI or NRTI combined with d4T or ZDV.	Excess adipose tissue in abdominal viscera, breast size, dorsocervical fat pad. Management: Tesamorelin ↓ in triglycerides & adiponectin levels *(CID 54:1642, 2012).*	Precise frequency unknown	Obesity prior to HIV infection; low CD4 count prior to therapy, older age; low baseline BMI.	Avoid combination of PI or NRTI with d4T or AZT. Switching from LPV/r to ATV/r ↓ visceral fat *(AIDS 23:1349, 2009).*	**What helps?** Growth hormone releasing factor (tesamorelin) ↓ visceral fat by 18% *(JAIDS 53:311, 2010; Med Lett 53:33, 2011).* FDA approved 2 mg sc once daily via restricted access program *(www.egrifta.com/AxisCenter.aspx).*

TABLE 6C (4)

Clinical Presentation	Implicated Drug Class or Drug(s)	Onset; Clinical Signs & Symptoms (S&S)	Estimated Frequency	Risk Factors	Prevention/ Monitoring	Clinical Management
ADVERSE EFFECTS THAT INFLUENCE QUALITY OF LIFE *(continued)*						
Gastrointestinal— Diarrhea	All protease inhibitors (PIs), didanosine (Videx)	Onset: 1st dose Symptoms: Perhaps worst with lopinavir/ritonavir, nelfinavir, & buffered didanosine	Varies	All patients	Antidiarrheals	Loperamide, diphenoxylate/ atropine, calcium tabs, psyllium products, pancreatic enzymes, L-glutamate.
Osteopenia & Osteoporosis (see Osteonecrosis, page 44)	Bone loss, 2° HIV, tenofovir, boosted atazanavir, EFV (JID 205 (Suppl 3);S391, 2012)	Months to years; increased risk of fractures	Unclear but higher than general population	Low vitamin D levels (CID 52;396, 2011)	Vitamin D supplements	Perhaps increased risk with stavudine & tenofovir; consider bisphosphonates
Peripheral neuropathy	**Didanosine (Videx), stavudine (Zerit)**	Onset: Weeks to months S&S: Usually legs. Numbness & paresthesias. Often irreversible even if drug(s) stopped.	Didanosine 12–34%; Stavudine 52%.	Pre-existing neuropathy; concomitant drugs that ↑ intracellular didanosine, e.g., ribavirin, tenofovir.	Avoid use, esp. in combination	If painful can try gabapentin or tricyclic antidepressants; lamotrigine, carbamazepine (watch for drug interactions), topiramate, tramadol, narcotics, topical capsacin.

TABLE 6D: OVERLAPPING TOXICITIES BETWEEN ANTIRETROVIRALS AND OTHER DRUGS COMMONLY USED IN HIV PATIENTS* (Anti-HIV Drugs are BOLD)

Bone Marrow Suppression	Peripheral Neuropathy	Pancreatitis	Nephrotoxicity	Hepatotoxicity	Rash	Diarrhea	Ocular Effects
Amphotericin B	**Didanosine**	Cotrimoxazole	Acyclovir (IV, HD)	Azithromycin	**Abacavir**	Atovaquone	Cidofovir
Cidofovir	Isoniazid	**Didanosine**	Adefovir	Clarithromycin	**Atazanavir**	Clindamycin	**Didanosine**
Cotrimoxazole	Linezolid	**Lamivudine** (child)	Aminoglycosides	**Darunavir**	Atovaquone	**Darunavir**	Ethambutol
Cytotoxic chemotherapy	**Stavudine**	Pentamidine	Amphotericin B	**Delavirdine**	Cotrimoxazole	**Fosemprenavir**	Linezolid
Dapsone		**Ritonavir**	Atazanavir (stones)	Didanosine (portal hypertension)	Dapsone	**Lopinavir/ritonavir**	Rifabutin
Flucytosine		**Stavudine**	Cidofovir	Dolutegravir	**Darunavir**	**Nelfinavir**	
Ganciclovir			**Cobicistat**	**Efavirenz**	**Delavirdine**	**Ritonavir**	
Hydroxyurea			Foscarnet	Fluconazole	**Efavirenz**	**Tipranavir**	
Interferon-alpha			**Indinavir**	Isoniazid	**Fosamprenavir**		
Linezolid			Pentamidine	Itraconazole	**Maraviroc**		
Peg-interferon alpha			**Tenofovir**	Ketoconazole	**Nevirapine**		
Primaquine				**Maraviroc**	**Raltegravir**		
Pyrimethamine				**Nevirapine**	Sulfadiazine		
Ribavirin				Didanosine (hepatic steatosis)	**Tipranavir**		
Rifabutin				**PIs** (esp. tipranavir)	Trimethoprim/ sulfamethoxazole		
Sulfadiazine				Rifabutin	Voriconazole		
Trimetrexate				Rifampin			
Valganciclovir				Voriconazole			
Zidovudine							

*Adapted from Guidelines for use of antiretroviral agents in HIV-1 infected adults and adolescents, DHHS, http://aidsinfo.nih.gov

TABLE 6E: ANTI-HIV DRUGS AVAILABLE VIA EXPANDED ACCESS PROGRAMS

(www.aidsinfo.nih.gov; 800-448-0440) No Drugs Available by Expanded Access at the present time

SELECTED DRUGS IN DEVELOPMENT

Drug Name(s), Number, (Manufacturer)	Drug Class (Site of Anti-HIV Activity)	Dose	Comments
Apricitabine (ATC)	nRTI	600 mg twice daily Dose being finalized in current studies	3TC-like agent with activity against virus harboring an M184V mutation. Antagonistic against 3TC and FTC. **Drug back in development.**
Pro-140	CCR5 Antagonist	324 mg SQ once weekly or biweekly	Studies underway to determine dose, safety, activity.
Cenicriviroc (TBR-652)	CCR5 - CCR2 Inhibitor	100 mg or 200 mg daily Dose still being determined	Phase III trials about to begin. CCR2 inhibition may produce anti-inflammatory effect.
Cobicistat (as single agent)	CYP3A4 inhibitor (boosting agent)	150 mg daily	Used as a 'ritonavir-like' boosting agent for selective PIs (e.g., Darunavir and Atazanavir. Likely to be co-formulated with these drugs
GS - 7340 (Tenofovir prodrug TAF)	nRTI	25 mg daily (Dose being finalized)	Compared to standard dose tenofovir DP (300 mg/d), tenofovir prodrug achieves 7-fold higher intracellular concentration, 90% lower circulating plasma levels. Being evaluated as fixed-dose combination with Elvitegravir, cobi, and FTC.

TABLE 6F: MANAGEMENT OF ANTIRETROVIRAL THERAPY FAILURE

Definition	**Therapeutic Failure:** Progression of clinical disease, virologic failure, or development of toxicity. **Virologic Failure:** Persistent (confirmed) HIV RNA (VL) > 200 c/mL 6 months after starting ART.
General approach to management	• Evaluate Adherence, tolerability, drug-drug interactions, and psychosocial issues • If tolerability/toxicity issue, identify the most likely offending agent and substitute another agent that is likely to have antiviral activity and not have overlapping toxicities or drug-drug interactions with remaining agents • Obtain/review antiretroviral drug history (including tolerability to prior agents used)
Management of virologic failure	**For documented HIV RNA > 200 but less than 500 c/mL** • Carefully review adherence / barriers to medication access • Improve PK if possible (boosting, drug-drug interactions) **For confirmed HIV RNA > 500 – 1000 c/mL** • Change regimen as soon as possible (prevent emergence of further resistance) • Obtain resistance test while on the failing regimen (genotype preferable in general; phenotype most helpful for complex treatment history) **If no resistance mutations noted:** Reassess adherence / drug-drug interactions/absorption issues. Check plasma drug levels (optional) **If resistance mutations observed:** • Change regimen based on findings (see below) and antiretroviral history • Expert discussion advised if unfamiliar with mutations or findings
Use of resistance test mutations	**General Rules** • Use at least 2 (and preferably 3) fully active agents; can be active drugs from prior regimen(s). However beware of archived resistant virus • Unclear how to 'count' partially active drugs. 3TC and FTC usually have residual partial activity and are often included in the new regimen (though not considered 'fully active' agents • Avoid 'double boosted' PIs (i.e., two PI agents + ritonavir) **If many options available** • Choose agent(s) most likely to be (1) better tolerated (2) more convenient/simpler (3) least drug-drug interaction **If only limited active drugs identified** • If 2 fully active drugs not identified / available, generally should defer changing therapy until newer agents are available. If clinical deterioration impending, switch to best alternative. Clinical judgment necessary • Treatment interruption should be avoided; even partially active regimens (~ 0.5 - 1.0 log reduction) are better than no therapy
Use of therapeutic drug monitoring (tdm)	**Rationale:** Drug levels can be highly variable (esp. PIs) **Which Drugs:** PIs, NNRTIs, maraviroc **Which Patients:** • Drug-drug interactions suspected • HIV agents with partial activity (desire to get optimal drug levels) • Pregnancy (selected cases) • Concentration-dependent toxicities • Unexplained absence of virologic response (e.g., wild type virus in pt with virologic failure) **Limitations** • Few prospective studies demonstrating benefit • Incomplete knowledge of therapeutic ranges • Considerable inter-individual variation of levels • Little / no role in nRTI medications owing to role of intracellular concentrations • Only a few qualified labs **Target Trough Concentrations for Selected Medications** (levels should be obtained at steady-state) • Atazanavir (150 ng/mL) • Fosamprenavir (400 ng/mL) • Indinavir (100 ng/mL) • Lopinavir (1000 ng/mL) • Nelfinavir (800 ng/mL) • Saquinavir (100-250 ng/mL) • Tipranavir (20,500 ng/mL) • Efavirenz (1000 ng/mL) • Nevirapine (3,000 ng/mL) • Maraviroc (> 50 ng/mL)

TABLE 6G: ANTIRETROVIRALS APPROVED OR TENTATIVELY APPROVED BY FDA FOR INTERNATIONAL AIDS RELIEF

The US FDA reviews international marketing applications for individual antiretroviral agents, fixed dose combinations & co-packaged ARVs, & grants approval (A) or tentative (T) approval (when products continue to have marketing protection) status to products that meet efficacy, safety & manufacturing standards for marketing in the US.

Generic name	Pharmaceutical Prep.	Supplier	Status
Single agents:			
Abacavir sulfate	300 mg tabs, 60 mg tabs, 20 mg/mL oral solution	Aurobindo Pharma, Ltd	T
	300 mg tabs, 60 mg tabs for oral suspension, 20 mg/mL oral solution	Cipla, Ltd	T
	300 mg tabs, 20 mg/mL oral solution	Hetero Drugs, Ltd	T
	300 mg tabs	Strides Arcolab, Ltd	T
	300 mg tabs, 60 mg tabs	Mylan Labs Ltd	T
Didanosine	200 mg, 250 mg, 400 mg delayed release caps	Barr Laboratories, Inc.	A
	125 mg, 200 mg, 250 mg, 400 mg delayed release caps	Aurobindo Pharma, Ltd	A
	125 mg, 200 mg, 250 mg, and 400 mg	Mylan Laboratories Ltd	T
Zidovudine (ZDV)	100 mg, 150 mg, 200 mg tabs	Aurobindo Pharma, Ltd	A
	10 mg/mL oral solution	Aurobindo Pharma, Ltd	A
	100 mg caps, 300 mg tabs, 60 mg tabs, 50 mg/5 mL oral solution	Aurobindo Pharma, Ltd	A
	100 mg caps, 50 mg/5 mL oral solution	Cipla, Ltd	A
	300 mg tabs	Cipla, Ltd	T
	300 mg tabs	HEC Pharm Inc	T
	300 mg tabs, 100 mg tabs	Mylan Laboratories, Ltd	A
	300 mg tabs	Hetero Labs Ltd	A
Lamivudine (3TC)	150 mg tabs	Ranbaxy Laboratories, Ltd	T
	150 mg tabs, 300 mg tabs	Mylan Laboratories, Ltd	T
	150 mg tabs	Aikem Laboratories, Ltd	T
	150 mg, 300 mg tabs	Aurobindo Pharma, Ltd	T
	10 mg/mL oral solution	Cipla, Ltd	T
	150 mg, 300 mg tabs	Hetero Labs Drugs, Ltd	T
	150 mg, 300 mg tabs	Macleods Pharmaceuticals, Ltd	T
Lamivudine (3TC) (cont.)	150 mg, 300 mg tabs	Strides Arcolab Ltd	T
	300 mg, 150 mg tabs	Micro Labs Ltd	T
	10 mg/mL oral solution	Hetero Labs Ltd	T
Emtricitabine	200 mg caps	Aurobindo Pharma, Ltd	T
	200 mg caps	Cipla, Ltd	T
	200 mg caps	Mylan Laboratories, Ltd	T
Stavudine (d4T)	15 mg, 20 mg, 30 mg, 40 mg caps, 1 mg/mL oral solution	Aurobindo Pharma, Ltd	A
	30 mg, 40 mg caps	Strides Arcolab, Ltd	T
	30 mg, 40 mg caps	Mylan Laboratories, Ltd	A
	1 mg/mL oral solution	Cipla, Ltd	A
	15 mg, 20 mg, 30 mg, 40 mg caps	Hetero Labs, Ltd	A
	40 mg caps	Emcure Pharmaceuticals, Ltd	T
Tenofovir Disoproxil Fumarate	300 mg tabs	Mylan Laboratories, Ltd	A
	300 mg tabs	Aurobindo Pharma, Ltd	A
	300 mg tabs	Cipla, Ltd	T
	300 mg tabs	Hetero Labs Ltd	A
	300 mg tabs	Strides Arcolab Ltd	T
Nevirapine	200 mg tabs	Ranbaxy Laboratories, Ltd	T
	50 mg, 100 mg tablets for oral suspension	Cipla, Ltd	T
	200 mg tabs	Cipla, Ltd	A
	200 mg tabs	Strides Arcolab, Ltd	A
	200 mg tabs, 50 mg/5 mL oral suspension	Aurobindo Pharma, Ltd	A
	50 mg tabs for oral suspension	Aurobindo Pharma, Ltd	T
	200 mg tabs	Huahai US, Inc	A
	200 mg tabs	Hetero Labs, Ltd	A
	200 mg tabs	Emcure Pharmaceuticals, Ltd	T

TABLE 6G (2)

Generic name	Pharmaceutical Prep.	Supplier	Status
Single agents *(cont.)*:			
Nevirapine *(cont.)*	200 mg tabs	Macleod's Pharmaceuticals, Ltd	T
	200 mg tabs	Mylan Pharms Inc	A
	200 mg tabs	Micro Labs Ltd	A
	200 mg tabs	Sciegen Pharms Inc	A
Efavirenz	200 mg caps, 600 mg tabs	Cipla, Ltd	T
	600 mg tabs	Edict Pharm	T
	200 mg, 600 mg tabs	Strides Arcolab, Ltd	T
	50 mg, 100 mg, 200 mg, and 600 mg tabs	Mylan Laboratories, Ltd	T
	600 mg tabs	Emcure Pharmaceuticals, Ltd	T
	600 mg tabs	Hetero Labs, Ltd	T
	50 mg, 100 mg, 200 mg caps; 600 mg and 100 mg tabs	Aurobindo Pharma, Ltd	T
	600 mg tabs, 200 mg, 50 mg caps	Micro Labs Ltd	T
Atazanavir sulfate	600 mg tabs	Macleods Pharm Ltd	T
	100 mg, 150 mg, 200 mg, 300 mg caps	Emcure Pharmaceuticals, Ltd	T
	150 mg, 300 mg caps	Mylan Labs Ltd	T
Atazanavir/Ritonavir	300 mg/100 mg caps	Mylan Labs Ltd	T
Lopinavir/ritonavir	200 mg/50 mg tabs	Mylan Labs Ltd	T
	200 mg/50 mg tabs; 80 mg/mL oral solution	Cipla, Ltd	T
	100 mg/25 mg tabs; 200 mg/50 mg tabs	Aurobindo Pharma, Ltd	T
	200 mg/50 mg tabs	Hetero Labs Ltd	T
Combinations and/or co-packaged products:			
Emtricitabine/Tenofovir Disoproxil Fumarate	Tabs: (200 mg FTC + 300 mg TDF)	Aurobindo Pharma, Ltc	T
	Tabs: (200 mg FTC + 300 mg TDF)	Mylan Labs, Ltd	T
	Tabs: (200 mg FTC + 300 mg TDF)	Strides Arcolab Ltd	T
	Tabs: (200 mg FTC + 300 mg TDF)	Hetero Labs Ltd	T

Generic name	Pharmaceutical Prep.	Supplier	Status
Lamivudine/Zidovudine	Tabs: (150 mg 3TC + 300 mg ZDV)	Aurobindo Pharma, Ltd	A
	Tabs: (30 mg 3TC + 60 mg ZDV)	Aurobindo Pharma, Ltd	T
	Tabs: (150 mg 3TC + 300 mg ZDV)	Pharmacare, Ltd	T
	Tabs: (150 mg 3TC + 300 mg ZDV)	Cipla, Ltd	T
	Tabs and tabs for oral suspension: (30 mg 3TC + 60 mg ZDV)	Cipla Ltd	T
	Tabs: (150 mg 3TC + 300 mg ZDV)	Emcure Pharmaceuticals, Ltd	T
	Tabs: (150 mg 3TC + 300 mg ZDV)	Mylan Labs, Ltd	T
	Tabs: (30 mg 3TC + 60 mg ZDV)	Mylan Labs, Inc.	T
	Tabs: (150 mg 3TC + 300 mg ZDV)	Hetero Labs, Ltd	T
	Tabs: (150 mg 3TC + 300 mg ZDV)	Macleods Pharmaceuticals, Ltd	T
	Tabs: (150 mg 3TC + 300 mg ZDV)	Strides Arcolab, Ltd	T
Lamivudine/Abacavir	Tabs: (300 mg 3TC + 600 mg abacavir) Tabs: (30 mg 3TC + 60 mg abacavir)	Aurobindo Pharma, Ltd	T
	Tabs: (300 mg 3TC + 600 mg abacavir)	Mylan Labs, Ltd	T
	Tabs for oral susp: 30 mg 3TC + 60 mg ABC)	Cipla, Ltd	T
	Tabs: (300 mg 3TC + 600 mg abacavir)	Cipla, Ltd	T
	Tabs: (30 mg 3TC + 60 mg abacavir)	Mylan Labs	T
Lamivudine/Stavudine	Tabs: (150 mg 3TC + 30 mg d4T)	Cipla, Ltd	T
	Tabs: (150 mg 3TC + 40 mg d4T)	Cipla, Ltd	T

TABLE 6G (3)

Generic name	Pharmaceutical Prep.	Supplier	Status
Combinations and/or co-packaged products (cont.)			
Lamivudine/Stavudine (cont.)	Tabs: (150 mg 3TC + 30 mg d4T); Tabs: (150 mg 3TC + 40 mg d4T)	Mylan Labs, Ltd	T
	Tabs: (150 mg 3TC + 30 mg d4T); Tabs: (150 mg 3TC + 40 mg d4T)	Pharmacare, Ltd	T
	Tabs for oral suspension: (60 mg 3TC + 12 mg d4T); Tabs for oral suspension: (30 mg 3TC + 6 mg d4T)	Cipla, Ltd	T
	Tabs: (150 mg 3TC + 30 mg d4T)	Hetero Labs, Ltd	T
	Tabs: (150 mg 3TC + 30 mg d4T)	Macleods Pharmaceuticals, Ltd	T
Lamivudine/Tenofovir Disoproxil Fumarate	Tabs: (300 mg 3TC + 300 mg TDF)	Mylan Laboratories Ltd	T
	Tabs: (300 mg 3TC + 300 mg TDF)	Hetero Drugs, Ltd	T
	Tabs: (300 mg 3TC + 300 mg TDF)	Aurobindo Pharma Ltd	T
	Tabs: (300 mg 3TC + 300 mg TDF)	Cipla Ltd	T
	Tabs: (300 mg 3TC + 300 mg TDF)	Ranbaxy Labs Ltd	T
	Tabs: (300 mg 3TC + 300 mg TDF)	Macleods Pharm Ltd	T
Lamivudine/Stavudine co-packaged with Nevirapine	Tabs: (150 mg 3TC + 40 mg d4T) with Tabs 200 mg nevirapine	Strides Arcolab, Ltd	T
Lamivudine/Stavudine/Nevirapine	Tabs: (150 mg 3TC + 30 mg d4T + 200 mg nevirapine); Tabs: (150 mg 3TC + 40 mg d4T + 200 mg nevirapine)	Cipla, Ltd	T
	Tabs: (150 mg 3TC + 30 mg d4T + 200 mg nevirapine); Tabs: (150 mg 3TC + 40 mg d4T + 200 mg nevirapine)	Strides Arcolab, Ltd	T

Generic name	Pharmaceutical Prep.	Supplier	Status
Lamivudine/Stavudine/Nevirapine (cont.)	Tabs: (150 mg 3TC + 30 mg d4T + 200 mg nevirapine); Tabs: (150 mg 3TC + 40 mg d4T + 200 mg nevirapine)	Pharmacare, Ltd	T
	Dispersible tabs: (30 mg 3TC + 6 mg d4T + 50 mg nevirapine); Dispersible tabs: (60 mg 3TC + 12 mg d4T + 100 mg nevirapine)	Cipla, Ltd	T
	Tabs: (150 mg 3TC + 30 mg d4T + 200 mg nevirapine); Tabs: (150 mg 3TC + 40 mg d4T + 200 mg nevirapine)	Emcure Pharmaceuticals, Ltd	T
	Tabs: (150 mg 3TC + 30 mg d4T + 200 mg nevirapine)	Hetero Labs, Ltd	T
	Tabs: (150mg/3TC + 30mg d4T + 200 mg nevirapine)	Macleods Pharmaceuticals, Ltd	T
Lamivudine/Stavudine co-packaged with Efavirenz	Tabs: (150 mg 3TC + 40 mg d4T) with Tabs 600 mg efavirenz	Strides Arcolab, Ltd	T
Lamivudine/Zidovudine co-packaged with Abacavir sulfate	Tabs: (150 mg 3TC + 300 mg ZDV) with Tabs 300 mg abacavir sulfate	Aurobindo Pharma, Ltd	T
Lamivudine/Zidovudine/Abacavir sulfate	Tabs: (150 mg 3TC + 300 mg ZDV + 300 mg abacavir sulfate)	Matrix Labs, Ltd	T
Lamivudine/Zidovudine co-packaged with Nevirapine	Tabs: (150 mg 3TC + 300 mg ZDV) with Tabs 200 mg nevirapine	Pharmacare, Ltd	T
	Tabs: (150 mg 3TC + 300 mg ZDV) with Tabs 200 mg nevirapine	Strides Arcolab, Ltd	T
	Tabs: (150 mg 3TC + 300 mg ZDV) with Tabs 200 mg nevirapine	Hetero Labs, Ltd	T
Lamivudine/Zidovudine/Nevirapine	Tabs: (150 mg 3TC + 300 mg ZDV + 200 mg nevirapine)	Aurobindo Pharma, Ltd	T

TABLE 6G (4)

Generic name	Pharmaceutical Prep.	Supplier	Status
Combinations and/or co-packaged products *(cont.)*			
Lamivudine/Zidovudine/ Nevirapine *(cont.)*	Tabs: (150 mg 3TC + 300 mg ZDV + 200 mg nevirapine)	Cipla, Ltd	T
	Tabs for oral suspension: (30 mg 3TC + 60 mg ZDV + 50 mg nevirapine)	Cipla, Ltd	T
	Tabs: (150 mg 3TC + 300 mg ZDV + 200 mg nevirapine)	Mylan Labs, Ltd	T
	Tabs for oral susp: (30 mg 3TC + 60 mg ZDV + 50 mg nevirapine	Mylan Labs, Ltd	T
	Tabs: (150 mg 3TC + 300 mg ZDV + 200 mg nevirapine) and tabs for oral suspension (30 mg 3TC + 60 mg ZDV + 50 mg nevirapine)	Strides Arcolab, Ltd	T
	Tabs: (150 mg 3TC + 300 mg ZDV + 200 mg nevirapine)	Macleods Pharms Ltd	T
	Tabs: (150 mg 3TC + 300 mg ZDV + 200 mg nevirapine)	Hetero Labs Unit III	T
Lamivudine/Zidovudine co-packaged with Efavirenz	Tabs: (150 mg 3TC + 300 mg ZDV) with Tabs: 600 mg efavirenz	Aurobindo Pharma, Ltd	T
	Tabs: (150 mg 3TC + 300 mg ZDV) with Tabs: 600 mg efavirenz	Strides Arcolab, Ltd	T
Lamivudine/Tenofovir Disoproxil Fumarate/Efavirenz	Tabs: (300 mg 3TC + 300 mg TDF + 600 mg efavirenz)	Mylan Labs, Ltd	T
Emtricitabine/ Tenofovir Disoproxil Fumarate/Efavirenz	Tabs: (200 mg FTC + 300 mg TDF + 600 mg efavirenz)	Mylan Labs, Ltd	T
	Tabs: (200 mg FTC + 300 mg TDF + 600 mg efavirenz)	Aurobindo Pharma Ltd	T
	Tabs: (300 mg 3TC + 300 mg TDF + 600 mg efavirenz)	Aurobindo Pharma Ltd	T
	Tabs: (300 mg 3TC + 300 mg TDF + 600 mg efavirenz)	Hetero Labs Ltd	T
Lamivudine/Tenofovir Disoproxil Fumarate co-packaged with Nevirapine	Tabs: (300 mg 3TC + 300 mg TDF) with Tabs: 200 mg Nevirapine	Mylan Labs Ltd	T

TABLE 6H: LIQUID FORMULATIONS OF ART DRUGS

Drug	Dosage Forms Available	Liquid Formulation	Special Instructions for Liquid Formulations	Crush Tablet or Open Capsule	Stability of Tablet/Capsule or Liquid when Mixed
Nucleos(t)ide Reverse Transcriptase Inhibitors (NRTIs)					
Didanosine (Videx)[1,2,3]	EC Capsules: 125 mg, 200 mg, 250 mg, 400 mg Generic EC capsules: 200 mg 250 mg, 400 mg Pediatric Powder for Oral Solution	Powder for oral soln: 2 gm or 4 gm btl (final conc 10 mg/mL)	Reconstitute powder to 20 mg/mL by adding 100 or 200 mL Purified Water to the 2 gm or 4 gm pwd btl. Then mix one part of the 20 mg/mL initial soln with one part Max Strength Mylanta for a final conc of 10 mg/mL. **Shake well and take on empty stomach.** Preferred dosing of liquid is twice daily dosing although once daily may be used to increase compliance—**more PK data to support BID dosing**[2].	Beads in capsules are enteric coated. Capsules may be opened and sprinkled on a small amount of food[3].	The Videx powder final admixture may be stored up to 30 days in **refrigerator**[1,2].
Lamivudine (Epivir)[1,2,3]	Tablets: 100 mg, 150 mg, 300 mg **Scored tablet:** 150 mg[2]	Oral Solution: 10 mg/mL	No reconstitution necessary	Tablets can be crushed and contents mixed with small amount of water or food and immediately taken[3].	Store oral solution at room temperature[2]
Stavudine (Zerit)[1,2]	Capsules: 15 mg, 20 mg, 30 mg, 40 mg (available as Brand and generic) Oral Solution	Powder for Oral Soln: 1 mg/mL (200 mL btl)	Add 202 mL purified water to powder container. Shake container vigorously until powder dissolves completely. This produces 200 mL of 1 mg/mL stavudine solution.	Capsules can be opened and contents mixed with small amounts of food or water (stable in solution for 24 hrs if kept refrigerated)[3].	Prepared solution may be stored up to 30 days in **refrigerator**[1,2]. Shake well prior to use. Capsule contents mixed with food or water and in solution are stable for 24 hours if kept refrigerated[3].
Abacavir (Ziagen)[1]	Tablet: 300 mg **Scored tablet** (available in '09–'10): 300 mg[2] Oral Solution.	Oral Solution: 20 mg/mL	No reconstitution necessary	Tablets may be crushed and contents mixed with a small amount of water or food and immediately ingested[3].	
Zidovudine (Retrovir)[1] All products available as generic	Tablet: 300 mg Capsule: 100 mg Oral Solution Intravenous Solution	Oral Solution: 10 mg/mL Intravenous soln: 10 mg/mL	No reconstitution necessary	Capsules may be opened and dispersed in water or onto a small amount of food and ingested immediately[2]. Tablets may be crushed and combined with a small amount of food or water and ingested immediately[3].	Capsules and/or tablets opened or crushed and mixed with food or water must be taken immediately[3].
Emtricitabine (Emtriva)[1,2]	Capsule: 200 mg Oral Solution	Oral Solution: 10 mg/mL	No reconstitution necessary. The solution bioavailability is 80% that of the capsule, therefore dose is 240 mg of solution vs 200 mg for capsule. Store in refrigerator.	No data	Oral solution should be stored in refrigerator.[2] Stable at room temperature for 3 months[2].
Tenofovir (Viread)[1]	Tablet: 300 mg	None		No data	

Footnotes on page 55. Courtesy of Jennifer Peterson and pharmacy staff at 1917 Clinic, UAB

TABLE 6H (2)

Drug	Dosage Forms Available	Liquid Formulation	Special Instructions for Liquid Formulations	Crush Tablet or Open Capsule	Stability of Tablet/Capsule or Liquid when Mixed
Non-Nucleoside Reverse Transcriptase Inhibitors (NNRTIs)					
Delavirdine (Rescriptor)[1]	Tablet: 100 mg, 200 mg	None		100 mg tablets may be dispersed in water; place 4 tablets in at least 90 mL, let stand then stir for uniform dispersion, consume promptly, rinse glass and swallow rinse to ensure entire dose; 200 mg tablets do **not** disperse in water.	Unknown – take **immediately** upon dispersion of 100 mg tablets in water[1].
Nevirapine (Viramune)[1]	**Scored tablet:** 200 mg. Oral Suspension.	Oral Suspension: 10 mg/mL.	No reconstitution necessary. Shake well before use. Store at room temperature[1].	Tablets can be crushed and combined with a small amount of food or water and administered immediately[1].	Crushed tablets mixed with food or water should be administered immediately[1].
Efavirenz (Sustiva)[1,2]	Capsules: 50 mg, 200 mg. Tablet: 600 mg	None. Liquid formulation is undergoing current studies[2].		Capsules may be opened and added to liquids or small amounts of food[2]. Capsules may have very peppery taste so may be better to mix with something sweet to disguise taste[3]	
Etravirine (Intelence)[1]	Tablet: 100 mg	None (but tablets can be dissolved to form liquid slurry)	Place two 100 mg tablets in a glass of water. Stir well until the water looks milky and drink it immediately. Rinse glass several times with water and swallow rinse each time[1,2].	Yes – Tablets may be dissolved.	Unknown, should be used immediately[2].
Rilpivirene	25 mg	None		No data	
Protease Inhibitors (PIs)					
Indinavir (Crixivan)[1]	Capsules: 100 mg, 200 mg, 333 mg, 400 mg	None		No data	
Nelfinavir (Viracept)[2]	Tablets: 250 mg, 625 mg. Powder for oral suspension. Crushed tablets are preferred over the powder for solution due to difficulties with powder[3].	Powder for oral suspension: 50 mg per one level gram scoop full (200 mg per one level teaspoon of powder). Dissolved tablets are usually better tolerated than pwdr for oral suspension[3].	For powder for oral suspension: powder **may** be mixed with water, milk, pudding, ice cream, or formula. Do **NOT** mix with acidic food/juice and do not add water to bottles of powder[2]. Must use scoop provided with oral powder for measuring purposes[3].	Tablets can be dissolved in a small amount of water. Once dissolved, cloudy mixture should be taken immediately. Rinse glass several times with water and drink rinse. Tablets can also be crushed and administered with pudding[2,3].	Mixture of powder with water, milk, pudding, ice cream, and formula is stable for up to 6 hours[2].
Ritonavir (Norvir)[2]	Capsules: 100 mg. Oral solution	Oral solution: 80 mg/mL (contains 43% alcohol by volume)	Solution should be stored at room temperature. Do NOT refrigerate. Shake well before use. Oral solution may be mixed with milk, chocolate milk, vanilla or chocolate pudding, or ice cream[2].	No	If oral solution is mixed with milk or other food, take immediately.

Footnotes on page 55. Courtesy of Jennifer Peterson and pharmacy staff at 1917 Clinic, UAB

TABLE 6H (3)

Drug	Dosage Forms Available	Liquid Formulation	Special Instructions for Liquid Formulations	Crush Tablet or Open Capsule	Stability of Tablet/Capsule or Liquid when Mixed
Protease Inhibitors (PIs) *(continued)*					
Saquinavir (Invirase)[1]	Capsule: 200 mg Tablet: 500 mg	None		No data	
Fosamprenavir (Lexiva)[2]	Tablets: 700 mg Oral Suspension	Oral Suspension: 50 mg/mL	Adults should take suspension **without** food. Pediatric pts should take suspension **with** food[2]. Shake well prior to use. Store at room temperature[2].	No data	
Lopinavir/ritonavir (Kaletra)[2]	Tablets: 200/50 mg Pediatric tablets: 100/25 mg Pediatric oral solution	Pediatric oral solution: 80/20 mg per mL (contains 42.4% alcohol by volume)	Oral solution should be administered **with** food[2].	**No** – tablets must be swallowed whole. Do not crush or split tablets[2,3].	Store oral liquid in refrigerator but stable at room temperature for 2 months[2].
Tipranavir (Aptivus)[2]	Capsule: 250 mg Pediatric oral solution	Pediatric oral solution: 100 mg/mL	Oral solution contains 116 IU per mL of vitamin E.	No	Oral solution should be stored at room temp. Must use solution within 60 days after opening bottle.
Atazanavir (Reyataz)[2]	Capsules: 100 mg, 150 mg, 200 mg, 300 mg	None		No data	
Darunavir (Prezista)[2]	Tablets: 75 mg, 400 mg, 600 mg (75 mg tab available in '09-'10)[2]	None		No data	
Entry/Fusion Inhibitors					
Enfuvirtide (Fuzeon)[3]	Injection for SQ	None		N/A	Reconstituted vial should be allowed to stand until powder goes completely into solution. Do not shake. Once reconstituted, vial should be used immediately or kept refrigerated until use but no more than 24 hrs. Do not draw up in syringe until time for use!
Maraviroc (Selzentry)[2]	Tablets: 150 mg, 300 mg	None		No data	
Integrase Inhibitors					
Raltegravir (Isentress)[1,2]	Tablet: 400 mg	None		No data	
Dolutegravir	Tablet: 50 mg	None		No data	
Combination Agents					
Zidovudine/Lamivudine (Combivir)[3]	**Scored tablet**	None—Liquid formulations are available as individual agents		Tablets can be crushed and mixed with a small amount of food or water and taken immediately[3].	Tablets in solution should be administered immediately[3].

Footnotes on page 55. Courtesy of Jennifer Peterson and pharmacy staff at 1917 Clinic, UAB

TABLE 6H (4)

Drug	Dosage Forms Available	Liquid Formulation	Special Instructions for Liquid Formulations	Crush Tablet or Open Capsule	Stability of Tablet/Capsule or Liquid when Mixed
Combination Agents *(continued)*					
Abacavir/zidovudine/ lamivudine (Trizivir)[1,3]	Tablet	None—Liquid formulations are available as individual agents		No[3]	
Emtricitabine/tenofovir (Truvada)[1]	Tablet	None		No	
Abacavir/lamivudine (Epzicom)[1]	Tablet	None—Liquid formulations are available as individual agents		No	
Emtricitabine/tenofovir/ efavirenz (Atripla)[1]	Tablet	None		No (current studies to see whether Atripla may be crushed are on-going – no results yet)	
Elvitegravir/Cobicistat/ tenofovir/Emtricitabine	Tablet 150 mg	None		No	

[1] Source: package inserts

[2] *Guidelines for the Use of Antiretroviral Agents in Pediatric HIV Infection, Feb 23, 2009, http://AIDSinfo.nih.gov*

[3] *http://www.cdc.gov/global/AIDS/docs/program_areas/pmtct/Peds%20Dosing%20Guide.pdf (Pediatric Antiretroviral Dosing in Resource Limited Settings, International Center for AIDS Care & Treatment Programs, Mailman School of Public Health, Columbia University, updated November 2006) Based on Guidelines published by the WHO.*

Footnotes on page 55. Courtesy of Jennifer Peterson and pharmacy staff at 1917 Clinic, UAB

TABLE 6I: ANTIRETROVIRAL DRUG COST COMPARISON
From Guidelines for the Use of Antiretroviral Agents in HIV-1 Infected Adults and Adolescents,
http://aidsinfo.nih.gov/guidelines (Can also be found at: *http://aids.about.com/od/treatmentquestions/a/
Wholesale-Price-Of-Hiv-Medications.htm* (accessed Sept 2013))

ARV Drug Generic (Brand) Name	Prep	Dosing	Tabs/Capsules/ ML Per Month	SWP* (Monthly)[a]
Nucleoside Reverse Transcriptase Inhibitors (NRTIs)				
abacavir (Ziagen)	300 mg tab	2 tabs daily	60 tabs	$670.37
	20 mg/mL soln	30 mL daily	900 mL	$674.60
didanosine DR (generic product) (Videx EC)	400 mg cap	1 cap daily	30 caps (≥ 60 kg)	$368.72
	400 mg cap	1 cap daily	30 caps (≥ 60 kg)	$478.08
emtricitabine (Emtriva)	200 mg cap	1 cap daily	30 tabs	$574.14
lamivudine (generic) (Epivir)	300 mg tab	1 tab daily	30 tabs	$429.66
	300 mg tab	1 tab daily	30 tabs	$498.89
	10 mg/mL soln	30 mL daily	900 mL	$509.28
stavudine (generic) (Zerit)	40 mg cap	1 cap twice daily	60 caps	$411.16
	40 mg cap	1 cap twice daily	60 caps	$512.62
tenofovir (Viread)	300 mg tab	1 tab daily	30 tabs	$998.80
zidovudine (generic) (Retrovir)	300 mg tab	1 tab twice daily	60 tabs	$360.97
	300 mg tab	1 tab twice daily	60 tabs	$557.83
Non-nucleoside Reverse Transcriptase Inhibitors (NNRTIs)				
delavirdine (Rescriptor)	200 mg tab	2 tabs three times daily	180 tabs	$365.45
efavirenz (Sustiva)	200 mg cap	3 caps daily	90 caps	$785.90
	600 mg tab	1 tab daily	30 tabs	$785.90
etravirine (Intelence)	100 mg tab	2 tabs twice daily	120 tabs	$978.64
	200 mg tab	1 tab twice daily	60 tabs	$978.64
nevirapine (Viramune)	200 mg tab	1 tab twice daily	60 tabs	$723.08
nevirapine XR (Viramune XR)	400 mg tab	1 tab daily	30 tabs	$670.63
rilpivirine (Edurant)	25 mg tab	1 tab daily	30 tabs	$804.38
Protease Inhibitors (PIs)				
atazanavir (Reyataz)	150 mg cap[b]	2 caps daily	60 caps	$1,222.10
	200 mg cap[b]	2 caps daily	60 caps	$1,222.10
	300 mg cap[b]	1 cap daily	30 caps	$1,210.56
darunavir (Prezista)	400 mg tab[b]	2 tabs daily	60 tabs	$1,230.20
	600 mg tab[b]	1 tab twice daily	60 tabs	$1,230.20
fosamprenavir (Lexiva)	700 mg tab	2 tabs twice daily	120 tabs	$1,988.96
		1 tab twice daily[b]	60 tabs	$994.48
		2 tabs once daily[b]	60 tabs	$994.48
indinavir (Crixivan)	400 mg cap	2 caps three times daily	180 caps	$548.12
		2 caps twice daily[b]	120 caps	$365.41
nelfinavir (Viracept)	625 mg tab	2 tabs twice daily	120 tabs	$879.84
ritonavir (Norvir)	100 mg tab	1 tab once daily	30 tabs	$308.60
		1 tab twice daily	60 tabs	$617.20
		2 tabs twice daily	120 tabs	$1,234.40
saquinavir (Invirase)	500-mg tab[b]	2 tabs twice daily	120 tabs	$1,088.84
tipranavir (Aptivus)	250-mg cap[b]	2 caps twice daily	120 caps	$1,335.14
Integrase Strand Transfer Inhibitor (INSTI)				
raltegravir (Isentress)	400-mg tab	1 tab twice daily	60 tabs	$1,228.69
elvitegravir (Stribild)	150/150/200/300 (FDC)	1 tab once daily	30 tabs	$2,810.96
dolutegravir (Tivicay)	50 mg tab	1 tab once daily	30 tabs	$1,175.00

TABLE 6I (2)

ARV Drug Generic (Brand) Name	Prep	Dosing	Tabs/Capsules/ ML Per Month	SWP[a] (Monthly)[a]
Fusion Inhibitor				
enfuviritide (Fuzeon)	90-mg inj kit	1 inj twice daily	60 doses (1 kit)	$3,248.72
CCR5 Antagonist				
maraviroc (Selzentry)	150-mg tab	1 tab twice daily	60 tabs	$1,259.82
	300-mg tab	1 tab twice daily	60 tabs	$1,259.82
Co-formulated Combination Antiretroviral Drugs				
abacavir/lamivudine (Epzicom)	600/300-mg tab	1 tab daily	30 tabs	$1,118.90
tenofovir/emtricitabine (Truvada)	300/150-mg tab	1 tab daily	30 tabs	$1,467.97
zidovudine/lamivudine (generic) (Combivir)	300/150-mg tab	1 tab twice daily	60 tabs	$931.61
	300/150-mg tab	1 tab twice daily	60 tabs	$1,081.70
abacavir/lamivudine/zidovudine (Trizivir)	600/150/300-mg tab	1 tab twice daily	60 tabs	$785.90
lopinavir/ritonavir (Kaletra)	200 mg/50-mg tab	2 tabs twice daily or	120 tabs	$871.36
	400 mg/100 mg per 5-mL soln	4 tabs once daily 5 mL twice daily	300 mL	$871.34
rilpivirine/tenofovir/emtricitabine (Complera/Eviplera)	200/25/300 mg	1 tab daily	30 tabs	$2,195.83
efavirenz/tenofovir/emtricitabine (Atripla)	300/200/600 mg	1 tab daily	30 tabs	$2,253.88

---

[a] SWP = Suggested Wholesale Price in 2013 (source is in 2012 *(source: First DataBank Blue Book AWP, accessed Sept 2013.)* Note that this price may not represent the pharmacy acquisition price or the price paid by consumers.

[b] Should be used in combination with ritonavir.

Key to Abbreviations: SWP = Suggested Wholesale Price; cap = capsule, DR = delayed release, EC = enteric coated, inj = injection,soln = solution, tab = tablet, XR = extended release

TABLE 7A: ACUTE HIV INFECTION

FIGURE 6   Natural History and Staging of Acute HIV Infection

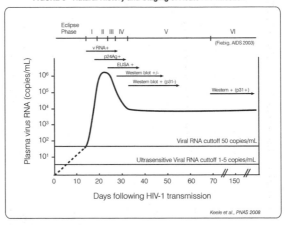

Keele et al., PNAS 2008

Acute (Recent or Primary) HIV Infection

- Definition: Initial burst of HIV viremia with undetectable anti-HIV antibody
- ART should be initiated as soon as HIV infection is recognized
- Perform genotype drug resistance testing (estimated 15% - 18% transmission of resistant virus)
- Use same regimens as recommended for treatment of chronic HIV infection
- **DHHS Guidelines recommend a PI-based regimen if ART started before resistance test results are known**
- Goal is suppression of viral load to below detectable limits
- Once ART is started, therapy should continue for life

Special Populations *(see www.aidsinfo.nih.gov)*

    a. **Injection drug users.** Active drug use may compromise adherence. Potentially co-existing neuropsychiatric symptoms & ↑ prevalence of Hep B & C add to risk of drug toxicities. Drug interactions may potentially cause ↑ or ↓ blood levels of ART drugs, & of methadone or drugs of abuse *(Mt Sinai J Med 67:429, 2000; see Table 16A).*

    b. **Co-infection with Hep B &/or C *(See Table 12, page 160).*** Co-infection with Hepatitis B is an indication for treatment of HIV. Lamivudine, emtricitabine & tenofovir are active against HBV *(CID 39:1062, 2004).* Two active anti-HBV agents are recommended for the treatment of HIV in HBV co-infected patients. **Therefore the use of TDF/FTC or TDF/3TC are the nucleoside backbones of choice in HIV/HBV co-infected pts** because of concerns about emergence of HBV resistance when 3TC or FTC is used without TDF, all patients with HIV/HBV coinfection TDF should be used in all patients if possible. When TDF cannot be used, entecavir should be added to the ARV regimen. If uncertain how to treat, seek expert consultation.

    Severe hepatitis flare *(see Black Box warnings)* may occur in pts with chronic Hep B after stopping any of these 3 drugs used for HIV therapy. In HCV/HIV co-infected pts, ↑ rate of progression to cirrhosis. Proper sequencing of rx for HIV/HCV important to avoid ↑ toxicities

    Changes in ART drug elimination with hepatic dysfunction may necessitate dosing changes *(CID 40:174, 2005; see Table 15B).* Therapeutic drug monitoring should be considered when there is significant liver dysfunction.

    c. **Adolescents:** Adult guidelines for ARV use are generally appropriate for post-pubertal adolescents. Dosage should be prescribed according to Tanner staging of puberty and not on the basis of age. If Tanner Stage I and II, dose according to Pediatric dosing recommendations; if late puberty Tanner V, dose according to Adult dosing recommendations. Youth in a growth spurt should continue with pediatric dosing initially. Adherence to medication is particularly challenging in adolescent populations and need to be managed carefully. Efavirenz should be used with caution among female adolescents owing to potential teratogenicity concerns.

TABLE 7B: MANAGEMENT OF EXPOSURE HEPATITIS B/C

OCCUPATIONAL EXPOSURE TO BLOOD, PENILE/VAGINAL SECRETIONS OR OTHER POTENTIALLY INFECTIOUS BODY FLUIDS OR TISSUES WITH RISK OF TRANSMISSION OF HEPATITIS B/C &/OR HIV-1 (E.G., NEEDLESTICK INJURY) *Inf Cont Hosp Epi 34:875-92,2013*

Free consultation for occupational exposures: call (PEPline) 1-888-448-4911.

General steps in management:
1. Wash clean wounds/flush mucous membranes immediately (use of caustic agents or squeezing the wound is discouraged; data lacking regarding antiseptics).
2. Assess risk by doing the following: (a) Characterize exposure; (b) Determine/evaluate source of exposure by medical history, risk behavior, & testing for hepatitis B/C, HIV; (c) Evaluate & test exposed individual for hepatitis B/C & HIV

Hepatitis B Occupational Exposure

Exposed Person*	Exposure Source		
	HBs Ag +	HBs Ag–	Status Unknown or Source Unavailable for Testing[†]
Unvaccinated	Give HBIG 0.06 mL per kg IM & initiate HB vaccine	Initiate HB vaccine	Initiate HB vaccine
Vaccinated (antibody status unknown)	Do anti-HBs on exposed person: If titer ≥10 milli-International units per mL, no rx If titer <10 milli-International units per mL, give HBIG + 1 dose HB vaccine**	No rx necessary	Do anti-HBs on exposed person: If titer ≥10 milli-International units per mL, no rx If titer <10 milli-International units per mL, give 1 dose of HB vaccine**

* Persons previously infected with HBV are immune to reinfection and do not require postexposure prophylaxis.
For known vaccine series responder (titer ≥10 milli-International units per mL, monitoring of levels or booster doses not currently recommended. Known non-responder (<10 milli-International units per mL) to 1° series HB vaccine & exposed to either HBsAg+ source or suspected high-risk source—rx with HBIG & re-initiate vaccine series or give 2 doses HBIG 1 month apart. For non-responders after a 2nd vaccine series, 2 doses HBIG 1 month apart is preferred approach to new exposure.
† If known high-risk source, treat as if source were HBsAG positive.
** Follow-up to assess vaccine response or address completion of vaccine series.

Hepatitis B Non-Occupational Exposure

Post-exposure prophylaxis is recommended for persons with discrete nonoccupational exposure to blood or body fluids. Exposures include percutaneous (e.g., bite, needlestick or mucous membrane exposure to HBsAG-positive blood or sterile body fluids, sexual or needle-sharing contact of an HBsAG-positive person, or a victim of sexual assault or sexual abuse by a perpetrator who is HBsAg-positive. If immunoprophylaxis is indicated, it should be initiated ideally within 24h of exposure. Postexposure prophylaxis is unlikely to be effective if administered more than 7 days after a parenteral exposure or 14 days after a sexual exposure. The hepatitis B vaccine series should be completed regardless. The same guidelines for management of occupational exposures can also be used for nonoccupational exposures. For a previously vaccinated person (i.e. written documentation of being vaccinated) and no documentation of postvaccination titers with a discrete exposure to an HBsAG-positive source, it also is acceptable to administer a booster dose of hepatitis B vaccine without checking titers. No treatment is required for a vaccinated person exposed to a source of unknown HBsAG status.

Hepatitis C Exposure

Determine antibody to hepatitis C for both exposed person &, if possible, exposure source. If source + or unknown and exposed person negative, follow-up HCV testing for HCV RNA (detectable in blood in 1-3 weeks and HCV antibody (90%) who seroconvert will do so by 3 months) is advised. **No recommended prophylaxis;** immune serum globulin not effective. Monitor for early infection, as therapy may ↓ risk of progression to chronic hepatitis. Persons who remain viremic 8-12 weeks after exposure should be treated with a course of pegylated interferon (*Gastro 130:632, 2006 and Hpt 43:923, 2006*). Case-control study suggested risk factors for occupational HCV transmission include percutaneous exposure to needle that had been in artery or vein, deep injury, male sex of healthcare worker (HCW), & was more likely when source VL >6 log10 copies/mL.

TABLE 7C: HIV EXPOSURE MANAGEMENT

A. HIV OCCUPATIONAL EXPOSURE *(See Infect Control Hosp Epidemiol 34:875, 2013)*
The decision to initiate post-exposure prophylaxis (PEP) is a clinical judgment made in concert with the exposed individual and is based on three factors:
1. Type of exposure
    a. Potentially infectious substances include: blood, unfixed tissues, CSF; semen and vaginal secretions (these have not been implicated in occupational transmission of HIV); synovial, pleural, peritoneal, ascitic, and amniotic fluids; other <u>visibly</u> bloody fluids.
    b. Fluids of low or negligible risk for transmission, unless visibly bloody include: urine, sweat, vomitus, stool, saliva, nasal secretions, tears, and sputum. **PEP is not indicated.**
    c. If the exposure occurred to intact skin, regardless of whether the substance is potentially infectious or not, and regardless of the HIV status of the source patient, **PEP is not indicated.**
    d. If the exposure occurred to mucous membranes (e.g., blood splash to the eye) or non-intact skin (e.g., abraded skin, open wound, dermatitis) or occurred percutaneously as a consequence of a needle stick, scalpel, or other sharps injury or cut, then **PEP may be indicated.** Human bites resulting in a break in the skin could theoretically transmit HIV, particularly if oral blood is present, although these have not been implicated in occupational transmission of HIV.
2. Likelihood that the source patient is HIV infected
    a. If the exposure constitutes a risk of HIV transmission as described above and the source patient is **known positive for HIV,** then **PEP should be instituted** immediately, within hours of exposure (Animal studies show PEP less effective when started > 72h post-exposure but interval after which PEP not beneficial is unknown; initiation of PEP after a longer interval may be considered if exposure risk of transmission is extremely high).
    b. If exposure constitutes a risk of HIV transmission, and the HIV status is **unknown,** but patient is **likely to be HIV infected** or there is a **reasonable suspicion** for infection based on HIV risk factors, then **PEP should be initiated pending confirmation of the source patient's HIV status.**
        i. If a rapid HIV test of the source patient can be performed, it is reasonable to withhold therapy pending results of this test and initiating PEP if the test is positive.
        ii. If rapid testing cannot be performed, PEP should be initiated pending results of source patient testing and discontinued if the test returns negative.
        iii. NOTE: Antibody testing is sufficient to rule out HIV infection, unless the source patient has suspected acute retroviral syndrome, in which case HIV viral load testing is recommended.
    c. If the **source is unknown** or the source is known but status and risk cannot be determined, the decision to initiate PEP should be made on a case-by-case basis in **consultation with an expert** (PEPline at *http://www.nccc.ucsf.edu/about_nccc/pepline/*), guided by the severity of the exposure and epidemiologic likelihood of HIV exposure.
3. Adverse effects and potential for drug interactions with the PEP regimen
    a. Newer agents are better tolerated and should allow a higher proportion of exposed healthcare providers to complete the prescribed four-week course of therapy.
    b. Information about drug interactions is available in Tables 16A and 16B, in the package insert and on-line at *hivinsite.ucsf.edu*
    c. Breast feeding and pregnancy are not contraindications to PEP (efavirenz is contraindicated during pregnancy).

FIGURE 7   PEP Algorithm

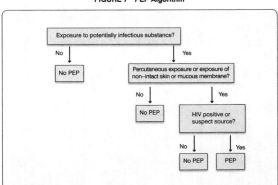

TABLE 7C (2)

REGIMENS FOR PEP: a 4-week course of 3 or more drugs now routinely recommended for all PEP

1. **Preferred regimen: Truvada** [combination of Tenofovir (TDF) 300 mg + Emtricitabine (FTC) 200 mg] po once daily + **Raltegravir** 400 mg po twice daily or dolutegravir 50 mg orally daily
2. **Alternative regimens:**
   a. Etravirine or Rilpivirine or Boosted protease inhibitor* + Truvada
   b. Etravirine or Rilpivirine or Boosted protease inhibitor* + TDF + Lamivudine (3TC)
   c. Etravirine or Rilpivirine or Boosted protease inhibitor* + Zidovudine (AZT) + 3TC
   d. Etravirine or Rilpivirine or Boosted protease inhibitor* + AZT + FTC
3. Abacavir, efavirenz, enfuvirtide, maraviroc should be used only in consultation with an expert
4. Didanosine, nelfinavir, tipranavir, stavudine (d4T) and nevirapine (contraindicated) are not recommended
5. If transmission of drug resistant virus is suspected, the regimen should be appropriately modified in consultation with an expert to include agents to which it is likely to be susceptible.

* Ritonavir 100 mg + [either Darunavir 800 mg or Atazanavir 300 mg or Fosamprenavir 1400 mg] once daily

FOLLOW-UP

1. Complete blood count, renal and hepatic panels recommended at baseline and repeated at 2 weeks with further testing if results are abnormal.
2. HIV antibody testing to monitor seroconversion should be performed at baseline, 6 weeks, 12 weeks, and 6 months post-exposure.
3. If a 4th generation p24 antigen-HIV antibody test is used, testing may be terminated at 4 months.
4. Extended follow-up for 12 months is recommended if HCV conversion occurred upon exposure to an HIV-HCV co-infected patient.

B. HIV NON-OCCUPATIONAL EXPOSURE

- Because the risk of transmission of HIV via sexual contact or sharing needles by injection drug users may reach or exceed that of occupational needlestick exposure, it is reasonable to consider PEP in persons who have had a non-occupational exposure to blood or other potentially infected fluids (e.g., genital/rectal secretions, breast milk) from an HIV+ source. Risk of HIV acquisition per exposure varies with the act (for needle sharing & receptive anal intercourse, ≥0.5%; approximately 10-fold lower with insertive vaginal or anal intercourse, 0.05–0.07%). Overt or occult traumatic lesions may ↑ risk in survivors of sexual assault.
- For pts at risk of HIV acquisition through non-occupational exposure to HIV+ source material having occurred ≤72 hours before evaluation, treatment is recommended with the same regimens used for occupational exposure (above). Areas of uncertainty: (1) while PEP not routinely recommended for exposures >72 hrs before evaluation, it may possibly be effective in some cases, (2) when HIV status of source patient is unknown, decision to treat & regimen selection must be individualized based on assessment of specific circumstances.
- Evaluate for exposures to Hep B, Hep C (*see Occupational PEP above*), & bacterial sexually-transmitted diseases & treat as indicated. DHHS recommendations for sexual exposures to viral and bacterial pathogens are available in *MMWR 55(RR-11), 2006*. Persons who are unvaccinated with or who have not responded to full HepB vaccine series should receive HBIG (hepatitis B immune globulin) preferably within 24 hrs of percutaneous or mucosal exposure to blood/body fluids of an HBsAg-positive person, along with HepB vaccine, with follow-up to complete vaccine series. Unvaccinated or not fully vaccinated persons exposed to a source with unknown HBsAG status should receive vaccine and complete vaccine series. For details and recommendations in other circumstances *see MMWR 55 (RR-11), 2006*.

C. PRE-EXPOSURE PROPHYLAXIS (PREP) FOR MEN WHO HAVE SEX WITH MEN (MSM)

Once daily Truvada (combination of FTC 200 mg + TDF 300 mg) resulted in a 44% decrease in incidence of HIV infection in one clinical trial (*NEJM 363:27, 2010*). Whether this is a practical approach to HIV prevention is unclear and it would be expensive: if applied in the US to 20% of a general MSM population, this could result in a 13% reduction in new HIV infections at a cost of $172,091 per quality life year gained (*Ann Intern Med 156:541, 2012*).

TABLE 8A: HIV/AIDS IN WOMEN/PREGNANCY

I.   **General Aspects**
   A.   Women represent half of persons with HIV/AIDS in the world. Among young people (15–24 yrs)
        in developing countries with HIV/AIDS, 64% are women.
   B.   Heterosexual transmission is dominant mode of transmission worldwide. Among new HIV/AIDS
        diagnoses among women in the U.S. in 2005: 80% heterosexual contact, 18% IDU.
   C.   Transmission of HIV from men to women occurs more readily than from women to men. Risk factors
        for male-to-female transmission: genital ulcers, partner with advanced disease, other STDs, trauma.
   D.   Risk after several years of unprotected sex with same infected partner is 10–45%.
   E.   Despite these aspects, relatively less is written about women's issues. Women are generally underrepresented
        in therapy trials.

II. **Initial Assessment:** See Table 2

III. **Clinical Manifestations** (Adapted from Newman, MD, Global HIV/AIDS Medicine 2008)
   A.   **AIDS-defining diagnoses:**
        • Disease progression similar in women & men (NEJM 333:751, 1995).
        • Survival is related to access to care, which may be worse for women.
        • Viral load at high CD4 counts tends to be lower in women (CID 35:313, 2002).
        • Gender difference narrows as CD4 drops.
   B.   **Human papillomavirus:**
        • HPV disease incidence increased! Cervical intraepithelial neoplasia (CIN) more prevalent in multiple studies.
          Prevalence increases with decreasing CD4 (CID 38:737, 2004).
        • Aggressive course, with high rate of progression to cancer if immunosuppressed.
        • Pap smear recommended for HIV+ women. If initial Pap smear is neg, repeat in 6 mos. If both are negative,
          annual Pap smears adequate (CDC Guidelines). We recommend every 6 mos for those with CD4 <200.
          Colposcopy recommended for any suspicious lesions. There are no contraindications to standard treatment
          modalities for CIN. Risk of recurrence higher after treatment.
        • Although many women with HIV are already infected with some HPV genotypes, there may be benefit
          to use of HPV vaccine according to recommendations for HIV negative women.
   C.   **Recurrent/refractory vaginal candidiasis**
        • May be early manifestation although poorly predictive of HIV infection (CD4 may be >500).
        • HIV diagnosis often missed because testing not offered.
   D.   **Other conditions**
        • PID may be more severe, 7–17% require hospitalization; tubo-ovarian abscess more likely.
        • Menstrual disorders (41% HIV+ women had menstrual abnormalities vs. 24% in controls) include irregular
          periods, heavier or scantier periods, early menopausal symptoms, ↑ in premenstrual symptoms.

IV. **Family Planning.** 85% of women with AIDS are in child-bearing years. Contraceptive and pre-conceptional planning are
     essential components of care. Hormonal contraceptives are generally safe in HIV+ women. However, women in Africa
     using depo-progesterone may be at increased risk of HIV acquisition and transmission. Condoms should be used with
     all forms of contraception (Ln ID 12:19, 2012). ARV drugs, especially Ritonavir, may decrease levels of some estrogens
     (Zeeman B, Hirschhorn LR, p. 616, in HIV Infection, Libman H, Witzburg RA. 3rd Ed., Little Brown & Co.).

Method of Contraception	Failure Rate	Risks
Sterilization	0.4	No HIV protection
Latex condom	12-15	HIV and STI protection
Diaphragm	16	Potential vaginal abrasions
Sponge	9-32	Potential vaginal abrasions
Oral Contraceptive	3-8	Drug interactions with ART decrease efficacy or increase side effects
Injectable depot progestin	3	No significant ART interactions. May increase HIV shedding. Use condoms in addition
Copper IUD	1	No HIV protection
Hormonal IUD	1	No HIV protection. May lower amprenavir levels. Other ART may change estrogen level
Implant	1	Progestin only no significant interactions
Vaginal ring	1-9	Effect of drug interactions on efficacy unknown

V.   **Treatment Issues**
   A.   **Inadequate gender-specific data!**
   B.   **Theoretical issues**
        • Baseline anemia (iron deficiency)
        • Low mean body weight, higher body fat, different hepatic metabolism compared to men
   C.   **Menstrual dysfunction**
        • Amenorrhea should be evaluated; start with pregnancy test
        • Premature menopause occurs frequently; consider short term hormone replacement therapy
   D.   **Recommended treatment regimens currently identical for men & women**
        • Rates of some side effects different in women (↑ rash and hepatitis on nevirapine with CD4 > 250.
          ↑ GI side effects on lopinavir/ritonavir)
        • **Efavirenz should be avoided in women who may become pregnant**
        • Lactic acidosis more common in women, associated with d4T & ddI

TABLE 8A (2)

VI. **HIV in Pregnancy: Care of the Mother**
  A. **Pre conception counseling**
  - All HIV + women should be asked if they are or might consider becoming pregnant
  - This may influence decision to start ART if CD4 > 350 or influence choice of agents (eg avoid efavirenz). Achieving stable viral load suppression to <50 copies/mL before conceiving is desirable
  - Consider folate supplement or multivitamin

  B. **Antepartum Care**
  - **All** pregnant women should be offered HIV testing & counseling **regardless** of risk factors. Include HIV in routine unless patient declines (opt-out testing)
  - Repeat HIV screening in the 3rd trimester for women with ongoing risk
  - Quantitative measure of **HIV RNA** initially 1 month after starting ART, then every 3 months
  - Obtain CD4 count and percent at outset & each trimester (some ↓ CD4 count in normal pregnancy)
  - **Screening tests** (HBsAg, RPR, chlamydia, gonorrhea) as in any pregnancy
  - Discourage illicit alcohol use, drug use, smoking, unprotected sex with multiple partners
  - Administer influenza, pneumococcal, Hep B, Hep A, and Tdap vaccines, as indicated *(MMWR 60 (RR 2, RR41), 2011)*
  - Assess need for OI prophylaxis

  C. **Use of antiviral therapy in pregnancy** *(www.aidsinfo.nih.gov)* (updated July 2012). Treatment of HIV in pregnancy requires attention to 2 separate but equal goals:
  - Provide optimal treatment to the woman that does not limit future options
  - Prevent transmission to the infant without drug toxicity
    1. Risk factors for mother-to-child transmission (MTCT)
       - Maternal viral load (outset & at delivery are independent predictors *(JID 183:539, 2001)*
       - Maternal CD4 count (risk of transmission ↑ 3-fold if CD4 <400)
       - Lack of antiviral therapy (independent of other factors) *(JID 183:539, 2001)*
       - Prolonged rupture of membranes (rate doubled if >4 hours) *(NEJM 334:1617, 1996)*
       - Mode of delivery
       - Breastfeeding (additional 10–14% transmission) *(JAMA 282:744, 1999)*
       - Shorter duration of antepartum ART *(AIDS 22:973, 2008)*
    2. General principles
       - Preventing MTCT should be integrated with obstetrical & HIV medical care for the mother. The mother should be informed & involved in decisions
       - Combination antiretroviral therapy ↓ risk of MTCT regardless of viral load
       - ARV is generally safe for the mother (avoid use of ddI with d4T—↑ risk of lactic acidosis; avoid efavirenz in 1st trimester)
       - Maximal viral suppression with combination therapy ↓ risk of resistance in mother & loss of future options, & is more effective than 1- or 2-drug regimens. **Preferred for all pregnant women**
       - Resistance testing recommended before beginning ART and if on therapy, but detectable viral load
       - Long-term safety of ART for infant exposed in utero is not fully known. Generally safe, although conflicting data on mitochondrial toxicity; myocardial function *(J Am Coll Cardio 57:76, 2011)*
       - Some data suggest ↑ rate of prematurity, low birth weight with PI use during pregnancy; given clear benefits, PIs should not be withheld
       - Optimal dosing in pregnancy has not been adequately studied for all agents
       - PI levels fall in third trimester (nelfinavir, indinavir, lopinavir/ritonavir, atazanavir). Consider obtaining levels
    3. **Combination therapy with 2 NRTIs + either an NNRTI or potent PI recommended** *(see http://www.aidsinfo.nih.gov):*
       a. **For all women for whom ARV therapy is otherwise appropriate**
       b. **For all pregnant HIV infected women regardless of CD4 count or viral load**
          - **Transmission in cohorts 0.7–2.0% with 3-drug ART**
          - **Regimen selection should be individualized based on resistance, side effect profile, convenience, hepatitis B status, likelihood of adherence, potential drug interactions, maternal toxicity and teratogenicity**
          - **Pregnant women receiving and tolerating an ARV regimen that is suppressing viral replication should continue the regimen including efavirenz-based regimens; however, the use of efavirenz should be avoided in the first trimester of pregnancy when possible.**
          - **Combination ARV regimens should include 1 or more NRTIs with high transplacental passage (ZDV, 3TC, FTC, TDF, ABC). The combination of d4T & ddI should be avoided**
          - **Tenofovir associated with decreased in growth and bone abnormalities in pregnant monkeys, but no evidence to date on humans. TDF is part of preferred ART regimens for Hep B coinfection and an alternative agent for Hep B negative women.**
          - **Preferred third agents are LPV/RTV or nevirapine. Alternative agents include boosted atazanavir and saquinavir HGC. Boosted darunavir appears to achieve adequate levels in pregnancy (CROI 2012, Abst 1012)**
          - **WHO recommends 2 NRTI backbones (ZDV + 3TC) and an NNRTI (nevirapine or efavirenz). Avoid EFV in 1st trimester. Alternative NRTI backbones include TDF + (FTC or 3TC)**
          - **While use of ZDV is recommended when possible based on trial data, choice of nucleoside regimen should consider the patient's viral resistance and ability to tolerate ZDV**
    4. Severe skin rash, ↑ transaminases & rarely fulminant hepatitis can occur after starting nevirapine. Rates higher in non-pregnant women than in men, esp. with higher CD4 count. Monitor LFTs, instruct mother to seek care for nausea, abdominal pain. Check transaminases in any woman who develops rash. **Consider non-nevirapine containing regimens if CD4 count >250 unless benefits clearly outweigh risks**

TABLE 8A (3)

5. Many trials have demonstrated significant efficacy of more limited regimens. Some may be more affordable or practical in specific settings. *(For detailed overview, see http://womenchildrenhiv.org/wchi?page=pi-10-02)*
6. **Stavudine & didanosine combination should not be used in pregnancy due to risk of lactic acidosis**

D. **Specific situations**

1. **For pregnant women not on therapy with an indication for ART:** Evaluate clinical, virologic, social factors, & previous therapy. Obtain resistance and Hepatitis B testing. Discuss options, risks, & benefits. Begin therapy as soon as possible, as long as adherence can be assured. Avoid efavirenz in 1st trimester and other drugs with teratogenic potential. Try to use at least one NRTI with good transplacental passage (ZDV, TDF, 3TC, FTC, ABC). Begin intravenous zidovudine continuous infusion at onset of labor while continuing oral ART, for women with HIV VL >400 copies/mL (or unknown VL). *See regimens in Table 6A.*

2. **For pregnant women not on therapy who do not otherwise require ART:** As for women who need therapy for their own health, evaluate clinical, virologic, social factors, & previous therapy. Obtain resistance testing. Combination therapy is strongly preferred. Consider starting ART as soon as possible, but deferring until after 1st trimester can be considered. Early initiation of ART may reduce perinatal transmission *(AIDS 22:973, 2008)*. Begin intravenous zidovudine continuous infusion at onset of labor for women with HIV VL >400 copies/mL or unknown VL. Avoid efavirenz in 1st tri and avoid nevirapine if CD4 count >250 unless benefits clearly outweigh risk.

3. **For women on ART when pregnancy is diagnosed:** If pregnancy detected in 1st trimester, ART should not be stopped. Some would substitute LPV/r for EFV, but DHHS panel recommends continuing EFV. If a woman is tolerating NVP, it should be continued regardless of CD4 count.

4. **For women in labor with no prior therapy:**
   - Intrapartum IV ZDV by continuous infusion & 6 weeks of oral ZDV for the infant.
   - Single-dose nevirapine for women in labor who have not received antepartum ARV agents are no longer recommended
   - Use of additional ARV agents for women in labor has not been well-studied, but can be considered with expert consultation
   - C-section is likely to provide additional benefit if membranes have not ruptured. There is no evidence of benefit in preventing MTCT for emergency C-section *(AIDS 22:973, 2008)*
   - Evaluate indications for ongoing maternal ART after delivery.

5. **For infants born to HIV-infected women who did not receive therapy or only intrapartum therapy:**
   - Begin oral ZDV as soon as possible & continue for 6 weeks.
   - Twice daily po dosing is now preferred for infants ≥ 35 weeks gestation.
   - Neonatal 2- or 3-drug ARV regimens are superior to ZDV alone for prevention of MTCT (CROI 2011, abst 124LB). ARV regimens studied were ZDV + 3 doses nevirapine (birth, dose 2 48h after dose 1, dose 3 96h after dose 2) and ZDV+3TC+nelfinavir. Nelfinavir powder is no longer commercially available in the US.
   - Although HTPN 040/PACTG 1043 studied ZDV + 3 doses nevirapine, some experts would consider also adding lamivudine for 2-4 weeks.
   - **EXPERT CONSULTATION RECOMMENDED** *(National (US) Perinatal Hotline: 1-888-448-8765)*

6. **HIV-infected women who are ARV experienced and not suppressed when becoming pregnant:**
   - Counsel about adherence, address issues contributing to difficulties. Discuss unknown safety and dosing of newer agents in pregnancy.
   - Obtain ARV history and viral resistance testing. Expert consultation recommended. For maternal health, constructing new regimen may be essential, despite uncertainties of new agents in pregnancy.
   - If viral load not <1000 copies/mL on new regimen, strongly consider scheduled elective C-section.
   - For infant prophylactic regimen, consult pediatric HIV specialist or Perinatal Hotline.

E. **Elective C-section before the onset of labor** ↓ transmission by 50% for women on no therapy or ZDV monotherapy *(NEJM 340:977, 1999)*. However, in recent cohorts on 3-drug therapy with suppressed HIV RNA, no apparent additional benefit of C-section was observed *(AIDS 22:973, 2008)*.
   - This should be discussed with the woman & she should be involved in the decision.
   - Elective C-section (before 38 weeks) should be considered if:
     - Maternal viral load >1000 at delivery despite ART. Possible benefit if >50 copies.
   - Unknown viral load at delivery
     - Mother received less than 3-drug therapy
     - Mother presents late in pregnancy
     - Obstetrical indications or maternal preference
   - Elective C-section is not cost-effective in resource-poor settings
   - Cefazolin prophylaxis recommended for C-section.
   - AROM, fetal scalp electrodes, operative delivery (forceps, vacuum extractor) and episiotomy should be avoided unless clear obstetric indications exist.

F. **PJP prophylaxis:** Recommended for women with CD4 count <200 or on prophylaxis. PJP during pregnancy can be more severe.
   - **TMP/SMX** may be used, although use in last trimester may be associated with ↑ bilirubin. Risk of kernicterus unknown but very small. TMP/SXZ reduced maternal & infant mortality among mothers with CD4 < 200 in resource poor setting. 1st trimester exposure might be related to small increase in birth defect rate.
   - **Dapsone:** no known adverse effects, although experience limited.
   - **Aerosolized pentamidine.** Little systemic absorption, although less effective in advanced disease. Effect of ventilation changes due to pregnancy on distribution is unknown. Can be used in 1st trimester.

TABLE 8B: HIV IN THE FETUS & NEWBORN

GENERAL:

- In 2010, only 143 new perinatal infections were reported in the U.S. An estimated 370,000 children newly infected with HIV worldwide in 2009 (a drop of 24% from 5 yrs earlier). In the U.S., 1005 children (age ≤ 14 yrs) were living with an AIDS diagnosis in 2009 & an additional 4095 are living with HIV. Worldwide, an estimated 2.5 million children are living with HIV.
- In the US in 2009, African Americans accounted for 77% of HIV diagnoses in children (age < 13 yrs) but only 15% of the population. Hispanics/Latinos accounted for 14% of HIV diagnoses; Caucasians accounted for 7% of HIV diagnoses, but 58% of the population.
- Thus, the success of HIV testing of pregnant women & intrapartum treatment in Western countries dramatically ↓ HIV infection in children. Universal testing & counseling **must be offered to all pregnant women** to improve this.
- At the same time, millions of children are infected in resource-poor settings.
- In 2006, an estimated 8700 infants were born to HIV-positive mothers in the US. This number has increased substantially (*JAIDS 57:218, 2011*).
- An increasing number of children with HIV in the U.S. are foreign born and at increased risk of TB, non-subtype B infection and intrapartum nevirapine resistance.

TRANSMISSION:

- **Over 90% of HIV+ children in U.S. acquired infection from their mothers perinatally:** in utero, during delivery, or postpartum through breastfeeding. Risk of transmission 13–40% (*http://aidsinfo.nih.gov/guidelines*).
- **Time of transmission:**
  - In utero: HIV has been identified in fetal tissues as early as 8 weeks. Probably in the majority, in utero transmission occurs late in pregnancy (*Lancet 345:518, 1995*).
  - Intrapartum: 50–70% of transmissions believed to occur through exposure to mother's blood, cervical secretions or amniotic fluid during delivery.
  - Postpartum acquisition rare in developed countries, important in developing countries. Breast-fed infants have a 10-14% add'l risk of becoming infected. In mothers seroconverting during lactation, risk is 1/3 (*Lancet 342:1437, 1993*).

DIAGNOSIS: *(See Table 8C, below)*

- HIV can be diagnosed in most infants by 1 mo & all infants by 6 mos of age by demonstration of virus by viral RNA PCR or DNA PCR. Viral culture is not used for routine diagnosis.
- HIV DNA PCR is sensitive and specific by 2-4 weeks of age (>90% sensitive). Quantitative RNA PCR assays are at least as sensitive and may better detect non-subtype B virus and provide viral load data. Low viral loads (< 5000 copies/mL) must be repeated and confirmed (*http://aidsinfo.nih.gov/ guidelines, JID 175:707, 1997; J AIDS 32:192, 2003*). Some experts perform both assays. Others use HIV RNA PCR to confirm positive HIV DNA PCR.
- Maternal anti-HIV IgG crosses the placenta & persists until 9–15 mos, so infants born to HIV-infected mothers may test positive for up to 15 mos regardless of infection. Assays for p24 antigen are less sensitive & less specific than PCR.
- PCR should be performed:
  - By age 48 hrs (not on cord blood) (Some clinicians omit this test)
  - At 2–3 wks
  - At 4-8 wks
  - Repeat at 4–6 mos if initial tests negative
- Any pos test should be repeated immediately along with quantitative HIV RNA PCR (viral load) before treatment begun.
- **Presumptive evidence of in utero infection is PCR positive in 1st 48 hours of life.** Intrapartum infection defined by negative test in 1st 48 hours and positive test (*NEJM 275:606, 1995*).
- If PCR is not available, HIV can be diagnosed by persistence of HIV antibody after 18 months of age.
- HIV infection can be presumptively excluded by 2 negative PCRs; one at > 14 days and one at > 1 month; HIV is definitively excluded (in absence of breast feeding) by at least 2 negative PCR tests; one at >1 month and one at >4 months.

NATURAL HISTORY:

- Bimodal distribution. Approximately 20-35% will be rapid progressors with onset of symptoms by median 8 months & median survival of <2 yrs.
- Median survival, untreated, for non-rapid progressors was 66 mos. Survival has greatly ↑ in the era of ART, & many perinatally infected children are reaching adolescence & young adulthood.

TABLE 8C: HIV INFECTION IN CHILDREN

1. HIV-Infected
   - Child <18 mos with positive virologic assays (HIV RNA or DNA PCR) on 2 separate determinations from one or more: HIV DNA PCR, HIV RNA PCR, p24 antigen.
   - Child ≥18 mos born to HIV+ mother or infected by blood products, sexual contact who is HIV antibody + by ELISA & Western blot or + PCR (2 separate samples).
2. Perinatally Exposed: A child who does not meet criteria above but
   - is HIV seropositive & <18 mos of age.
   - unknown antibody status but born to HIV+ mother.
3. Seroreverter: (CDC definition): A child born to HIV+ mother: Documented HIV negative (2 or more neg. EIA at 6–18 mos, or 1 neg. EIA at >18 mos) & no other lab evidence of infection & not had an AIDS-defining condition
4. HIV-uninfected (definitive): Child with 2 or more HIV PCR assays which are neg: 1 after 1 month and 1 after 4 mo of age, or HIV antibody negative after 6 months (2 separate specimens).

1994 CDC PEDIATRIC HIV CLASSIFICATION[1]

Immunologic Categories	Clinical Categories (Level of Signs/Symptoms)			
	N: None	A: Mild	B: Moderate	C: Severe
1: No evidence of suppression	N1	A1	B1	C1
2: Evidence of moderate suppression	N2	A2	B2	C2
3: Severe suppression	N3	A3	B3	C3

Immunologic Categories (CD4 counts change with age)

	Age of Child					
	<12 mos		1–5 yrs		6–12 yrs	
Immunologic Category	CD4/µL	(%)	CD4/µL	(%)	CD4/µL	(%)
1: No evidence of suppression	≥1,500	(≥25)	≥1,000	(≥25)	≥500	(≥25)
2: Evidence of moderate suppression	750–1,499	(15–24)	500–999	(15–24)	200–499	(15–24)
3: Severe suppression	<750	(<15)	<500	(<15)	<200	(<15)

REVISED WHO STAGING SYSTEM FOR HIV INFECTION & DISEASE IN CHILDREN
(See http://www.who.int/HIV/paediatric/infants2010/en)

Clinical Stage 1:	Asymptomatic
Clinical Stage 2:	Mild
Clinical Stage 3:	Advanced
Clinical Stage 4:	Severe

TABLE 8D: CHILDREN: INITIAL EVALUATION, INITIATION OF ANTIRETROVIRAL THERAPY, PJP PROPHYLAXIS & SUPPORTIVE THERAPY *(http://aidsinfo.nih.gov/guidelines)*

A. **Initial evaluation of the HIV-infected child**
   1. Document actual HIV infection
   2. History
      - General well-being
      - Infections and HIV-related conditions
      - Disclosure status
      - Growth and Developmental status
      - Psychiatric history
      - Medications (including over-the-counter and other supplements/complementary meds)
      - Social history including parent/caregiver's health, drug use, insurance
      - Sexual and drug use history
      - Risk factors for opportunistic infections including places of residence, travel, pets
      - Immunization history and documentation
   3. Comprehensive Physical Exam
      - Plot height, weight, BSA
      - Attention to lymph nodes, cardiac, dermatologic, developmental, neurologic exams
   4. Baseline Laboratory Evaluation
      - Complete blood count
      - Complete metabolic panel including BUN, creatinine, LFT's, cholesterol
      - RPR, TB testing (eg. Quantiferon TB Gold), CMV antibody, Hepatitis B surface antibody (HBsAb), HBsAg, Hepatitis C antibody, perhaps vitamin D level
      - For adolescents, chlamydia/gonorrhea nucleic antibody testing

[1] 1994 revised classification system for HIV infection in children less than 13yrs of age *[MMWR 43(RR-12):1–10, 1994]*

TABLE 8D (2)

5. HIV staging
   * CD4 count and CD4 percent, quantitative HIV RNA, genotypic resistance testing
6. Initial Health Maintenance
   * HIV risk reduction as age appropriate. Include contraception and safer sex for adolescents
   * Psychosocial support
   * Immunization update *(See Table 19)*

B. **P. jiroveci Prophylaxis—Revised Guidelines**
   1. In infants with perinatally acquired HIV, PJP occurs most frequently at 3–6 mos, often acute in onset with poor prognosis. HIV+ infants <1 yr of age at risk even with CD4 ≥1500.
      * Identify infants born to HIV+ mothers promptly (screen mothers during pregnancy), obtain PCR as described above.
      * Begin PJP prophylaxis at 4-6 wks in infants born to HIV-infected mothers who are HIV positive or who remain indeterminate.
      * Stop prophylaxis in children found to be presumptively HIV-negative (e.g., 2 negative PCRs; one obtained after 14 days and one after 1 mo of age).
      * Continued PJP prophylaxis in HIV-infected children (age >1 yr) depends on immunologic stage *(see above)*. Recommended for all children Immunologic Category 3. In resource poor settings, WHO recommends for all HIV-exposed children age < 2 yr, WHO Clinical Stage 2, 3 or 4, or CD4% < 25%.
   2. Drug Regimens for PJP Prophylaxis in Children ≥4 wks of Age:
      * **TMP/SMX (150 mg TMP/M2/day)** po divided twice daily 3x/wk on consecutive days (i.e., Mon., Tues., Wed.). Alternatives: same daily dose 1x/day. Once-daily regimen may be best for adherence.
      * If TMP/SMX not tolerated:
         * **Dapsone 2 mg/kg po 1x/day** or 4 mg/kg po q wk
         * **Aerosolized pentamidine (children ≥5 yrs) 300 mg** via Respirgard II inhaler monthly
         * **Atovaquone 30 mg/kg po q24h** for children 1–3 mos old. Atovaquone 45 mg/kg po q24h for children 4–24 mos.

C. **Antiretroviral Therapy (ART) in Children**
   1. **When to start:** This decision is more complex in children than in adults. Data specific to outcomes in children are limited, & clinical trial data do not address when to start. Natural history studies in children & extrapolation from adult studies are used to derive guidelines. Some factors argue for early treatment in children:
      * 25–35% of HIV-infected children will be rapid progressors
      * Viral load & CD4 are associated with rapid progression but cannot accurately identify all rapid progressors in first year of life
      * The CHER study in South Africa demonstrated improved survival in asymptomatic infected infants when therapy was started at < 12 months compared to waiting for symptoms *(4th AIDS Conference on HIV Pathogenesis, Treatment and Prevention 2007 Sydney Abstract LB WES103)*
      * Immune control of virus limited in first year of life
      * HIV encephalopathy, other neurological disease & cardiac involvement may occur at young age
      * Some trials of early therapy have shown promising results
      * CD4 count thresholds are most helpful in deciding when to start ART *(AIDS 24:1213, 2010)*

      Some factors to consider before institution of therapy:
      * Slow progressors may maintain good immune function for many years without treatment
      * Limited number of drugs with liquid formulation
      * Highly variable & inadequately understood pharmacokinetics of ARV drugs in children may lead to inadequate levels & drug failure
      * Metabolic complications, including abnormal lipids, glucose intolerance, fat redistribution & possibly bone mineral abnormalities can occur in children
      * Children may have excellent immune reconstitution on treatment even with advanced disease
      * Difficulties with adherence are common & lead to drug failure
      * Children may rapidly run out of treatment options

TABLE 8D (3)

Three sets of guidelines have been developed. They share several features. In infants who are known to be HIV-infected, they favor starting therapy in all infants, due to the inability to identify rapid progressors. In older children, the guidelines favor treatment, especially when the child shows immune deterioration. All emphasize the need for education to ensure adherence, & routine monitoring for efficacy & safety:

RECOMMENDATIONS FOR BEGINNING TREATMENT IN INFANTS & CHILDREN

Age Group	DHHS 2012	PENTA 2009	WHO 2010
< 12 months	**Treat** All (AI)	**Treat** All	**Treat** All
12-<24 months 24-<36 months	**Treat** • CDC stage B* or C (AI) • Asymptomatic or mild symptoms <u>and</u> • CD4 < 1000 cells/µL <u>or</u> CD4% <25% (AII) **Consider** • Asymptomatic or mild symptoms <u>and</u> • CD4 ≥ 1000 cells/µL or CD4 ≥25% (BIII)	**Treat** • CDC stage B or C • WHO stage 3 or 4 • CD4 < 1000 cells/mL • CD4% < 25% **Consider** • HIV RNA ≥100,000 copies/mL	**Treat** • WHO stage 3 or 4 • CD4 < 750 cells/mL • CD4% < 25%
36 months <5 years	**Treat** • CDC stage B* or C (AI) • CD4 < 750 cells/µL or CD4% <25% (AII) **Consider** • Asymptomatic or mild symptoms <u>and</u> • CD4 ≥ 750 cells/µL or CD4 ≥25% (BIII)	**Treat** • CDC stage B or C • WHO stage 3 or 4 • CD4 < 500 cells/mL • CD4% < 20% **Consider** • HIV RNA ≥100,000 copies/mL	
> 5 years	**Treat** • CDC Stage B* or C (A1) • Asymptomatic or mild symptoms <u>and</u> • CD4 ≤ 350 cells/µL (AI) • CD4 350-500 cells/µL (BII) **Consider** • Asymptomatic or mild symptoms <u>and</u> • CD4 ≥ 500 cells/µL	**Treat** • CDC stage B or C • WHO stage 3 or 4 • CD4 < 350 cells/mL **Consider** • HIV RNA ≥100,000 copies/mL	**Treat** • WHO Stage 3 or 4 • CD4 < 350 cells/mL

DHHS: Panel on Antiretroviral Therapy and Medical Management of HIV-Infected Children. Guidelines for the Use of Antiretroviral Agents in Pediatric HIV Infection. Nov 5, 2012. Available at *http://aidsinfo.nih.gov/ContentFiles/PediatricGuidelines.pdf*
PENTA: PENTA Steering Committee. PENTA 2009 guidelines for the use of antiretroviral therapy in pediatric HIV-1 infection. *HIV Medicine (2009), 10, 591–613*
WHO: WHO. Antiretroviral therapy of HIV infection in infants and children: towards universal access: recommendations for a public health approach - 2010 revision. Available at *http://www.who.int/hiv/pub/paediatric/infants2010/en/index.html* (The strength of the recommendation [A-C] and the strength of the evidence [I-III] is shown for the DHHS recommendations)

* Excludes LIP or single episode of serious bacterial infection

2. **Recommended therapy**

Combination therapy with at least 3 antiretroviral drugs is recommended for all children started on therapy. Choice of drugs depends on supporting data, age of the patient, local availability, & need for liquid formulation. WHO guidelines emphasize initial use of NNRTI-based regimens because of costs, local availability, & to complement adult guidelines. U.S. & European guidelines recommend either PI-based or NNRTI-based initial regimens, but recognize the risk of NNRTI-resistant virus being transmitted from mother to child *(see below)*.

If available, resistance testing should be obtained for children before starting ART, especially if an NNRTI is being considered. If the local prevalence of resistance is known, it may influence the need for resistance testing.

If abacavir therapy is being considered, HLA B*5701 screening can virtually eliminate risk of hypersensitivity reaction and should be obtained if available.

TABLE 8D (4)

RECOMMENDED FIRST-LINE THERAPY FOR HIV-INFECTED INFANTS & CHILDREN

	DHHS	PENTA	WHO
Preferred	2 NRTIs[1] **plus** lopinavir/ritonavir (if ≥ 14 days) **or** 2 NRTIs[1] **plus** efavirenz[2] (if ≥ 3 yrs)**or** 2 NRTIs[1] **plus** atazanavir + low-dose ritonavir (if ≥ 6 yrs)	2 NRTIs[3] **plus** one PI (lopinavir/ritonavir) **or** 2 NRTIs[3] **plus**1 NNRTI (nevirapine if < 3 yrs; efavirenz if age > 3 yrs)	If age < 2 yrs and not exposed to maternal **or** infant nevirapine: 2 NRTIs[4] + nevirapine
Alternative regimens	2 NRTIs[1] **plus** nevirapine[5] **or** 2 NRTIs[1] **plus** darunavir + low-dose ritonavir (if ≥ 3 yrs) **or** 2 NRTIs[1] **plus** fosamprenavir + low-dose ritonavir (if ≥ 6 months)		If age < 2 yrs and exposed to nevirapine: 2 NRTIs[4] + lopinavir/ritonavir

If age > 3 yrs: 2 NRTIs[4] + (nevirapine or efavirenz) |

	DHHS
Use in special circumstance	• 2 NRTIs[1] **plus** atazanavir unboosted (for treatment-naive adolescents ≥ 13 yrs and 39 kg) **or** • 2 NRTIs[1] **plus** fosamprenavir unboosted (if ≥ 2 yrs) **or** • 2 NRTIs[1] **plus** nelfinavir (if ≥ 2 yrs) **or** • Zidovudine + lamivudine + abacavir
Not recommended or Insufficient data to recommend for initial therapy	• Etravirine-containing regimens • Efavirenz-containing regimens if < 3 yrs • Tipranavir-, saquinavir-, or indinavir-containing regimens • Maraviroc-, rilpivirine-, raltegravir- or enfuvirtide-containing regimens • Triple-class regimens • Triple-NRTI regimens (except ZDV+3TC+ABC) • Dual (full-dose) PI regimens • Tenofovir-containing regimens if < 12 yrs or ≥ 12 yrs and Tanner 1[6] • Full-dose ritonavir or ritonavir as sole PI • Nelfinavir-containing regimens if < 2 yrs • Unboosted atazanavir-containing regimens if < 13 yrs and/or < 39 kg • Once-daily dosing of lopinavir/ritonavir, boosted darunavir, or fosamprenavir (boosted or unboosted)

AVOID: monotherapy; dual-NRTI alone; TDF + ABC + (3TC or FTC); TDF + ddl + (3TC or FTC); ATV + IDV; dual-NNRTI; 3TC + FTC; d4T + ZDV; EFV in 1st trimester pregnancy or adolescents at risk of pregnancy; NVP in adolescents if CD4 > 250 (girls) or > 400 (boys); unboosted SQV, DRV, or TPV

[1] **DHHS preferred NRTI combinations:** ABC + (3TC or FTC) [if ≥ 3 months]; TDF + (3TC or FTC) [if Tanner Stage 4 or 5]; ZDV + (3TC or FTC). **DHHS alternative NRTI combinations:** ddl + (3TC or FTC); TDF + (3TC or FTC) [if ≥ Tanner Stage 3]; ZDV + ABC; or ZDV + ddl. **DHHS NRTI combinations for special circumstances:** d4T + (3TC or FTC); TDF + (3TC or FTC) [if < 12 yrs and Tanner Stage 2]. **DHHS NRTI combinations not recommended or insufficient data to recommend for initial therapy:** ABC+ddl, ABC+TDF, ddl+TDF, and ddl+d4T
[2] Must be able to swallow capsules
[3] PENTA acceptable NRTI combinations: **3TC+ABC (preferred);** ZDV+3TC; TDF+FTC (adolescents only)
[4] WHO acceptable NRTI combinations: **ZDV+3TC (preferred);** ABC+3TC; d4T+3TC
[5] NVP should not be used in postpartum females with CD4 > 250 cells/mm³ unless benefit clearly outweighs risk
[6] The use of tenofovir carries an increased risk of bone toxicity in prepubertal patients. May consider its use in special circumstances when benefits outweigh risks.

3. **Monitoring of children on antiretroviral therapy**

   Children should be monitored at 1-2 weeks after beginning a new antiretroviral regimen to check for adherence and adverse effects. When nevirapine is started, serum transaminases should be monitored at 2 and 4 weeks and then monthly for 3 months.

   Children on antiretroviral therapy should be followed at regular intervals, usually every 3 mos.

   Clinical parameters:
   • Weight & height growth
   • Nutritional status (including Vitamin D levels)
   • Developmental milestones & neurological symptoms
   • Adherence & side effects
   • No consensus on bone mineral density testing by DEXA but considered by some experts

   Laboratory monitoring should include: CBC with differential, CD4 % & count. If available, viral load, liver enzymes, creatinine, glucose, electrolytes, & total cholesterol should be monitored.

4. **Therapeutic drug monitoring**

   Age-related changes in drug metabolism & wide interpatient variability of drug levels along with generally low success rates suggest that therapeutic drug monitoring may be very useful for PIs & NNRTIs. In some European countries, therapeutic drug monitoring has become routine. Information on laboratories & on laboratory participation in quality assurance programs is available at www.hivpharmacology.com. Target minimum trough concentrations in *Table 6F* and in the *DHHS Guidelines for the Use Antiretroviral Agents* at www.aidsinfo.nih.gov.

5. **When to change antiretroviral therapy**

   Deciding on when to change therapy can be a complex process that takes into account the remaining options, the level of adherence, the social situation & the clinical status. The goal of initial therapy is to suppress viral load to the lowest level possible, usually below the limits of quantification, & to allow the immune system to reconstitute. Ongoing viral replication permits the selection of resistant mutants, & will lead to increasing drug resistance. When initial therapy "fails", good treatment options are usually available. With subsequent treatment

TABLE 8D (5)

regimens, the number of remaining options becomes progressively limited.

Ideally, the goal of subsequent regimens is to re-establish maximal viral suppression. With the availability of enfuvirtide, tipranavir, darunavir, raltegravir, maraviroc and etravirine, it has become possible to construct regimens for many treatment-experienced adults that will control viral load to below the level of quantification. Many of these agents are now available for children but require high pill burden.

The availability of new drugs makes it often possible to construct a suppressive regimen. However, poor adherence is the most common cause of ART failure. Starting a new regimen without addressing behavioral or social causes of non-adherence will lead to development of additional resistance. The decision on when to start a new regimen will depend on remaining options, clinical status, family preference, & family situation.

Considerations on when to change are divided into virologic, immunologic, & clinical. These are not absolute. Clinical changes, however, are the clearest & most non-controversial indications for change of therapy:

Virologic failure	• **Incomplete response:** Less than a minimally acceptable virologic response after 8–2 wks of therapy (defined as a < 10-fold (1.0 $\log_{10}$) decrease from baseline HIV RNA levels • HIV RNA not suppressed to < 200 copies after 4–6 mos of antiretroviral therapy • **Viral Rebound:** Repeated detection of HIV RNA in children who initially had undetectable levels in response to antiretroviral therapy. Consider observation and repeat testing if rebound is to low level (< 1000 copies) • A reproducible ↑ HIV RNA copy number among children who have had a substantial HIV RNA response but still have low levels of detectable HIV RNA. Such an ↑ would warrant change in therapy if, after achieving a virologic nadir, a >3-fold (> 0.5 $\log_{10}$) ↑ in copy number for children aged > 2 yrs & > 5-fold (>0.7 log10) ↑ is observed for children aged < 2 yrs
Immunologic failure	• **Incomplete immunologic response to therapy:** Failure of a child with severe immune suppression (CD4 percentage < 15%) to ↑ CD4 % by at least 5 points above baseline or, if > 5 years, ↑ CD4 count by at least 50 cells/mL above baseline over first year • **Immunologic decline:** Persistent ↓ of 5 percentage points in CD4 % or ↓ to below pre-therapy baseline in CD4 cell count > 5 yrs at baseline
Clinical failure	• Progressive neurodevelopmental deterioration* (2 or more of: impaired brain growth, cognitive decline, or motor dysfunction) • Growth failure: persistent decline in weight-growth velocity despite adequate nutritional support & without other explanation* • Severe or recurrent infection or illness – Recurrence or persistence of AIDS-defining conditions or other serious infections*
Toxicity	• It may be desirable to control some side effects (e.g., diarrhea) rather than changing therapy. If a single drug can be associated with the toxicity, it is acceptable to change the offending agent

* Criteria marked with asterisk are from WHO guidelines (& may overlap with DHHS recommendations). These may be particularly helpful in the resource-limited setting.

6. **What to use as alternate therapy** *(see also Table 6F)*
   There are limited data on sequencing antiviral therapy in HIV-infected children. Several general principles are useful:
   a. When treatment failure occurs, always assess adherence to the treatment
   b. Try to address adherence problems before changing regimens
   c. If adherence has been good, assume viral resistance has developed, but it may not have developed to all agents. Viral resistance testing, if available, should be performed. If possible, obtain viral resistance testing while on failing regimen. Without testing, all 3 drugs should be changed if possible
   d. Take into account predicted cross-resistance
   e. Avoid dose reduction for toxicity unless levels can be measured
   f. Treatment failure may occur due to inadequate absorption or drug levels
   g. Consider enrolling in clinical trial
   h. **The use of at least 2 new active drugs with non-overlapping resistance best predicts response. Never add a single drug to a regimen that is clearly failing**
   i. **Consider likelihood of availability of (or ability to use) new drugs in near future and try and construct regimen with 2-3 active drugs**
   j. If regimen with 2 active drugs cannot be constructed or adherence cannot be assured and clinically stable, consider waiting and maintaining partially suppressive regimen, e.g., lamivudine monotherapy
   k. If adherent patient is failing in absence of severe resistance, consider measuring drug levels and addressing pharmacokinetic issues

D. **Supportive Treatment & Prophylaxis**
   1. Intravenous gamma globulin (IVIG)
      a. Not routinely used. Recommended for infants & children with evidence of humoral immune defects (hypogammaglobulinemia or documented failure to form specific antibody responses) IVIG 400 mg/kg q28 days is recommended.
      b. Thrombocytopenia (<20,000/mm³) on antiretroviral therapy: IVIG 0.5–1 gm/kg/dose x 3–5 days *(See Table 22 for Winrho®)*
   2. Immunization: See Table 19
   3. Pneumocystis jiroveci: See above, Section A
   4. Mycobacterium avium complex: prophylaxis recommended *[MMWR 46(RR-12), 1997]*. Begin if CD4 <50 for children ≥6 yrs; for children 2–6 yrs, begin if CD4 <75; for 1–2 yrs if CD4 < 500; <1 yr CD4 <750. Clarithromycin 7.5 mg/kg po q12h or azithromycin 20 mg/kg po once weekly is preferred. Rifabutin now used as 3rd-line, 5 mg/kg po once daily (only for children ≥6 yrs). Dose of rifabutin should not exceed 300 mg/day
   5. Psychosocial support *(see Am Acad Pediatrics, Red Book, 1994)*: School attendance, child/foster care, adolescent education

TABLE 8E: CLINICAL SYNDROMES, OPPORTUNISTIC INFECTIONS IN INFANTS & CHILDREN, WHICH DIFFER FROM ADULTS
In HIV-infected infants & children, disease progression is manifest by decrements in growth & delayed neurodevelopment as well as opportunistic infections as occur in adults
(J Ped 128:58, 1996)

CLINICAL SYNDROME	INFANT/CHILD	ADULT	CLINICAL FEATURES (in children)/COMMENTS
Central Nervous System			
Encephalopathy			General: HIV encephalopathy is a syndrome that includes motor & cognitive dysfunction seen in pts with advanced HIV. Administration of ArV therapy has been shown to be beneficial in treating children with HIV encephalopathy.
Static course	Common	0	25% children show cognitive & motor deficits. Most have head circumference in 10–25th percentile. Problems with verbal expression, attention deficits, hyperactivity. Mild ↑ reflexes in legs to spastic diplegia. IQ stable.
Plateau course	Uncommon	0	Infants or child's gain of cognitive or motor skills plateaus. Motor deficits are common. IQ usually only 50–79
Subacute progressive course	Uncommon	AIDS dementia common	Gradual progressive decline in motor, language, adaptive function. Early, child is alert, wide-eyed, with a paucity of facial movements. Endstage: mute, dull-eyed, quadriparetic. CSF: mild pleocytosis, ↑ protein, may be + for HIV antibody & virus. CT: atrophy, progressive calcification in basal ganglia (most common in infants & young children).
Focal brain diseases: seizures, focal neurologic deficits			
Infections			
Toxoplasmosis	V. rare	Common	Toxo is uncommon in infants & children since it is most often due to reactivation.
Progressive multifocal leuko-encephalopathy (JC virus)	V. rare	Common	PML is uncommon in infants & children since it is most often due to reactivation.
Endocrine			
Failure to thrive & growth retardation	Common	Wasting syndrome common	33/36 HIV+ children showed failure to thrive, not purely related to diarrhea & malnutrition. Known causes of growth failure are growth hormone deficiency, hypothyroidism, & glucocorticoid excess. 1/3 of HIV+ children have abnormal thyroid function (↑ thyrotropin, ↑ TBG) which correlates with disease progression (J Ped 128:70, 1996).
Eye			
Cytomegalovirus retinitis	Uncommon	Common	CMV chorioretinitis in 1.6% children vs. 10–20% in adults (Arch Ophthal 107:978, 1989). In children, it usually occurs with generalized CMV infection, viremia & multiple organ involvement. When present, ocular lesions are same as in adults, Table 11A, page 102.
Retinal depigmentation, on ZDV	~5%	0	Asymptomatic peripheral retinal depigmentation (dosages >300 mg/M/day).
HIV-associated "cotton wool" spots	Rare	Common	Seen only in children >8–10 yrs, while seen in 60–70% of adults.
Gastrointestinal Tract			
Mouth			
Kaposi's sarcoma	V. rare	Common	More prevalent in HIV+ children in areas of Africa.
Esophagus	Uncommon	Common	When pain/difficulty occur, children more likely to refuse to eat. CMV—odynophagia, Candida—dysphagia.
Dysphagia, odynophagia			
Diarrhea	Common	Common	Most common agents: rotavirus 24% (more common in inpatient setting); salmonella (19%), campylobacter (8%) (more common in outpatients). Presence of blood &/or WBC in stool has high positive predictive value for salmonella or campylobacter (PIDJ 15:876, 1996).
Heart			
Cardiomyopathy	Common	Common	Abnormal ECG changes (ventricular hypertrophy & non-specific ST-T changes) in 55–93% HIV+ children.
	Common	Uncommon	Left ventricular dysfunction 29–74% (most important cardiac change). 20% transient or chronic congestive failure. Unexpected cardiorespiratory arrests in 8/81 (JAMA 269:2869, 1993). Pericardial effusions & tamponade have been noted frequently in children (PIDJ 15:819, 1996).

TABLE 8E (2)

CLINICAL SYNDROME	INFANT/CHILD	ADULT	CLINICAL FEATURES (in children)/COMMENTS
Hematologic			
Hypergammaglobulinemia	**Common**	**Uncommon**	By age 6 mos, almost all HIV+ children have ↑ gamma-globulins.
Protein S (coagulation inhibitor)	Common	Common	19/26 children had ↓ levels, but risk of thrombosis low (*Ped IDJ 15:106, 1996*). Adults, ↑ protein S in 27–73%, thrombotic complications in 12%.
Hepatobiliary	Rare	Common	Very few reports relating to children. Etiologies such as AIDS cholangiopathy, peliosis hepatis (bacillary angiomatosis) not reported. 2 cases of fatal hepatic necrosis associated with adenovirus reported (*Rev Inf Dis 12:303, 1990*).
Lung			
Tuberculosis	Uncommon	Common	Virtually all are primary infections. Clinical: fever, cough. X-ray: often focal infiltrates with hilar adenopathy, cavitation uncommon.
Lymphocytic interstitial pneumonitis (LIP)	Common	V. rare	LIP occurs in 40% of children with perinatally acquired HIV. HIV & EBV antigens have been demonstrated in lung tissue. Usually diagnosed in children >1 yr as compared with PJP which is most common in first year. LIP has better prognosis than PJP. Median survival is ~5x shorter in children diagnosed with PJP than in children with LIP (*Lancet 348:866, 1996*). Clinical: slowly progressive tachypnea, cough, wheezing, hypoxemia. Rales are infrequent. Clubbing of digits is characteristic. Generalized lymphadenopathy, hepatosplenomegaly & parotid swelling. X-ray: diffuse reticulonodular infiltrates associated with hilar lymphadenopathy. Bacterial superinfection is common. Diagnosis by lung biopsy. Rx: steroids may be of some benefit.
Cryptococcosis	Uncommon	Common	Disseminated infection or localized process of the lungs. Intermittent fever is most common presenting manifestation. All pts have low CD4, history of previous OIs, & onset of cryptococcosis most commonly in 2nd decade of life (*PIDJ 15: 796, 1996*).
Congestive heart failure	Common	Uncommon	See *Heart*, above.
Leiomyosarcoma	Rare (but ↑)	V. rare	EBV demonstrated by PCR in tumors (*NEJM 332:12, 1995*)
Renal			
Nephropathy	Common	Rare	Nephropathy observed in 29% children with perinatal AIDS (*Kidney 31:1167, 1987*). In children may present with nephrotic syndrome with a course of 12–18 mos (*NEJM 321:625, 1989*). Steroid rx may be of value.
"Sepsis"	Common	Uncommon	25% of symptomatic HIV+ children will have bacteremic episodes, most due to bacteremic pneumonia or bacteremia without a focus (*Pediatric AIDS, Eds. P.A. Pizzo, C.M. Wilfert, Ch. 13, page 199, 1991*).
Fungemia (a nosocomially-acquired infection)	Common	Uncommon	Risk factors: central venous catheter (>90 days), prior antibiotic therapy (>3 different antibiotics, parenteral ↑ risk), parenteral hyperalimentation, hemodialysis, prolonged neutropenia, colonization by Candida species (*CID 23:515, 1996*)
Skin			
Impetigo	Common	Uncommon	Due to Staph. aureus or Group A strep. Clinical: areas of erythema with "honey crusting". May be widespread & evolve into "cellulitis". Increasing incidence of MRSA skin & soft tissue infections.

TABLE 8F: SELECTED DRUGS COMMONLY USED IN CHILDREN WITH HIV INFECTION

INDICATION/DRUG	DOSAGE	FORMULATIONS	COMMENTS
Antifungal Drugs			
Amphotericin B	0.5–1 mg/kg/day IV (same as adult, see Table 12, page 145)	Same as adult	
Ampho B lipid complex	5 mg/kg/day IV as for adults		
Caspofungin	75 mg/M² IV q24h loading dose, then 50 mg/M² IV q24h	Same as adult	
Fluconazole		Oral suspension (orange-flavored), 50 mg/5 mL (teaspoon)	
Oral/esophageal candidiasis	6–12 mg/kg/day		
Systemic candidiasis	12 mg/kg/day IV or po		
Cryptococcal meningitis			
Treatment	12 mg/kg po 1st day, then 6 (to 12) mg/kg/day po		
Suppression	6 mg/kg/day po		
Itraconazole	3 mg/kg po q24h (capsules) 5 mg/kg po q24h (suspension)	Oral suspension 10 mg/mL	Efficacy & safety not established Extensive drug-drug interactions Bioavailability of capsules is low & variable Administer suspension on empty stomach with 4–6 oz of Coca-Cola.
Voriconazole	6 mg/kg q12h x 2 then 4 mg/kg q 12h (FDA approved but 8-9 mg/kg may be needed)	Capsules 50 mg, 200 mg Oral suspension 40 mg/mL	Extensive drug-drug interactions Reversible visual disturbance in 20% Measure trough level: goal is 1-6 mcg/mL
Anti-HIV Drugs[1]			
Nucleoside analogue reverse transcriptase inhibitors (NRTIs)			
Abacavir (Ziagen)	Age ≥3 mos: 8 mg/kg 2x/daily not to exceed 300 mg Neonatal dose unknown Wt-based dosing: 14-21 kg: ½ tablet po qAM, ½ tablet po qPM >21 to <30 kg: ½ tablet po qAM, 1 tablet po qPM >30 kg: 300 mg (1 tablet) po 2x/day Adolescent/adult dose: 300 mg 2x/day or 600 mg 1x/day	Solution 20 mg/mL 300 mg tablets Fixed combination 600 mg with 300 mg lamivudine (Epzicom) Fixed combination 300 mg with 300 mg zidovudine & 150 mg lamivudine (Trizivir)	Hypersensitivity reaction in ~5%, may be difficult to recognize. Rechallenge may be fatal. Hypersensitivity associated with HLA B*5701. Screening for HLA B*5701 virtually eliminates hypersensitivity reactions and should be obtained before starting if available.
Didanosine (ddI, Videx)	120 mg/M² q12h not to exceed 200 mg per dose. 240 mg/M² q24h not to exceed 400 mg per dose if > 3 and treatment naive Body weight 20-25 kg: 200 mg once daily Body weight 25-60 kg: 250 mg once daily Body weight > 60 kg: 400 mg once daily Neonatal dose (2 weeks-<3 months): 50 mg/M² q12h Infant dose (age 3-8 mos): 100 mg/M² q12h	Pediatric powder (when reconstituted with antacid): 10 mg/mL Delayed-release capsules (enteric-coated beadlets): Videx EC 125, 200, 250, 400 mg Generic delayed-release capsules 200, 250, 400 mg	Dose on empty stomach. Reduce didanosine dose if combined with tenofovir. Do not administer with ribavirin Increased risk of pancreatitis. Risk higher if co-administered with tenofovir or stavudine.

Fluconazole COMMENTS (right column):

	Adult Dose	Pediatric Equivalent
	100 mg	3 mg/kg
	200 mg	6 mg/kg
	400 mg	12 mg/kg (not to exceed 600 mg/day)

[1] Adolescents ≥ Tanner 4 should be dosed according to adult dosing (see Table 6B)

TABLE 8F (2)

INDICATION/DRUG	DOSAGE	FORMULATIONS	COMMENTS
Anti-HIV Drugs/Nucleoside analogue reverse transcriptase inhibitors (NRTIs)	*(continued)*		
Emtricitabine (Emtriva) (oral solution)	6 mg/kg 1x/day 3 months of age to 17 years or 33 kg 200 mg 1x/day if > 33 kg Neonatal dose: 3 mg/kg once daily Adolescent/adult dose 200 mg 1x/day	Solution 10 mg/mL Tablet 200 mg Fixed combination 200 mg with 300 mg tenofovir (Truvada) Fixed combination 200 mg with 300 mg tenofovir, 600 mg efavirenz (Atripla) Fixed combination 200 mg with 300 mg tenofovir, 25 mg rilpivirine (Complera) Fixed combination 200 mg with 300 mg tenofovir, 150 mg elvitegravir, 150 mg cobicistat (Stribild)	Screen for HBV infection before starting. Oral solution stable for 3 months in at up to 77F/25C.
Lamivudine (3TC, Epivir)	4 mg/kg 2x/day (>30 days max 150 mg 2x daily) Neonatal dose (<30 days): 2 mg/kg 2x/day Wt based recommendations for tablet Body weight 14-21 kg: 75 mg po 2x/day 21-30 kg: 75 mg AM/150 mg PM >30 kg: 150 mg po 2x/day Adolescent/adult dose (weight >30 kg): 150 mg 2x/day or 300 mg once daily	Solution 10 mg/mL (Epivir) 5 mg/mL (Epivir HBV) Tablets 100 mg, 150 (scored), 300 mg Fixed combination 150 mg with 300 mg ZDV (Combivir) Fixed combination 150 mg with 300 mg ZDV, 300 mg abacavir (Trizivir) Fixed combination 300 mg with 600 mg Abacavir (Epzicom)	Screen for HBV infection before starting. Consider switching to 8-10 mg po 1 x 1 day if > 3 years and undetectable viral load (max 300 mg po 1 x/day)
Stavudine (d4T, Zerit)	Body weight <30 kg: 1 mg/kg 2x/day >30 kg: 30 mg 2x/day Neonatal dose birth to 13 days 0.5 mg/kg 2x/day	Solution 1 mg/mL Capsules 15, 20, 30, 40 mg (Generic approved for sale in U.S.)	Better tolerated than zidovudine but more strongly associated with lipoatrophy, peripheral neuropathy, mitochondrial toxicity. Combination with ddI associated with increased risk of lactic acidosis
Zidovudine (ZDV, AZT, Retrovir)	160 mg/M² q8h or 180-240 mg/M² q12h Adolescent/adult dose 300 mg 2x/day Neonatal dose (age <6 wks) 4 mg/kg po q12h; 1.5 mg/kg IV q6h Premature infant 30-35 wks: 2 mg/kg po 2x/day or 1.5 mg/kg IV q 12h; increase to 3 mg/kg po q 12h or 2.3 mg/kg IV at 14 days of age. Premature infant <30 weeks: 2 mg/kg po q 12h or 1.5 mg/kg IV; increase to 3 mg/kg po q 12h or 2.3 mg/kg IV at 4 weeks of age Body wt based dose: 4-9 kg: 12 mg/kg 2x daily 9-<30 kg: 9 mg/kg 2x daily > 30 kg: 300 mg 2x daily	Syrup 10 mg/mL Capsules 100 mg Tablets 300 mg Generic syrup 10 mg/mL & tablets 300 mg 10 mg/mL IV Fixed combination 300 mg with 150 mg 3TC (Combivir, generic) Fixed combination 300 mg with 150 mg 3TC, 300 mg abacavir (Trizivir) Concentrate for IV use 10 mg/mL	

TABLE 8F (3)

INDICATION/DRUG	DOSAGE	FORMULATIONS	COMMENTS
Nucleotide reverse transcriptase inhibitor (NtRTI)			
Tenofovir (Viread)	8 mg/kg po once daily (age ≥ 2 yrs) maximum 300 mg 1 scoop powder = 40 mg Use tablets for children > 17 kg who can swallow tablets Wt-based dosing: 17–22 kg: 150 mg once daily 22–<28 kg: 200 mg once daily 28–<35 kg: 250 mg once daily ≥35 kg: 300 mg once daily Adult dose 300 mg 1x/day	Tablets 150 mg, 200 mg, 250 mg, 300 mg Tablets dissolve in water, orange or grape juice Powder formulation 40 mg/gm Fixed combination 300 mg with 200 mg emtricitabine (Truvada) Fixed combination 300 mg with 200 mg emtricitabine and 600 mg efavirenz (Atripla) Fixed combination 200 mg with 300 mg tenofovir, 25 mg rilpivirine (Complera) Fixed combination 200 mg with 300 mg tenofovir, 150 mg rilpivirine, 150 mg cobicistat (Stribild)	Screen for HBV before starting. Monitor renal function. ↓ bone mineral density observed in young animals. ↓ BMD was prevalent in HIV-infected children before treatment; small ↓ in BMD in 5/15 at 1 yr in 1 study (Pediatrics 116:e846, 2005). No change compared to controls at 1 yr in another (JAIDS 40:448, 2005). Use with caution & decrease dose if any renal impairment. Decrease ddI dose if used with tenofovir. Consider Vitamin D level and Vitamin D supplement.
Non-nucleoside reverse transcriptase inhibitors (NNRTIs)			
Efavirenz (Sustiva)	10–15 kg, 200 mg; 15–20 kg, 250 mg; 20–25 kg, 300 mg; 25–32.5 kg, 350 mg; 32.5–40 kg, 400 mg; >40 kg, 600 mg—all 1x/day Neonatal dose unknown/not approved for infants Adult dose 600 mg 1x/day	Capsules 50, 200 mg Tablets 600 mg Fixed combination 600 mg with Tenofovir 300 mg/Emtricitabine 200 mg (Atripla) Liquid preparation used in PACTG 382 (contact BMS to check on availability)	Give at night to reduce CNS side effects. Capsules can be opened & added to food or liquid but contents have peppery taste. Atripla should be administered on an empty stomach. Minimum weight for Atripla 40 kg. Lowers concentration of unboosted PIs, LPV/ritonavir, voriconazole. Increase dose of EFV if given with RIF. Pregnancy Class D. Avoid if possibility of pregnancy.
Etravirine (Intelence)	Age > 6 to 17 yrs: Wt-based dosing: ≥ 16–<20 kg: 100 mg 2x/day 20–<25 kg: 125 mg 2x/day 25–<30 kg: 150 mg 2x/day ≥30 kg: 200 mg 2x/day	Tablets 25 mg, 100 mg, 200 mg	Administer with food. Tablets disperse in water. Glass should be rinsed with water and the rinses swallowed to ensure consuming the entire dose. Do not co-administer with efavirenz, atazanavir or tipranavir due to interactions. Multiple other drug interactions.
Nevirapine (Viramune)	<8 yrs of age, 7 mg/kg 2x/day or 200 mg/M² >8 yrs of age, 4 mg/kg 2x/day or 150 mg/M² **Note:** Initiate dosing once daily x 14 d. If no rash, increase to 2x/day. **Dosing by M² preferred** Neonatal dose 5 mg/kg or 120 mg/M² 1x/day x 14 d, then 120 mg/M² 2x/day x 14 d, then 200 mg/M² 2x/day Adolescent/adult dose 200 mg 1x/day x 14 d then 200 mg 2x/day Neonatal prophylaxis: 2 mg/kg at birth and age 3 days	Suspension 10 mg/mL Tablets 200 mg, 400 mg extended release	Do not dose-escalate in presence of rash. If rash is associated with fever, oral lesions, conjunctivitis, blistering, or hepatitis, stop medication immediately. Severe cholestatic hepatitis & Stevens-Johnson syndrome are rare but life-threatening complications that may occur in the 1st 6 wks. In adults, risk of severe toxicity increased in women with CD4 > 250 & men with CD4 > 400. Lowers concentration of LPV/ritonavir. Risk of rash and hepatotoxicity higher when CD4% > 15%.
Rilpivirine (Edurant)	Not approved in children. No PK or dosing data available. Trial underway for age 12–18 years. Adolescent/adult dose: 25 mg once daily with food	Tablets 25 mg Fixed combination 25 mg with tenofovir 300 mg/emtricitabine 200 mg (Complera/Eviplera)	Administer with food. Metabolized by CYP3A. Do not administer with rifampin, rifabutin, rifapentine, PPIs.

TABLE 8F (4)

INDICATION/DRUG	DOSAGE	FORMULATIONS	COMMENTS
Protease Inhibitors			
Atazanavir (Reyataz)	Age > 6 yrs: 15 kg–<20 kg: ATV 150 mg + RIT 100 mg once daily 20 kg–<32 kg: ATV 200 mg + RIT 100 mg once daily 32 kg–<40 kg: ATV 250 mg + RIT 100 mg once daily ≥40 kg: ATV 300 mg + RIT 100 mg once daily Neonatal use not recommended Adolescent/adult dose 400 mg 1x/day or 300 mg + 100 mg ritonavir both 1x/day	Capsules 100, 150, 200 mg, 300 mg	Administer with food. Wide variability in levels in children with unboosted atazanavir. Ritonavir-boosted atazanavir may give more consistent levels. If using unboosted atazanavir in adolescents, consider TDM. Avoid in infants due to ↑ bilirubin. Avoid use with proton pump inhibitors if possible. If PPI must be used, no more than 20 mg omeprazole should be given, 12 hrs after atazanavir/ritonavir. Boost with ritonavir If co-administered with tenofovir or efavirenz. **Do not co-administer with nevirapine.**
Darunavir (Prezista)	FDA approved for age > 3 yrs. Wt-based dosing: For children weighing 10–15 kg, dosing is based on darunavir (DRV) 20 mg/kg + ritonavir (RIT) 3 mg/kg 2x/day: 10–<11 kg: DRV 200 mg (2 mL) + RIT 32 mg (0.4 mL). 11–<12 kg: DRV 220 mg (2.2 mL) + RIT 32 mg (0.4 mL). 12–<13 kg: DRV 240 mg (2.4 mL) + RIT 40 mg (0.5 mL). 13–<14 kg: DRV 260 mg (2.6 mL) + RIT 40 mg (0.5 mL). 14–<15 kg: DRV 280 mg (2.8 mL) + RIT 48 mg (0.6 mL). For children > 15 kg who can swallow tablets: 15–29 kg: darunavir 375 mg + ritonavir 50 mg 2x/day 30–39 kg: darunavir 450 mg + ritonavir 60 mg 2x/day >40 kg: Adult dose Adult/adolescent dose 600 mg + ritonavir 100 mg 2x/day (treatment experienced) 800 mg + ritonavir 100 mg (treatment naive adults only) once daily	Tablets 75 mg, 150 mg, 400 mg, 600 mg Oral suspension 100 mg/mL	Administer with food. Active against many strains with extensive protease inhibitor resistance. Potential for many drug-drug interactions. Review other medications. May substitute ritonavir 100 mg tablets for children 20–40 kg instead of ritonavir liquid. Do not use in children < age 3 years because of concerns related to seizures and death in infant rats. Do not use once daily in children age < 12 years.

TABLE 8F (5)

INDICATION/DRUG	DOSAGE	FORMULATIONS	COMMENTS
Anti-HIV Drugs/Protease Inhibitors *(continued)*			

Fosamprenavir (Lexiva)	2-5 yrs naive only: 30 mg/kg 2x/day (not to exceed adult dose of 1400 mg 2x/day). Not recommended 6-18 naive only unboosted 30 mg/kg (not to exceed 1400 mg) 2x daily
	2 x day:
	<11 kg: FPV 45 mg/kg + RIT 7 mg/kg
	11-<15 kg: FPV 30 mg/kg RIT 3 mg/kg
	15-<20 kg: FPV 23 mg/kg + RIT 3 mg/kg
	20 kg FPV 18 mg/kg + RIT 3 mg/kg (not to exceed adult dose of 700 mg + 100 mg ritonavir 2x/day)
	Neonatal use not recommended
	Adolescent/adult dose:
	Antiretroviral naive:
	  1400 mg 2x/day (>47 kg)
	  700 mg + 100 mg ritonavir 2x/day
	  1400 mg + 100 or 200 mg ritonavir 1x/day
	Antiretroviral experienced: 700 mg +
	  100 mg ritonavir 2x/day
		Tablet 700 mg (equivalent to 600 mg amprenavir)
		Oral suspension 50 mg/mL
			Administer tablets with or without food if used alone. Administer solution with food and when boosting with ritonavir.
			Once daily dosing is not recommended for children. FDA approved for children as young as 4 weeks but DHHS panel does not recommend for children < 6 months.

Indinavir (Crixivan)	500 mg/M² q8h (not approved) Adolescent/adult dose 800 mg q8h or 800 mg + ritonavir 100 or 200 mg 2x/day	Capsules 100, 200, 333, 400 mg	Response associated with Cmin. *(AAC 44:1029, 2000).* Consider measuring Cmin if available & adjusting dose. Nephrolithiasis in 20% of children. Ensure hydration.
Lopinavir/Ritonavir (Kaletra)	Age 14 days - 12 months: 300 mg lopinavir/75 mg r/M² 2x/day Age 12 months - 18 years: 230 mg lopinavir/57.5 mg r/ M² 2x/day if not taking efavirenz, nevirapine or fosamprenavir. Increase to 300 mg lopinavir/75 mg/ M² 2x/day if taking above drugs but many prefer this dose for all children. Alternate wt based for oral soln: <15 kg: 12 mg/3 mg/kg 2x/day 15-40 kg: 10 mg/2.5 mg/kg 2x/day >40 kg: Adult dose Tablet Dosing: 15-25 kg: 2 tablets (100 mg lopinavir/25 mg r) 2x/day 25-30 kg: 3 tablets 2x/day 30-45 kg: 4 100/25 mg tab or 2 200/50 mg tab 2x/day >45 kg: Adult dose Adult adolescent dose: 400 mg lopinavir/100 mg r 2x/day if not receiving NVP, EFV, fosamprenavir. Increase dose in patients on NVP, EFV, FPV	Pediatric solution 80 mg lopinavir/20 mg ritonavir per mL (contains alcohol and polyethylene glycol) Tablets 100 mg lopinavir/25 mg ritonavir 200 mg lopinavir/50 mg ritonavir	Administer tablets with or without food. Do not split or crush. Oral solution should be administered with food. Oral solution should be refrigerated but stable up to 2 months at room temp. For adults who are treatment naive, tablets can be dosed as 400 mg/100 mg once daily in naive PI naive patients; this has not been evaluated in adolescents who might have more rapid clearance. Higher doses (eg 300 mg/M² or 600 mg/140 mg 2x/day should be considered in treatment-experienced patients with PI resistance mutations. Standard dose of 230 mg/M² gives trough lower than target associated with response in treatment experienced adults (5.7 mcg/mL CROI 2008 abstr 574). Crushed tablets give lower exposure: not recommended **(CROI 2010 abst 871).** **Life threatening events including heart block reported in premature infants.** Should not be used in premature infants until 2 weeks beyond due date or in term infants 14 days unless benefits clearly outweigh risks.

TABLE 8F (6)

INDICATION/DRUG	DOSAGE	FORMULATIONS	COMMENTS
Anti-HIV Drugs/Protease Inhibitors (continued)			
Nelfinavir (Viracept)	Age 2-13 yrs: 45–55 kg 250 mg q12h (8th CROI, 2001, Abst. 250). Approved dose of 30 mg/kg q8h may lead to inadequate levels. Neonatal wt-based dosing: 1.5-2 kg: 100 mg 2x/day 2-3 kg: 150 mg 2x/day > 3 kg: 200 mg 2x/day Adolescent/adult dose 1250 mg q12h	Powder for oral suspension 50 mg/level scoop Tablets 250, 625 mg	Take with meal to ↑ absorption. Large variability in levels. Crushed or dissolved tablets more reliably absorbed. Consider measuring C_{min} if available & adjusting dose. Maintaining ↑ trough > 0.8 mcg/mL associated with improved response in one study.
Ritonavir (Norvir)	350-400 mg/M² 2x/day Neonatal dose not established; 450 mg/M² 2x/day led to lower exposure than target in adults Adolescent/adult dose 600 mg 2x/day	Solution 80 mg/mL Capsules 100 mg Tablets 100 mg	Full dose ritonavir is rarely used. Dose should be escalated over 1st 7 days to ↓ side effects. Use lower dose as pharmacokinetic enhancer. Solution is unpleasant tasting. High levels of side effects in older children and adults relative to other PI's. Refrigerate capsules; stable 30 days at room temperature.
Saquinavir (Invirase) Note: Soft-gel capsules no longer available.	Under study: Not approved in infants or children, but Saquinavir Wt based dose (limited data): 5-15 kg: 50 mg/kg + ritonavir 3 mg/kg 2x daily 15-40 kg: 50 mg/kg + ritonavir 2.5 mg/kg 2x daily >40 kg: 50 mg/kg + ritonavir 100 mg 2x daily Adolescent/adult dose: 1000 mg + 100 mg ritonavir 2x/day With Lopinavir/ritonavir: Saquinavir 1000 mg + Lopinavir/ritonavir 400 mg/100 mg both 2x/day	Hard-gel capsules 200 mg Film-coated tablets 500 mg	Consider measuring C_{min} if available & adjusting dose. (C_{min} >100 ng/mL associated with response.) Should only be used with ritonavir enhancement. Not recommended for children with prolonged QT interval.
Tipranavir (Aptivus)	Not approved in 2 yrs of age. 375 mg/M² + ritonavir 150 mg/M² 2x/day wt-based: 14 mg/kg + ritonavir 6 mg/kg 2x/day Adolescent/Adult dose: 500 mg with 200 mg ritonavir 2x/day	Capsule 250 mg Solution 100 mg/mL with 116 IU Vit E/mL	Administer with food. Active against many virus strains with extensive PI resistance, & used only in patients with extensive prior experience. Most effective when given with other active agents, such as enfuvirtide. Activity and tolerability in PACTG1051 similar to adult trials (Intl AIDS Conf 2006 Abstr WEA60301) Induces metabolism of other PIs & should not be co-administered with them. Possible association with intracranial hemorrhage
Fusion Inhibitors			
Enfuvirtide (Fuzeon)	6-16 yrs 2 mg/kg 2x/day, maximum dose 90 mg (1 mL) injected subcutaneously <6 yrs not approved Adolescent/adult dose 90 mg (1 mL) 2x/day injected subcutaneously	Injection: lyophilized powder for injection 108 mg of enfuvirtide when reconstituted with 1.1 mL sterile water to deliver 90 mg/mL.	Most effective when started with 1–2 new drugs to which virus is sensitive. Must be reconstituted & used within 24 hrs. Inject in upper arm, abdomen, anterior thigh—rotate site. Common injection site reactions include tender itchy nodules.

TABLE 8F (7)

INDICATION/DRUG	DOSAGE	FORMULATIONS	COMMENTS
CCR5 Inhibitors			
Maraviroc (Selzentry)	Not approved in children Adolescent/adult doses: 150 mg 2x/day when given with strong CYP3A inhibitors (with or without CYP3A inducers) including all PIs (except tipranavir/ritonavir) 300 mg twice daily when given with NRTIs, enfuvirtide, tipranavir/ritonavir, nevirapine, raltegravir 600 mg twice daily when given with CYP3A inducers, including efavirenz, rifampin, phenobarbital, etravirine, phenytoin, etc. (without a CYP3A inhibitor)	Tablets 150 mg, 300 mg	Tropism assay should be used before prescribing to exclude X 4/dual tropic virus. Cytochrome P450 substrate. Do not use in patients with CrCl < 30 mL/min who are receiving potent CYP3A4 inhibitors
Integrase Inhibitors			
Raltegravir (Isentress)	Age and Wt-based dosing: 6-12 yrs and > 25 kg: 400 mg tablet 2x/day day **OR** 2-<12 yrs chewable tablet dosing: 10-<14 kg: 3 x 25 mg 2x/day 14-<20 kg: 1 x 100 mg 2x/day 20-<28 kg: 1.5 x 100 mg 2x/day 28-<40 kg: 2 x 100 mg 2x/day > 40 kg: 3 x 100 mg 2x/day Infants 6 mo-2 yrs: Not approved Adolescent/adult dose 400 mg 2x/day	Tablets 400 mg Chewable tablet 25 mg and 100 mg scored Granules 6 mg/kg 2x/day under study.	Give with or without food Chewable tablets may be chewed or swallowed whole Efavirenz and etravirine may decrease raltegravir concentrations
Elvitegravir	No pediatric dosing currently Adult dose 1 tablet once daily	Fixed dose combination Elvitegravir 150 mg, Cobicistat 150 mg, TDF 300 mg, FTC 200 mg	Give with food
Dolutegravir (Tivicay)	Adults and children >12 years and >40 kg 50 mg po once daily if INSTI-Naive 50 mg po bid if INSTI-experienced or with efavirenz, fosamprenavir/ritonavir, tipranavir/ritonavir or rifampin	Tablets 50 mg. Granules under study	Give with or without food
Antimycobacterial Drugs			
M. tuberculosis			
Ethambutol	15-25 mg/kg/day po	No pediatric formulation	Not approved in children <13 yrs but can be given. Monitor for closely for visual change
Isoniazid	Neonates: 10 mg/kg po q24h. Infants/Children: 10-20 mg/kg po q24h (maximum 300 mg/day)	50 mg/5 mL syrup	Can give IM
Pyrazinamide	20-40 mg/kg po q24h as 1 or more doses (maximum 2 gm/day)	No pediatric formulation	
Rifampin	10-20 mg/kg po q24h (maximum 600 mg/day)	No pediatric formulation. Ad hoc solution can be made by pharmacy	Can give po or IV. Do not use with protease inhibitors. Reduced dose rifabutin can be substituted
Streptomycin	10-20 mg IM q12h (max. 1 gm/day)		

TABLE 8F (8)

INDICATION/DRUG	DOSAGE	FORMULATIONS	COMMENTS
MAC—Mycobacterium avium-intracellulare complex			
Azithromycin	5 mg/kg/day for treatment 20 mg/kg once weekly, not to exceed 1200 mg	Oral suspension 100 or 200 mg/5 mL, 250 mg, 600 mg capsules	
Clarithromycin	15 mg/kg/day divided q12h po (not to exceed 500 mg po q12h)	Granules for oral suspension (125 or 250 mg/5 mL) (DO NOT refrigerate suspension)	
Clofazimine	1-2 mg/kg/day po to max. of 100 mg/day	No pediatric formulation	
Rifabutin	10-20 mg/kg/day po (max 300 mg/day)	No pediatric formulation	↓ dose with protease inhibitors, inc with NNRTI's
Antifungal Drugs			
Pneumocystis pneumonia (PCP)			
Prophylaxis (See Table 8D)			
TMP/SMX OR	150 mg/M² TMP component po divided q12h on 3 consecutive days (M, T, W) each week. Abbreviated schedules: Table 8D	Oral suspension (cherry or grape flavored), 40 mg TMP/200 mg SMX/5 mL (teaspoon); 80 mg TMP/400 mg SMX tablet (single strength)	Breakthrough episodes of PJP: TMP/SMX 3%, dapsone 15% or higher, aerosol pentamidine 15%, IV pentamidine 25% (J Ped 122:163, 1993)
Dapsone OR	2 mg/kg/day po (not to exceed 100 mg)	No pediatric formulation	
Aerosolized pentamidine—only if ≥5 yrs old	300 mg with Respirgard II inhaler 1x monthly		Used as young as 8 mos (PIDJ 12:958, 1991)
Treatment			
Atovaquone suspension	30-40 mg/kg po q24h. Dosing interval not established	Not FDA-approved for pediatric use	Efficacy in children not established. CNS levels <1%.
Pentamidine isethionate	4 mg/kg/day IV or IM x 12-14 days		Start with IV in all but mildest cases
TMP/SMX	Children >2 mos 20 mg TMP/100 mg SMX/kg/day divided q6h po or IV in same dose q6-8h		

TABLE 8F (9)

INDICATION/DRUG	DOSAGE	FORMULATIONS	COMMENTS
Antiviral Drugs—other than anti-HIV			
Cytomegalovirus			
Cidofovir	No studies in children.	IV solution only	Must follow guidelines for hydration & probenecid.
Induction	5 mg/kg once a week for two doses		Dose adjust for renal disease
Maintenance	5 mg/kg every 14 days		
Foscarnet			No studies reported in children. Deposited in teeth &
Induction	180 mg/kg/day divided q8h		bone of growing animals. Dose adjust for renal disease
Maintenance	90–120 mg/kg IV q24h		
Valganciclovir	7 mg × m² × CrCl (2x/day induction (max 900 mg)	Tablets 450 mg	Dose adjust for renal diseases
Induction	900 mg po 2x/day for 21 days	Solution 50 mg/5 mL	
Maintenance	900 mg po q day		
Ganciclovir		Adult capsule or IV solution	Has potential carcinogenicity
Induction	5 mg/kg IV q12h		Dose adjust for renal disease
Maintenance	5 mg/kg IV q24h		
Herpes simplex virus			
Acyclovir	30 mg/kg IV q8h (age <12 yrs)	200 mg/5 mL oral suspension (banana flavored) available	Daily urine output should be 1 mL/1.3 mg of acyclovir
	15 mg/kg IV q8h (age >12 yrs)	if appropriate	
Influenza			
Oseltamivir	<1 year: 3 mg/kg/day po q 12h	30, 45, 75 mg capsule and oral suspension 12 mg/mL	
	≥ 1 year and		
	≤15 kg: 30 mg po q12h		
	16-23 kg: 45 mg po q12h		
	24-40 kg: 60 mg po q12h		
	>40 kg: 75 mg po q12h		
Varicella zoster (<2 yrs old)			
Acyclovir	500 mg/M² IV q8h		

For additional data on drugs for pain &/or nutritional management, see www.aidsinfo.nlh.gov/guidelines, Supplements to Pediatric Guidelines Mar 2008.

TABLE 8G: PROPHYLAXIS FOR FIRST EPISODE OF OPPORTUNISTIC DISEASE IN HIV-INFECTED INFANTS & CHILDREN

PATHOGEN	INDICATION	PREVENTIVE REGIMENS*	
		FIRST CHOICE	ALTERNATIVES
Pneumocystis pneumonia (PCP)	HIV-infected or HIV-indeterminate infants aged 1–12 mos	TMP/SMX 150/750 mg/M²/day in 2 div. doses po 3x/wk on consecutive days (A2)	Aerosolized pentamidine (children aged ≥5 yrs) 300 mg 1x monthly via Respirgard II nebulizer (C3); dapsone (children aged ≥1 mo.) 2 mg/kg (max 100 mg) po q24h (C3). Atovaquone 30 mg/kg po q24h for 1–3 mos old & >24 mos old; 45 mg/kg po q24h for 4–24 mos old; IV pentamidine 4 mg/kg every 2–4 wks if other options are unavailable (C3)
	HIV-infected children aged 1–5 yrs with CD4 count <500 or CD4 percent <15%	Acceptable alternative dosage schedules: (A2) Single dose po 3x/wk on consecutive days or daily	
	HIV-infected children aged 6–12 yrs with CD4 <200 OR CD4 percent <15%	2 div. doses po q24h; 2 div. doses po 3x/wk on alternate days	
Mycobacterium tuberculosis Isoniazid-sensitive	TST reaction ≥5 mm prior positive TST result without treatment OR contact with case of active tuberculosis	Isoniazid 10–20 mg/kg (max. 300 mg) po OR IM q24h x 9 mos. (A1) OR 20–40 mg/kg (max. 900 mg) po 2x/wk x 9 mos. (B3)	Rifampin 10–20 mg/kg (max. 600 mg) po or IV q24h x 12 mos. (B2) (Rifampin duration of rx is 4–6 mos. according to 1999 USPHS guidelines.)
Isoniazid-resistant	Same as above; high probability of exposure to isoniazid-resistant tuberculosis	Rifampin 10–20 mg/kg (max. 600 mg) po OR IV q24h x 12 mos. (B2)	Uncertain
Multidrug (isoniazid & rifampin)-resistant	Same as above; high probability of exposure to multidrug-resistant tuberculosis	Choice of drug requires consultation with public health authorities	None
Mycobacterium avium complex	For children aged ≥6 yrs, CD4 <50; 2–6 yrs, CD4 <75; 1–2 yrs, CD4 <500; <1 yr, CD4 <750	Clarithromycin 7.5 mg/kg (max. 500 mg) po q12h (A2) OR azithromycin 20 mg/kg (max. 1200 mg) po 1x/wk (A2)	Children aged ≥6 yrs, rifabutin 300 mg po q24h (B1); <6 yrs, 5 mg/kg po q24h when suspension becomes available (B1); azithromycin 5 mg/kg (max. 250 mg) po q24h (A2)
Varicella zoster virus	HIV-infected children who are asymptomatic & not immunosuppressed	Varicella zoster vaccine	None
	Significant exposure to varicella with no history of chickenpox, shingles, or varicella vaccine	Varicella zoster immune globulin (VZIG), 1 vial (1.25 mL)/10 kg (max. 5 vials) IM, administered ≤96 hrs after exposure, ideally within 48 hrs (A2)	

* See Table 4A for HIV classification

TABLE 9A: EPIDEMIOLOGY OF HEPATITIS C (HCV)

1. **Caseload**

   180 million cases of Hepatitis C virus (HCV) worldwide in 2011. Highest rates in Africa and Asia. Egypt > 15% prevalence. 4.1 million cases in the U.S. (1.6%). Most patients infected prior to 1990 *(Hepatology 49:1335, 2009)*. Approximately 20,000 new infections/year in the U.S. Most HCV infected persons do not know their status.

2. **Risk of Transmission**. Intravenous drug users (IVDU) > blood products recipients > homosexual > heterosexual.

Sexual transmission	Number of sexual partners (2.2-2.9 relative risk (RR)). For persons with preexisting Herpes simplex (HSV) (3.85RR). Preexisting trichomonas (3.3 RR)
HIV	1.9-4.4 RR
Healthcare workers	Primary needle stick injury. Risk of HBV ≥ HCV > HIV, if not vaccinated for HBV.
Vertical transmission	

   FIGURE 8   Risk of Transmission of HCV

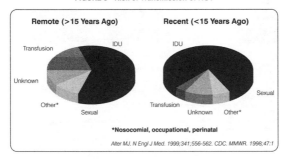

   ***Nosocomial, occupational, perinatal**

   Alter MJ. N Engl J Med. 1999;341;556-562. CDC. MMWR. 1998;47:1

TABLE 9B: DIAGNOSIS OF HCV INFECTION

1. **Testing**

   Categories of HCV diagnostic tests and test type:
   - HCV Antibody Test: EIA assay.
   - HCV Quantitative Viral Load (HCV RNA): PCR.
   - HCV Genotype 1-6: Sequencing.

   HCV Quantitation Tests:

Assay (Mfg)	Method	Genotypes Detected	Linear Range (IU/mL)	Limit of Detection (Genotype 1 in Plasma)(IU/mL)	Lower Limit of Quantitation (IU/mL)
COBAS® TaqMan® HCV Test v2 (For use with High Pure System) (Roche Diagnostics)	Semi-automated RT-PCR	1-6	43-69,000,000	15	25
COBAS® AmpliPrep COBAS® TaqMan® HCV Test	Automated RT-PCR	1-6	25-300,000,000	7.1	43
Versant HCV RNA 3.0 Assay (Siemens Health Care Diagnostics)	Semi-automated bDNA signal amplification		615-7,700,000		615
Abbott RealTime HCV (Abbott Diagnostics)	Semi-automated RT-PCR		12-100,000,000		12

TABLE 9B (2)

2. **Testing Algorithm** *(Modified from: Cleveland Clinic J Med 70:S7, 2003)*

FIGURE 9   HCV Testing Algorithm

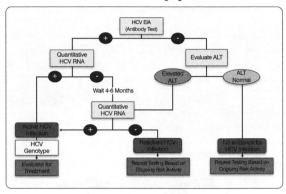

TABLE 9C: NATURAL HISTORY OF HCV

1. **Acute HCV**

    Usually asymptomatic. If symptomatic, usually abates in days to weeks; rarely associated with hepatic failure.
    Typically leads to chronic infection–in 60-80% of cases (elevated transaminases).

    Factors associated with natural clearance include: HLA-DRB1*1101 and DQB1*0301 haplotypes;
    Favorable **IL-28B** genetic status *(See Table 9E);* Low HCV viral load.

    Treatment of acute HCV usually results in "cure" (sustained virologic response–SVR). Therefore, Rx should
    be initiated within first 6 mos of infection when possible.

2. **Chronic HCV**

FIGURE 10 Chronic HCV Progression

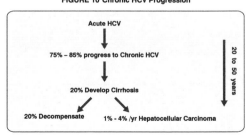

Associated With Faster Progression

- Older age at time of infection
- Male gender
- Alcohol use
- HIV Co-infection
- HBV Co-infection
- Acquisition or re-infection post-transplant

Survival

- With compensated cirrhosis: 5 year survival = 91%
  (10 year = 79%)
- With decompensated cirrhosis: 5 year survival = 50%.

TABLE 9D: CLINICAL PRESENTATION OF HEPATITIS C INFECTION

1. **Symptoms.** Usually asymptomatic. When symptomatic, common complaints include: fatigue, nausea, anorexia, myalgias, arthralgias, asthenia, Weight loss (except where ascites). Note: there is poor correlation between symptoms and disease stage or transaminase elevations

2. **Signs.** Depends on stage of disease. Skin disorders: spider angiomas, porphyria cutanea tarda (PCT). Stigmata of cirrhosis: ascites, jaundice, hepatomegaly, splenomegaly, peripheral edema, hemorrhoids

3. **Laboratory Abnormalities.** Transaminase elevation: 1/3 normal transaminase levels, only 25% have > 2X ULN, poor correlation between transaminase elevation and liver histology. Otherwise, no specific lab abnormalities except when cirrhotic or hepatic decompensation: low albumin, elevated bilirubin, AST/ALT ratio > 1, low platelet count, cryoglobulinemia

4. **Extrahepatic Manifestations.** Lymphoma, mixed cryoglobulinemia, glomerulonephritis (membranoproliferative), auto-antibody disorders, e.g. thyroiditis, PCT and Lichen planus, diabetes mellitus

5. **Staging.**

   - **Liver Biopsy.** Liver Biopsy is the gold standard for HCV staging.

     Metavir Classification System

Staging	F0	No scarring
	F1	Minimal scarring
	F2	Scarring outside immediate area that contains blood vessels
	F3	Bridging fibrosis; spreading and connecting to other areas containing scarring
	F4	Cirrhosis; advance scarring of liver
Histological Activity Score (Knodell Score)	0	No inflammation
	1-4	Minimal inflammation
	5-8	Mild inflammation
	9-12	Moderate inflammation
	13-18	Marked Inflammation

   - **Non-Invasive Tests (in lieu of Liver Biopsy; also *see 9I (2) page 91* of this Guide).** Modified from *Martinez, Hepatology 53:325, 2011.*
     AUC = area under ROC curve: indicates relative correlation with biopsy findings (F0-F4).

Score	Serum Markers	≥ F2 (%)	AUC ≥ F2	F4 (%)	AUC F4
FibroTest	Multiple	33-74	0.74-0.89	3-25	0.82-0.92
Forns	Multiple	32-59	0.75-0.91	3-20	-
APRI	Multiple	27-74	0.69-0.88	3-25	0.61-0.94
FIB-4	Multiple	21-36	0.74-0.85	7	0.91
Hepascore	Multiple	39-79	0.74-0.86	6-34	0.80-0.94
Fibrometer	Multiple	41-56	0.78-0.89	4-15	0.94
ELF	Multiple	27-64	0.77-0.87	12-16	0.87-0.90
Fibroscan	Liver Elastography	37-74	0.72-0.91	8-25	0.87-0.98

6. **Model for End-Stage Liver Disease (MELD) Score / Child-Pugh Score (A, B, or C)**
   - MELD score used to determine End-Stage Liver Disease MELD = $3.78 \times \log_e$ (bilirubin in mg/dl) + $11.2 \times \log e$ (INR) + $9.57 \times \log_e$ (creatinine in mg/dL) + 6.43. If MELD score > 10, refer to hepatologist for transplantation

   Child-Pugh Score (Add score from each Clinical Feature below)

Clinical Feature	Score: 1	Score: 2	Score: 3
Encephalopathy *(see below)*	None	Grade 1-2	Grade 3-4
Albumin	>3.5 gm/dL	2.8-3.5 gm/dL	<2.8 gm/dL
Total bilirubin	<2 mg/dL	2-3 mg/dL	>3 mg/dL
(If taking indinavir or if Gilbert's syndrome)	<4 mg/dL	4-7 mg/dL	>7 mg/dL
Prothrombin time/INR	<4/<1.7	4-6/1.7-2.3	>2.3

   Grade of Encephalopathy

Grade	Description
1	Mild confusion, anxiety, restlessness, fine tremor, slow coordination
2	Drowsiness, asterixis
3	Somnolent but arousable, marked confusion, speech incomprehensible, incontinent, hyperventilation
4	Coma, decerebrate posturing, flaccidity

   Child-Pugh score Classification

MELD Score	Class
5-6	A
7-9	B
>9	C

TABLE 9E: HCV TREATMENT REGIMENS AND RESPONSE WITH AND WITHOUT HIV COINFECTION

1. **Treatment Setting.** Indications for treatment of HCV must take into account both relative and absolute contraindications. Response to therapy reflects defined terms. Duration of therapy is response guided based on Genotype. Recommended follow-up during and post-treatment.

2. **Indications for Treatment.** Assuming use of Pegylated Interferon (Peg-IFN) + Ribavirin in the regimen: motivated patient, acute HCV infection, biopsy: chronic hepatitis and significant fibrosis, cryoglobulinemic vasculitis, cryoglobulinemic glomerulonephritis, stable HIV infection, compensated liver disease, acceptable hematologic parameters, creatinine < 1.5 (GFR > 50) With emergence of newer Direct Acting Agents (DAAs) treatment with IFN-based regimens should be reserved only for those who absolutely need treatment now. Otherwise, should wait for approval of new agents (by mid-2014).

3. **Contraindications for Treatment.** Contraindications (both relative and absolute) also assume use of Pegylated Interferon (Peg-IFN) + Ribavirin in the regimen.
   a. **Relative Contraindications.** Hgb < 10, ANC < 1000, PTLs < 50K, hemodialysis and/or GFR < 50, active substance and alcohol use, anticipated poor compliance, untreated mental health disorder, e.g. depression, stable auto-immune disease, Thalassemia and sickle cell anemia, sarcoidosis, HIV co-infection (CD4 < 200, concurrent zidovudine)
   b. **Absolute Contraindications.** Uncontrolled, active, major psychiatric illness, especially depression; hepatic decompensation (encephalopathy, coagulopathy, ascitis); severe uncontrolled medical disease (DM, CHF, CAD, HTN, TB, cancer); untreated thyroid disease; pregnancy, nursing, child-bearing potential (anticipated pregnancy, no birth control); active untreated autoimmune disease; HIV co-infection (CD4 < 100, concurrent ddI)

4. **Response to Therapy.** Predictors of successful response to therapy include: recent infection with HCV, Genotype 2 or 3 infection, favorable IL-28B haplotype, less severe liver disease on biopsy, HCV viral load < 800,000.

5. **Definitions of Response to Therapy.**

Null	Failure to decrease HCV VL by >2 log at week 12.
Non-Responder	Failure to clear HCV RNA by week 24.
Partial Response	>2 log ↓ HIV RNA by week 12 but not undetectable at week 24.
Early Virologic Response (EVR)	>2 log ↓ at week 12 and undetectable at week 24; **Complete EVR** = undetectable at both week 12 and 24.
Rapid Virologic Response (RVR)	Undetectable by week 4 and sustained through course of Rx
Extended Rapid Virologic Response (eRVR)	New terminology with Direct Acting Agents (DAAs). Undetectable after 4 weeks of DAA treatment (e.g., week 4 for telaprevir or week 8 for boceprevir), with sustained undetectable HCV RNA at weeks 12 and 24.
End of Treatment Response (ETR)	Undetectable at end of treatment.
Relapse	Undetectable at end of therapy (ETR) but rebound (detectable) virus within 24 weeks after therapy stopped.
Sustained Virologic Response (SVR)	CURE! Still undetectable at end of therapy and beyond 24 weeks after therapy is stopped.

FIGURE 11 Peginterferon and Ribavirin: Response to Therapy

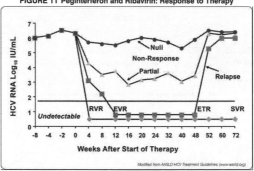

Modified from AASLD HCV Treatment Guidelines (www.aasld.org)

6. **Response Guided Therapy:** The use of viral decay on therapy to guide total length of therapy. A key factor in minimizing drug exposure with maximum therapeutic benefit.

7. **IL-28B Genotype:** Gene locus on chromosome 19 predicts response to Interferon Therapy, especially in patients with genotypes 1 and 4: For SNP Rs129798620 **Genotype CC: most favorable response;** Genotypes CT and TT, less favorable. Other SNPs for IL-28B have different favorable alleles (e.g., SNP Rs8099917 where TT genotype associated with more favorable response).

TABLE 9E (2)

FIGURE 12 Response to IFN based Therapy Based on IL-28B Haplotype

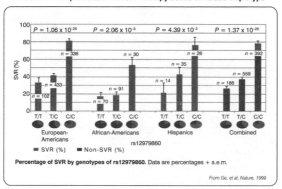

Percentage of SVR by genotypes of rs12979860. Data are percentages + s.e.m.

From Ge, et al, Nature, 1999

8. **Treatment Regimens**

* **Sofosbuvir** (400 mg po 1 tab qd with food) and **Simeprevir** (150 mg po 1 cap qd) were FDA approved in late 2013 for in combination therapy for treatment of Genotype 1 HCV. **Please consult Sanford Guide digital editions for the most current updates regarding recommended use of these new agents.**

* Biopsy is a 'gold standard' for staging HCV infection and is helpful in some settings to determine the ideal timing of HCV treatment. When bx not obtained, "non-invasive" tests are often employed to assess the relative probability of advanced fibrosis or cirrhosis. Fibroscan approved by FDA for use to stage degree of cirrhosis in 2013.

* Resistance tests: Genotypic resistance assays are available that can determine polymorphisms associated with reduction in susceptibility to some DAAs (Direct Acting Agents, e.g., protease inhibitors). **However, resistance tests are not routinely recommended in pts naïve to Rx and are reserved for selective use in patients who have received prior unsuccessful treatment with a DAA.**

* **IMPORTANT NOTE REGARDING TREATMENT DECISION-MAKING:** Newer drugs are in development. **Emerging data suggest a high probability that newer regimens that spare the use of pegylated Interferon (peg-IFN) and/or Ribavirin (RBV) will be successful and available by mid-2014 (or sooner).** Therefore, the timing of the decision to initiate HCV therapy needs to be individualized based on: the patients current clinical status, the viral genotype, the pt's ability to tolerate peg-IFN/RBV based therapies, and the likelihood of disease progression over the next 5 years while newer treatments are developed. The Ultimate Goal for treatment of HCV: no Interferon or Ribavirin, only Direct Acting Agents (DAA).

Genotype	Regimen
All*	• Either Pegylated Interferon (PEG-IFN) alfa 2a (Pegasys) 180 mcg SQ weekly OR • PEG-IFN Alfa 2b (PEG-Intron) 1.5 mcg/kg SQ weekly **(Sofosbuvir + Ribavirin will be approved for use in early 2014 for genotype 2 and genotype 3 infections. Check Sanford Guide Website for frequent updates: http://webedition.sanfordguide.com)**
	PLUS
2, 3	• Ribavirin 400 mg bid (if using response guided Rx, dose Ribavirin as for Genotype 1, 4)
1, 4	• Ribavirin 600 mg bid (wt > 75 kg) OR • Ribavirin 400 mg qAM + 600 mg qPM (wt < 75 kg)
	PLUS

1 Only*	• Telaprevir (Incivek) 750 mg (2 tabs) po tid (with food–not low fat) for 12 wks only
	    ▪ Start immediately with PEG-IFN + Ribavirin at recommended doses
	    ▪ Must stop Telaprevir at week 12 and continue PEG-IFN + Ribavirin for remainder of duration of therapy

	OR

1 Only*	• Boceprevir (Victrelis) 800 mg (4 caps) po tid (with food–meal or light snack)
	    ▪ Start 4 weeks after starting PEG-IFN + Ribavirin at recommended doses
	    ▪ Continue along with PEG-IFN + Ribavirin for full duration of therapy

WARNINGS:	• **Never use Telaprevir or Boceprevir as monotherapy** • **Never Dose Reduce Either Telaprevir or Boceprevir** • **Never Combine Telaprevir or Boceprevir** • **Never use either drug in sequence owing to shared resistance profiles**

* Recommendations likely to change to non-IFN based regimens in 2014. Check Sanford Guide Web Edition for frequent updates: *http://webedition.sanfordguide.com)*

TABLE 9E (3)

9. Duration of Therapy

Genotype	Response Guided Therapy (for PEG-INF based regimens)

2, 3	• If RVR: Treat for 16-24 weeks of total therapy*
	   ■ Check for SVR at week 40 or 48 depending on duration of therapy (16 or 24 weeks)
	• If EVR: Treat for 24 weeks of total therapy
	   ■ Check for SVR at week 48
	• If Partial or Null Response: Discontinue therapy at week 12 (treatment failure)

4	• If eRVR or EVR: Treat for 48 weeks of total therapy ■ Check for SVR at week 2 • If Partial or Null Response: Discontinue at weeks 24 and 12, respectively.

1**	• If eRVR: Continue therapy for 24 weeks (week 28 for boceprevir)
	   ■ Check for SVR at week 48 (week 52 for boceprevir)
	• IF EVR: Continue therapy for 48 weeks
	   ■ Check for SVR at week 72
	• If Null, Partial Response, or **NOT complete EVR:** Discontinue therapy at week 12 therapy at week 12

  *   Similar SVR rates for 16 vs. 24 wks but higher relapse with 16 wks of therapy. Re-treatment in such settings usually results in SVR with longer (24 wk) duration.

 ** Assuming use of Direct Acting Agents (DAA), e.g., Telaprevir or Boceprevir. If DAAs are not being used, treatment duration is the same as for Genotype 4.

10. Recommended Follow up Schedule

Week*	CBC	CMP	TSH	HCV RNA	CD4	HIV RNA	Depress Screen	MD Visit
0	X	X	X	X	X	X	X	X
2	X	X						
4	X	X		X		X	X	X
8	X	X						X
12	X	X	X	X	X	X	X	X
18	X	X						X
24	X	X	X	X	X	X	X	X
30	X	X						X
36	X	X	X	X		X	X	X
42	X	X						X
48	X	X	X	X	X	X	X	X
PT-4**	X	X				X	X	X
PT-12**	X	X			X	X		
PT-24**	X	X	X	X	X	X		X

  * Treatment week   ** Post-treatment (PT) week

Key: **CBC:** Complete Blood Count (watch for anemia in first 2 weeks of Rx);
         CMP: Comprehensive Metabolic Panel **TSH:** Thyroid Stimulating Hormone

• **Note:** HIV RNA and CD4 count only for those with HCV/HIV co-infection.

• **Schedule is modified based on duration of therapy. Schedule is also modified for those taking boceprevir; should check HCV RNA at weeks 8 and 16 to assess RVR and EVR, respectively.**

11. Coinfection: HCV and HIV

• Screen all HIV patients for presence of HCV antibody
• ART benefits host defense against HCV
    o In untreated HIV with CD4 > 500, consider treating HCV before starting ART
    o In untreated HIV with CD4 < 200, start ART and defer HCV therapy until CD4 count rises
• Avoid combining ribavirin with d4T or ddI: severe mitochondrial toxicity
• Ribavirin + AZT aggravates anemia.
• Boceprevir and telaprevir OK with raltegravir, but not recommended with several HIV PIs (see package inserts)

TABLE 9E (4)

FIGURE 13 Genomic Structure of HCV

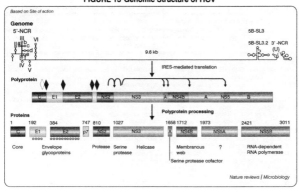

Nature reviews | Microbiology

TABLE 9F: HCV DRUGS IN DEVELOPMENT

HCV DRUGS IN DEVELOPMENT			
Site (Class)	**Drug**	**Study Phase**	**Mfgr**
NS3 / 4 **(Protease Inhibitors)**	Simeprevir	Approved	Janssen
	Faldaprevir (BI 1335)	III	Boehringer Ingelheim
	Vaniprevir	II	Merck
	Narlaprevir	IIa	Merck
	Danoprevir/r	II	InterMune/Roche
	Asunaprevir (BMS 650032)	III	Bristol Myers Squibb
	Sovaprevir (ACH 1625)	II	Achillion
	GS 9526	II	Gilead
	ABT-450/r	III	Enanta/Abbott
	IDX 320	II	Idenix
	GS-9451	II	Gilead
	ACH-2684	Pre-clinical	Achillion
	MK-5172	II	Merck
NS5B **(Nucleosides/tides)**	R7128	II	Roche
	ALS-2158	I	Vertex
	Sofosbuvir (Solvadi)	Approved	Gilead
	GS-938	IIb	Gilead
	VX-222	II	Vertex
	VX 135 (ALS-2200)	I	Vertex
	Mericitabine	IIb/III	Roche
	IDX 184	II (FDA hold)	Idenix
NS5B **(Non-nucleosides)**	Tegobuvir (GS 9190)	II	Gilead
	TMC7055	II	Janssen
	BMS-1325	II	BMS
	GS-9669	II	Gilead
	BI-7127	IIb/III	BI
	VX 2221	IIb	Vertex
	ABT-333	III	Abbott
	IDX-370	Ib	Idenix
	Setrobuvir (ANA 598)	II	Roche
	PPI 383	IIa	Presidio
NS5A Inhibitors	Daclatasvir (BMS-052)	III	Bristol Myers Squibb
	PPI-668	Ib/II	Presidio
	Ledipasvir (GS 5885)	III	Gilead
	GS 5816	Ib / II	Gilead
	ABT 267	III	Abbott
	MK 8742	Ib/II	Merck
	GSK 805	II	GSK
	ACH 3102	Ib/II	Achillion
	IDX 719	II	Idenix
Cyclophilin Inhibitors	SCY-635	Dropped	Scynexis
	Alisporivir	2b (FDA hold)	Novartis
Peg-IFN	Peg-Lambda	III	BMS
Toll-like Receptor 7 Inhibitor	GS 9620	II	Gilead

TABLE 9G: EPIDEMIOLOGY OF HEPATITIS B (HBV)

1. **Caseload.** 350,000,000 cases worldwide, at least 1.25 million in US; defined as persons Hepatitis B surface antigen (HBsAg) positive for more than 6 months *(Am J Pub Health 89:14-18, 1994; MMWR 54 (RR-16): 1- 31, 2005).* 15-40% of Carriers will develop complications, including cirrhosis, hepatic decompensation, and hepatocellular carcinoma.

2. **Risk of Transmission.** Hepatitis B virus (HBV) replicates to high titers in the blood, especially during initial (acute) infection. Any parenteral or mucosal exposure can transmit the virus. HBV is transmitted via perinatal, percutaneous, sexual exposure, and close person-to-person contact (e.g., open cuts or sores). It is ~ 100-fold more efficiently transmitted than HIV. HBV is present in most tissues and body fluids (serum, saliva, semen, vaginal secretions) and can survive for long periods of time on environmental surfaces.

3. **Virology & Life Cycle.** DNA virus: HBV is a partially double stranded hepadnavirus. Once within the cell nucleus, the HBV DNA causes the liver cell to produce surface (HBs) proteins, the core (HBc) protein, DNA polymerase, the HBe protein, HBx protein and other as yet undetected proteins and enzymes. HBV has a unique mechanism of replication via reverse transcription of pregenomic RNA by its DNA polymerase. The lack of proofreading function leads mutant virions that can fuel antiviral resistance. Produces full virion (42 nm complete virus; Dane Particle) and smaller (22 nm) HBsAg particles in large quantities. Primarily infects hepatocytes, although believed to infect lymphocytes as well. HBV amplifies via reverse transcription of an RNA intermediate. Enters nucleus; forms covalently closed circular (CCC) DNA. May, but does not always, integrate into host DNA.

4. **Eight Genotypes.**
   o **A** (N. America / Europe / Parts of Africa): More responsive to IFN Rx
   o **B** (Asia): More responsive to IFN Rx
   o **C** (Asia): More severe liver disease; slower HBsAg clearance; more HCC; Less responsive to IFN Rx
   o **D** (India / Middle East / Mediterranean / Africa): Less responsive to IFN Rx
   o **E** (Africa)
   o **F** (S. America)
   o **G** (Undetermined)
   o **H** (Undetermined)

TABLE 9H: NATURAL HISTORY OF HBV

1. **Acute HBV Infection.** Usually asymptomatic (incubation period of 1 – 4 months). If symptomatic, usually abates in days to weeks; rarely associated with hepatic failure (unless co-infected with Hepatitis Delta Virus, HDV). Factors associated with natural clearance include: Cellular Immune Responses (NK cell; NK T-cell; and virus specific CD4 T cells and CD8 cytotoxic T lymphocytes). Those who resolve the acute infection maintain broad and strong CTL responses.
   Note: HBV DNA can persist at low levels for > 20 years and those who seem to clear infection likely are not truly cured of HBV infection. Subsequent chemotherapy or immune suppressive therapy: risk factors for re-emergence of HBV replication.

2. **Three Phases of Infection.** Not all patients successfully make it through all 3 phases: Immune tolerant phase (+HBeAg, +HBsAg, High level HBV DNA); Inflammatory phase (reduction in HBV DNA; Elevated transaminases); Non-Replicative phase (loss of HBeAg; reduction of HBV DNA; Normalization of ALT/AST).

3. **Diagnostic Test Panels.**

Interpretation of Diagnostic Test Panels					
	Acute HBV	Inactive chronic HBV	Active Chronic HBV	Vaccinated / Immune	Cleared / Latent Infection
HBsAg	+ + +	+	+ +	-	-
Anti-HBs	-	-	-	+ +	+ +
Anti-HBc (IgM)	+ +	-	-	-	-
Anti-HBc (IgG)	+ + +	+	+	-	+
HBeAg	+ + +	-	+/-	-	-
Anti-HBe	-	-	+/-	-	+/-
HBV DNA	+ + +	+	+ +/+ + +	-	-
ALT / AST	Elevated	Normal	Elevated	Normal	Normal

4. **Progression of Disease.** The following factors are associated with faster progression (and higher rates of HCC): level of HBV DNA (strongest predictor of development of cirrhosis), family history of HCC or cirrhosis, older age, male, alcohol use, HIV co-infection, HCV co-infection.

TABLE 9I: HEPATITIS B (HBV), CLINICAL PRESENTATION

1. **Symptoms.** Patients with HBV are usually asymptomatic. When symptomatic, common complaints include: fatigue, nausea, anorexia, myalgias, arthralgias, asthenia, weight loss (except where ascites). Poor correlation between symptoms and disease stage or transaminase elevation. **Note: For patients with cirrhosis, abrupt change in clinical symptoms or lab findings suggests spontaneous bacterial peritonitis (SBP): tap ascites!**

2. **Signs.** Depends on stage of disease. Skin disorders: spider angiomas. Stigmata of cirrhosis: ascites, jaundice, hepatomegaly, splenomegaly, peripheral edema, hemorrhoids, caput medusa.

3. **Laboratory Abnormalities.** Transaminase elevation: 1/3 normal transaminase levels, only 25% have > 2x ULN, poor correlation between transaminase elevation and liver history. Otherwise, no specific lab abnormalities except when cirrhotic or hepatic decompensation: low albumin, elevated bilirubin, AST/ALT ratio>1, low platelet count, cryoglobulinemia.

TABLE 9I (2)

4. **Extrahepatic Manifestations.** Lymphoma, mixed cryoglobulinemia, glomerulonephritis (membranoproliferative), auto-antibody disorders (e.g., thyroiditis), PCT and Lichen planus, diabetes mellitus, polyarteritis nodosum.

5. **Staging.** Current treatment recommendations depend, in part, on the amount of liver fibrosis and hepatic inflammation.
   a. **Liver biopsy is the gold standard.** *See Table 9D, page 85,* for Metavir Classification System (staging and histologic activity score).
   b. **Inflammation and fibrosis.** Battery of enzymes and serum proteins are used as a surrogate marker of hepatic inflammation and fibrosis. One example is the Fibrosure Index. Correlation with liver biopsy fibrosis is shown in the Figure. Accuracy of Fibrosure result is best at the lower (<0.2) or higher (>0.8) values.
   c. **Child-Pugh Score and Model for End Stage Liver Disease (MELD).** *See Table 9D, page 85.*

FIGURE 14 Fibrosure Index Correlation to Fibrosis Stage

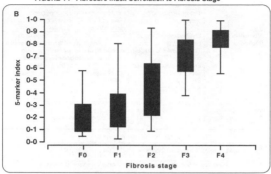

(From Imbert-Bismut, Lancet 2001.)

TABLE 9J: HBV TREATMENT (WITH & WITHOUT HIV COINFECTION)

1. **Indications for Treatment.** Decision to treat HBV infection is based on evidence of HBV viral replication and magnitude of liver fibrosis.

2. **When to Treat.** The following are key indicators: HBeAg status, HBV viral load (HBV DNA), elevated liver enzymes (ALT level), cirrhosis. For HBeAg+ patients, treatment is typically deferred for 3-6 months to observe spontaneous seroconversion from HBeAg+ to negative.

				When to Treat HBV	
HBeAg status	HBV DNA: "viral load"	ALT	Fibrosis*	Treatment** IFN = interferon; NUC = nucleoside/ tide analogue	Comments
+	> 20,000	< 2xULN	F0 –F2	Observe	Low efficacy with current Rx; biopsy helpful in determining whether to Rx. Lean toward Rx if older age or + Family Hx HCC
+	> 20,000	< 2x ULN	F3-F4	**Treat: IFN or NUC**	**No IFN if decompensated cirrhosis**
+	> 20,000	> 2x ULN	Any	**Treat: IFN or NUC**	INF has higher chance of seroconversion to HBeAg Negative and HBsAg Negative status.
-	< 2000	< 1xULN	Any	Observe	Might Treat if F4; **No IFN if decompensated cirrhosis.**
-	2000-20,000	< 2x ULN	F0 – F2	Observe	
-	2000-20,000	< 2x ULN	F3 – F4	**Treat: NUC or (IFN)**	NUCs favored if HBeAg negative; Treatment duration ill-defined. Certainly > 1 year, likely chronic Rx (indefinitely)
-	> 20,000	> 2xULN	Any	**Treat: NUC or IFN**	NUCs favored if HBeAg negative; Treatment duration chronic / indefinite

Modified from *AASLD HBV Treatment Guidelines (www.aasld.org); and EASL Guidelines (J Hepatology 57:167, 2012)*
* Liver Biopsy or fibrosure assay is helpful in determining when and how to treat
** Treatment options listed below

TABLE 9J (2)

3. **Treatment Regimens.**
   - HBV alone: single drug therapy is usually sufficient
   - HBV-HIV coinfection: combination therapy recommended

	Drug/Dose	Comments
Preferred Regimens	**Pegylated-Interferon-alpha 2a** 180 μg sc once weekly OR **Entecavir** 0.5 mg po once daily OR **Tenofovir** 300 mg po once daily	PEG-IFN: Treat for 48 weeks Entecavir: Do not use Entecavir if Lamivudine resistance present. Entecavir/Tenofovir: Treat for at least 24-48 weeks after seroconversion from HBeAg to anti-HBe. Indefinite chronic therapy for HBeAg negative patients. Renal impairment dose adjustments necessary.
Alternative Regimens	**Lamivudine** 100 mg po once daily OR **Telbivudine** 600 mg po once daily OR **Emtricitabine** 200 mg po once daily (investigational) OR **Adefovir** 10 mg po once daily	These alternative agents are rarely used except in combination. **When used, restrict to short term therapy owing to high rates of development of resistance.** Not recommended as first-line therapy. Use of Adefovir has mostly been replaced by Tenofovir.
Preferred Regimen for HIV-HBV Co-Infected Patient	**Truvada** (Tenofovir 300 mg + Emtricitabine 200 mg) po once daily + another anti-HIV drug	ALL patients if possible as part of a fully suppressive anti-HIV/anti-HBV regimen. Continue therapy indefinitely.

- The goal of therapy for HBeAg+ patients is seroconversion from positive to negative (but this rarely occurs). For HBeAg negative patients, the goal is suppression of HBV DNA to < 50 IU/mL.

Summary of Sustained Viral Response After One Year of Therapy Note: low frequency of loss of HBeAg loss.						
	PEG-INF 2a	Lamivudine	Adefovir	Entecavir	Telbivudine	Tenofovir
HBeAg Seroconversion	27%	16-21%	12%	21%	22%	21%
HBV DNA <50 IU/mL	25 -63%	60-73%	51-64%	67-90%	60-88%	80-95%
ALT normalization	39%	41-75%	48-61%	68%	60%	77%
HBeAg loss	3%	<1%	0	2%	<1%	3%
Viral Resistance	0	15-30%	Minimal	0	6%	0

Modified from Hepatology 45:507, 2007.

4. **Comments.**
   - **All patients with HBV infection should be vaccinated against Hepatitis A.**
   - **All patients with HBV should be evaluated for presence of Hepatitis D (HDV or Delta) virus infection.**
   - Interferon best used in HBeAg+ patients; much higher conversion rates from HBeAg+ to HBeAg- and from HBsAg+ to HBsAg- with IFN compared to nucleoside regimens.
   - **IFN therapy** favored in **Genotype A (and B)** patients; and those who have lower HBV DNA, higher ALT, younger age, and women, all have higher seroconversion response rates.
   - For those who seroconvert from HBeAg to anti-HBe, if consolidation therapy for one additional year, 20% will serorevert back to HBeAg+ status within 1 – 3 years. Ongoing monitoring is required for all patients.
   - **NOTE: Return to active HBV replicative state, including HBsAg seroreversion, spikes in HBV DNA, and liver inflammation/damage, can occur when HBV infected patients receive chemotherapy or immunomodulating agents!** This is especially a concern when using Rituxan or for those patients receiving Stem Cell Transplantation. Use of a nucleoside agent recommended prior to the initiation of chemotherapy and /or immunotherapy in HBsAg positive patients and in selected HBsAg-, anti-HBS+, anti-HBc+ patients.
   - All patients with cirrhosis, HBeAg+ status, older patients, and those with a positive family history of HCC should have periodic (every 6 – 12 month) screening for HCC with an ultrasound and alpha-fetoprotein assay.
   - **Resistance:** Lamivudine, Telbivudine, and Adefovir, when used as monotherapy are associated with high level resistance. Frequency of emergence of mutations increases with duration of therapy (> 6 months). Reviewed in Lancet Inf Dis. 12: 341, 2012.
   - **Combination Therapy:** Under investigation. Early studies demonstrate higher rates of virologic success (HBV DNA < 50 IU/ml), HBeAg seroconversion, and possibly less emergence of resistance. Not yet recommended as primary mode of therapy except where resistance already exists, in patients with HIV-HBV co-infection, and for those with advanced disease and decompensated cirrhosis.

TABLE 10: PRIMARY PROPHYLACTIC ANTIMICROBIAL AGENTS AGAINST OPPORTUNISTIC PATHOGENS IN ADOLESCENTS & ADULTS

Prevention of First Episode of Disease (for 2nd, see Table 12). [For 2004 USPHS/IDSA Guidelines for Prevention of OIs in HIV, see MMWR 53:RR-15, 2004].

Lowest CD4 Count	Pathogen	Preventive Regimens		Comments
		Primary	Alternative	
All patients regardless of CD4 level	**Mycobacterium tuberculosis:** TST: ≥5 mm or prior untreated pos. TST or contact with case of active TB. Positive gamma interferon release assay. Newer IGRAs appear to be as good as TSTs for detection of latent TB in HIV-infected patients, but there are conflicting reports as to the value of IGRAs for predicting subsequent active TB (AJ 182:1826, 2010; CID 48:954, 2009; Eur Resp J 35:1346, 2010; JCM 49:2086, 2011).	**[INH** 5 mg/kg/day po, maximum 300 mg] po, + **pyridoxine** 50 mg po q24h x 9 mos.] or **[INH** 900 mg po + **pyridoxine** 100 mg po 2x/wk x 9 mos]	**RIF**** 600 mg po q24h or **RFB**** 300 mg po q24h x 4 mos²	See Table 11A, page 115. 12 dose weekly rifapentine 15 mg/kg/dose (max dose 900 mg) is an option in HIV-positive patients not on antiretroviral therapy. REF: NEJM 3655:11, 2011
	As above but high probability of exposure to INH-resistant TB	**RIF**** 600 mg po q24h or **RFB**** 300 mg po q24h x 4 mos.		
	Exposure to multi-drug resistant TB	Consultation recommended		
CD4 <200/mm³	**Pneumocystis pneumonia (PCP):** (See Table 11A page116) **DC prophylaxis when CD4 count >200 for >12 wks in response to ART.** Current data also suggests it is likely safe to dc prophylaxis in patients on combined ART who also have CD4 counts of 101-200 (CID 51:611, 2010).	**Trimethoprim/sulfamethoxazole (TMP/SMX)-DS:** one tab po q24h or 3x/week or **TMP/SMX-SS** one tab po q24h or **Dapsone** 100 mg po q24h	**Aerosolized pentamidine** 300 mg q month via Respirgard II nebulizer (if toxo pos, see below) OR **Atovaquone** suspension1500 mg po q24h	TMP/SMX superior to other rx in actual practice (incidence of failure 0.0002/100 person yrs) vs. dapsone or inhaled pentamidine or atovaquone (0.001/100 person yrs). Atovaquone = pentamidine but had 1 rx-limiting adverse events.
CD4 <100/mm³ REF: CID 40 (Suppl. 3), 2005	**Toxoplasma gondii:** (in pts with + IgG toxo, antibody titer). DC primary prophylaxis in toxo Ab+ pts with CD4 >200 for >12 wks in response to ART.	**TMP/SMX-DS** one po q24h.	**Dapsone** 100 mg po q24h + **pyrimethamine** 50 mg po q week + **leucovorin** (folinic acid) 25 mg po q week	Another option: Atovaquone 750 mg po q6–12h + pyrimethamine 25 mg q24h + leucovorin 10 mg po q24h.
	Histoplasmosis: Not routinely recommended. Can be considered for patients at high risk because of occupational exposure or who live in a hyperendemic region for histoplasmosis (≥10 cases/100 patient-years).	**Itraconazole 200 mg twice daily**		If used, primary prophylaxis can be stopped once CD4 >150 for 6 months for patients on ART and restarted if CD4 falls below 150.
CD4 <50/mm³	**Mycobacterium avium-intracellulare³:** (See Table 12, page 119.) **DC prophylaxis when CD4 count >100 sustained for 3 mos. in response to ART.**	Chronic suppression: **Clarithromycin** 500 mg po q12h or **azithromycin** 1200 mg po weekly (both assoc. with emergence of resistant respiratory flora).	Rifabutin 300 mg po q24h	See Table 12, page 137. Single daily dose of 500 mg of clarithro better than rifabutin but no direct comparison available between std. q12h dosage (ATS/IDSA Consensus Statement: AJRCCM 175:367, 2007).
	Cytomegalovirus: (See Table 12, page 158.) Authors feel it is reasonable to observe pts closely, rx active CMV infection. Preemptive rx of pts with CMV viremia without evidence of organ involvement generally not recommended. May safely **dc CMV preventive therapy** when CD4 count > 100–150 per mm³ and HIV viral load has been suppressed on ARVs for > 6 mos. Restart if CD4 drops ≤100–150/mm³	Chronic suppression: **Valganciclovir** 900 mg po q24h (see Comment)	Oral ganciclovir 1 gm po q8h	See Table 12, page 158, primary prophylaxis. If plasma PCR for CMV pos, 43% risk of disease (↓ to 26% on oral ganciclovir); if PCR neg., 14% (↓ to 1% on oral ganciclovir). Therefore, some use prophylaxis in gay males when PCR pos.
	Candida species, cryptococcus: Not routinely recommended prior to 1st fungal infection [MMWR 51(RR-8):15, 2002]	Patients with positive CRAG, even with low titers, and other evidence of disease should be treated for cryptococcal infection		

¹ TST = tuberculin skin test (Mantoux).
² Interaction with protease inhibitors to be considered; see Table 12, pg 136. For options regarding concurrent use of protease inhibitors & RIF or RFB.
³ Authors think it reasonable to observe pts closely, rx strongly suspected or active MAC, then institute chronic suppression (see Table 12, page 137).
⁴ Interaction with protease inhibitors to be considered; see Table 12, page 136.

TABLE 11A:[1] DIAGNOSIS & DIFFERENTIAL DIAGNOSIS OF CLINICAL SYNDROMES, OPPORTUNISTIC INFECTIONS & NEOPLASMS

(For Treatment, see Table 12)

CLINICAL SYNDROME, ETIOLOGY, EPIDEMIOLOGY	CLINICAL PRESENTATION, DIAGNOSTIC TESTS, COURSE
Acute HIV infection (primary HIV infection, acute retroviral syndrome)	**Symptoms:** Occur in 50-90%, others have asymptomatic seroconversion; diagnosis made in <10% Time from exposure to sx usually 2-6 wks.

Acute HIV infection (primary HIV infection, acute retroviral syndrome)

Differential diagnosis includes: EBV mononucleosis, CMV mononucleosis, toxoplasmosis, rubella, viral hepatitis, syphilis, primary HSV, drug reactions

Think acute HIV when mononucleosis suspected but serological tests for mono negative.

NOTE: During acute retroviral syndrome, individuals have very high plasma & genital secretion viral titers and **are highly infectious both from sexual activity & needle sticks.**

Drug-resistant virus commonly isolated in acute retroviral syndrome.

Symptoms: Occur in 50-90%, others have asymptomatic seroconversion; diagnosis made in <10% Time from exposure to sx usually 2-6 wks.

Symptoms	Frequency (%)	Symptoms	Frequency (%)	Lab Abnormalities	Freq (%)
Fever	>95	Headache	33	↑ ALT, AST	50
Adenopathy	75	Hepatosplenomegaly	15	↓ platelets	45
Pharyngitis	75	Neuropathy	6	↓ lymphs (CD4)	35
Macular or papular rash	70	Oral/genital ulcers	<5	Atypical lymphs (↑ CD8)	35
Myalgias/arthralgias	80	Esophageal ulcers	<5		
N, V, or diarrhea	30-60	Palpable purpura	<5		
		Conjunctivitis	<5		

Up to 50% have neurological manifestations from severe headache to signs of meningitis or encephalitis. Those with acute neurologic syndromes have 10x higher CSF viral loads than those without neurologic symptoms. OIs are rare.

Course/Prognosis: symptoms usually resolve in 1-2 wks & rarely up to 10 wks. The occurrence of the acute retroviral syndrome, a short incubation period to symptoms (fever, fatigue, myalgias), & duration of illness >14 days correlate with more rapid progression to AIDS. See Table 6A.

[1] These summaries initially used the 6th Edition of *The Medical Mgmt of AIDS*, edited by Merle A. Sande & Paul A. Volberding, W.B. Saunders & Co., 1999. *See Table 12* for details of treatment/disease entity.

TABLE 11A (2)

CLINICAL SYNDROME, ETIOLOGY, EPIDEMIOLOGY	CLINICAL PRESENTATION, DIAGNOSTIC TESTS, COURSE

Central Nervous System CNS invasion occurs early in HIV infection. ART produced ↓ CNS AIDS-defining events (*Eur J Neurol 18:527, 2011*) but mortality is high when these occur and other CNS conditions may be increasing (immune reconstitution leukoencephalitis, chronic "burnout" VZV encephalitis, toxoplasma or PML).

Cognitive Disorders, Diffuse Brain Dysfunction

Declining mental acuity with preservation of alertness

HIV-1 associated dementia (HAD or HIVD), also known as AIDS dementia complex (ADC), multinucleated giant cell encephalitis, or HIV-1-associated cognitive/motor complex. Frequency: 1/3 of adults, ½ children with AIDS. Most common cause of dementia worldwide in adults < 40 years of age	Impaired short-term memory, ↓ concentration, clumsiness, slowness, apathy, irritability, & personality changes. **Process is slowly progressive, weeks to months** (usually occurs after AIDS defining diagnosis) **& CD4 count usually <200/mm³**. Degree of intellectual impairment & stage of ADC correlates with CSF HIV RNA. Higher levels of HIV RNA in CSF predict progression of neuropsychological impairment & postmortem evidence of HIV encephalitis.

Stage 0: normal
Stage 1: mild, can work
Stage 2: moderate but cannot work
Stage 3: severe, cannot work, major intellectual disability
Stage 4: vegetative (**In AIDS dementia complex, a "vegetative" patient can be aroused to a level of alertness. This is an important distinction between AIDS dementia complex & many other potential etiologies)**

Neuro exam: non-focal	Early	Late
Cognition	Inattention ↓ concentration Forgetfulness, slowing of thought processing	Global dementia
Motor	Slowed movements Clumsiness Ataxia	Paraplegia
Behavior	Apathy Blunting of personality Agitation	Mutism

CSF: Normal 30–50%, ↑ WBC (monos) 5–10% [CSF abnormalities: pleocytosis, ↑ protein or ↑ immunoglobulin levels reported in 30% asymptomatic HIV+ individuals].

MRI scan: Early is typically normal. **Cerebral atrophy, occ. with diffuse fluff ("spilled milk"), edema of antral white matter & basal ganglia, best seen on T-2 weighted imaging.** No mass effect. Normal gadolinium rules out most cases of primary brain lymphoma & toxo but does not rule out other infections (neurosyphilis, cryptococcal meningitis, MAC encephalitis).

Pts receiving antiretroviral therapy (ART) have fewer cognitive abnormalities than untreated pts, & when impaired may show marked improvement with rx. Symptoms of acute meningoencephalitis may reflect failure of ART with ↑ CSF HIV viral load & may respond to change in ART.

Progressive multifocal leukoencephalopathy (PML) in early-stage disease (see page 98).	Dementia is rare, occurs only late.

TABLE 11A (3)

CLINICAL SYNDROME, ETIOLOGY, EPIDEMIOLOGY	CLINICAL PRESENTATION, DIAGNOSTIC TESTS, COURSE
Central Nervous System/Cognitive Disorders, Diffuse Brain Dysfunction/Declining mental acuity with preservation of alertness (continued)	
Declining mental acuity with concomitant depression of alertness (without focal findings)	Depression of alertness occurs only in advanced disease.
AIDS dementia complex (ADC) (as above, Stage 3 or 4.)	Late stage
Cryptococcal disease (see meningitis, page 73; Eye, page 71)	Often assoc. with ↑ CSF pressure
	Usually focal findings
Toxoplasmic encephalitis	**Pts usually alert in early stages of disease; can become depressed later**
Progressive multifocal leukoencephalopathy (PML) (see page 98)	
Primary CNS lymphoma (see page 97)	Rare without focal findings, occurs when deep structures in brain involved
Cytomegalovirus (CMV) encephalitis (CD4 <50/mm3) Frequency not well defined. Overall CMV ~20%, clinical encephalitis occurs in ~1% of CMV cases. **Diagnosis made by detection of CMV DNA by PCR in CSF.** Response to rx variable. CMV can cause apoptosis of neuronal, glial, & endothelial cells of the CNS (J. Clin Viro 32:218, 2005).	Onset subacute: delirium/confusion 90%, apathy & withdrawal 50%, focal neurologic signs 50%. Antecedent CMV disease is common. Metabolic abnormalities: hyponatremia, hyperkalemia, hypo-osmolality, hypernatremia secondary to dehydration. **Non-specific CSF:** no cells or mildly ↑ cells, ↑ protein, mild ↓ glucose. Typical neuropathologic feature is ventriculoencephalitis with periventricular necrotic lesions. Micronodular encephalitis with microglial nodules involving parenchyma, cerebellum, spinal cord also occurs; meninges may be involved. **MRI with contrast: meningeal enhancement, focal ring-enhancing lesions, or periventricular enhancement with gadolinium; lacks sensitivity and may be normal despite advanced CMV disease. PCR for CMV DNA ~90% sensitive & 90% specific.**
Tuberculosis. See meningitis, page 73.	Always consider in 3rd World (esp. Africa) or immigrant from a region with a high prevalence of TB with symptoms of altered mental status, headache, lethargy or coma.
Neurosyphilis (general paresis, meningovascular)	Serum VDRL & FTA/ABS + in >90%. Diagnosis established by presence of CSF lymphocytic pleocytosis, high protein or positive CSF serology in presence of compatible clinical syndrome and/or + FTA-ABS in serum. CSF VDRL sensitivity ranges from 10–89%. CSF FTA-ABS highly sensitive in HIV- cases (>95%), with similar sensitivity likely in HIV+ cases. MRI: cortical infarcts. (Clin Radiol 61:393, 2006). Indications for CSF examination: neurologic, ophthalmic, or otologic symptoms; evidence of acute tertiary syphilis; treatment failure (4-fold increase in nontreponemal serology after treatment or lack of 4-fold decrease within 12 mo. after treatment). Routine CSF examination does not improve outcome. CSF examination indicated for those with serological evidence of syphilis and neurological symptoms, isolated ophthalmic syphilis, or < 4-fold decrease in RPR titers after treatment (MMWR 59(RR-12; 2010 and CID 53:S110, 2011).
Herpes simplex virus (HSV) encephalitis Frequency & role still undefined but probably no more common than in non-AIDS population (Clin Radiol 61:393, 2006).	Clinical presentation: confusion, fever & headache, anxiety & depression, memory loss, aphasia. CSF: virus seldom cultured from CSF. Definitive dx requires brain biopsy or CSF PCR test for HSV DNA (98% sensitive during 1st wk of disease). HSV2 encephalitis also reported (AIDS Reader 17:67, 2007).
Causes not directly related to HIV Drugs: sedative/hypnotic, alcohol, 'street drugs'; hypoxemia; sepsis; Metabolic: hypothyroidism, vitamin B₁₂ deficiency, electrolyte imbalance	Associated clinical features may suggest etiology but may be subtle, esp. in advanced HIV.

TABLE 11A (4)

CLINICAL SYNDROME, ETIOLOGY, EPIDEMIOLOGY	CLINICAL PRESENTATION, DIAGNOSTIC TESTS, COURSE
Central Nervous System/Focal brain dysfunction (continued)	
Focal brain dysfunction: seizures &/or focal neurologic findings (hemiparesis, cerebrovascular abnormalities, blindness).	Risk of focal brain lesions ↓ with ART but most dramatic ↓ with primary CNS lymphoma & toxo. PML slight ↑.
Abrupt onset Cerebrovascular events: transient ischemic attack (TIA), cerebrovascular accident (stroke, CVA); risk of ischemic/hemorrhagic stroke may be increasing in ART era *(Eur J Neurol 113:233, 2006; AIDS Care 19:492, 2007).*	Causes of focal brain lesions include atherosclerosis, embolism, vasculitis, hypercoagulable state *(Neurol 17:1267, 2007).* Exclude meningovascular syphilis, VZV, lymphoma, cryptomeningitis, cocaine use with vasospasm ischemic events. ↑ life expectancy & metabolic side effects leading to atherosclerosis from ART; expect ↑ incidence of strokes.
Subacute course (days)	
Toxoplasmic encephalitis (TE). First or second most common neurologic disorder in untreated AIDS and frequent AIDS-defining illness, even during ART era. Frequency ↓ with use of TMP/SMX prophylaxis vs. *P. jiroveci* and ART. Seroprevalence varies widely among countries: from 10-20% to 50% or higher, especially in African countries.	Symptoms: Headache 50-70%, altered mental status 70%, hemiparesis &/or other focal signs 60%, seizures 30%. Fever, confusion, coma also seen. Symptoms may recur with immune reconstitution from ART even with successful rx for toxo. **Lab: CD4 <100/mm³ in 80%.** Toxoplasma serum IgG is + in essentially all pts who develop TE (frequency 85-99%) & titer predictive of development of disease: Relative risk ↑ with >150 intl units/mL IgG and CD4 <200. Specific prophylaxis is protective. Scan: MRI more sensitive than CT. **Multiple spherical ring-enhancing lesions,** corticomedullary junction, basal ganglia, thalamus often involved and mass effect common. Lesions often identified even without concomitant neurologic findings. **Course:** >85% will respond to specific anti-toxo treatment *(Cochrane Database System Rev Jul19:CD005420, 2006),* most within 7 days. **If no improvement after 7-10 days of rx—biopsy.** Primary CNS lymphoma common in 'non-responsive' cases. Brain biopsy indicated earlier (in <7 days) in patients with CD4 >100 or if negative toxo antibody titer, single lesion & progression of symptoms on antitoxo rx. If improvement, biopsy not required. Neurologic deficits often persist *(Clin Microbiol Infect 13:510, 2007).*
Primary CNS lymphoma ↓ Incidence from 8.0/1000 person-years pre-ART to 2.3/1000 person-yrs post-ART. Epstein-Barr virus DNA present in nearly all.	Symptoms: Usually afebrile, headache, confusion, focal neurologic deficits, seizures. Often alert, but with mass effect may have more global mental dysfunction. **Lab:** CSF: Normal 30-50%, protein 10-150 mg/dL, cells (monos) 0-40/mm³, cytology + in <5%. PCR for detection of **EBV DNA has sensitivity >90%, but lacks specificity and may have a poor positive predictive value** *(CID 38:1629, 2004).* Scan: White matter more often involved than gray matter. One or a few weakly enhancing irregular lesions, typically in periventricular region with mass effect. Biopsy necessary for definitive diagnosis. **Course:** median survival time poor (< 3 mo); improved survival with ART.
Tuberculous/non-tuberculous mycobacterial brain abscess (see meningitis, page 73)-tuberculoma Cryptococcoma *(see meningitis, page 73)* May coexist or be confused with toxo encephalitis	Uncommon. Usually concomitant with cryptococcal meningitis, CRAG of CSF & serum positive, but with an isolated cryptococcoma, CRAG (serum & CSF) may be negative.
Varicella zoster virus (VZV) encephalitis *(AIDS Reader 17:64, 2007)* Less common complication of dermatomal zoster with ART.	Often associated with dermatomal zoster or vesicular rash. Signs and symptoms: headache, altered mental status, seizures, cranial nerve palsies. CSF: 0-300 WBCs, predom. lymphs, mild ↑ in protein. **PCR detection of VZV DNA sensitive & specific.** >50% recovery with antiviral therapy.

TABLE 11A (5)

CLINICAL SYNDROME, ETIOLOGY, EPIDEMIOLOGY	CLINICAL PRESENTATION, DIAGNOSTIC TESTS, COURSE
Central Nervous System/Focal brain dysfunction/Subacute course *(continued)*	
Cytomegalovirus (CMV) infection	See above.
Aspergillosis • ↑ in pts with ↓ WBC & rx with corticosteroids • Direct extension from sinuses or orbits—also from lung.	Nonspecific neuro symptoms including headache, cranial or somatic nerve weakness or paresthesias, altered mental status & seizures. High mortality; medical rx usually unsuccessful. Scan—CT reveals hypodense lesions.
Herpes simplex virus (HSV) encephalitis	See page 96
Bartonella henselae, with neurologic complications	Encephalitis, dementia. Scan: Contrast-enhancing mass lesion.
Chagas' Disease (*Trypanosoma cruzi*) (*Ann Trop Med Parasitol 101:31, 2007*).	Reactivation in 20%, chronic Chagas in 28%.
Nocardia brain abscess	Rare; can be confused with tuberculosis.
Chronic course (weeks)	
Progressive multifocal leukoencephalopathy (PML) Frequency 4–7% of AIDS patients. Caused by JC virus (a papovavirus), which infects oligodendrocytes, the myelin-producing cells of the CNS. CD4 usually ≤100/mm³. Prolonged survival & remission reported with highly effective antiretroviral rx but not consistently. Although typically non-inflammatory, inflammatory lesions from immune reconstitution syndrome upon institution of ART may worsen and lead to a fatal outcome (*Acta Neuropathol 109:449, 2005; Scand J Infect Dis 39:347, 2007*).	**Symptoms: Develops insidiously with a single focus** (limb weakness 1/3, ataxia 13%, visual defects 1/3, altered mental status 1/3) but afebrile & arousable (preservation of alertness until late into disease course). With progression, multiple foci occur. Seizures found in 20% in one series. **Lab:** CSF: Normal (pleocytosis in 20%, ↑ protein 30%). **JC IgM antibody & PCR of CSF for JCV 82% sensitive, 100% specific.** JC viral load in CSF predictive of disease state & progression but not in patients Rx with ART (*CID 40:738, 2005*). **MRI Scan: Multiple fluffy or diffuse hypodense non-contrast enhancing lesions in subcortical white matter, no mass effect.** High signal intensity on T-2 images in hemispheric white matter, ill-defined margins (CT/MRI—clinical dissociation, images worse than pt. symptoms). May become contrast-enhancing with immune reconstitution assoc. with ART. Occ. inflammation present without ART. Brain biopsy is definitive diagnostic procedure (demyelination, JCV on electron microscopy), sensitivity 40–96%, but not required if MRI is characteristic & JC PCR positive. **Course:** Death usual within 6 mos but spontaneous sustained remissions occur in 5–10. **Immune reconstitution with ART may have serious consequences due to ↑ inflammatory changes in area of PML lesion. No clear consensus on management of PML currently exists.**

Most Common Peripheral Nerve Syndromes in HIV Disease by Stage: The following are organized according to stage of HIV infection and relative prevalence.

Peripheral neuropathies are common (6–13%) in HIV/AIDS. They most commonly affect the sensory nerves & are caused by either HIV, opportunistic infections, drugs or are idiopathic. They present as part of several discrete syndromes & vary according to stage of disease.

Acute retroviral syndrome:	*See Acute retroviral syndrome, page 94*
Neuropathy (6–8%)	Headache/retro-orbital pain, often ↑ with eye movement (30%), photophobia. Myelopathy, peripheral neuropathy, brachial neuritis, facial palsy, cauda equina & Guillain-Barré syndrome. Course: Usually self-limited, but persistence reported.

TABLE 11A (6)

CLINICAL SYNDROME, ETIOLOGY, EPIDEMIOLOGY	CLINICAL PRESENTATION, DIAGNOSTIC TESTS, COURSE
Central Nervous System/Most Common Peripheral Nerve Syndromes in HIV Disease by Stage *(continued)*	
Early (asymptomatic HIV; CD4 > 200)	
Inflammatory demyelinating polyneuropathy (IDP) (occurs <5%) *(see below)*	
Subacute (Guillain-Barré syndrome) or acute inflammatory demyelinating polyradiculoneuropathy (AIDP).	Ascending paralysis with preservation of sensory function—global limb weakness. Probably represents autoimmune phenomenon. Nerve conduction studies show demyelinating features. One pt with CMV-associated Guillain-Barré responded to ganciclovir + ART. May be associated with immune reconstitution.
Chronic (chronic inflammatory demyelinating polyneuropathy) (CIDP or IDP) (may also occur late)	Progressive weakness in arms & legs, paresthesias with minor sensory loss, may be asymmetrical, absent DTRs. Demyelinating polyneuropathy, CSF ↑↑ protein, mild to moderate lymphocytic pleocytosis (10–50 cells/mm³), EMG shows demyelination.
Mononeuritis, multiplex (MM) (also occurs late) (rare)	Facial weakness, foot or wrist drop. EMG, multifocal axonal neuropathy, multifocal cranial & peripheral neuropathies, thought to be immune mediated or vasculitis.
Multiple sclerosis-like syndrome (rare) (*Neurologist 13:154, 2007*).	Waxing & waning course, multifocal defect, may rarely represent immune reconstitution inflammatory syndrome (IRIS).
Late (symptomatic HIV, CD4 <200)	
Weakness/spasticity:	
Vacuolar myelopathy (occurs in as many as 40% of patients at autopsy) & is the most common form of spinal cord disease in HIV-infected individuals; under-recognized clinically. Infectious causes of myelopathies: HTLV-1, herpesviruses (VZV, HSV2, CMV), enteroviruses, *T. pallidum*, TB, various fungi, & parasites.	Progressive painless gait disturbance with ataxia & spasticity. Also rarely occurring in upper extremities. CSF normal or ↑ protein, 5–10 cells/mm³. Imaging usually normal. Use of somatosensory-evoked potentials in pts with absent ankle DTRs valuable dx tool in differential dx of myelopathy from neuropathy.
CMV, Progressive lumbosacral polyradiculopathy/myelitis (DDx: VZV, syphilis, spinal lymphoma)	Subacute onset. Back & radicular pain, ascending weakness, areflexia, bladder & sphincter dysfunction, variable sensory loss but may produce "saddle anesthesia." May progress rapidly to flaccid paralysis. CMV PCR in blood and CSF positive.
Mononeuritis multiplex due to CMV	Multifocal sensory & motor deficits in major peripheral or cranial nerves (esp. laryngeal nerves & upper > lower extremities—acute onset over 1 mo), usually painful. CD4 <50. CMV PCR in blood and CSF positive.
Numbness/burning: Distal sensory loss with neuropathic pain (most common neuropathy). Symptoms: pain (often described as excruciating unremitting pain), paresthesias, ↓ ankle reflexes, ↓ vibratory or pinprick sensation.	
Distal predominantly sensory symmetrical polyneuropathy (DSP) (occurs in up to 50% of pts with late-stage HIV) (*Neurology 66:1679, 2006*). Risk factors include age >40, diabetes, white race, nadir CD4 <50 & 50–199, VL >10,000 copies/mL at 1ˢᵗ measurement plus ETOH abuse, drugs (vincristine, INH & halidomide & ritonavir) (*CID 40:148, 2005; Neurology 66:1679, 2006*). ↓ incidence with ART (*CID 40:148, 2005*)	Hyperesthesia, "**burning**" **feet**, distal numbness with ↓ ankle DTR, stocking/glove sensory loss. Severity of symptoms (pain) correlates with plasma HIV-1 RNA levels. Suppression of HIV may improve symptoms.

TABLE 11A (7)

CLINICAL SYNDROME, ETIOLOGY, EPIDEMIOLOGY	CLINICAL PRESENTATION, DIAGNOSTIC TESTS, COURSE
Central Nervous System/Most Common Peripheral Nerve Syndromes in HIV Disease by Stage *(continued)*	
Toxic neuropathy from antiretroviral drugs (TNA) (ddI > d4T > 3TC) (occurs >5%) but has been reported to occur in up to 30% of pts on ddI. Frequency associated with dose & duration of exposure; d4T in combination with ddI doubles risk. FDA warning for ribavirin + ddI ± d4T assoc. with mitochondrial toxicity. Disease progression & host factors (mitochondrial haplogroup & age) all predispose individuals to neurotoxic effects of antiretroviral drugs *(CID 40: 148, 2005, AIDS 19;1341, 2005).* Protease inhibitors may also potentiate neuronal damage & toxic neuropathy *(Ann Neurol 59:876, 2006).* Etiology associated with NRTI selective inhibition of γ-DNA polymerase leading to depletion of mitochondrial DNA & degeneration of mitochondria of neurons & Schwann cells.	**Aching feeling of feet, burning sensation.** ↑ serum lactate levels discriminated d4T neuropathy from DSP neuropathy (90% sensitivity, 90% specificity). **EMG:** axonal neuropathy; symptoms (pain) may worsen for up to 4 wks after discontinuation of rx. Some pts able to continue drugs with full or reduced dose & neuropathy may improve or resolve; however, substantial portion of pts continue to experience debilitating pain. **Lamotrigine** (an anticonvulsant drug) ↓ pain vs. placebo in 227 pts. Rash a common side effect. Results confirmed in 92 pts receiving ART. No difference from placebo in 135 pts with DSP without ART. Coenzyme Q actually ↑ pain. Rx with acetyl-l-carnitine (1500 mg q12h po) up to 33 mos. assoc. with ↓ symptoms & peripheral nerve regeneration in 21 HIV+ pts with TNA *(HIV Clin Trials 6:344, 2005).*
Weakness/myalgias:	
Myopathy due to drugs: HIV, zidovudine [ZDV + ddC > ZDV + ddI]	Weakness without sensory finding, DTRs intact with myalgias. EMG: irritative myopathy, ↑ CPK, muscle biopsy, myofibril degeneration + inflammation.
Electrolyte & Metabolic Abnormalities	
Hyponatremia	About 20% of ambulatory & 50% of hospitalized patients have serum Na of <135 mmol/L. On admission ½ due to GI loss & hypovolemia. During hospitalization ½ due to SIADH (PJP, bacterial pneumonias, CNS infection); patients are edema-free, with hypertonic urine with low serum osmolality & high urinary sodium.
Volume depletion 2° to diarrhea and hypo-osmolar fluid replacement	
Chronic cirrhosis	
Syndrome of inappropriate secretion of antidiuretic hormone (SIADH) (2° to pulmonary or CNS infections)	
Adrenal insufficiency, primary	
Hyporeninemic hypoaldosteronism	
Nephrotoxic drugs: pentamidine, amphotericin B, foscarnet	
Hyperkalemia	20-53% pts on TMP/SMX or TMP + dapsone for treatment of PJP develop hyperkalemia. TMP is a sodium channel inhibitor & functions as a K-sparing diuretic agent.
Trimethoprim	
Hypoaldosteronism−ketoconazole	
Adrenal insufficiency	
Hypokalemia	Hypokalemia in tenofovir-related Fanconi syndrome *(See CID 56:567, 2013 for effects of tenofovir on renal function).*
Drug-related (diuretics, Amphotericin), diarrhea, hypomagnesemia	
Hypercalcemia	Lab: ↑ serum 1,25-dihydroxy vitamin D concentrations with ↓ levels of intact parathormone.
Lymphoma	
Granuloma formation associated with immune reconstitution.	
Hypocalcemia	Neuromuscular irritability, carpal or pedal spasm. Foscarnet forms complex with ionized calcium. Ampho B & aminoglycosides may lead to Mg²⁺ wasting with inhibition of parathyroid hormone release & action.
Drug-related: Foscarnet, amphotericin B, aminoglycosides	
Endocrine System:	
Pituitary gland	25% of advanced but non-AIDS HIV+ patients have ↓ pituitary reserve. Functional pituitary insufficiency is very uncommon. Useful diagnostic tests: Corticotropin-releasing hormone (CRH) test; testing for several hormones simultaneously: insulin + thyrotropin-releasing hormone (TRH) + gonadorelin (GnRH)); measure glucose, cortisol, GH, TSH, prolactin, LH, FSH & ACTH. Iatrogenic Cushing's from use of corticosteroids with ritonavir.
Infectious involvement of anterior pituitary, e.g., CMV, P. jiroveci (carinii), Toxoplasma gondii	

TABLE 11A (8)

CLINICAL SYNDROME, ETIOLOGY, EPIDEMIOLOGY	CLINICAL PRESENTATION, DIAGNOSTIC TESTS, COURSE
Electrolyte & Metabolic Abnormalities (continued)	
Thyroid gland (see CID 45: 488, 2007 for etiologies and test use) Chronic illness HIV infection	Lab: ↓ T_3 with reciprocal ↑ rT_3 (reverse T_3), T_4 usually normal. Useful diagnostic tests: T_3, T_4, thyroid-binding globulin, rT_3. In an Italian study, 12.6% of 182 HIV+ patients on ART had subclinical hypo thyroidism vs. 0% of 20 naïve patients. Stavudine Rx most significant risk factor (Clin Endocrinol 64:375, 2006). P. jiroveci and other fungi may involve the thyroid rarely (Mycoses 50: 443, 2007; Mayo Clin Pro 83:1046, 2008). Coccidioides thyroiditis (following pneumocystis (JCM 50:2535, 2012).
Graves' disease associated with immune reconstitution from ART (AIDS 20:466, 2006)	
Adrenal gland (the most commonly affected endocrine gland) Primary adrenal failure; causes include: • CMV adrenalitis (found in 33–88% of AIDS pts at autopsy) • HIV infection of adrenal • Infiltration by Kaposi's sarcoma, lymphoma or infection (MAC, crypto, histo, pneumocystis) • Drug-induced: ketoconazole (impairs steroid synthesis), fluconazole (1 report: 800 mg q24h x 68 days, J Microbiol Immun Inf 37:250, 2004); 6 cases of overt Addison's diseases on withdrawal of inhaled corticosteroids (fluticasone) with ritonavir (J Clin Endocrinol Metab 90:4394, 2005), megestrol (prolonged use) (AnIM 122:843, 1995) • Pituitary insufficiency (see above) • Iatrogenic Cushings Syndrome o Use of glucocorticosteroids with ritonavir boosted protease inhibitors (J Asthma 47:830, 2010).	**Addison's disease: fever, hypotension, abdominal pain, hyponatremia, hyperkalemia.** Overt Addison's disease is uncommon, although blunted responses to ACTH are common. Addisonian crisis may be precipitated by excessive stress or ketoconazole. CMV antigenemia assoc. with adrenal insufficiency. Suboptimal response to ACTH stimulation & ↓ stress cortisol serum levels should receive stress doses of corticosteroids where there is infection, trauma, etc. (Endocr J 49:641, 2002).
Pancreas	
Pancreatitis Drug-associated: pentamidine, didanosine (ddI) 2–6%, stavudine (d4T) 1%, lamivudine (3TC) more common in children, ddI/d4T. Other drugs implicated, including those used to treat OIs and malignancies.	Typical presentation (nausea, vomiting & abdominal pain). Insulin-dependent diabetes mellitus may develop. Rarely pancreatic infections: tuberculosis (J. Pancreas 10:64, 2009) or cryptosporidium (Rev Soc Bras Med Trop 37:182, 2004).
Hyperglycemia: Insulin resistance common in ART; see Table 6C Drug-induced [especially protease inhibitor 6%, megestrol acetate, & corticosteroids (J AIDS & Human Retro 17:46, 1998)]. See Table 6B & Table 6C	Other diabetogenic drugs frequently taken by HIV+ patients: dapsone, rifampin, sulfamethoxazole in patients with renal failure, octreotide, ganciclovir (AnIM 118:529, 1993). 6% of pts receiving ART with PI developed DM over a 1-yr period (Ann Pharmacother 34:580, 2000). ART may cause ↓ insulin secretion and ↑ insulin resistance (JAIDS 50:499, 2009). In D:A:D study, incidence was 5.72 cases/1000 pt-yrs; ↑ with cumulative exposure and d4T use (Diab Care 31:1224, 2008).
Hypoglycemia Drug-induced [Pentamidine (IV), 2%].	During destruction of islets, insulin release may cause hypoglycemic coma. Co-trimoxazole associated with severe hypoglycemia resulting from increased insulin levels suggesting a sulfonylurea-like effect: 14 cases reported, renal insufficiency in 93%, most were receiving 2 double-strength tabs twice a day for Rx of PJP (Lancet ID 6:178, 2006).

TABLE 11A (9)

CLINICAL SYNDROME, ETIOLOGY, EPIDEMIOLOGY	CLINICAL PRESENTATION, DIAGNOSTIC TESTS, COURSE
Electrolyte & Metabolic Abnormalities *(continued)*	
Gonads	
Testes Primary testicular failure (see *CID 33:857, 2001 & AIDS P Care STDs 19:655, 2005*). Drug-associated: ketoconazole, megestrol (↓ testosterone; *AIDS Pat Car STD 13:149, 1999*).	↓ libido & impotence common. Gynecomastia is rare (1.8%). Efavirenz also assoc. with gynecomastia in a retrospective case-controlled study in 3 pts (*AIDS Reader 14:29, 2004*). ART may ↓ libido in males and is assoc. with ↓ estradiol levels (*Int J AIDS/HIV 15:234, 2004*). Erectile dysfunction found in 74% of HIV+ urban men (*AIDS Pt Care STDs 20:75, 2006*). Lab: ↓ free testosterone levels, ↑ LH & FSH, normal. Testosterone replacement useful & ↑ muscle mass, ↑ mood with ↓ depression symptoms & ↑ bone density (*AIDS Reader 13:515, 2003*).
Ovaries Menstrual irregularities are common, esp. with advanced HIV/AIDS (CD4 <200/mm³) & wasting. ART use associated with ↓ rates of menstrual problems (*J Womans Health 15:591, 2006*).	In 69 HIV-infected women, weight loss >10% max. weight was significant predictor of low free testosterone serum level, thus ↓ androgen level common in women with wasting (*CID 36:499, 2003*). Testosterone replacement (patches 2x/wk), ↑ testosterone levels but had little physiological effect in a randomized double-bind study in 52 women (*JCEM, Dec. 21, 2004*).
Eye: Ocular manifestations occur in up to 75% of HIV infected pts. Introduction of ART has significantly reduced significance of ocular disease but has introduced immune-recovery uveitis associated with CMV (*Ocul Immunol Inflamm 13:213, 2005*) and lesions related to the metabolic alterations induced by ART; chalazion, diabetic & hypertension retinopathy, lipid arc of the cornea and glaucoma (*Eur J Opth 16:728, 2006*). Cataracts, uveitis and optic nerve disorders are common causes of significant vision loss in Uganda (*JAIDS 53:95, 2010*).	Differential Dx: CMV papillitis, VZV—rapidly progressive retinal necrosis (*AIDS 16:1045, 2002*), syphilis, cryptococcal meningitis, TBc, toxo (*Ophth 111:716, 2004*), endophthalmitis (bacterial or fungal) (*CID 26:34, 1998*).
Acute loss of vision	
Eyelids (*Ln 348:525, 1996*) Herpes zoster ophthalmitis, Molluscum contagiosum	Solitary lesions of molluscum contagiosum may persist after ART (*Br J Ophthal 87:1427, 2003*) or may regress with pronounced injection (IRS) (*Graefes Ar Clin Exp Ophth 242:951, 2004*). Lid ptosis (+/- external ophthalmoplegia) described in pts with lipodystrophy on long-term ART (*CID 47:845, 2008*).
Posterior Segment Infections	
Cytomegalovirus (CMV) retinopathy: Fx: See *Table 12, page 158* Marked reduction with ART (*J AIDS 22:228, 1999; HIV Med 2:255, 2001*), but less so with advanced disease (*AnIM 135:17, 2001*). **ART markedly improves survival & success of anti-CMV rx.** (*J AIDS & HR 19:13, 1998; AIDS 12:613, 1998*) but vision loss from immune recovery uveitis (epiretinal membrane, cystoid macular edema or cataract) reported in up to 63% (*Retina 25:633, 2005*) (See *Table 11B*) but account for <10% of causes of vision loss from CMV (*Ophthal 113:1441, 2006*). ART reduces vision loss from CMV retinitis by approximately 50% (*Ophthal 113:1432, 2006 & 113:684, 2006*). Rates of 2ʳᵉ eye involvement ↓ with ART but not if CD4 stays <50/mm³ (*Ophthalmology 111:2232, 2004*).	**Peripheral retinitis, CD4 count is <50/mm³.** Course: Usually begins with unilateral "floaters" to ↓ visual acuity to blindness. **Ophthal.: Findings are usually initially in the periphery, moving centrally until macula &/or optic disc involved. Lesions are large creamy to white areas with granular borders & perivascular exudates & hemorrhages ("cottage cheese & ketchup" appearance) with little overlying vitreous reaction. If redness or pain of the eye, photophobia or irregular-shaped pupil develops, suspect infection other than CMV retinopathy.** Dx: Based on clinical features, CMV DNA+ in serum; ↓ with effective anti-CMV rx (*CID 15:1756, 2001*). ↑ CMV-specific CD4 &/or CD8 cells predict prevention of recurrence after ART (*AIDS Res Hum Retrovir 17:1749, 2001; JID 184:256, 2001*), while failure to ↑ CMV-specific CD4 response assoc. with multiple relapses (*JID 183:1285, 2001*). Mortality from CMV correlates with CMV DNA in plasma (*JCI 101:Y97, 1998*). CMV genome not found in aqueous humor by PCR in immune recovery uveitis (*Ophthalmologia 218:43, 2004*).

TABLE 11A (10)

CLINICAL SYNDROME, ETIOLOGY, EPIDEMIOLOGY	CLINICAL PRESENTATION, DIAGNOSTIC TESTS, COURSE
Eye / Posterior Segment Infections (continued)	
Primary CMV papillitis	**Rapid ↓ in visual acuity.** Swelling of optic nerve head, atrophy within 4 wks. Consider pulsed systemic steroids + ganciclovir or foscarnet (Am J Ophth 108:691, 1989). Dx & Rx: See CMV peripheral retinitis, above, & Table 12, page 159.
Herpes zoster/simplex virus (VZV) retinitis (mean CD4 24) 5/10 pts presenting to eye clinic in Nigeria with HZ ophthalmicus were HIV+ (West Afr J Med 22:136, 2003).	**May not be associated with cutaneous zoster.** (1) **Acute retinal necrosis (ARN) syndrome:** rapidly progressive necrosis of peripheral retina (often 360°) with occlusive vasculopathy, marked vitreous & anterior chamber inflammation, optic neuritis & scleritis. Complete visual loss in involved eye. May be associated with retrobulbar optic neuritis (Am J Neuroradiol 25:1722, 2004). (2) Ill-defined areas of peripheral retinal whitening without granular borders, minimal vitreous reaction, no pain or foveal lesions (confused with CMV). Report of progressive outer retinal necrosis (PORN) treated with ART, systemic, and intra-vitreal anti-virals (J Clin Virol 38:254, 2007). PORN typically occurs at very low CD4 counts, but has also been described after starting ARV therapy (e.g., VZV-positive rapidly progressive necrosis with no vitreal inflammation, 2 months after starting ARV therapy when CD4 was 127) (J Med Assoc Thai 92, Suppl 3: S52, 2009).
HIV-associated "cotton wool" spots (CWS) CWS occurs in about 50% of patients with non-infectious microvascular retinopathy. Nonspecific findings & seen in many other conditions (Med 82:187, 2003).	Usually asymptomatic but occur more in late-stage disease. Ophthal. exam: Small fluffy white lesions with indistinct margins without exudates or hemorrhages. Lesions do not progress & usually regress spontaneously, do not require treatment. CWS may indicate ↑ risk for onset of CMV retinitis.
Initis secondary to cidofovir (CID 25:337, 1997; CID 28:156, 1999)	Common with intravitreal injection but recurrent episodes with IV also reported
PEG interferon alfa-2b—ribavirin ocular changes	8/23 (35%) receiving PEG INF-Rib for Hep C rx developed visual/ocular abnormalities, including cotton wool spots, cataracts, ↓ color vision (AIDS 18:1805, 2004). Uveitis, vascular occlusions reported (World J Gastroenterol 13:3137, 2007).
Retinal depigmentation	5% of children on didanosine (ddI) usually at >300 mg/M²/day developed retinal depigmentation (RW Price, ch 14, The Medical Management of AIDS, 6th Ed). Asymptomatic.
Retinal deposits of clofazimine	Clofazimine deposits in pigmented tissues. May result in brownish refractile crystals in retina.
Rifabutin-associated uveitis Reported in 1–2% pts on 600 mg/day (NEJM 330:438, 1994). Also rarely on 300 mg/day (AnIM 121:510, 1994).	↑ common with use of protease inhibitors (↑ rifabutin serum levels) (see Table 16A, Drug/Drug Interactions).
Syphilis in HIV: **Think syphilis (Int J STD AIDS 12:754, 2001** Eye June 3, 2005). Uveitis in HIV: bilateral in 80%, evidence of optic neuritis or chorioretinitis, or combinations of these. Focal anterior scleritis with retinitis caused by syphilis uncovered with immune reconstitution (Clin Exp Ophthalmol 32:526, 2004).	**In HIV+, syphilitic ocular disease is more common, more severe & often bilateral.** Sx may include blurred or ↓ vision, scotomata, redness, pain (Amer J Med 119:448, 2006). **Necrotizing retinitis with hemorrhage may be confused with CMV. Cream-colored posterior plaques may be seen with mucocutaneous lesions in 2° syphilis.** May present as bilateral exudative retinal detachment (Ocul Immunol Inflamm 13:459, 2005). CSF examination indicated to r/o neurosyphilis. Lab: Reactive VDRL & FTA/ABS on serum. Course: Rx failures or relapses reported with penicillin used intravenously for 2-week courses (CID 51:468, 2010).
Toxoplasmic chorioretinitis Ocular involvement uncommon in AIDS. Lesions may be single or multifocal, usually discrete, perivascular in location.	Pre-existing chorioretinal scars usually absent. Hemorrhages are absent or minimal. Vitritis & iridocyclitis (red, painful eye) are common. May occur without intraretinal lesions. Lab: PCR for toxo DNA in vitreous fluid may be of value (Ophthal 106:1554, 1999; Ophthal 111:716, 2004). Course: Response to rx usually good, prolonged suppression required. Oral steroids not used.

TABLE 11A (11)

CLINICAL SYNDROME, ETIOLOGY, EPIDEMIOLOGY	CLINICAL PRESENTATION, DIAGNOSTIC TESTS, COURSE
Fever of Unknown Origin (FUO) Definition: Temp > 38.3oC, duration > 4 wk for out-patient or > 3d for inpatient (*Am J Med Sci, Apr 3, 2012*). Prolonged fever is a common finding in AIDS pts. The etiology varies with geography (*AIDS 16:909, 2002*), frequency↑ with ↓ CD4 counts & ↓ with ART (*Eur J Clin Micro Inf Dis 21:137, 2002*). **Etiology of FUO in AIDS:** **In US:** primary HIV infection, M. tuberculosis, atypical mycobacteria, Pneumocystis jiroveci pneumonia, CMV, Hodgkins lymphoma, non-Hodgkins lymphoma, cryptococcosis, syphilis, bartonellosis, disseminated histoplasmosis, coccidioidomycosis, immune reconstitution inflammatory syndrome (IRIS). **In Spain, TBc identified in 42%,** leishmaniasis in 14% (less common with ART—*CID 37:973, 2003*) & MAC in 14% (*CID 20:872, 1996*). **In Brazil,** TBc in 33%, 25% have multiple etiologies. Monocytic ehrlichiosis reported (*Braz J Infec Dis 10:7, 2006*). Among 50 ART-naive HIV+ patients in Brazil with ≥2 symptoms of prolonged fever, weight loss, hepatomegaly or abnormal LFTs, percutaneous liver biopsy revealed TB in 12, cryptococcus in 5, and both in 1. Co-infection with HIV and visceral leishmaniasis also described in Brazil (*J Parasitology 95:652, 2009; PMID 19642802*). Most (80%) had CD4 <200. Cases were diagnosed by bone marrow examination. **In Thailand & Vietnam,** TBc, crypto, Penicillium marneffei (*Sante 13:149, 2003*). **In Thailand,** 26% of HIV pts with FUO had infection with ≥ 2 organisms (*Int J STD AIDS 19:232, 2008*). **In Africa, TBc most common by far,** crypto, malaria, others include histoplasmosis, salmonella bacteremia, bacterial pneumonia. Pts with fever & peripheral adenopathy, think TBc & Burkitt's lymphoma (*Int J Cancer 92:687, 2001*). **In India,** TBc 63%, crypto 10%, PJP 7%, others include bacterial pneumonia, amebic liver abscess, histoplasmosis, & cerebral toxo (*Natl Med J India 22:52, 2004*). **In areas of high prevalence, malaria should be ruled out,** but HIV+ pts with fever are frequently rx for malaria delaying dx of above. Co-infection with both common: frequency of falciparum malaria fever↑ with ↓ in CD4 count (*JID 192:984, 2005, Ln 362:1008, 2003*). Malaria assoc. with ↑ VL (*Lancet 365:233, 2005*). **M. avium** is the most common cause of FUO in the U.S. when CD4 count <50. It appears to be rare in East Central Africa (*JID 162:208, 1990, J AIDS 8:195, 1995*) but point prevalence 10% in South Africa (*CID 33:2069, 2002*). Infection due to Mycobacterium avium-intracellulare complex [M. avium 52%, M. intracellulare 21%, M. xenopi 7%, M. fortuitum 2% (*CID 20:73, 1995*)] [M. genavense, an unrelated organism which clinically behaves like MAC].	**Sensitivity of AFB bc related to CD4 count:** <100 19% +, 101–200 7% +, >200 0% +, 17% of febrile pts in Malawi had pos. AFB blood cultures (*Int J Tuberc Lung Dis 6:1067, 2002*). **Fungal bc of limited value:** Serum CRAG + in 3%; all <200 CD4. **Chest x-ray** of value when respiratory sx present 85–95% sensitive but specificity only 16–30%. **Urine culture** of value with dysuria. In pts with atlon LFTs, liver bx revealed cause of fever in 13/24 pts (*CID 20:606, 1995*). **Diagnostic value of bone marrow aspirate & biopsy appears to vary from study to study, geographical location, & likely availability of other dx tests. Bone marrow bx** pos. in 52/123 FUO pts in Spain but could have probably been dx through other means (*AIM 157:1577, 1997*). In Brazil, specific dx in 33/99 with AFB in 12, histo 5, & lymphoma 6 (*Pathol Res Pract 200:591, 2004*). In London yield of BM exam was 30% in pts on ART and 23% without ART. ↑ yield with fever & cytopenias (*Int J STD AIDS 16:686, 2005*). In 72 pts with AIDS & FUO in U.S., BM exam of low diagnostic yield even with abnormal hematological parameters (*J AIDS 37:1599, 2004*). In endemic areas when **LDH >600 units/L,** 32% had pos. bone marrow stain for histoplasmosis vs. 8% with LDH <600 (*South Med J 93:692, 2000*). In pts with high-prolonged fever & ↑ bilirubin, bone marrow aspiration, biopsy & culture more sensitive & rapid for dx mycobacteria & histo than blood cultures (*Am J Hematol 67:100, 2001*). When fever assoc. with hepatosplenomegaly & pancytopenia; think leishmania in endemic areas or in returning travelers from these areas (*Scand J Int Dis 41:777, 2009*); bone marrow smear pos. for amastigotes (*Hum Pathol 31:75, 2000*). Think lymphoma with prolonged fever, cytopenias & hemophagocytic syndrome (*AIDS Pt Care STDs 17:495, 2003*). M. avium usually presents as disseminated infection with symptoms of fever, weight loss, night sweats, **diarrhea, anemia & neutropenia,** but may be asymptomatic even with positive blood cultures. Lab: Colonization of respiratory secretions & GI tract is common & may precede disseminated disease. When symptomatic, blood cultures are usually positive for MAC (BACTEC system is very sensitive). Dual infection with M. tbc recognized.

TABLE 11A (12)

CLINICAL SYNDROME, ETIOLOGY, EPIDEMIOLOGY	CLINICAL PRESENTATION, DIAGNOSTIC TESTS, COURSE
Gastrointestinal Tract (Review: Gut 57:861, 2008)	
Mouth (Adapted from J. S. Greenspan and D. Greenspan, chapter 10, The Medical Management of AIDS, 6th edition). (Bull World Health Organ 83:700, 2005, Top HIV Med 13:143, 2006; Adv Dent Res 19:63 & 57, 2006). Oral manifestations very common in HIV-infected persons worldwide.	
Oral lesions without soreness (or mild soreness) Acute retroviral syndrome (see Acute HIV, page 58)	Oral ulcerations (aphthous ulcers), enanthems and oral candidiasis.
Candidiasis (majority have CD4 <200) Cigarette smoking a risk factor for oral candidiasis; OR 2.5 in 631 adults (Community Dental Oral Epidemol 33:35, 2005). **Pseudomembranous form** (thrush) (most common form)	Response to ART with ↑ CD4 assoc. with ↓ oropharyngeal candidiasis. The presence of Oral Candidiasis predicted immune failure in patients on ART (AIDS patient Care STDS 19:70, 2005). Small 1–2 mm to large white plaques on any mucosal surface. Can be wiped off, leaving erythematous to bleeding base. Lab: Dx established by KOH prep of scraping & culture. Oral candidiasis was predictor for TB in Thailand (J Oral Pathol Med 31:163, 2002).
Erythematous form	Smooth red patches on soft or hard palate, dorsal tongue &/or buccal mucosa. Lab: Dx established as above.
Angular chelitis	Erythematous cracks & fissures at corner of mouth. Lab: Dx established as above.
Hyperkeratotic form (candidal leukoplakia)	White lesions on tongue, palate &/or buccal mucosa that cannot be wiped off. Clinically resembles hairy leukoplakia (see below). Lab: Biopsy of lesion will show fungi.
Kaposi's sarcoma (100% had CD4 <200)	Red to purple macules, papules or nodules, occasionally the same color as adjoining tissue, on tongue, palate or buccal mucosa. Usually asymptomatic but may become painful with ulceration & inflammation (Oral AIDS 9 (Suppl 2), 88, 2002). Sublingual ranula may be HIV-associated finding in HIV+ children in Zimbabwe (Oral Dis 10:229, 2004). Lab: Biopsy necessary for dx since bacillary angiomatosis may have similar appearance.
Hairy leukoplakia (HLP) (majority have CD4 <200) Epstein-Barr virus can be detected by immunochemistry, in situ hybridization or EBV-DNA by PCR in nearly 100% of lesions (J Oral Pathol Med 29:118, 2000; Am J. Clin Pathol 114:395, 2000).	Lesions usually asymptomatic. **White thickening of oral mucosa &/or lateral tongue margins with vertical folds or corrugations.** Lesions range from few mm to covering entire dorsal surface of the tongue. ↑ frequency in smokers (J AIDS 21:236, 1999). Cannot be scraped off. **Lab: Biopsy: epithelial hyperplasia with thickened parakeratin layer with hair-like projections & vacuolated prickle cells.**

TABLE 11A (13)

CLINICAL SYNDROME, ETIOLOGY, EPIDEMIOLOGY	CLINICAL PRESENTATION, DIAGNOSTIC TESTS, COURSE
Gastrointestinal Tract/Mouth/Oral lesions without soreness (or mild soreness) *(continued)*	
Warts [human papillomavirus (HPV)] Oral warts ↑ in size & frequency in response to ART *(Oral Dis 8 (Suppl. 2):91, 2002) (AIDS Pt Care STD 18:443, 2004; Am J Med Sci 328:57, 2004).*	Usually asymptomatic. Present as single or multiple papilliform warts with multiple white spike-like projections, or as flat lesions resembling focal epithelial hyperplasia. Lab: Biopsy. Types 7, 13 & 32, but usually not 6, 11, 16 & 18 which are associated with anogential warts. Rx with topical cidofovir gel 1% successful in 1 recalcitrant case *(Cutis 73:191, 2004). (For detailed rx modalities, see MMWR 58: RR-4, 2009).*
Secondary syphilis (often multiple). *(Med Oral 9:33, 2004)*	Dx by VDRL &/or biopsy of lesion *(see Clinics Sao Paulo 61:161, 2006).*
Lymphoma	Poorly demarcated swelling on alveolar ridges &/or discrete oral masses. Lab: Biopsy. May be EBV+ *(Oral Oncol 38:96, 2002).* Plasmablastic lymphoma often presents with oral lesions *(Am J Hematol 83:804, 2008).*
Carcinoma, squamous cell: ↑ risk, suggested by 3 epidemiological studies especially of lips & tongue *(Adv Dent Res 19:57, 2006).*	Squamous cell carcinoma of tongue reported in HIV disease. Lab: Biopsy
Cytomegalovirus (CMV) oral ulcers	A rare manifestation of CMV *(AnIM 119:924, 1993).* Usually with disseminated infection. Lab: Biopsy & immunohistochemistry.
Histoplasmosis, Geotrichosis, Cryptococcosis, Penicillium marneffei, Leishmaniasis.	Rare in occurrence. Lesions painless, clean ulcerations on palate, gingiva, tongue and/or oropharynx. Lab: Biopsy; organism identified on culture & stains.
Sore mouth without discrete lesions **HIV-associated gingivitis & periodontitis:** Common with advanced HIV. Pts at all stages of HIV infection have ↑↑ numbers of PMNs & mast cells throughout the gingiva & ↑ macrophages below the gingival epithelium *(AIDS 16:235, 2002).* Chronic periodontitis assoc. with ↑ cells with ↑ expression of HIV receptors/co-receptors/α defensins perhaps ↑ susceptibility of HIV infection via oral route *(J Dent Res 11:232, 2006).* Response to Rx improved with ART *(Eur J Med Res 11:232, 2006).*	Marked halitosis, spontaneous bleeding & deep-seated gingival pain are usual. Gingiva show fiery red margins with necrosis & ulceration of interdental papillae. May rapidly progress to loss of gingival soft tissue & destruction of supporting bone leading to loss of teeth & necrotizing stomatitis, is similar to noma (gangrenous stomatitis). Consider in the differential oral disease due to methamphetamine use (Xerostomia, extensive caries, periodontal disease, pain) *(Oral Dis 15:27, 2009).* Dx: Based on clinical features. Cultures not helpful. Entamoeba gingivalis has been isolated, ? significance *(CID 27:471, 1998).* Rx: Start with curettage/debridement, followed by topical povidone-iodine (Betadine) irrigation, then chlorhexidine gluconate (Peridex) mouthwash + oral antibiotics effective against anaerobes (metronidazole, clindamycin, AM/CL).
Oral lesions, painful **Recurrent aphthous ulcers (RAU)** More common in HIV disease, last longer & produce more painful symptoms than in immunocompetent persons *(Am J Clin Dermatol 4:669, 2003).* See Table 12, page 163.	Recurrent crops of superficial painful ulcers (1 mm to 1 cm) on non-keratinized oral or oropharyngeal mucosa. Lab: Biopsy; shows only non-specific inflammation. See Table 12, page 163.
Herpes simplex virus (HSV) — *See rx, page 160.* HSV-1 most common cause; rarely HSV-2; both can be shed in oral secretions *(Sex Trans Inf 80:272, 2004).*	Recurrent crops of small painful vesicles that ulcerate, usually on palate or gingiva. Usually heal but tend to recur. Herpetic geometric glossitis [extremely tender longitudinal fissures occur, heal with acyclovir IV *(NEJM 329:1859, 1993)*]. Lab: Smears from lesions reveal multinucleate giant cells, + for HSV on immunofluorescent staining.

TABLE 11A (14)

CLINICAL SYNDROME, ETIOLOGY, EPIDEMIOLOGY	CLINICAL PRESENTATION, DIAGNOSTIC TESTS, COURSE
Gastrointestinal Tract/Mouth (continued)	
Xerostomia (dry mouth)	Clinical: Dry mouth occurs in 2% of patients on didanosine (ddI). PI-based ART was a risk factor for ↓ saliva and salivary gland enlargement in HIV-positive women (Oral Dis 15:52, 2009; PMID 19017280).
Sjögren's-like syndrome—may be drug-associated	See Salivary gland enlargement, below.
	Rx: Saliva substitutes (electrolytes in carboxymethylcellulose base) & nasal spray may help.
Salivary gland enlargement	
Benign parotid lymphoepithelial lesions (diffuse infiltrative CD8 lymphocytosis syndrome or DILS; may have systemic features) (ArthrRheum 55:466, 2006)	Presents as painless (80%) bilateral parotid swelling due to infiltration with CD8 + T lymphocytes. Submandibular glands not involved. 80% have generalized lymphadenopathy, bilateral cervical. Resembles Sjögren's syndrome with sicca symptoms (dry mouth & eyes). Associated findings may include lymphocytic interstitial pneumonia (60%), aseptic meningitis. Most black pts were HLA-DR5. In contrast to Sjögren's,
↑ prevalence in Africans with HIV infection reported (Arch Path Lab Med 124:1773, 2000)	none had anti Ro/SS-A or anti La/SS-B antibodies, rheumatoid factor usually negative. Dx based on fine needle aspiration. More common in children.
Other possibilities: CMV (17%), candida, PJP, adenovirus, lymphoma, Kaposi's sarcoma, tuberculosis; 10 cases reported (J Oral Pathol Med 34: 407, 2005). MAC, sarcoid	Uni- or bilateral painful parotid swelling (CID 22:369, 1996). KS present as painless mass in parotid or submandibular region (Cancer 88:15, 2000).
Esophagus (Adapted from J.P. Cello, chapter 13, The Medical Management of AIDS, 5th edition). Esophageal motility disorders common (16/18, 88%) with or without symptoms of dysphagia or odynophagia (Dig Dis Sci 48:962, 2003)	
Dysphagia (difficulty swallowing with a sensation of food sticking)	
Candidiasis	For therapy, see Table 12, page 148. If no response to therapy for candida, then endoscope to r/o CMV
Frequency 50–70%, decline in ART era (Am J Gastro 100:1455, 2005)	or aphthous ulcers.
The most common cause of dysphagia in HIV+ patients (42–79% of pts).	X-ray: Barium swallow: typically evidence of plaques & ulceration ("moth-eater" appearance). Findings supportive but not diagnostic.
	Endoscopy: Large yellow-white plaques usually seen throughout the esophagus.
	Biopsy/brushing: Will show tissue-invasive pseudohyphae.
	Secondary prophylaxis: Recurrence rates (20–80%) in 45–90 days. See Table 12, page 148.
Odynophagia (pain on swallowing) or esophagospasm (retrosternal episodic pain without swallowing)	
Cytomegalovirus (CMV) esophagitis	Symptoms are odynophagia, usually without dysphagia, weight loss.
	Endoscopy: Large solitary (>10 cm² in surface area), shallow, superficial ulcers especially in distal esophagus. Histology necessary to establish diagnosis. If no inclusions, rx as aphthous ulcer.
Idiopathic (aphthous) esophageal ulceration (IEU)	Pts present with odynophagia. Differential diagnosis: CMV, HSV, drug-induced ulcers.
	Endoscopy: Large discrete ulcers.
	Rx: Prednisone 40 mg po q24h, taper by 10 mg/wk, total course 4 wks. Thalidomide (200 mg po q24h x 14 d).
Herpes simplex virus (HSV) esophagitis	Clinical: Acute onset, intense pain, widespread involvement. May be associated with oral herpes (AIDS Clin Care 7:2, 1995). Median CD4 15/mm³ (CID 22:926, 1996).
	Endoscopy: Shallow erosive ulcers (like reflux esophagitis).
	Rx: Acyclovir

TABLE 11A (15)

CLINICAL SYNDROME, ETIOLOGY, EPIDEMIOLOGY	CLINICAL PRESENTATION, DIAGNOSTIC TESTS, COURSE

Gastrointestinal Tract/Esophagus/Odynophagia (continued)

Esophageal ulcers associated with acute HIV infection

Clinical: Acute retroviral syndrome (fever, myalgia, macular or papular rash) (page 94) + odynophagia or dysphagia. Lesions heal spontaneously. Pts are not predisposed to recurrent esophageal ulceration. Endoscopy: One or more discrete ulcers. On biopsy: retroviral virions. Rx: Viscous lidocaine may ↓ symptoms.

Lymphoma, Kaposi's sarcoma, squamous cell carcinoma, histoplasmosis, leishmaniasis. Non-infectious causes include Crohn's, Behçet's, drugs (bisphosphonates, tetracyclines).

Abdominal pain, acute onset (J Emer Med 23:111, 2002)

Pancreatitis (See page 122)
- Drug-associated most common (46%), e.g., didanosine, pentamidine, lamivudine (3TC) in children, ddI & d4T, and others.

APACHE II criteria best predicted outcome in severe cases—accuracy 75% (Glasgow 69%, Ranson 48%), similar to pancreatitis in non-HIV infected populations (Am J Gastro 98:1278, 2003).

Bowel perforation/peritonitis
Most common cause is CMV in advanced HIV infection

AIDS pts with perforation usually febrile, with rigid abdomen, rebound tenderness. Perforations most common in large bowels. Also lymphoma, typhlitis, KS, tuberculosis, salmonellosis. Immune reconstitution from ART assoc with perforation of ileocecal TB (Dis Col Rect 15:977, 2002).

Small bowel disease: cramping paraumbilical abdominal pain, weight loss, large volume diarrhea

Diarrhea is a common complication and presenting feature of HIV infection. Diarrhea lasting more than 5 days should be evaluated by microscopic exam (wet mount for Isospora and E. histolytica, modified acid fast for cryptosporidia and cyclospora, modified trichrome for microsporidia); cultures for salmonella, shigella, campylobacter, and enteropathogenic E. coli; PCR or toxin assay for C. difficile; stool antigen for giardia. If studies are negative consider upper endoscopy and colonoscopy for CMV, MAC, KS, lymphoma. Non-infectious causes include antiretroviral therapy, protease inhibitors in particular, HIV enteropathy, pancreatic insufficiency (CID 55:860, 2012).

Acute infectious diarrhea (for specific treatment, see Table 12)

Agent	Prevalence/CD4 Stage	Clinical Features	Diagnostic Clues/Comments
Campylobacter jejuni, C. coli, C. upsaliensis (Emerg Inf Dis 8:237, 2002)	Any CD4	Watery or bloody diarrhea, fever, ± fecal WBC	Stool culture, most labs cannot detect C. cinaedi, C. fennelli, C. fennelli. ↑ sensitivity using membrane filter technique on non-selective blood agar.
Clostridium difficile	**Most common cause of bacterial diarrhea among persons infected with** Any CD4	Watery diarrhea, fecal WBC, fever, leucocytosis, cramps, hypoalbuminemia, disease spectrum: nuisance diarrhea, colitis, megacolon. Endoscopy usually shows pseudo-membranous colitis but may be normal. C. difficile toxin usually positive. Both toxin A&B should be tested. PCR more sensitive than EIA, 95% vs 80%, and is becoming test of choice (Curr Gastroenterol Rep 13:344, 2011). CT scan shows colitis with thickened mucosa. May present with leukemoid reaction.	Antibiotic exposure: most common—cephalosporins, clindamycin, FQs, ampicillin; rare—TMP/SMX, ZDV, albendazole, rifampin. Proton-pump inhibitors also identified as a risk factor. Curr Opin Infect Dis 25:405, 2012
Enteric viruses: Noro, rota, adeno, corona, astro, picobirna, & calicivirus	4-15% Any CD4 In a study of adults presenting to three US medical centers with acute gastroenteritis, comprehensive detection methods identified norovirus (26%) and rotavirus (18%) as the most frequent pathogens (JID 205:1374, 2012).	Acute watery diarrhea but 1/3 becomes chronic.	Stool electron microscopy: detection of viral particles has limited value in clinical practice.

TABLE 11A (16)

Agent	Prevalence/CD4 Stage	Clinical Features	Diagnostic Clues/Comments
Gastrointestinal Tract/Diarrhea/Acute infectious diarrhea *(continued)*			
Enteroadherent E. coli Enteroaggregative E. coli & entero-invasive E. coli.	Any CD4	Watery diarrhea, weight loss, ↓ D-xylose absorption, acute but may be chronic, usually in right colon, most pts on TMP/SMX prophylaxis. A large outbreak of infection occurred in Europe in 2011 due to E coli O104:H4, an enteroaggregative strain that also produced Shiga-toxin, was associated with an unusually high proportion of cases with HUS *(NEJM 365:1771, 2011)*.	Adherence to Hep-2 cells (research labs only). Cytotoxic phenotypes assoc. with diarrhea in AIDS pts *(Trans R Soc Med Hyg 97:523, 2003)*.
Idiopathic	25–40%. Variable CD4. Non-infectious causes; rule out drugs, diet, inflammatory bowel disease, anxiety, food poisoning.	Chronic, watery diarrhea most common but may mimic infectious causes.	Negative studies include culture, ova & parasites, C. difficile toxin assay.
Salmonella S. enteritidis S. typhimurium	5–15% 100x ↑ when compared to general population, any CD4 count, more common with lower CD4	Watery diarrhea, fever, ± fecal WBC.	Blood culture, stool culture (sensitivity approx. 90%).
Shigella	2%, ↑ in HIV+, MSM, direct oral-anal contact & foreign travel *(CID 44:327, 2007)*. Any CD4	Watery or bloody diarrhea, fever, fecal WBC.	Stool culture
Certain parasites may also cause acute diarrhea, including Isospora belli & Entamoeba histolytica/dispar *(Int J STD AIDS 14:487, 2003)*.			
Chronic infectious diarrhea 10% of pts with CD4 <200—unchanged with ART but with change in etiology: ↓ OI (53 to 13%) & ↑ non-infectious causes (30 to 70%)			
Cryptosporidia Appear to be spread sexually between men who have sex with men *(Sex Trans Inf 79:412, 2003)*.	CD4 <150	Enteritis: watery diarrhea, noninflammatory diarrhea (fecal WBC neg.), afebrile, malabsorption, wasting, large stool volume with abdominal pain, remitting symptoms for months, years.	Water-borne, low infectious dose, in healthy adults only 132 oocysts. AFB smear of stool to show **oocyst 4–6 μm.** DFA available. In pts with CD4 >180/mm³ C. parvum cleared spontaneously in 7–28 days; with CD4 <180, 87% persisted. Rx: See Table 12.
Cyclospora cayetanensis	US <1%, Haiti 11% CD4 <100	Enteritis, watery diarrhea, up to 18x q24h for 10 mos.	Stool AFB smear, oocyte 8–10 μm, resembles cryptosporidia.
Cytomegalovirus (CMV)	13–20% CD4 <100	Fever, fecal WBC, ± blood, enteritis, colitis, perforation with toxic megacolon, solitary rectal ulcer, small bowel mass. Most common cause of lower GI bleeding.	Sigmoidoscopy with rectal biopsy (best initial invasive test), 10–30% of CMV colitis will affect only right side, further steps include colonoscopy with small bowel biopsy. CT segmental lesions or pancolitis. Rx: See Table 12.

TABLE 11A (17)

Agent	Prevalence/CD4 Stage	Clinical Features	Diagnostic Clues/Comments
Gastrointestinal Tract/Diarrhea/Chronic infectious diarrhea *(continued)*			
Entamoeba histolytica	1–3%. Any CD4 count.	Colitis, bloody stool, cramps, pos. fecal WBC, most are asymptomatic carriers. Course may be protracted (*J Clin Gastro 33:64, 2001*).	Travel history (Latin America, SE Asia). Sic×l ova & parasites. Metronidazole or tinidazole were 97% effective in treating invasive amoebiasis (IA). HepC antibody positivity associated with risk of recurrence of IA; newly diagnosed syphilis tended to be associated with recurrence, suggesting possibility of acquisition of new infection (*PLoS Negl Trop Dis 5:1318 2011*).
Giardia	1–5% Any CD4 count	Enteritis, watery diarrhea, flatulence, bloating, malabsorption	History of drinking mountain stream water. Stool ova & parasites. DFA available.
Idiopathic	More common with lower CD4 (<200).	Watery diarrhea, malabsorption, no fecal WBC	Biopsy shows villous atrophy, crypt hyperplasia, no identifiable cause despite endoscopy with biopsy & electron microscopy for microsporidia
Isospora belli	U.S. 1.5% developing countries 10–12%. CD4 <100	Enteritis, watery diarrhea, wasting, noninflammatory diarrhea (no fecal WBC), no fever.	AFB stool smear, **oocysts 20–30 µm,** or seen on biopsy or exam of intestinal secretions.
Microsporidia Septata intestinalis Enterocytozoon bienausi hellum	20% CD4 <100	Enteritis, watery diarrhea, noninflammatory diarrhea (fecal WBC neg.), fever is uncommon, remitting disease over years, malabsorption, wasting common. Pts improve with response to ART. May disseminate to kidneys, brain, lungs, etc.	Food/water-borne infection **spores 1–2 µm,** fluorescence with calcofluor (excellent screening test), confirmation with Giemsa stain. Special trichrome stain also diagnostic. Complications: disseminated disease, biliary disease.
Mycobacterium avium (cause & effect for diarrhea not always clear)	10% CD4 <50	Enteritis, watery diarrhea, no fecal WBC, common fever & wasting (*Curr Opin Gastroenterol 22:18, 2006*), diffuse abdominal pain in late stage.	Stool culture unreliable, colonization may occur without diarrhea. Diagnosis: positive blood cultures, biopsy may show changes like Whipple's disease, hepatosplenomegaly, adenopathy, thickened small bowel.
Small bowel bacterial overgrowth		Watery diarrhea, malabsorption, wasting, often associated with hypochlorhydria.	Hydrogen breath test, culture of small bowel aspirate.

CLINICAL SYNDROME, ETIOLOGY, EPIDEMIOLOGY

CLINICAL PRESENTATION, DIAGNOSTIC TESTS, COURSE

Diarrhea due to alternative mechanisms (1 to 70% with ART)
(non-infectious diarrhea ref: CID 55:860, 2012) — Considerations: HIV disease per se, autonomic denervation, Crohn's disease, pancreatic insufficiency (*HIV Med 1:33, 2005*), overgrowth of normal bowel flora, & antiretroviral drugs (may be the most common cause). Rx of latter: d/c or some success reported with oat bran, psyllium, loperamide, and others.

Typhlitis *(acute cecitis, inflammation of cecum)* — Clinically resembles acute appendicitis, but involves the cecum, which is ulcerated, edematous, necrotic. Associated with Clostridium septicum & Pseudomonas aeruginosa. Can be a manifestation of C. difficile. Consider especially in severely neutropenic patients.

Colorectal disease: left lower quadrant &/or suprapubic cramping, rectal urgency (tenesmus), frequent small volume stools, occasional proctalgia & dyschezia (painful defecation)

Drug-associated diarrhea *(CID 28:701, 1999)* — **Diarrhea is a common complication of rx with antimicrobial agents (including antiretroviral agents).** May be a direct effect of drug on GI motility (macrolides), overgrowth of GI flora, See adverse effects: Table 6B & Table 13. Thalidomide (200 mg po q24h × 21 d), improvement in 2/2 pts (*CID 20:250, 1995*). See Table 12, page 163. C. difficile.

Infectious agents (as above)

Idiopathic (aphthous) proctitis — Adenovirus has been found on biopsy & easily overlooked. Biopsy to exclude other causes. Thalidomide (200 mg po q24h × symptoms.

Colorectal disease — Endoscopy—large, discrete ulcers. Biopsy to exclude other causes.

TABLE 11A (18)

CLINICAL SYNDROME, ETIOLOGY, EPIDEMIOLOGY	CLINICAL PRESENTATION, DIAGNOSTIC TESTS, COURSE
Gastrointestinal Tract/Diarrhea/Colorectal disease (continued)	
Cytomegalovirus (CMV)	Endoscopy—focal ischemic colitis with submucosal hemorrhages & discrete ulcers in distal colonic mucosa. Ganciclovir is effective in most patients. Rx: See Table 12.
Herpes simplex virus (HSV) Types 1 & 2	Painful recurrent small to persistent progressive large necrotizing ulcers in perirectal area. Emergence of acyclovir-resistant strains on rx can occur. Lab: Smears from lesions reveal multinucleate giant cells. + for HSV on immunofluorescent staining.
Histoplasmosis (Diag Microbiol Infect Dis 55:193, 2006).	Diarrhea, fever, abdominal pain & wt loss. Most commonly involving colon or cecum. Bx of lesions + 89%, blood or other site culture + 72%. Median CD4 34.
Mycobacterium tuberculosis.	Tuberculosis in ileocecal area & colon may be seen in HIV patients without evidence of pulmonary TBc on chest x-ray.
Other considerations: idiopathic inflammatory bowel disease (ulcerative colitis), Kaposi's sarcoma, lymphoma, epidermoid carcinoma & other neoplasms	Kaposi's sarcoma may be confined to the rectum & present as hemorrhagic rectocolitis.
Proctitis	Lab: Numerous PMNs on smear of exudate. Specific diagnosis depends on laboratory studies.
Neisseria gonorrhoeae	Empiric rx for GC & chlamydia recommended but should also consider herpes & syphilis.
Herpes simplex virus	Note that diagnosis of LGV requires 3-week course of doxycycline (MMWR 59 (RR-12): 1, 2010).
Syphilis, primary or secondary	
Lymphogranuloma venereum (LGV)	
Chlamydia trachomatis (non-LGV immunotypes)	
Human papillomaviruses	
Cytomegalovirus	
Enteric pathogens, e.g., Shigella, Entamoeba histolytica, Campylobacter	
Genital Tract/Sexually Transmitted Diseases [MMWR 59 (RR-12), 2010]	
Cervicitis/Urethritis: N. gonorrhoea and/or C. trachomatis	**Males:** Painful urination and purulent urethral discharge; gram stain sensitive (>95%) and specific (>99%). **Females:** May not have cervical discharge. Gram stain less reliable. For both males and females: NAAT on urine, urethral swab and/or cervical swab for both N. gonorrhoea and C. trachomatis.
High frequency of dual infection. Ref: MMWR 61:590, 2012.	
Genital ulcers (For H. simplex, see genital vesicles)	
Chancroid: H. ducreyi. Discrete outbreaks; cofactor for HIV transmission; 10% coinfected with syphilis or HSV	**Painful** genital ulcer + tender suppurative lymphadenopathy. Do darkfield to rule out syphilis. Even with special culture media, culture sensitivity is <80%. Retest for syphilis 3 months after treatment. All sex partners of pts with chancroid should be examined and treated if they have evidence of disease or have had sex with index pt within the last 10 days.
Granuloma inguinale: Klebsiella (Formerly Calymmatobacterium) granulomatis. Rare in US	**Painless** progressive ulcerative lesions without regional lymphadenopathy. Ulcers bleed easily. Hard to culture; rely on visualization of Donovan bodies on biopsy.
Lymphogranuloma venereum: C. trachomatis C. trachomatis serovars L1, L2 or L3. NAAT test for C. trachomatis will be positive.	Unilateral inguinal/femoral lymphadenopathy. Self-limited papule/ulcer at site of inoculation. Rectal exposure leads to proctitis (rectal discharge, pain, constipation, fever and/or tenesmus) (Dis Colon Rectum 52:507, 2009). Can result in fistulas or stricture. **Diagnosis:** Based on serology; biopsy contraindicated because sinus tracts can develop.

TABLE 11A (19)

CLINICAL SYNDROME, ETIOLOGY, EPIDEMIOLOGY	CLINICAL PRESENTATION, DIAGNOSTIC TESTS, COURSE
Genital Tract/Sexually Transmitted Diseases *(continued)*	
Pelvic Inflammatory Disease (PID):	Any combination of **endometritis, salpingitis, tubo-ovarian abscess** and **pelvic peritonitis.** Early diagnosis
Acute: N. gonorrhea and C. trachomatis – esp. 1st episode	and treatment important to avoid scarring of upper genital tract with sequelae (infertility, dyspareunia).
Acute or recurrent: vaginal flora (anaerobes, enteric gm-neg bacilli, Streptococcus	**Diagnosis:** Tender with cervical motion or uterine palpation or adnexal bimanual exam. Majority have mucopurulent
agalactiae). *MMWR;59(RR-12); 2010.*	cervical discharge. Urine nucleic acid amplification test for N. gonorrhoea and C. trachomatis.
Perihepatitis (Fitzhugh-Curtis syndrome): Either N. gonorrhea and C. trachomatis	Right upper quadrant pain. Do NAAT for N. gonorrhea and C. trachomatis on urine and/or cervical swab.
Proctitis, proctocolitis:	Proctitis: Anorectal pain, tenesmus and/or rectal discharge.
Proctitis: N. gonorrhea, C. trachomatis, to include LGV. T. pallidum & HSV	Proctocolitis: Proctitis plus diarrhea and abdominal cramps.
Proctocolitis: Campylobacter, shigella, E. histolytica & rarely LGV	Try to make a specific diagnosis: Urine NAAT for N. gonorrhoea & C. trachomatis, stool C&S, stool ova
AIDS pts: add CMV, MAI, cryptosporidium, microsporidia and isospora.	& parasites, antigen detection for cryptosporidia, whole blood CMV-PCR.
Venereal (genital) warts: human papillomavirus (HPV)—multiple types,	Diagnosis is usually by appearance: flat, papular or pedunculated growth (condylomas) on genital mucosa.
but type 6 & 11 most common to worry about oncogenic types.	Can cause warts and/or malignancy at a variety of sites: cervix, vagina, vulva, penis, anus, oropharynx.
Heart (Note: Many reports of cardiovascular disease preceded availability of ART. Hence, current relevance is unclear.)	
Pericarditis:	Most frequent cardiovascular disease (CVD) in patients with AIDS (10-40%); most small and asymptomatic.
Many possible etiologies: typical/atypical mycobacteria, fungi, S. aureus, nocardia,	Fever, "pleuritic" chest pain, friction rub; less commonly signs and symptoms of tamponade. Often need tissue
listeria, rhodococcus, neoplasms: lymphoma & Kaposi's sarcoma.	to make definitive diagnosis. Worldwide, in roughly 25%, no etiology established. M. tuberculosis most common.
Myocardial disease:	Ranges from myocarditis at autopsy to clinical myocardiopathy. Only 10% have symptomatic heart failure.
Etiology: variety of opportunistic pathogens in 10-15%. Speculate remainder	Diagnosis can be complicated by concurrent use of cocaine, alcohol and/or methamphetamine. Drugs used
due to cardiotropic viruses, e.g., coxsackie, CMV, EBV and perhaps HIV.	to treat HIV and OIs may be directly toxic to myocardium: e.g., pentamidine and zidovudine (AZT).
Pulmonary hypertension (AIDS patients):	Fatigue, dyspnea, right heart failure. Cardiac: ECHO: RVH, RVD, tricuspid insufficiency and pulmonary hypertension.
Multifactorial etiology: multiple lung infections, esp. PJP, toxic effects of illicit drugs	Poor prognosis; may benefit from ART.
(cocaine), recurrent thromboembolism, veno-occlusive disease and idiopathic.	HIV infection itself is a risk factor for heart failure *(Arch Int Med 171:737, 2011).*
Hematologic abnormalities:	
Anemia (etiologies by category):	
Infection:	Infiltrate bone marrow. Inhibit RBC progenitor cells. Diagnosis by culture and biopsy.
Disseminated mycobacteria & fungi	Infects RBC precursors in marrow with subsequent maturation arrest. Bone marrow shows giant pronormoblasts.
Parvo B19 virus	**Diagnosis:** serology and blood PCR.
B12 & Folate:	Due to poor dietary intake and reduced intestinal absorption.
Iron: anemia of chronic disease	Chronic disease: Decreased serum iron, decreased iron binding capacity but normal or increased serum ferritin
	True iron deficiency: Decreased serum iron, increased iron binding capacity and decreased ferritin.
Hemolysis: With AIDS, positive direct Coomb's common (18%) but hemolysis rare.	Ref on positive Coombs: Transfusion 46:1237, 2006. Dapsone and primaquine precipitate hemolysis if G6PD deficient.
Can be drug-induced if G6PD deficient pt.	
Drug-induced bone marrow suppression: Zidovudine & less often ganciclovir,	Zidovudine most common: majority of pts develop macrocytosis & roughly 25% develop anemia.
valganciclovir, ampho B and TMP-SMX.	

TABLE 11A (20)

CLINICAL SYNDROME, ETIOLOGY, EPIDEMIOLOGY	CLINICAL PRESENTATION, DIAGNOSTIC TESTS, COURSE

Hematologic abnormalities (continued)

Neutropenia (etiologies by category): Defined as absolute neutrophil count (ANC) less than 1000/μL. Infection risk increases with ANC < 500/μL.

In nearly 1/3 of HIV pts. But presence **does not** correlate with ANC.

Marrow dysfunction due to infiltration by, or influence of, systemic infection or malignancy.

Antineutrophil antibodies	
Ineffective granulopoiesis	*Drugs commonly involved:* Ganciclovir / Ribavirin / Valganciclovir
Drugs contribute in 80% of patients.	5-flucytosine / Pentamidine / TMP/SMX / Zidovudine
	Ampho B / Pyrimethamine

Eosinophilia (etiologies in alphabetical order):

Drug reaction:	Malignancy: e.g., Hodgkins disease
Ecto-parasite: e.g., Norwegian scabies	Parasites: e.g., round worm like strongyloides
Fungal infection: e.g., Coccidioidomycosis.	Skin disease: e.g., HIV-associated eosinophilic folliculitis.

Thrombocytopenia:

Primary HIV-associated thrombocytopenia (PHAT): Three etiologic factors:

Mechanism: Antiplatelet antibodies in serum & on platelet surface.

Reduction in platelet life span	Coated platelets removed by RES macrophages.
Doubling of splenic uptake	HIV can infect megakaryocytes, associated with increased apoptosis.
Decrease in platelet production	*Common drug causes of* Ganciclovir / Pyrimethamine / Rifampin
Secondary thrombocytopenia: Differential diagnosis includes malignancy, OIs,	*decreased platelets:* Pentamidine / Pyrizinamide / TMP/SMX
co-morbid disease (e.g. hepatic cirrhosis) and drug toxicity.	Acyclovir / Rifabutin / Valganciclovir

Hepatic Disease (↑ transaminase levels in 2-3.8% of asymptomatic HIV+ pts)

Drug-associated hepatic dysfunction
(Avoid acetaminophen)

Multiple drugs used in HIV patients are associated with abnormalities in LFTs: TMP/SMX (½ pts), acyclovir, nevirapine, didanosine (ddl), ZDV, ddC, all PIs, ganciclovir, foscarnet, ketoconazole, fluconazole, INH, rifampin (see *Table 12*). Most require dose reduction or discontinuation if abnormalities exceed about 5x normal values.

Clinical: Predictors of drug-induced hepatotoxicity: baseline ↑ aminotransferases, concomitant hepatotoxic medications, thrombocytopenia, renal insufficiency & Hep C coinfection (OR 2.7). (*J Acq Imm Def Synd 43:320, 2006*). Inconsequential increase of indirect bilirubin in pts given atazanavir or indinavir. Hepatic necrosis & death has been reported with nevirapine. **Nevirapine hepatotoxicity may be severe, esp. in pts with ↑ CD4 counts (CD4 > 250 in women; > 400 in men). Co-infection with Hep B & C, ↑ baseline ALT elevation & previous hx of parenchymal liver disease ↑ likelihood of drug toxicity.**

Peliosis hepatis (bacillary angiomatosis). *Manifestation of Bartonella henselae in AIDS patients.*

Clinical: Fever, abdominal pain, weight loss, hepato- & splenomegaly. About ½ pts will have skin lesions: painful, erythematous plaques or nodules. ⅓ have lymphadenopathy. 2/3 pts give history of cat bite or scratch. Etiologic agent: Bartonella henselae (usual). B. quintana (uncommon). Can be isolated from blood, 5–15 days of incubation and then lysis-centrifugation on blood agar under CO₂. Rx: *Table 12, page 131.*

Viral hepatitis

Hepatitis A (HAV).
Hep A in HIV-infected persons is clinically indistinguishable from Hep A in HIV-uninfected persons but viremia lasts longer and alkaline phosphatase is higher. (*CID 34:380, 2002*). Risk factors include homosexual activity, injection drug use. Hepatitis A and Hep B vaccine indicated for non-immune homosexual men.

HIV/HBV co-infection & progression of liver disease/HIV:
- Co-infected patients have increased risk of cirrhosis.
- No accelerated progression of HIV in co-infected pts.
- Immune reconstitution inflammatory syndrome (IRIS): IRIS described in co-infected pts treated with ART. Can be life threatening if limited residual hepatic function.
- Administer Hep A vaccine if non-immune

TABLE 11A (21)

CLINICAL SYNDROME, ETIOLOGY, EPIDEMIOLOGY	CLINICAL PRESENTATION, DIAGNOSTIC TESTS, COURSE
Hepatic Disease/Viral hepatitis (continued)	

Hepatitis B (HBV): JAC 65:10, 2010; see Tables 9G-9J

Diagnostic Issues: Tests & interpretation are same in HIV-infected and non-infected patients

Serologic markers and HBV DNA in response to HBV infection*

	HBsAg	HBeAg	IgM Anti-HBc	IgG Anti-HBc	Anti-HBs	Anti-HBe	HBV DNA	Interpretation
Acute Hep B:								
	+	+	+				+++	Early infection
	+		+	+			+++	
			+	+			±	'Core' window
				+	+	+		Recovery
Chronic Hep B:								
	+	+		+			+++	Active replication
	+	±		+			±	Low/non-replicative
	+			+		+		Chronic HBV flare
	+			+			++	Pre-core/core promoter mutants

* Blank space means negative test. Hepatitis D not included "Occult Hep B" (*JAIDS 44:309, 2007*)

Isolated positive test for Anti HBc (*JID 195:1437, 2007*):
• More common in HIV pts, especially if HBV/HCV coinfection
• Unclear as to whether occult HBV viremia is occurring.
• Unclear whether to give HBV vaccine.

Pathogenesis & HIV:
• After recovery from acute disease, can detect HBV nucleic acid by PCR.
• HBV controlled by cellular & humoral immunity.
• Flares of HBV can occur with immunosuppression.
• HBV DNA levels and reactivation rates higher in HIV pts than pts with only HBV. HIV pts more likely to develop chronic infection.

1) Cirrhosis and decreased cytochrome p450 activity leads to toxic drug levels; 2) IRIS can occur;
3) Lamivudine withdrawal can lead to flare of hepatitis.

• Screen pts for exposure to HAV & HBV. **If no evidence of past infection, give HAV & HBV vaccines.**
• Look for occult HBV—order antibody to HB core (IgG Anti-Hbc). Co-infection with HB and HC increases risk of hepatocellular carcinoma (*AnIM 146:649, 2007*).
• Assess degree of hepatic fibrosis by liver biopsy or consider non-invasive marker of fibrosis: e.g., panels of common laboratory tests or liver stiffness by elastography (Fibroscan).
• For differential diagnosis of glomerular disease in pts with HCV/HIV co-infection, see *NEJM 362:636, 2010.*
• Emerging data: polymorphisms adjacent to IL28B gene determines degree of spontaneous clearance and response to interferon rx (*Nature 461:399, 2009; Nature 461:798, 2009*).

Do anti-HDV serology at baseline and/or with flares of hepatitis. Ref: *CID: 44:988, 2007*

HIV/HBV co-infection & ART associated liver toxicity:
Applies to HIV/HCV co-infection as well. *CID 38 (Suppl. 2):S90, 2004.*

Hepatitis C(HCV)/HIV co-infection:
• HCV induced liver injury complicates treatment of HIV: concomitant HIV accelerates progression of HIV-induced liver injury (*Ln 9:775, 2009*).
• Liver ultrasound and serum alpha-fetoprotein every 6-12 months to check for hepatocellular carcinoma.
• Determine HCV quantitation and genotype.
• HCV infection increases hepatic toxicity of ART: see *Hep B above & CID 38 (Suppl. 2):S90, 2004.*
• Treatment: see Table 9E.

Hepatitis D (delta agent): defective virus; requires chronic Hep B co-infection. Antibodies to delta agent in 25% of HIV+, HIV- individuals.

Hepatitis E (HEV): usually acute and self-limited. Can cause chronic infection & cirrhosis in AIDS pts (*NEJM 361:1025, 2009*).

HEV antibodies by EIA found in 33/162 (20%) homosexual men (Italy), 60/198 (30%) (Spain) (*Ln 344:1433, 1994; Ln 345:127, 1995*). In the U.S., HEV prevalence is <1%.

Hepatitis G
• Related to Hep C
• Replication in lymphocytes; poorly in hepatocytes
• 2% of blood donors wiremic, & 13% have antibodies

So far, no association with any clinical illness. Transmitted sexually, by contaminated blood and mother to child. Infections (past or current) with **HGV were associated with ↑ CD4 counts & better AIDS-free survival rates** in hemophilia pts with HIV (*AnIM 132:959, 2000*), & slower progression & ↓ mortality in others.

Hepatitis, viral, other

There are isolated reports of hepatitis associated with other viruses: EBV

TABLE 11A (22)

CLINICAL SYNDROME, ETIOLOGY, EPIDEMIOLOGY	CLINICAL PRESENTATION, DIAGNOSTIC TESTS, COURSE
Lipomatosis/Lipodystrophy (See Table 6C & Table 11B)	
Lung Most common causes are Pneumocystis (jiroveci (carinii) pneumonia, bacterial pneumonia, tuberculosis. Viral pneumonia dx increasingly common in older adults but not unique in HIV infected patients. Decreased incidence in ART era (0.8/100 pt. yrs). Risk factors: ↑ age, IVDU, smoking, non-adherence to ART.	In pts with chronic productive cough or recurrent pneumonia in same site, consider bronchiectasis. BOOP rare in HIV+ but described (J Inf 49:159, 2004).
Bronchitis, bronchiectasis, bronchiolitis obliterans (BOOP) HIV & CD4 >200, spectrum of pathogens similar to non-HIV pts.	
Pneumonia • Clinical syndrome ranges from abrupt onset of chills, fever and productive cough to weeks of cough, fever, night sweats and weight loss to months of gradually progressive dyspnea. • Clinical syndrome depends on pathogen, co-morbidities (other than HIV) and especially the patient's CD4 T lymphocyte count. • Need detailed epidemiologic history, e.g., TB exposure, influenza immunization, exposure to endemic area of deep fungi. • Pattern of illness varies with degree of immunocompromise.	• The lower the CD4 count, the broader the differential diagnosis, the more severe the illness and the more aggressive the diagnostic effort. • Clinical presentation can be acute or chronic. • Patterns of infection change as CD4 counts falls. Risk of Immune Response Inflammatory Syndrome (IRIS) increases as CD4 count falls. • Spectrum of potential pathogens broadens as AIDS patients are susceptible to opportunistic pathogens as well as neoplastic disease.
Any CD4 count (high or low):	**Clinical presentation varies with stage of HIV infection:**
Pulmonary tuberculosis (Mycobacterium tuberculosis): **Common:** ANY PT SUSPECTED OF TB SHOULD BE ISOLATED [private room, negative pressure, health care workers (HCW) & visitors entering should wear high efficiency disposable marks] [See Table 23]. Concomitant HIV and M. tuberculosis infections remain a major problem in the developing world where they are a significant cause of mortality, especially in patients with multi-drug resistant and extensively drug-resistant strains (JID 198:1582, 2008; JAMA 300 423, 2008; EID 15:258, 2009; CID 48:829, 2009; CMR 24:351, 2011). Note that in certain areas such as CA & Mexico – 25% of HIV-associated TB is caused by M. bovis (esp. abd TB) rather than M. tuberculosis (CID 51:1343, 2010). In the 3rd World TBc & HIV are closely linked: HIV and TBc coinfection as high as 50% (CID 50:1377, 2010). Nearly 20% of patients starting ART in Durban, SA, had undiagnosed, culture positive TB in 2008 (CID 51:823, 2010).	• **Early HIV infection** (CD4 >400/mm³): Reactivation. Typical presentation **with upper lobe cavitary disease most common.** Extrapulmonary disease uncommon. PPD (5 TU) is + (≥5 mm induration) in 80%. Always consider in pts with chronic cough. • **Late HIV infection** (CD4 <400/mm³): Either reactivation or progressive primary disease (30–50%). Clinical: Fever, cough (may be absent), shortness of breath, weight loss, night sweats but a small proportion of HIV+ patients (esp. in developing countries) have minimal or no symptoms of TB (CID 50 (Suppl. 3): S23, 2010). **X-ray: Mediastinal-hilar adenopathy most common with progression to diffuse, somewhat coarse interstitial densities or localized infiltrates,** especially in mid or lower lung fields. Pleural effusion in 10–20%. Disseminated (reticulonodular infiltrates, not classic 'miliary' since 'millets' are granulomata, usually not seen in HIV with low CD4) the most common with CD4 <200/mm³. Hilar/peritracheal adenopathy is uncommon with PJP or bacterial pneumonia, common in TB. Sputum: Smears + for AFB in 40–50% pts with pulmonary TB, BAL +, in 50–60%, culture +, in 80–90%.

TABLE 11A (23)

CLINICAL SYNDROME, ETIOLOGY, EPIDEMIOLOGY	CLINICAL PRESENTATION, DIAGNOSTIC TESTS, COURSE
Lung/Pulmonary tuberculosis (continued)	
Tuberculosis often occurs before the pt has AIDS-defining illness, but ART sig ↓ risk. Most cases due to reactivation but primary tuberculosis being recognized with increasing frequency. MDR and XDR TB emerging threats in sub-Saharan Africa (Trop Med Int Health 15:1052, 2010).	Rx with ART results in immune reconstitution inflammatory syndrome (IRIS) characterized by worsening of chest x-ray after 1–5 wks about a third of patients. Severe respiratory failure reported. **Most recent data shows that initiation of ART during TB therapy improves survival despite risk if IRIS** (NEJM 362:697, 2010; CID 50:1377, 2010). IRIS assoc. with 1 CD4, 1 ratio of CD4 to CD8 1 month after ART & with dissemination of TB (CID 39:1709, 2004). Rx. Table 12, page 132.
Community-Acquired Pneumonia (CAP), Not hospitalized, No co-morbidities	
• Picture of atypical pneumonia: minimally productive cough, low-grade fever, lung infiltrates. • Potential etiology: mycoplasma, C. pneumoniae, mild Legionella. Zoonotic causes atypical pneumonia. Psittacosis, Q-fever, tularemia.	• Cough major symptom. • If no hospitalization, diagnostic tests often not done. • Can diagnose mycoplasma with antibody level, PCR or quantitative cold agglutinins. C. pneumoniae PCR available. Legionella urine antigen or throat swab for PCR.
Community-Acquired Pneumonia (CAP), Hospitalized, COPD	
• Major pathogens: S. pneumoniae, H. influenzae, M. catarrhalis. If influenza season, S. aureus a concern. Rarely Legionella.	• Classically, abrupt onset of chills, fever and productive cough with variable degrees of impaired oxygenation. • Culture sputum and blood. Urine antigen testing for S. pneumoniae and Legionella pneumophila. • Nasopharyngeal swab for respiratory viruses. • Management similar to treatment of CAP in HIV-negative patients (CID 44 (Suppl. 2); S27, 2007; MMWR 58 (RR-4), 2010).
Community- or Hospital-Acquired, Alcoholic + Cirrhosis/Protracted Mechanical Ventilation (w/w/o Tracheostomy)	
• Clinical setting increases risk of pneumonia due to P. aeruginosa and other aerobic gram-neg. bacilli.	• Patients present with fever, purulence in airway, new pulmonary infiltrates and neutrophilia. • Culture airway secretions and blood. Many prefer bronchoscopy to obtain quantitative cultures of lower airway secretions. Guidelines for children CID 53:617, 2011. Guidelines for children CID 53:617, 2011.
CD4 Count ≤200 cells/mm³:	
Pneumocystis pneumonia (PCP)	
• Dry cough, fever and progressive dyspnea over period of several weeks. • With effective ART dramatic ↓ in incidence of PJP. Most cases now in pts. with previously undiagnosed HIV/AIDS or pts. who are non-compliant with ART. • Remember, may co-exist with TB. • Also, same organisms, i.e., S. pneumoniae, common in absence of HIV/AIDS also common in pts. with HIV/AIDS.	**S&S:** Dry cough, progressive dyspnea and fever. **Chest X-ray:** Most often—diffuse bilateral symmetrical fine reticular infiltrates. Less common—focal nodules without cavitation, thick wall cysts, pneumatoceles/pneumothorax. **Pulmonary physiology:** Low PaO₂, decreased vital capacity and diffusing capacity. **Diagnosis:** Presence of organism on induced sputum or BAL. PCR also sensitive. Beta-D-glucan sensitive for screening (J Clin Microbiol 50:7-15, 2012).

TABLE 11A (24)

CLINICAL SYNDROME, ETIOLOGY, EPIDEMIOLOGY	CLINICAL PRESENTATION, DIAGNOSTIC TESTS, COURSE

Lung/CD4 Count ≤200 cells/mm³ *(continued)*

Comparison of clinical features of bacterial pneumonia (Bact Pn), PJP and M. tuberculosis (TBC) *(AIDS 16:85, 2002)*

	Diagnosis ( ) = # of Pts					
	Bact Pn (94)		PJP (101)		TBC (37)	
Clinical Feature	%	OR	%	OR	%	OR
(OR=Odds Ratio)						
Fever >7 days	11%	1.0	34%	4.3¹	54%	9.9¹
Cough >7 days	20%	1.0	50%	3.9¹	51%	4.2¹
Yellow-green sputum	54%	2.8¹	30%	1.0	30%	1.0
DOE	43%	1.5	81%	9.0¹	32%	1.0
Weight loss	23%	1.0	44%	2.2¹	68%	6.8¹
Night sweats	23%	1.0	46%	2.7¹	54%	3.9¹
Tachycardia	57%	2.8¹	39%	1.3	32%	1.0
Abn auscultation	77%	3.5¹	62%	1.8	49%	1.0
LDH >400	29%	1.0	62%	4.0¹	43%	1.9
pO₂ <75	36%	1.8	66%	6.0¹	24%	1.0
Interstitial infiltrate	17%	1.3	69%	14.5¹	14%	1.0
Lobar infiltrate	54%	59¹	22%	1.0	32%	24.8¹

OR 95% CI does not include 1.0 when indicated by †

Kaposi's sarcoma (KS) (in lung)
Etiology is HHV-8 (KS-associated herpes virus)

Clinical: Usually but not always associated with cutaneous &/or mucosal KS. Present with cough (92%), dyspnea (82%) & fever (67%); less likely than pts with concurrent OI to have temp >38.3 & RR >20 breaths/min. Symptoms may be prolonged.
X-ray: Findings are somewhat distinctive: **coarse, poorly defined nodular densities throughout the lungs with concomitant coarse linear densities in the perihilar regions.** Nodules increase slowly in size, rapid ↑ suggests hemorrhage. Pleural effusions common (up to 50%). Hilar adenopathy rare (<10%).
Dx: Bronchoscopy will usually show typical violaceous endobronchial lesions.
Rx: *Table 18*. May respond to antiretroviral rx or specific antiviral Rx (*Curr Top Microbiol Immunol 312:289, 2007*).

Lymphoma: HHV-8 also identified in body cavity lymphomas— see above

Lymphomas associated with advanced HIV infection are increasingly common, are usually non-Hodgkin B cell type, with extranodal involvement the rule. Thoracic involvement is uncommon (10%) but when it occurs it produces pleural effusion in 50%, hilar &/or mediastinal adenopathy in ⅓ & either reticulonodular interstitial infiltrates or alveolar consolidation in 25%.

Lymphoid interstitial pneumonia (LIP) (children) *(Chest 112:2150, 2002)*

A disease of unknown etiology which may present with shortness of breath in children with HIV infection (see *Table 8E*). **X-ray: Resembles PJP with diffuse or focal, fine to medium reticular interstitial infiltrate. Findings gradually worsen over mos.**
Dx: Lung biopsy is necessary for dx: shows an accumulation of lymphocytes & plasma cells in interstitial areas.
Rx: Corticosteroids may be beneficial.

Pulmonary alveolar proteinosis
Nocardiosis (Nocardia asteroides)
Uncommon. CD4 <200/mm³

Fever, malaise, cough, weight loss. Chest x-ray: 83% abnormal. cavitation 62%, lobar consolidation 52%, pleural effusion 33%, reticulonodular infiltrates 33%. Lab: Blood cultures rarely +. Diagnosis requires biopsy.

TABLE 11A (25)

CLINICAL SYNDROME, ETIOLOGY, EPIDEMIOLOGY	CLINICAL PRESENTATION, DIAGNOSTIC TESTS, COURSE
Lung *(continued)*	
CD4 Count <100 cells/mm³	
Cryptococcosis *(Cryptococcus neoformans)* (common)	Site of entry is usually the lungs & pneumonia has been reported. X-ray: Variable pattern: single or multiple well-defined nodules with or without cavitation or diffuse reticular infiltrates &/or hilar/mediastinal adenopathy. Occasionally a reticulonodular pattern or isolated pleural effusion may occur. Dx: Isolation of C. neoformans from respiratory secretions or blood cultures. Serum CRAG may be positive. Rx: *Table 12, page 149.*
Coccidioidomycosis *(Coccidioides immitis)* (common—endemic areas) Risk factors include Afro-American race & ↑ level of immunosuppression. Reactivation or primary infection in patients from "cocci belt" (southwest U.S.) with CD4 <150/mm³.	**Presentation is similar to histoplasmosis—fever, chills, night sweats & weight loss; severe shortness of breath is common.** Cutaneous lesions common: generalized, erythema nodosum, granulomatous dermatitis and Sweet's syndrome. X-ray: Diffuse bilateral reticulonodular infiltrate (65%) similar to histoplasmosis or focal pulmonary infiltrate (14%) or normal (16%). Dx: While complement fixation antibody tests are frequently positive (68%), dx is established by identification of large spherules of C. immitis in sputum, BAL, biopsy or on culture. Rx: *Table 12, page 148.*
Histoplasmosis *(Histoplasma capsulatum)* (common—endemic areas) Reactivation infection common when CD4 <200/mm³ in pts with geographical history of having been in the "histo belts" (Ohio-Mississippi River Valley, southeastern U.S., St. Lawrence River Valley, Central America & northern South America).	Presents with nonspecific systemic complaints: fever, weight loss, night sweats and dyspnea. Hepatosplenomegaly & focal cutaneous pustules or ulcers may be presenting findings. Pts may also present with "septic shock" including DIC. CD4 count <150. X-ray: Commonly shows diffuse, bilateral poorly defined small (1-2 mm) nodular infiltrates with or without hilar/mediastinal adenopathy. Diagnosis: 95% of pts. have detectable histo antigen in urine (Mira Vista: Tel 866-647-2847). Organism sometimes visible in PAS or silver stains of peripheral blood or bone marrow. Serologic tests also available.
Blastomycosis (uncommon)	Uncommon; largest series is 15 cases *(AnIM 116:847, 1992)*. CD4 <200/mm³: Pulmonary (7 cases), 2 chest pain, CXR 3 focal, 3 diffuse reticulonodular. BAL cultures + Disseminated (8 cases): CNS involvement (5 cases), multiple organs (6 cases).
Paracoccidioidomycosis (South America)	Rx: *Table 12, page 151.* Reported in Brazil. Lymphadenopathy, interstitial lung disease, with papule-nodular skin lesions with central ulceration, ulcerative lesions of the mouth *(Clin Dermatol 30:616, 2012)*.
Mycobacterium kansasii *(may also occur at higher CD4 counts)*	Clinical: Fever, cough, weight loss, dyspnea, night sweats. X-ray: Infiltrates "atypical", alveolar, interstitial or diffuse parenchymal or pleural effusion. Upper lobe cavities. ½ have extrapulmonary dissemination. Cavitation more common at ↑ CD4 counts, hilar adenopathy with dissemination more common at ↓ CD4 counts.
Mycobacterium genavense	Presents with fever, weight loss, diarrhea, abdominal pain, hepatosplenomegaly, anemia, pancytopenia, & occ. painful cutaneous nodules *(Ann Int Med 128:409, 1998)*.
Penicillium marneffei	Primarily presents as fever, anemia, weight loss & skin lesions (70%) with lymphadenopathy but ⅓ have cough & organism cultured from lung in 15%. Pulmonary infiltrates (densities, abscesses & cavities) have been seen. Essentially all cases from SE Asia. Dx by isolation from skin, blood or bone marrow. Rx: *Table 12, page 151.*
Rhodococcus equi (uncommon) Can be confused with TBC.	Rhodococcus presentations vary: slowly progressive mass lesion which cavitates, consolidation with & without cavitation, ground glass opacities, peribronchial nodules and centrilobular nodules ("tree in bud" pattern). Rx: *Page 142.*

TABLE 11A (26)

CLINICAL SYNDROME, ETIOLOGY, EPIDEMIOLOGY	CLINICAL PRESENTATION, DIAGNOSTIC TESTS, COURSE
Lung/CD4 Count <100 cells/mm³ *(continued)*	
Toxoplasma gondii (uncommon)	Rare in U.S., in France represents up to 5% of cases of suspected PJP. Febrile illness, minimal cough, ↑ dyspnea. Chest x-ray: Diffuse interstitial or diffuse coarse nodular infiltrates (resembles PJP). Pleural effusion occurs. Lab: ↑ transaminase, ↑ LDH. Sputum: BAL - for T. gondii. Rx: *Table 12, page 155.*
CD4 <50 cells/mm³	
Aspergillosis (uncommon) • Aspergillus sp. are commonly isolated but rarely invasive. AIDS & neutropenia increases risk.	Fever, cough, hemoptysis, fungus invades blood vessels and lung infiltrates and/or cavities. **Diagnosis:** serum or BAL galactomannan; airway culture; sometimes need biopsy.
Cytomegalovirus (CMV) • CMV pneumonia is rare.	Diagnosis of pneumonia more likely if CMV inclusions, with no other pathogens, seen on lung biopsy. Positive blood RT-PCR for CMV supports diagnosis.
Hilar adenopathy, mediastinal adenopathy M. tuberculosis, M. avium-intracellulare (MAI, MAC). Fungal: Histoplasmosis, coccidioidomycosis, cryptococcosis, blastomycosis Lymphoma, Kaposi's sarcoma.	Following ART & ↑ CD4, IRIS may manifest as hilar adenopathy with MAC, M. Tbc, crypto & other pathogens. Clinical predictors of etiology in 110 HIV+ pts: • Cough + necrosis of nodes = mycobacteria (51) • >7 days symptoms, dyspnea, airway disease = bacterial pneumonia (26) • ≤5 days symptoms, no cough or pulmonary nodules = lymphoma (2) *(J AIDS 31:291, 2002)*
Mass lesion ± necrosis (abscess) Histoplasmosis, coccidioidomycosis, cryptococcosis, anaerobes, S. aureus, M. kansasii, Rhodococcus equi, Mycobacterium tuberculosis, Pneumocystis jiroveci (carinii), lymphoma, Kaposi's sarcoma, aspergillus, MAC, Nocardia asteroides, P. aeruginosa, CMV all possible etiologies.	Broad differential diagnosis. Frequent etiology: aspergillus; mycobacteria; bacteria (e.g. P. aeruginosa, R. equi). Less common etiology: crypto, cocci, histo among others.
Mycobacterium avium-intracellular complex (MAI, MAC) • Usually presents as FUO with fever, night sweats and weight loss.	**Diagnosis:** positive mycobacterial blood cultures. Following initiation of ART, pts with MAC at risk for IRIS. Manifests as: painful generalized lymphadenopathy, massive abdominal & thoracic adenopathy, pulmonary infiltrates, fever, leucocytosis & cutaneous nodules *(see Table 11B)*.
Pleural effusion *(Sex Trans Infect 76:122, 2000)* **Infections** (66–70%): Bacterial pneumonia .... 31–57% Pneumocystis pneumonia .... 15% M. tuberculosis .... 8–16% Others (each <5%): Septic embolism, aspergillosis, C. neoformans, MAC, nocardia, all rare **Non-infectious** (31%): *(see Curr HIV Res 1:385, 2003)* KS .... 10–40% Hypoalbuminemia .... 19% Heart failure .... 5% Others: Kaposi's sarcoma (10% in 1 series), non-Hodgkins lymphoma (18% in 1 series), atelectasis, uremia, ARDS, pulmonary emboli (4%)	Large effusions & bilateral effusions suggest Kaposi's sarcoma & lymphoma. Tuberculosis more likely when effusions suggest miliary nodules or mediastinal adenopathy. Dx usually requires pleural tap for histology & culture.

TABLE 11A (27)

CLINICAL SYNDROME, ETIOLOGY, EPIDEMIOLOGY	CLINICAL PRESENTATION, DIAGNOSTIC TESTS, COURSE
Lung/CD4 Count <50 cells/mm³ *(continued)*	
Pneumocystis pneumothorax	
• More common after aerosolized pentamidine	High mortality rate if associated with PJP.
Pulmonary eosinophilia (Loeffler's syndrome)	Can be caused by drugs commonly used in HIV+ pts: sulfonamides, dapsone, penicillin.
Pulmonary nodules (1 or more on CT scan)	Lengthy differential **diagnosis:** neoplasia, bacteria, mycobacteria and fungi all possible. Culture sputum and blood. May need tissue.
Community-acquired Pneumonia by Organism	
Selected Bacterial Etiologies:	
Bordetella bronchiseptica	Respiratory illness (ranges from mild URI to pneumonia. May be associated with pets.
Chlamydia pneumoniae (another cause of "atypical" pneumonia)	**Diagnosis:** disease mild so usually not pursued. Sequential antibody titers or RT-PCR for diagnosis.
Haemophilus influenzae (increased incidence in tobacco users with chronic bronchitis)	Can present as acute exacerbation of COPD with associated bronchopneumonia. Only rarely encapsulated (type B) Haemophilus, non-typable haemophilus species more common.
Legionella sp.	Legionella pneumophila in 85% (positive urine antigen); 18% of Legionella not pneumophila and are urine antigen negative. PCR detects all Legionella sp.
Mycoplasma pneumonia (uncommon but may cause flu-like illness; common presentation is as "atypical" pneumonia with severe persistent cough of 2-3 wks duration)	**Diagnosis:** due to long incubation period, antibody usually positive at presentation. Quantitative cold agglutin elevated. RT-PCR available. Macrolide resistance reported in M. pneumonia (AAC 52:348, 2008).
Pseudomonas aeruginosa	Fever, new pulmonary infiltrates and neutrophilia. Often in ICU.
Staphylococcus aureus (highly virulent strain circulating (USA 300 MRSA); can develop post-viral tracheobronchitis, haematogenously in IDU, or de novo)	**Diagnosis:** ideally, qualitative culture by protected specimen brush technique. Variable severity of illness: subacute to chronic cavitary pneumonia due to overwhelming necrotizing pneumonia with/w/o toxic shock, endocarditis and/or haematogenous seeding of vertebral column. **Diagnosis:** sputum gram stain and culture, blood culture.
Streptococcus pneumoniae [most common etiology of CAP in both HIV+ and HIV negative pts. pneumococcal vaccine is protective (NEJM 362:812, 2010)]	Fever, chills, productive cough; pleuritic chest pain & dyspnea at all stages of HIV infection. **Most (up to 95%) of HIV+ pts with pneumococcal pneumonia will have positive blood cultures.**
Selected Viral Etiologies: [most common etiology of CAP in both HIV+ and HIV negative pts. pneumococcal vaccine is protective (NEJM 362:812, 2010)]	X-ray usually consolidation (homogeneous densities) with either segmental or lobar distribution.
Adenovirus (different serotypes have variable severity of viral pneumonia—winter & spring.)	Fever, cough, new infiltrate. On BAL, 19% positive for at least one respiratory virus. Recent outbreaks of severe pneumonia due to adenovirus—14. No predilection for HIV pts.
Human herpesvirus 6 (HHV-6)	HHV-6 infected cells detected in tissues obtained at necropsy in 9/9 pts, probably primary cause of fatal pneumonitis. Relevance is that HHV-6 infections treatable with ganciclovir & foscarnet (Ln 343:577, 1994).
Influenza A or B (common in outbreaks; vaccine effective: incidence 6.1% in vaccinated vs. 21.2% in unvaccinated (p=0.001); Ab response ↑ when CD4 count >200 or ART; immunization recommended (JAIDS 39:167, 2005)]	No evidence that influenza in general is more severe in HIV+ pts. **Diagnosis:** rapid nasal/oropharyngeal swabs only 50% sensitive. Need nasal RT-PCR to optimize sensitivity.
Varicella	Pneumonia common with typical diffuse reticulonodular infiltrates.

Selected Viral Etiologies: (59 pts with HIV & mean CD4 cell count of 55 (2-650). Fever, cough, new infiltrate. On BAL, 19% positive for at least one respiratory virus:
1 corona, 2 influenza, 3 parainfluenza & 1 bocavirus, metapneumovirus & rhinovirus [AIDS 22:701, 2008].

TABLE 11A (28)

CLINICAL SYNDROME, ETIOLOGY, EPIDEMIOLOGY	CLINICAL PRESENTATION, DIAGNOSTIC TESTS, COURSE
Lymph Nodes	
Generalized lymphadenopathy **(applies to lymphadenopathy without an obvious primary source)** Etiologies: acute HIV infection, TB, atypical mycobacteria, histoplasmosis, coccidioidomycosis, lymphoma, Kaposi's sarcoma, syphilis, Epstein-Barr virus, toxoplasma, tularemia, sarcoid, CMV, & Castleman's disease.	History & physical exam direct evaluation. If nodes fluctuant, aspirate & base rx on Gram & acid-fast stains. Pts receiving ART may demonstrate fever & generalized lymphadenopathy from MAC infection following robust ↑ CD4 cells; **immune reconstitution inflammatory syndrome (IRIS).**
Musculoskeletal System	
Pyomyositis Staphylococcal; aerobic Gm-neg. bacilli (uncommon).	May follow exercise, local trauma or injections. Swelling in muscular area, localized pain & fever. ESR usually ↑. Erythema often absent, can be indolent. ↑ bilateral in HIV. WBC may be normal & blood cultures usually negative Diagnosis: CT or MRI. Rx for Staph (MRSA), see Table 12, pg 143.
Osteomyelitis S. aureus, Strep. species, enterobacteriaceae, M. kansasii, H. capsulatum, nocardia	Diagnosis: blood cultures, if positive; if not, bone biopsy necessary to establish diagnosis.
Septic arthritis	Septic arthritis has a similar course in HIV+ & non-HIV pts. M. kansasii ↑ in AIDS. Think MRSA & mycobacteria. Rx for Staph (MRSA), see Table 12, pg 143; mycobacterial rx, Table 12, pg. 137.
Osteonecrosis (avascular necrosis): osteoporosis, & osteopenia, assoc. with advanced HIV & traditional risk factors (↓ body mass, weight loss, steroid use, & smoking). Likely a complication of HIV itself, not ART.	Evaluate for osteonecrosis in pt with persistent groin & hip pain. Plain films not usually revealing; usually requires MRI for definitive diagnosis. Risk factors: ↑ lipids, alcoholism, pancreatitis, **corticosteroid rx,** hypercoagulable state. Multiple joints often involved. MRI best test for diagnosis. Hip replacement surgery usually required for optimal treatment outcomes. In a prospective multicenter randomized open-label study, alendronate 70 mg qw + Vit. D 500 intl units q24h & calcium 1000 mg q24h improved lumbar bone mineral density & minimized femoral bone mineral density decrease after 52 wks vs. Vit. D & calcium alone in 41 HIV+ persons on ART (HIV Clin Trials 5:269, 2004). Other studies also confirm use of bisphosphonates while hormonal therapies such as raloxifene, testosterone and growth hormone-releasing hormone promising but require more study (see CID 42:108, 2006).
Arthritis, polyarticular Reiter's syndrome: urethritis or cervicitis, conjunctivitis, arthritis, & mucocutaneous lesions (circinate balanitis, keratoderma blennorrhagica).	Typically, non-bacterial urethritis 7–14 days after sexual exposure. Asymmetric polyarticular arthritis involving large joints of legs, including toes, develops over several weeks. Typically resolves in 3–4 mos but ~50% have recurrences. HLA B27 uncommon in Africans but reactive spondyloarthropathies still common in HIV+ persons. Lab: Synovial fluid typically is translucent, 2000–100,000 cells/µl, >50% PMNs. culture negative, glucose <50 mg/dl lower than blood glucose. Rx: Since often assoc. with C. trachomatis, empirical rx for chlamydia (see Table 12, pg 131) is appropriate. In non-HIV+ patients, methotrexate or folic acid antagonists have been used; they should not be used in HIV+ pts.
Psoriatic arthritis	Psoriasis noted in 1–5% HIV+ population. Frequency of arthritis ↑ in HIV+ pts with psoriasis.
"Lightning pain" syndrome	Severely painful acute attack of arthralgia or myalgia lasts a few hours to a few days. Often requires narcotics for relief. Clinical exam normal. Cause unknown, no sequelae (Med J Aust 158:114, 1993).

TABLE 11A (29)

CLINICAL SYNDROME, ETIOLOGY, EPIDEMIOLOGY	CLINICAL PRESENTATION, DIAGNOSTIC TESTS, COURSE
Musculoskeletal System (continued)	
Rheumatoid arthritis	Virtually never occurs in pts with HIV. Several pts with rheumatoid-factor positive RA have gone into remission after infection with HIV.
Systemic Lupus Erythematosis	Also not reported in HIV patients.
Arthritis, oligoarticular Review: Clin Exp Rheum 26:799, 2008	Usually asymmetrical, lower limbs. HLA B27 negative. Synovial fluid: low WBC with PMNs. HIV-associated arthritis occurred in 7.8% of 270 pts at various stages of HIV. Course was acute, of short duration (2 wks), without recurrences or erosive changes. Septic arthritis also usually monoarticular, MRSA & mycobacteria most common.
Myopathy (progressive proximal muscle weakness)	
HIV-1 associated myopathy	Proximal muscle weakness, ↑ creatinine kinase levels. Muscle biopsy: inflammatory infiltrates. Rule out statin toxicity, especially simvastatin with ritonavir (increased simvastatin levels).
Drug-associated: zidovudine (ZDV), ddI & ddC; may be assoc. with d4T, lactic acidosis & mitochondrial toxicity.	Proximal muscle weakness & atrophy (legs >arms, "baggy butt syndrome") with ZDV > 6 months. Creatinine kinase ↑. Typically associated with high-dose zidovudine use in the past. Muscle biopsy: "Ragged red fibers" on histology, abnormal mitochondria on EM. Improves with discontinuation of ZDV, recurs with rechallenge. ddC other NRTIs can cause a selective loss of mitochondrial DNA in vitro. Rhabdomyolysis rarely associated with TMP-SMX.
Polymyositis—also reported from IRIS (Clin Exp Rheumatol 22:651, 2004; Sex Trans Inf 80:315, 2004)	A dermatomyositis-like disease has been described in AIDS (Rheum Dis Clin NA 17:117, 1991; ArIM 159:1012, 1999).
Pancreatitis (see above Endocrine System/Pancreas) **Hyperamylasemia with or without abdominal pain:** Etiologies: Alcohol-related; gallstones; drugs: pentamidine, ddI, TMP/SMX, 3TC; CMV, MAC.	Pancreatitis due to ddI can be fatal (0.35%). All NRTIs implicated & likely due to mitochondrial toxicity. Pts rx for both Hep C & HIV receiving ribavirin & ddI + d4T at ↑ risk for mitochondrial toxicity including pancreatitis. Also reported in primary HIV infection. In a recent review of 8,451 subjects enrolled in ACTG trials, overall pancreatitis rates were 0.61 per 100 person-years. Highest rates seen in pts on indinavir/DDI/d4T (J AIDS 39:159, 2005). IV pentamidine is associated with pancreatic islet cell damage (hypoglycemia with later diabetes mellitus.
Peritoneal Disease	
Ascites, sudden onset	Symptoms & signs of underlying process.
Transudative ascitic fluid (<3 gm protein/100 mL) Concomitant hepatic cirrhosis (alcoholic), congestive heart failure, inferior vena cava obstruction, Budd-Chiari syndrome, hypoalbuminemia, vasculitis, hep B or C	
Exudative ascitic fluid (>3 gm protein/100 mL) (>500 cells/mm **suggests infection, neoplasm)** Tuberculosis, lymphoma, cytomegalovirus, nocardia, strongyloides.	Collect large volume (500–1000 mL), centrifuge, may reveal AFB on smear. Biopsy. Etiology most often found on biopsy. Rx for TB, see Table 12, pg. 133.

TABLE 11A (30)

CLINICAL SYNDROME, ETIOLOGY, EPIDEMIOLOGY	CLINICAL PRESENTATION, DIAGNOSTIC TESTS, COURSE
Renal. Review of HIV-associated renal disease, see *Curr HIV/AIDS Rep 9:187, 2012.*	
HIV-associated nephropathy (glomerulosclerosis) (HIVAN) Incidence HIVAN 8/1000 person yrs for HIV+ but 26.4/1000 person yrs in those with AIDS. ART ↓ risk of HIVAN. (Etiology likely due to direct infection of HIV. HIV also shown to infect renal tubular epithelial cells with production of the various proinflammatory mediators.	**HIVAN is an indication for urgent initiation of ARV therapy.** Usually occurs in advanced HIV with ↑ viral load *(CID 43:377, 2006).* Massive proteinuria of sudden onset, hypoalbuminemia, renal insufficiency rapidly progressing to endstage renal disease. Peripheral edema & hypertension minimal or absent. Biopsy recommended to differentiate from other causes of GN. Renal bx: Focal glomerulosclerosis with mesangial deposits of C3 & IgM, tubular ectasia & tubulo-interstitial disease. Significance of antiglomerular basement membrane antibody uncertain *(Am J Kidney Dis 48:e55, 2006).* Bx often of value in HIV+ pt with varying degrees of proteinuria. 6 of 25 pts from S. Africa with classic findings of HIVAN had only microalbuminuria and in 6 of 7 with persistent microalbuminuria *(Kidney Int 69:2243, 2006).* Treatment: **Antiretroviral therapy is imperative!** 60 mg prednisone for 1 mo. followed by 2 mos. taper ↓ serum creatinine, ↓ proteinuria, & preserved renal function at 6 mos. in 7/13 pts vs. 0/8 control *(Kidney Int 58:1253, 2000).* Angiotensin-converting enzyme (ACE) inhibitor has also had some limited success *(Pharmaco Therapy 25:1761, 2005).* ART rx improves outcome of HIV-assoc. nephropathy *(AntiM 139:214, 2003; AIDS Reader 14:443, 2004; Kidney Int 66:145, 2004; Clin Nephrol 64:124, 2005).* **Renal Transplant:** Survival rates at 1 and 3 yrs were 95% and 88% among HIV+ transplant recipients; graft survival rates were 90% and 74%, respectively. Survival rates are similar to non-HIV+ individuals, rejection rates are a bit higher *(NEJM 2010; 363:2058-2059).*
HIV-associated IgA nephropathy Rarer than HIV glomerulosclerosis. Majority of pts are white.	Microscopic hematuria, minimal proteinuria. ↑ serum IgA. Progression of disease is slow. Thought to be immune complex disease *(Kid International 81:833, 2012).*
Nephrotoxic drugs: pentamidine, foscarnet, aminoglycosides, amphotericin B; tenofovir, cidofovir, adefovir.	Causes renal tubular damage. Cobicistat causes increase in serum creatinine of 0.1 - 0.15 mg/dl but NO concomitant decrease in GFR (as determined by Iohexol clearance). Cobi inhibits multidrug and toxin extrusion protein 1 (MATE1) in the proximal tubule and has no effect on kidney function. Dolutegravir inhibits a different proximal tubule extrusion molecule resulting in a mild increase in serum creatinine without any impact on glomerular filtration.
Hemorrhagic cystitis	Hem. cystitis caused by adenovirus reported.
Urolithiasis: Renal colic in pts on PIs.	Causes of nephrolithiasis in HIV+ pts: indinavir-containing stones, Ca oxalate, urate. Reports of kidney stones with atazanavir.
Immune reconstitution syndrome (IRIS) *(See Table 11B)*	Inflammatory response following 8 wks of ART in pt with miliary TB with AFB urinary shedding, developed acute renal failure *(CID 38:e32, 2004).*
"Sepsis"/Bacteremia (M. tuberculosis, non-typhi salmonella & S. pneumo were most common causes in Nairobi, Kenya *(CID 33:248, 2001)*	
Disseminated pneumococcal disease	30-85% of pts with pneumococcal pneumonia have bacteremia. Rate of S. pneumoniae bacteremia is 100-fold ↑ in HIV+ pts.
Disseminated histoplasmosis may mimic sepsis syndrome	See page 120
Haemophilus influenzae bacteremia	Rx: *Table 12, pg. 150.*
Causes include those seen in the non-HIV+ patient, especially the febrile neutropenic patient; enterobacteriaceae, Pseudomonas sp., Staph. aureus, Staph. epidermidis.	↑ nasopharyngeal carriage rates for Staph. aureus in higher in HIV. ↑ rates of Staph aureus bacteremia. Nosocomial bacteremia still common in ART era.
Recurrent bacteremia	
Non-typhi salmonella, especially S. typhimurium (outside of U.S., Salmonella typhi)	In U.S. 20-fold ↑ in risk in HIV+ individuals. With CD4 >200/mm³ clinical presentation & response to rx similar to HIV-negative individuals. With CD4 <200/mm³, diarrhea is a less prominent symptom. Relapses occur. Rx: See *Table 12, pg. 142.*
Mycobacterium avium-intracellulare (MAC).	Rx: See *Table 12, page 137.*
Bartonella henselae, quintana	Rx: See *Table 12, page 131.*
Rhodococcus equi	See *Table 12, page 142.*

TABLE 11A (31)

CLINICAL SYNDROME, ETIOLOGY, EPIDEMIOLOGY	CLINICAL PRESENTATION, DIAGNOSTIC TESTS, COURSE
Sinuses, paranasal	
Sinusitis: Common in AIDS. Microbial flora similar to HIV-negative (S. pneumoniae, H. influenzae, M. catarrhalis) plus other Gram-positives (Staph. epidermidis, P. acnes), aerobic Gram-negatives (Pseudomonas aeruginosa), fungi (aspergillus, rhizopus (mucor), Alternaria alternata, H. capsulatum). Rarely parasites (microsporidium, cryptosporidium, CMV, & mycobacteria.	Sinusitis may be part of acquired atopy in AIDS. 2/3 pts are symptomatic (fever, nasal congestion, discharge). X-ray: 79% had air fluid level, usually more than one sinus. Despite rx, recurrent or persistent infections are common. Antral puncture required for accurate cultures & indicated if rx against common pathogens fails. Think fungal if facial pain or headache out of proportion to clinical or x-ray findings, if CD4 <50 & ANC <1000, indolent course & subtle x-ray findings of invasion. Most common fungus Aspergillus fumigatus.
Skin/Hair' (See Dermatol Clin 24:473, 2006 for excellent review)	
HIV-associated pruritus Etiology: Skin infections or infestations; papulosquamous disorders; photodermatitis; xerosis; drug reactions; rarely lymphoproliferative disorders	One of the most common symptoms in pts with HIV. Workup with careful exam of skin, nails, hair & mucous membranes to establish primary dermatological diagnosis; biopsy skin if necessary. ART may improve idiopathic HIV pts but some may flare with immune reconstitution.
Eosinophilic folliculitis (see J Am Acad Dermatol 55:215, 2006) Low CD4 counts & marked extremities, 90% above nipple line. ↑ eos, ↑ IgE. CD4 usually <250. Metronidazole 250 mg q8h for 3–4 wks works in some. May represent auto-immune reaction to sebum. Difficult to differentiate from infective folliculitis; bx is useful. In large study of 878 HIV-infec women, ART ↓ folliculitis.	pruritus, discrete, erythematous urticarial, follicular painless papules on trunk, head, neck, proximal
Macular or papular lesions	
Acute retroviral syndrome	Lesions 5–10 mm diam. symmetrical, esp. on face or trunk (may involve palms & soles), erythematous, non-pruritic. Stevens-Johnson syndrome, see page 94. Constitutional 'mono-like symptoms: fever (87%), skin rash (68%). Average duration of symptoms/signs 21 days.
Insect bites (scabies—axilla, groin, fingerweb; fleas—lower legs; mosquitoes—arms & legs).	Erythematous, urticarial papules. Intensely pruritic lesions are scabies until proven otherwise. Heaped up, scaly eruption is Norwegian Scabies; highly infectious! (See "crusted lesions" below) Rx with topical therapy. **Permethrin** 5% total body (Chin to toes) overnight; alternative **ivermectin** 200 mcg/kg po 1X; may need to be repeated 14 days later.
Drugs: Common cause of rash (esp. TMP/SMX & nevirapine) HIV+ have ↑ frequency of skin reactions to most drugs.	Drug-associated rashes occur in about 5% of those initiating ART. Overall, ART assoc. with ↓ of dermatological manifestations.
Molluscum contagiosum More common in young women (CID 38:579, 2004)	Occurs in 8–15% AIDS pts. 2–5 mm pearly flesh-colored papules, often with central umbilication on face, anogenital region. Disseminated cryptococcosis, P. marneffei, granuloma annulare may mimic. Rx: see Table 12, page 161
Syphilis, secondary	See above, Genital Tract. Rx: see Table 12, page 144.
Candidiasis (47% of AIDS pts had mucocutaneous candidal infections in 1 series).	Children: diaper-rash type rash involving trunk & extremities. Adults: red, hemorrhagic macular or papular lesions. Rx: see Table 12, page 147.
Cryptococcosis	Common. Widespread skin-colored, dome-shaped translucent papules 1–4 mm in diameter. Resemble Molluscum contagiosum. Rx: see Table 12, page 149.
Histoplasmosis	Slightly pink 2–6 mm cutaneous papules to larger reddish plaques & multiple shallow crusted ulcerations, usually in febrile patient. Rx: see Table 12, page 150.
Mycobacterial infections: M. tuberculosis, M. avium-intracellulare, M. kansasii, M. marinum, M. haemophilum, M. genavense (see page 118).	Vary from acneiform plaques, pustules or indurated verrucous plaques to ulcerative nodular lesions. See page 115. Lupus vulgaris, from disseminating Mtbc or BCG. Rx: see Table 12, page 132.

TABLE 11A (32)

CLINICAL SYNDROME, ETIOLOGY, EPIDEMIOLOGY	CLINICAL PRESENTATION, DIAGNOSTIC TESTS, COURSE
Skin/Hair/Macular or papular lesions *(continued)*	
Mycobacterium leprae	Clinical presentation of borderline leprosy similar in HIV+ & HIV–, but rx for neuritis less successful in HIV+. Rx: *see Table 12, page 140.*
Penicillium marneffei *(Curr Opin Infect Dis 21:31, 2008)*	Clinically present with fever, weight loss, small umbilicated macular or papular skin lesions (2/3 pts). hepatosplenomegaly, adenopathy. Almost all pts lived or traveled in Southeast Asia. Rx: *see Table 12, page 151.*
Cutaneous Pneumocystis jiroveci (carinii)	Rare but reported with underlying PJP and advanced AIDS. More common if on aerosolized pentamidine. Typically verrucous translucent papules anywhere on body. Rx: *see Table 12, page 151.*
Human papillomavirus (warts, condyloma acuminatum)	Diffuse flat & filiform lesions, often in unusual sites. *See GI & Genital Tract, above.* Rx: *see Table 12, page 161.*
Kaposi's sarcoma (CD4: mean 87/mm³, median 37/mm³)	Early lesions are round or irregular pinkish-red to violaceous macules to papules, usually non-tender. Often symmetrical along skin tension lines. *See Table 18.*
Lymphoid papulosis (LyP) Rare cutaneous lymphoproliferative disorder	Chronic recurrent pruritic eruption of papules & nodules that undergo spontaneous regression. Usually benign with minority progressing to lymphoma. May resemble pityriasis but histologically resembles lymphoma (Anaplastic T-cell or HD).
Nodular, verrucous, &/or ulcerative lesions	
Mycobacterial infections	*See above*
Bacillary angiomatosis *(Clin Dermatol 27:271, 2009)*	Friable vascular papules, cellulitis, plaques & subcutaneous nodules, usually tender. Pts may be febrile. May be confused with KS. Etiology: Bartonella henselae & B. quintana. May be isolated from blood (5–15 days incubation of lysis centrifugation cultures on blood agar, 5% CO₂), & identified with Warthin Stary stain. Rx: *see Table 12, page 131.*
Acanthamoeba, disseminated	Rare.
Sporotrichosis	Uncommon, but reported. May cause multiple lesions with dissemination. Rx: *see Table 12, page 152.*
Cryptococcosis	As above
Histoplasmosis	As above
Furunculosis can be severe	Most due to MRSA. Contagious. Spread with households, partners. Rx: *see Table 12, page 142.*
Kaposi's sarcoma: Kaposi-associated herpesvirus (KSHV) now called HHV 8 is found in biopsy samples & blood mononuclear cells of pts with AIDS-related or classical KS.	Skin usually 1st site of presentation. Lesions palpable, firm, non-tender nodules. Early lesions may resemble ecchymoses. Typically violaceous, hyperpigmented, involving head, neck. Later become confluent, form large tumor masses & occur throughout the body. Up to 40% GI involvement. Oral lesions may precede skin lesions. Responds to ART.
Non-Hodgkins lymphoma	Skin involved in 15% of pts with non-Hodgkin lymphoma. Lesions are usually papules or nodules.
Mycobacterium avium-intracellulare (MAI/MAC)	Fever & extensive cutaneous nodules (granulomas or focal necroses) have been reported in pts infected with MAC who responded to ART **with immune reconstitution** (↓ CD4 counts & ↓ viral load). Steroids may be useful rx *(Table 11B).*
Leishmania	May produce a wide spectrum of localized or disseminated cutaneous, mucosal or diffuse lesions. Most lesions are small, papular with ulceration but with HIV may widely disseminate with hundreds of lesions. Common in the Middle East/Iraq, other endemic regions.
Vesicular bullous or pustular lesions	
Herpes simplex virus	Grouped vesicles on erythematous base rapidly evolve into ulcerations or fissures. May persist as chronic large ulcerative lesions, esp. in perianal area. Rx: *see Table 12, page 160.*
Varicella zoster virus: Common in HIV+ pts & frequently precedes AIDS; 10–20% frequency overall.	Grouped vesicles on erythematous base. May be verrucous. In chronic form may persist as hyperkeratotic lesions. Dermatomal distribution. May be multidermatomal. Rx: *see Table 12, page 162.*

TABLE 11A (33)

CLINICAL SYNDROME, ETIOLOGY, EPIDEMIOLOGY	CLINICAL PRESENTATION, DIAGNOSTIC TESTS, COURSE
Skin/Hair/Vesicular bullous or pustular lesions *(continued)*	
Cytomegalovirus	Rare. Small reddish-purple macules that ulcerate. May present with non-healing perianal ulceration. Rx: see *Table 12, page 158.*
Staphylococcal impetigo	Erythematous-crusted papules may be pruritic on face, trunk, groin. Rx: *see Table 12, page 142.*
"Typical scabies"	Extremely pruritic, papular & vesicular lesions characterized by linear or serpentine burrows most commonly on hands, wrists, elbows, ankles. Average number of mites is 11. As above. Rx: see *Table 12, page 156.*
Stevens-Johnson syndrome	Most often drug-related: TMP/SMX, fluconazole, ddI, anti-TBc drugs.
Porphyria cutanea tarda	Association with HIV described but the co-occurrence may reflect coexistence of risk factors, esp. alcohol use, Hep C, rather than causal association. Lesions especially over sun-exposed areas.
Papulosquamous lesions	
Seborrheic dermatitis	Occurs in 20–80% HIV+ individuals, dandruff to patches & plaques of erythema with indistinct margins & yellowish scale on "hairy" areas. Malassezia furfur may be causative agent.
Xerotic eczema (dry-skin syndrome). ↑ with ↓ CD4 counts	Occurs in 5–20% HIV+ individuals. Often severely pruritic & resistant to antihistamines
Dermatophytosis (*T. rubrum* most common, then *T. mentagrophytes* & *E. floccosum*)	Occurs in 20–35% HIV+ individuals. Widespread, often severe with scaly red pruritic papules & plaques.
Tinea versicolor	Patchy areas of fine scale & hypopigmentation. CD4 often >300/mm³ Usually resistant to topical agents.
Psoriasis	Presents as (1) discrete plaques or (2) a diffuse dermatitis often associated with palmoplantar keratoderma. Distribution may be atypical: groin, axilla & scalp rather than elbows & knees. Common nail changes & psoriatic arthritis.
Crusted (Norwegian) scabies Occurs in 1.3–5% HIV+ individuals.	**Highly contagious** to close contacts (health care workers). Usually occurs in patients with severe immunodeficiency. Characterized by erythema, hyperkeratosis & crusting. Pruritus is typically present but hyperkeratotic, crusted form may be absent. Burrows usually not seen. Gross nail thickening & subungual debris common. Alopecia, hyperpigmentation, pyoderma & eosinophilia may occur. Dx is based on demonstration of heavy mite burden (1000s) on scraping vs. a few in typical scabies. Crusted scabies is resistant to therapy and treatment failure is common. Concomitant oral and topical treatment is most effective: permethrin 5% cream + oral ivermectin or topical benzyl benzoate emulsion with ivermectin *(Indian J Dermatol Venereol Leprol 75;340, 2009.*
Folliculitis	
Staphylococcal folliculitis	An uncommon presentation is violaceous plaques (up to 10 cm) in groin, axilla & scalp. Rx: see *Table 12, page 142.*
Eosinophilic folliculitis	See above, *Skin, eosinophilic folliculitis.*
Skin discoloration (reddish-brown, occ. black or bluish)	Seen in 75–100% of pts on clofazimine, but also think Addison's disease, toxoplasmosis, etc.
Pressure ulcers (PUs) Incidence 2.3/100 hospital admissions: ↑ with female sex, length of hospital stay (1.06/100 pt days), advanced HIV. Mortality 50% with PU vs. 7.2% without PU with attributed mortality of 42.8.	Aggressive preventive strategies should be implemented.
Hair disease: Diffuse thinning, premature greying, elongated eyelashes. In African-Americans peculiar straightening of previously curly hair has been observed in advanced HIV	
Nail disease	
Onychomycosis	
Longitudinal pigmented nail bands	Seen in almost ½ pts on higher-dose ZDV, more common in dark-skinned patients, occurs within 4–8 wks of starting rx.

TABLE 11A (34)

CLINICAL SYNDROME, ETIOLOGY, EPIDEMIOLOGY	CLINICAL PRESENTATION, DIAGNOSTIC TESTS, COURSE
Splenomegaly	23% of 70 consecutive HIV/+ pts were found to have splenomegaly on physical exam & 66% by ultrasound. Pts with liver disease were more likely to have ↑ (RR=1.84, P<0.001). ↑ spleen was not predictive of any clinical event during a 1-yr follow-up or with developing AIDS in a 6-yr follow-up. **Massive splenomegaly: think leishmaniasis!**
Systemic, wasting syndromes 'Slim' disease (enteropathic AIDS), rule out: Cryptosporidium & other causes of chronic diarrhea Mycobacterium avium–intracellulare complex (MAC) Mycobacterium tuberculosis Histoplasma capsulatum Kaposi's sarcoma Non-Hodgkin lymphoma	Weight loss is common (29% in one series). Causes: opportunistic infections, chronic diarrhea, psychosocial factors, drug associated, unexplained. Rapid weight loss (>4 kg in <4 mos.) accompanied by anorexia is usually a sign of secondary infection, slower weight loss (>4 kg in >4 mos.) is often due to GI disease with diarrhea, less marked weight loss may be due to ↓ caloric intake. Responds to ART. **Watch for 'refeeding syndrome'** in those with profound malnutrition and weight loss (*PLoS ONE* 5(5): e10687, 2010).

TABLE 11B: IMMUNE RECONSTITUTION & NOVEL SYNDROMES ASSOCIATED WITH ART

Antiretroviral Therapy (ART) has led to a marked improvement in the control of HIV infections & significant reduction in mortality from AIDS *(CID 44:599, 2007)*. In addition, ART has led to reconstitution of the immune deficiencies in the majority of patients receiving this therapy. As a result of this, the incidence of opportunistic infections & AIDS-defining illnesses has also declined *(JAMA 296:292, 2006; CID 50:1, 2010)*. The incidence of certain other infections including invasive S. pneumoniae has also declined in the US since the advent of ART *(JID 191:2038, 2005)*. Interestingly, in developed countries, non-HIV related causes of death (especially cardiovascular disease, non-HIV-related cancer and substance abuse) caused 25% of all deaths in patients receiving ART between 1999 and 2004 *(Ann Int Med 145:397, 2006)*. HIV-infected patients with the metabolic syndrome are at increased risk for ASCVD *(CID 44:1368, 2007)*. In addition to the direct antiretroviral effects of ART, a number of novel clinical syndromes have been seen as well. Among the syndromes associated with ART are adverse effects due to protease inhibitors & other components of ART, new syndromes associated with immune reconstitution, & the clinical effects of ART on opportunistic disorders.

1. **Adverse effects due to drugs used in ART**

   Many of the most important adverse events directly related to the agents used in ART (such as renal lithiasis due to indinavir, gastrointestinal events related to ritonavir & other protease inhibitors) are detailed in *Table 6B*. In addition, a number of unusual syndromes (not necessarily related to a specific agent, but to classes of agents used in ART) have been described in the past several years. Included among these syndromes (some of which may cause serious morbidity or even death) are lactic acidosis, abnormalities in glucose metabolism, disorders of lipid metabolism, lipodystrophy syndromes such as lipoatrophy & lipohypertrophy, osteopenia & possibly aseptic necrosis of the hip. These complications are covered in detail in *Table 6C*.

2. **New syndromes associated with immune reconstitution**

   Patients receiving ART have reduced plasma HIV-1 viral load & increased CD4 T-lymphocyte counts. Despite this AIDS-defining events may develop within the first several months after initiation of ART. It is unclear at this point as to whether this is related to a delay in restoration of immune function or the fact that ART may actually promote clinical development &/or expression of such infections as well as AIDS-related malignant disease. More commonly, however, one sees a variety of inflammatory reactions associated with immune reconstitution *(Med 81:213, 2002; JAC 51:1, 2003)*. This syndrome is often termed the **immune reconstitution inflammatory syndrome (IRIS)** & occurs in up to 25% of patients with an underlying opportunistic infection after initiation of ART *(JAC 57:167, 2006)*. The most frequent manifestations are dermatological, particularly involving genital herpes and warts *(CID 42:418, 2006)* or systematic reactions in patients with mycobacterial disease *(Lancet ID 5:361, 2005)*. In patients with disseminated MAC disease, elevations in CD4 cells & associated immune reconstitution may be coupled with the development of painful generalized lymphadenopathy resembling scrofula. Massive mesenteric adenopathy with severe abdominal pain & thoracic adenopathy associated with pulmonary infiltrates & endobronchial proliferative lesions have also been described. These patients are often systemically ill with fever, leukocytosis & malaise sufficient to require hospital admission. IRIS is also a well-known complication of the initiation of antiretroviral therapy in patients infected with M. tuberculosis where it may be associated with a paradoxical worsening of treated TB (Hectic fevers, lymphadenopathy, worsening chest film) or presentation of non-TB *(JID 196:S63, 2007; JID 202:1728, 2010)*. Corticosteroid therapy may be considered in severe cases *(CID 48:101, 2008)*. IRIS may also be seen in patients with underlying sarcoid or autoimmune disease, both of which appear to have immunopathology different from that of "classic" IRIS *(CID 48:101, 2009)*.

   The development of symptomatic cytomegalovirus retinitis shortly after initiation of ART is likely a manifestation of the same phenomenon. Flares in hepatitis in patients chronically infected with hepatitis B & C viruses are likely also the result of improvement in immune status. Note that this syndrome must be distinguished from the mild hepatotoxicity associated with drugs used to treat ART. The symptoms of the immune reconstitution syndromes usually subside spontaneously with continued therapy for the underlying disease or with the use of nonsteroidal anti-inflammatory agents. Occasionally reactions may be severe enough to be life-threatening & may require corticosteroid therapy. The incidence and severity of IRIS when ART is initiated after an AIDS-defining opportunistic infection (OI) has recently been determined and varies considerably with the OI. Cumulative 1 year incidence of IRIS was 29% for Kaposi's sarcoma (KS), 16% for tuberculosis, 14% for Cryptococcus, 10% for MAI complex and 4% for PJP (now PJP). Morbidity and mortality was highest for visceral KS *(CID 54:424, 2012)*.

3. **Selected effects of ART on opportunistic infections or other complications of HIV infection**
   (See next page and also see Table 11A for individual OIs)

TABLE 11B (2)

Opportunistic Infection	Common Clinical Presentation	Presentation After Highly Active Antiretroviral Therapy (ART)
Castleman disease	Fever, lymphadenopathy	Clinical recovery with resolution of lymphadeno-pathy. However, late relapse (fatal) after initial response described in 5 patients despite immune reconstitution.
Cryptococcus neoformans	Meningitis usually indolent, cerebrospinal fluid leukocytosis uncommon	Overt meningitis, marked cerebrospinal fluid leukocytosis. IRIS seen in 13% of patients with cryptococcal meningitis and was associated with elevated baseline serum cryptococcal antigen (CID 49:931, 2009).
Cryptosporidiosis, microsporidiosis	Diarrhea	Clinical, microbiological resolution associated with significant reduction in viral load.
Cytomegalovirus	Retinitis, vitreitis, uveitis uncommon	Atypical (non-retinitis) manifestations of CMV, including pneumonitis, pseudotumoral colitis, adenitis & symptoms of viremia. Immune recovery uveitis.
Eosinophilic folliculitis	Inflammatory reaction involving new hair follicles—especially on face and trunk	Inflammatory reaction to Dermodex folliculorum mites. May respond rapidly to ivermectin.
Hepatitis B (chronic)	Asymptomatic or nonspecific symptoms	Acute flare of clinical hepatitis 5–12 wks after beginning ART. Usually resolves without change in therapy.
Hepatitis C (chronic)	Asymptomatic	Acute hepatitis, cirrhosis or HCV-associated disorder such as cryoglobulinemia within 1–9 months after initiation of ART.
Herpes simplex (ano-genital)	Painful ulcerated lesions	Recrudescence of recurrent episodes of ano-genital lesions.
Herpes zoster	May be severe accompanied by complications	Mild presentation, uncomplicated. May see increased incidence of zoster after initiation of ART, possibly due to ↑ CD8 cells.
HIV-1 associated nephropathy	Impaired renal function	Reversal of pathology & recovery of function.
HIV-associated non-Hodgkin's lymphoma	Typical Stage I-IV lymphoma	Improved clinical outcome & survival.
Human papillomavirus (HPV) infection in women	Genital warts, squamous intraepithelial lesions (SILs) of cervix, cervical cancer.	Effective and adherent ART associated with reduced burden of HPV infection and SILs (JID 201:681, 2010).
Kaposi's sarcoma	Skin lesions, disseminated disease, oral lesions	Regression of lesions coincident with significant reduction in viral load. Laryngeal obstruction from mucosal edema is rare complication of ART. ↓ incidence in US after introduction of ART (JAMA 305:1450, 2011).
Lymphoepithelial parotid cysts	Parotid cysts	Resolution on antiretroviral therapy.
Molluscum contagiosum	Disseminated skin lesions	Resolution of severe disease coincident with 10-fold increase in CD4 cells.
Mycobacterium avium complex	Disseminated disease, weight loss, diarrhea, mycobacteremia	Focal lymphadenitis, granulomatous masses, endobronchial proliferative lesions, abdominal lymphadenopathy & pain (see above for more details), clearance of bacteremia without antimycobacterial therapy, development of cavitation in pulmonary nodules. Immune reconstitution lymphadenitis may occur despite azithromycin prophylaxis (CID 42:418, 2006). Intraabdominal disease results in greater morbidity than peripheral lymphadenitis.
M. tuberculosis	Subclinical disease	Can develop "unmasked TB-IRIS syndrome" after initiation of ART (JID 199:437, 2009). May also occur in patients with drug-resistant infections (CID 48:667, 2009).
Oral candidiasis	White plaques on oral & pharyngeal mucosa (thrush)	Clinical resolution of oral candidiasis without antifungal therapy. This is independent of immune reconstitution & may be a direct effect of PIs.
Oral warts	Relatively rare oral lesions	Marked ↑ in oral warts which are progressive & recur after removal.
Chronic parvovirus B-19 infection	Anemia; AIDS wasting syndrome; encephalitis	Anecdotal case reports of response in patients with each syndrome receiving ART.
Progressive multifocal leukoencephalopathy	Neurologic deficits, MRI demonstration of hypodensities without contrast enhancement	Neurologic deficits; neurologic deficits with enhancing lesions on MRI, frequently with peripheral enhancement; long-term, see remission of neurologic symptoms & improvement of radiographic findings & increased survival in approx. 50% of cases. Fatal, paradoxical worsening of PML (non-responsive to steroids) has also been described in pts shortly after initiation of ART.

TABLE 11B (3)

Opportunistic Infection	Common Clinical Presentation	Presentation After Highly Active Antiretroviral Therapy (ART)
Pulmonary tuberculosis	Pulmonary infiltrates	Fever, lymphadenopathy, worsening pulmonary infiltrates. Note: incidence of Tbc decreased with ART.
Sarcoidosis	Cutaneous lesions; diffuse pulmonary involvement; adenopathy	Flares of preexisting or new onset sarcoidosis described in patients on ART.
Systemic lupus erythematosus	Incidence of SLE decreased in immuno-suppressed AIDS pts	Anecdotal reports of new onset of SLE & flares of preexisting SLE following ART.
Tegumentary leishmaniasis	No lesions or few erythematous papules	Worsening of prior lesions or development of disseminated lesions.
Visceral leishmaniasis	Fever, hepatosplenomegaly	Long-term remission; development of post-kala-azar dermal leishmaniasis.

4. **Effect on incidence of AIDS-related opportunistic infections.** The immune reconstitution associated with ART has clearly led to a striking decline in the incidence of AIDS-related opportunistic infections, although the spectrum of these diseases, in general, has not been altered. The incidence is highest immediately after starting ART & declines progressively thereafter. There has been a significant decrease in AIDS-defining malignancies (KS, NHL) since introduction of ART *(JAMA 305:1450, 2011)*. ART may be a more common cause of diarrhea than formerly frequent opportunistic pathogens and cardiovascular complications are less frequent.

5. **Discontinuation of prophylaxis for opportunistic infections** *(Also see Table 10)*. Data have now accumulated that it is possible to stop primary prophylaxis for MAI, PJP, & toxoplasmosis in patients with sustained responses (CD4 cell counts >100–200) to ART. It is also now possible to stop secondary prophylaxis for PJP, MAI [especially in patients who received at least 1 year of macrolide-based therapy], toxoplasmosis, cryptococcosis, & CMV retinitis in patients with sustained CD4 cell responses. Rare instances of recurrence of MAI infection following immune reconstitution & cessation of therapy for disseminated MAI have been described. The same may be true for patients in whom secondary prophylaxis for PJP is discontinued. However, discontinuance of cotrimoxazole prophylaxis in Ugandan patients with CD4 counts > 200 led to increased incidence of malaria and diarrhea *(CID 54:1204, 2012)*.

6. **Infectivity.** Data suggest that HIV-infected persons with undetectable viral load are less infectious and may be less likely to transmit HIV via sexual contact. However, it is also clear that this potential reduction in HIV transmission within a population does not translate to elimination of risk within individual couples. Thus, the CDC makes the following recommendations:
   - Use of ART may be a promising tool for slowing transmission of HIV within populations if prevention benefits are not offset by increases in risk behavior. Success of such a program will depend critically upon 1) widespread testing and early identification of infected persons, 2) ongoing counseling to support maintenance of safer sexual behaviors, 3) adequate clinical follow-up to monitor for adverse effects of ART and 4) geographic and financial accessibility of treatment for affected persons.
   - In accordance with DHHS guidelines, clinicians may consider the potential benefit of decreased risk of HIV transmission to others in deciding whether to initiate ART on infected persons (even with CD4 counts >350 cells/mL).
   - The risk of sexual transmission is substantially reduced for individual couples in which the infected partner is on effective ART and has achieved undetectable plasma HIV viral load, but is not completely eliminated. Sexual transmission of HIV may still occur when the infected partner is on ART. In Feb 2008 CDC reiterated that people living with HIV who are sexually active use condoms with all sexual partners.
   - For couples in which both partners are infected, the potential implications of superinfection are unclear. Use of condoms is recommended in this setting as well *(CDC Guidelines, Sept 2009, http://www.cdc.gov/hiv/resources/press/020108.htm)*. Note also that while acyclovir treatment for HSV-2 genital infections also decreases plasma HIV viral load, it has no impact on transmission of HIV *(NEJM 362:477, 2010)*.

131

TABLE 12: TREATMENT OF SPECIFIC INFECTIONS IN HIV+/AIDS PATIENTS *(MMWR 58(RR-4), 2009)*

CAUSATIVE AGENT/DISEASE	MODIFYING CIRCUMSTANCES	SUGGESTED REGIMENS		COMMENTS
		PRIMARY	ALTERNATIVE	
BACTERIAL INFECTIONS				
Bartonella **Bacillary angiomatosis; Peliosis hepatis—patients with AIDS** Ref: *AAC 48:1921, 2004; CID 41:969, 2005*	Etiology: B. henselae, B. quintana	(**Clarithro** 500 mg q12h or **clarithro ER** 1 gm q24h) or (**doxy** 100 mg q12h po) x 3 months.	(**Erythro** 500 mg q6h po or **doxy** 100 mg q12h po) x 3 months.	CNS infection or non-CNS but severe: doxy 100 mg po/IV q12h ± RIF 300 mg po/IV x 16 wks. Risk of Jarisch-Herxheimer reaction in 1st 48 hrs. Ref: *AAC 48:1921, 2004*.
Endocarditis	Etiology: B. henselae, B. quintana (Ref: *Circulat 111:3167, 2005*).	Suspected Bartonella endocarditis: [**Ceftriaxone** 2 gm IV q24h x 6 wks + **gentamicin** 1 mg/kg q8h x 14 days] + **doxycycline** 100 mg IV/po bid x 14-d. If **Gent** toxicity precludes use, substitute **RIF** 300 mg IV/po bid x 14d. Surgery: Over ⅓ pts require valve surgery; relation to cure unclear.		Diagnosis: immunofluorescent antibody titer ≥ 1:800; blood cultures only occ. Positive, or PCR of tissue from surgery. B. Quintana transmitted by body lice among homeless. Asymptomatic presence in RBCs described (*Ln 360:226, 2002*).
Trench fever	B. quintana	**Doxy** 100 mg bid. Doxy alone is OK if no endocarditis		
For chronic suppression in AIDS patients	With CD4 count <200	**Erythro** 250-500 mg po q6h (see Comments)	**Clarithro** or **azithro** in above doses	Suppression until CD4 T-lymphocyte count above 200/mm³
Campylobacter jejuni; Campylobacter coli	Severity ↑ in elderly, pregnancy, bloody stools, assoc. inflamm bowel disease.	**Azithro** 500 mg po q24h x 3 days. Treat bacteremia for 14 days. Treatment meta-analysis: *CID 44:696, 2007*.	(**Erythromycin stearate** 500 mg po q12h x 5 days or **CIP** 500 mg po q12h) x 5 days.	Macrolide resistance rare, **worldwide resistance to FQs** up to 80% (*CID 48:1500, 2009; EID 10:1102, 2004; AAC 54:1232, 2010*).
Chlamydia trachomatis (non-gonococcal or post-gonococcal urethritis, cervicitis) Refs: *MMWR 59 (RR-12): 44, 2010*	NOTE: Assume concomitant GC. **Evaluate & treat sexual partners.**	**Doxycycline** 100 mg po q12h x 7 days OR **Azithro** 1 gm po (single dose) In pregnancy: **azithro** 1 gm po x 1 or **Erythro** base 500 mg po q6h x 7 days	**Erythro** base 500 mg po q6h x 7 d OR **Ofloxacin** 300 mg po q12h x 7 d OR **Levo** 500 mg po q24h x7 days.	Diagnosis: Nucleic acid amplification test on urine, urethral swab, or cervical swab. Follow-up: Do not repeat NAAT immediately post-treatment. Early recurrence/failure secondary to re-infection. Should retest 3+ months post-treatment.
Clostridium difficile toxin-mediated diarrhea (*CID 51:1306, 2010*)	See Sanford Guide to Antimicrobial Therapy for more detail	**Metronidazole** 500 mg po q8h or 250 mg po q6h x10-14 d. If severe use **vanco** po q6h x10-14 d (*CID 40:1588, 159 & 1598, 2005 & 45:302, 2007*)	**Vancomycin** 125 mg po q6h x 14 days - use if WBC > 15,000	Avoid anti-motility agents. **Relapse occurs in 10-20% of patients**; consider Fidaxomicin 200 mg bid x 10 days for recurrence. Isolate patient.
Granuloma inguinale (Calymmatobacterium granulomatis or donovanosis) *MMWR 59 (RR-12):25, 2010*	Now: Klebsiella granulomatis	**Doxycycline** 100 mg po q12h x minimum of 3-4 wks or **TMP/SMX** 1 DS tablet (160 mg TMP) po q12h x 21 d	[(**Erythro** 500 mg po q6h x 21 d (can be used in pregnancy) or (**CIP** 750 mg po q12h x 3 wks) or (**azithro** 1 gm po qwk x 3 wks)	Rare in U.S. Should see clinical response after 1 wk. If no improvement, consider adding Gent 1 mg/kg IV q48h. **Rx until all lesions healed—may require 4 wks of rx.** Rx failure/relapse seen with doxy & TMP/SMX.
Haemophilus ducreyi (chancroid) *MMWR 59 (RR-12):19, 2010*	Painful genital ulcer(s)	**Ceftriaxone** 250 mg IM (single dose) or **azithro** 1 gm po single dose	**CIP** 500 mg po q12h x 3 d or **Erythro** 500 mg po q6h x 7 d	Uncircumcised males & HIV + pts do not respond as well as circumcised or HIV neg. Check HIV antibody & syphilis serology. See *MMWR 59 (RR-12), 2010*.
Listeriosis (Meningitis) Ref: *CID 43:1233, 2006*	Bacteremia, meningitis, focal infections, diarrhea	**Ampicillin** 2 gm IV q4h + **gentamicin** 2 mg/kg load dose, then 1.7 mg/kg q8h.	If pen allergic: **TMP/SMX** 20 mg/kg/day (TMP component) IV divided in q6-8h dosage	Synergy with ampicillin + an aminoglycoside (gentamicin). Duration of rx 2-4 wks. **(Cephalosporins not active vs. L. monocytogenes.**
Lymphogranuloma venereum *MMWR 59 (RR-12) 26, 2010*	Etiology: C. trachomatis, serovars. L1-L3	**Doxycycline** 100 mg po q12h x 21 d	**Azithro** 1 gm po once weekly x 3 weeks (clinical data lacking) or **Erythro** 500 mg po q6h x 21 d	Dx based on serology, biopsy contraindicated. Presents with rectal ulcer and anal discharge (*Dis Colon Rectum 52:707, 2009*).

TABLE 12 (2)

CAUSATIVE AGENT/DISEASE	MODIFYING CIRCUMSTANCES	SUGGESTED REGIMENS		COMMENTS
		PRIMARY	ALTERNATIVE	
BACTERIAL INFECTIONS (continued)				
Mycobacterium tuberculosis: Treatment of latent infection (LTBI) [previously known as preventive treatment, infection without disease (pos tuberculin test)] or **HIV+ pts with anergy & high risk for tuberculosis** (AnM 119: 185, 1993). HIV+ pts with anergy need prophylaxis only if exposed to active TB (NEJM 337: 315, 1997) or if they fall into a group at high risk for TBc (e.g., HIV-infected IV drug abusers) (AIDS 13: 2069, 1999). Therefore use of anergy testing in conjunction with PPD testing not recommended for routine screening programs for TB among HIV-infected pts in U.S. (MMWR 46/RR-15;1, 1997; JAMA 283:2003, 2000). Treatment of LBTI effective in HIV+ patients (JID 196:S52, 2007; NEJM 364:1441, 2011).	Organisms likely to be INH-susceptible	**INH** 5 mg/kg/day (max. 300 mg/day 2x/wk x 9 mos + **pyridoxine** (B6) 25-50 mg po x 9 mos For children, see Table 9F, page 79.	If compliance problem: **INH** by DOT, 15 mg/kg 2x/wk x 9 mos (MMWR 52:735, 2003) **RIF** if not possible, options: **RIF+PZA** x 2 mos no longer recommended due to reports of severe & fatal hepatitis (MMWR 52:735, 2003) OR **RFB** 300 mg po q24h x 4 mos is as effective as 9 mos INH regimen (CID 49:1883, 2009). 12 dose INH + Rifapentine regimen may be used in HIV+ patients NOT on ART, but not recommended for pts on ART (MMWR 60:1650, 2011; NEJM 365:2155, 2011).	For pts given ddC + INH, suggest 50 mg pyridoxine/day. Duration of preventive therapy: INH x 9 mos preferred, recommendations range from 2–12 mos. Ugandan study suggests 6 mos of INH or INH + RIF also ↓ risk of TB disease (AIDS 15:2137, 2001), 12 mos regimens of RIF + PZA or RFB + PZA also shown to be effective (AJRCCM 155:1497, 1997; MMWR 52:735, 2003). Monitoring for cofactors did not seem to allow prediction of fatalities (CID 42:346, 2006). Therefore, regimen is no longer recommended by CDC for LTBI (CID 42:735, 2003; CID 39:484, 2004). Not all agree with CDC recommendations and recent study suggests short course therapy is safe with monitoring and more likely to be completed than longer Rx (CID 43:271, 2006). 3 & 4 month INH & RIF regimens also safe and effective as 9 mos. of INH in children (Peds CID 45:715, 2007). Resistant TBc occurred in HIV+ pts given INH + RIF by DOT—presum. due to malabsorption (NEJM 332:336, 1995; AJM 127:289, 1997; CID 25:1044, 1997). Although 1 study failed to detect direct effect on bioavailability of antimycobacterial drugs in pts with AIDS ± diarrhea (CID 25: 104, 1997). INH (Isoniazid) reported to ↓ progression of HIV (Lancet 342:268, 1993). Late "failures" of INH "prophylaxis" usually due to reinfection, not primary failure of regimen (CID 34:386, 2002). 4 months rx with RIF (10 mg/kg/day) produced fewer adverse effects than 9 months of INH (AIM 149:689, 2008).
	INH-resistant (or adverse reaction to INH), RIF-sensitive organisms likely	**RIF** 600 mg po q24h or **RFB** 300 mg po q24h x 4 mos		

---

[1] **Tuberculin test (TST):** The standard is the Mantoux test, 5 TU (intermediate) in 0.1 mL diluent stabilized with Tween 80. Read at 48–72hrs, measuring the maximum diameter of induration (not erythema). A reaction ≥5 mm is defined as + in the HIV+ pt. For HIV+, the reaction is cut-off for a +. Pt history is critical. BCG ≥10 mm is cut-off for a +. In HIV+ or persons w/chest x-ray findings, a reaction ≥5 mm is + (Brit Med J 304:1231, 1992). Note that BCG immunization in HIV+ children carries significant risk of causing disseminated BCG disease (CID 42:548, 2006). Moreover, HIV infection severely impairs BCG-specific T cell response may provide little, if any, vaccine-induced benefit in HIV-infected infants (JID 199:982, 2009). Because up to 25% of patients with HIV are anergic, the decrease in proportion of false-negative TST results obtained by reducing cutoff for positivity from 10 to 5 mm is limited (CID 43:634, 2006). See also Table 23 for details of PPD testing. **Interferon Gamma Release Assays (IGRAs):** IGRAs detect T-cell response when exposed to M. tuberculosis antigens. Four such tests have now been approved by the U.S. FDA. • QuantiFERON-TB (QFT) (approved 2001, but discontinued in 2005) • QuantiFERON-TB Gold (QFT-G) (approved 2005) • QuantiFERON-TB Gold In-Tube Test (QFT-GIT) (approved 2008) • T-Spot (approved 2008). As with TST, using with IGRAs in low prevalence populations lend insight into false-positive results (CID 53:234, 2011). QFT-G, QFT-GIT & T-Spot each measures different aspects of immune response so test results are not always interchangeable. IGRAs are relatively specific for MTBc and should not cross-react with BCG or most nontuberculous mycobacteria. CDC recommends IGRAs can be used in place of (but not in addition to) TST in persons unlikely to return for reading TST in past (e.g. homeless, drug abusers), or have received BCG. TST is preferred in children age <5 yrs (but IGRAs is acceptable). IGRA or TST may be used without preference for recent contacts of TB with special ability for follow-up testing (since IGRAs do not produce booster effect). May also be used without preference over the other for serial testing for occupational exposures. QFT-GIT & T-Spot 90.9% sensitive for active TB in HIV-positive patients (CID 49:954, 2009). For detailed discussion of IGRAs, see MMWR 59 (RR-5), 2010; JCM 49:2086, 2011; CID 52:1031, 2011. **Nucleic acid amplification tests (NAAT)** can reliably detect M. tuberculosis in clinical specimens 1 or more weeks earlier than conventional cultures. They are particularly useful in detecting MTBc from smear-positive specimens. Sensitivity from each patient for whom diagnosis of TB is being considered but has not yet been established by conventional means; recommend NAA testing be performed on at least one respiratory specimen from each patient for whom the first test result would alter case management or TB control activities (MMWR 58:7, 2009). For discussion of new diagnostic tests, see CID 50(S3):S173, 2010. **Rapid (24-hr) diagnostic tests** for M. tuberculosis: (1) the Amplified Mycobacterium tuberculosis Direct Test amplifies and detects M. tuberculosis ribosomal RNA; (2) the AMPLICOR Mycobacterium tuberculosis detects M. tuberculosis DNA. Sensitivities of these tests are ~95% in smear-positive, AFB-positive specimens and ~48–53% in smear-negative specimens; specificity remains >95% but sensitivity is 40–77% (AJRCCM 155:1497, 1997; MMWR 58:7, 2009). Note that MTD is more sensitive and specific. **Xpert MTB/RIF** is a rapid test (2 hrs.) for MTBc in sputum samples which also detects RIF resistance with specificity of 99.2% and sensitivity of 72.5% in smear negative patients (NEJM 363:1005, 2010). Can be effectively used in low resource settings (Lancet 377:1495, 2011). Current antibody-based and ELISA-based rapid tests for MTBc are less accurate than microscopy + culture (LnID 11:736, 2011). MTD is not recommended by WHO because they are less accurate.

* See end of section for options regarding concomitant use of protease inhibitors & **RIF** or **RFB**.

NOTE: All dosage recommendations are for adults (unless otherwise indicated) & assume normal renal function.

TABLE 12 (3)

CAUSATIVE AGENT/DISEASE	MODIFYING CIRCUMSTANCES	SUGGESTED REGIMENS		COMMENTS
		PRIMARY	ALTERNATIVE	
BACTERIAL INFECTIONS/Latent TB treatment *(continued)*				
For more details, see USPHS recommendations [AnM 137 No. 5 (Suppl. Part 2), 2002; CID 37-1686, 2003; NEJM 350:2060, 2004; JAMA 293:2776, 2005].	INH+ & RIF-resistant organisms likely	Efficacy of all regimens unproven. **PZA** 25-30 mg/kg/day max. of 2 gm/day + **ETB** 15-25 mg/kg/day po x 12 mos.	**PZA** 25 mg/kg/day to max. of 2 gm/day + **ETB** 15-25 mg/kg/day + **CIP** 750 mg q12h OR **oflox** 400 mg q12h OR **levo** 500 mg/day, all po, x 6-12 mos.	If ETB used in dose over 15 mg/kg/day, monitor pt for retro-bulbar neuritis. (Visual acuity & red/green color test: ≥10% loss considered significant.) **Consultation recommended.**

Treatment, active tuberculosis

[In developing countries, 10–20% of pts who are HIV + & have active TBc are bacteremic (AIDS 13: 2193, 1999). Overlapping TB (especially MDR TB) and HIV remains a major problem in developing countries (JAMA 300:423, 2008; EID 15:256, 2008). Patients who have dx of TB during first 3 months of ART are 3.25 times more likely to die than those without TB (CID 48:829, 2009).

Isolation essential *(See Table 11A, page 115).* Older observations on infectivity of susceptible & resistant MTBc before & after rx (Am Rev Resp Dis 85:511, 1962) may not be applicable to MDR MTBc or the HIV+ individual. Extended isolation may be appropriate. [MMWR 54(RR-17), 2005]

General references on therapeutic options: CID 40 (Suppl. 1): S1, 2005; JID 196 (Suppl. 1):S35, 2007; CMR 24:351, 2011; JID 204:817, 2011; JID 205 (Suppl 2):S141, 2012; CID 50:1288, 2010; The Medical Letter 10 (116):29, 2012; 2012 DHHS Guidelines on ART in Adults and Adolescents: http://www.aidsinfo.nih.gov/ContentFiles/AdultandAdolescentGL.pdf (p. J12).

General principles TBc therapy in pts co-infected with HIV (See 2012 DHHS Guidelines cited under general references):
- Rx of TBc in pts with HIV infection should follow same principles as for persons without HIV.
- Presence of active TBc requires immediate initiation of rx. All HIV-infected pts with active TB should receive ART.
- In antiretroviral-naïve pts, delay of ART for 4–8 wks after initiation of TBc rx permits better definition of causes of adverse reactions & paradoxical reactions, but most recent data shows that initiation of ART with TB rx significantly improves survival despite risk of IRIS (paradoxical reactions). [NEJM 362:697, 2010].

Specific recommendations on timing of ART:
- In pts with CD4 < 50, start ART within 2 wks of starting TB treatment.
- In pts with CD4 > 50 and clinical disease of major severity, start ART within 2-4 wks after starting TB treatment.
- In pts with CD4 > 50 but without severe clinical disease, ART can be delayed beyond 2-4 wks of starting TB treatment, but not beyond 8-12 wks.
- All HIV-infected pregnant women with active TB should receive ART as early as feasible.
- In HIV-infected pts with documented MDR-TB or XDR-TB, start ART within 2-4 wks of confirmation of TB drug resistance & initiation of 2nd-line TB therapy.

- Directly observed therapy strongly recommended for HIV/TB co-infected.
- Rifampin/rifabutin-based regimens should be given at least 3x weekly in pts with CD4 <100/mm³. Rifabutin is preferred rifamycin for pts on PIs.
- Rifapentine is not recommended in HIV-infected pts unless in the context of a clinical trial.
- Despite drug interactions, a rifamycin should be included in pts receiving ART, with dosage adjustment as necessary.
- Paradoxical reaction should be treated with continuation of rx for TBc & HIV, along with use of NSAIDs.
- In severe cases of paradoxical reaction, some suggest use of high-dose prednisone (www.aidsinfo.gov). However, adjunctive prednisone of no benefit in HIV+ patients with CD4 counts >200 (JID 191:856, 2005) or in patients with TBc pleurisy. [JID 190:869, 2004].

Multiresistant (MDR) TBc: *defined as resistant to at least 2 drugs including INH and RIF [JID 196 (Suppl. 1):S86, 2007; AIM 149:123, 2008]* For reviews of therapy of MDR TB see JAC 54:593, 2004; Med Lett 2:83, 2004; For reviews of therapy see MMWR 56:250, 2007; NEJM 359:359, 2008; CID 50 (Suppl. 3): S195, 2010; NEJM 363:1050, 2010; The Medical Letter 10 (116):29, 2012.

Extensively Drug-Resistant TB
(XDR-TB): defined as resistant to INH & RIF plus any FQ and at least one of 3 second-line drugs: capreomycin, kanamycin or amikacin (MMWR 56:250, 2007; CID 45:338, 2007; JID 198:1577, 2008; Lancet ID 9:19, 2009).

NOTE: All dosage recommendations are for adults (unless otherwise indicated) & assume normal renal function.

TABLE 12 (4)

BACTERIAL INFECTIONS/Treatment, active tuberculosis (continued)

NOTES:

1. Clinical & microbiologic response same as in HIV-neg patient.

2. Post-treatment long-term suppression not necessary for drug-susceptible strains.

3. Short course (6 mos) therapy, including 2x weekly DOT regimens in HIV+ pts effective. However, because of **possibility of developing resistance to rifampin in pts with low CD4 cell counts who receive weekly or biweekly doses of rifabutin.** It is recommended that such pts receive daily (or at least 3x-weekly) doses of RFB for initiation & continuation phase rx of TBc.

INITIAL PHASE[a] — SEE COMMENTS FOR DOSAGE

Regimen[1,2]	Drugs	Interval/Doses (min. duration)[b]
1	INH RIF** PZA ETB	7 d/wk x 56 doses (8 wk) or 5 d/wk x 40 doses (8 wk)[c]
2	INH RIF** PZA ETB	7 d/wk x 14 doses (2 wk), then 2x/wk x 12 doses (6 wk) or 5 d/wk x 10 doses (2 wk)[c] then 2x/wk x 12 doses (6 wk)
3	INH RIF** PZA ETB	3x/wk x 24 doses (8 wk)
4	INH RIF**	7 d/wk x 56 doses (8 wk) or 5 d/wk x 40 doses (8 wk)[c]

CONTINUATION PHASE OF THERAPY (in vitro susceptibility known)[b]

Regimen	Drugs	Interval/Doses (min. duration)[a,b]	Range of Total Doses (min. duration)[b]
1a	INH/RIF	7 d/wk x 126 doses (18 wk) or 5 d/wk x 90 doses (18 wk)[c]	182-130 (26 wk)
1b	INH/RIF	2x/wk x 36 doses (18 wk)	92-76 (26 wk)[e]
2a	INH/RIF	2x/wk x 36 doses (18 wk)	62-58 (26 wk)[e]
3a	INH/RIF	3x/wk x 54 doses (18 wk)	78 (26 wk)
4a	INH/RIF	7 d/wk x 217 doses (31 wk) or 5 d/wk x 155 doses (31 wk)[c]	273-195 (39 wk)
4b	INH/RIF	2x/wk x 62 doses (31 wk)	118-102 (39 wk)

COMMENTS — Dose in mg/kg (max. daily dose)

Regimen*	INH	RIF**	PZA	ETB	SM	RFB**
Daily:						
Child	10-20 (300)	10-20 (600)	15-30 (2000)	15-25 (1600)	20-40 (1000)	10-20 (300)
Adult	5 (300)	5 (600)	15-30 (2000)	15-25 (1600)	15 (1000)	5 (300)
2x/wk (DOT):						
Child	20-40 (900)	10-20 (600)	50-70 (4000)	50 (4000)	20-30 (1500)	10-20 (300)
Adult	15 (900)	10 (600)	50-70 (4000)	50 (4000)	25-30 (1500)	5 (300)
3x/wk (DOT):						
Child	20-40 (900)	10-20 (600)	50-70 (3000)	25-30 (2000)	25-30 (1500)	NA
Adult	15 (900)	10 (600)	50-70 (3000)	25-30 (2000)	25-30 (1500)	NA

Second-line anti-TB agents can be dosed as follows to facilitate DOT:

Cycloserine 500-750 mg po q24h (5x/wk)

Ethionamide 500-750 mg po q24h(3-5x/wk)

Kanamycin or capreomycin 15 mg/kg IM/IV q24h(3-5x/wk)

CIP 750 mg po q24h (5x/wk)

Ofloxacin 600-800 mg po q24h (5x/wk)

Levofloxacin 750 mg po q24h (5x/wk)

For reviews of therapy see MMWR 56:250, 2007; NEJM 359:359, 2008; CID 50 (Suppl. 3): S195, 2010

* Footnotes are on page 136.

** See end of Section regarding concomitant use of protease inhibitors & **RIF** or **RFB**.

NOTE: All dosage recommendations are for adults (unless otherwise indicated) & assume normal renal function.

TABLE 12 (5)

BACTERIAL INFECTIONS/Treatment, active tuberculosis *(continued)* Review of therapy for MDR TB. *JAC 54:593, 2004; Med Lett 2:83, 2004.*

MODIFYING CIRCUMSTANCES	SUGGESTED REGIMENS	DUR. OF TREATMENT (MO.)	SPECIFIC COMMENTS	COMMENTS
INH (± SM) resistance	**RIF, PZA, ETB** (an **FQ** may strengthen the regimen for pts with extensive disease). Emergence of FQ resistance a concern (*Ln ID 3:432, 2003; AAC 49:3178, 2005*)	6	In Brit. Medical Research Council trials, 6 mos regimens have yielded ≥95% success rates despite resistance to INH if 4 drugs were used throughout. RIF + ETB or SM was used throughout. Add'l studies suggested results were best if PZA also used throughout 6 mos. FQs not employed in BMRC studies, but may strengthen regimen for pts with extensive disease. INH should be stopped in cases of INH resistance [see *MMWR 52(RR-11):1, 2003 for add'l discussion*].	**NOTE:** FQ resistance may be seen in pts previously treated with FQ. WHO recommends using Moxifloxacin (if MIC ≤2) if resistant to earlier generation FQs (*AAC 54:4765, 2010*). Linezolid has excellent in vitro activity, including MDR strains.
Resistance to INH & RIF (± SM). (Expert consultation strongly advised)	**FQ, PZA, ETB, IA**, ± alternative agent[1]	18–24	In such cases, extended rx is needed to ↓ the risk of relapses. In cases with extensive disease, the use of an additional agent (alternative agents) may be prudent to ↓ the risk of failure & additional acquired drug resistance. Resectional therapy may be appropriate.	
Resistance to INH, RIF (± SM), & ETB or PZA (Expert consultation strongly advised)	**FQ** (**ETB** or **PZA** if active), **IA**, & 2 alternative agents[1]	24	Use the first-line agents to which there is susceptibility. Add 2 or more alternative agents in case of extensive disease. Surgery should be considered. Survival ↑ in pts receiving active FQ & surgical intervention (*AJRCCM 169:1103, 2004*).	
Resistance to RIF	**INH, ETB, FQ** supplemented with **PZA** for the first 2 mos. (an IA may be included for the first 2–3 mos. for pts with extensive disease).	12–18	Daily & 3x/wk regimens of INH, PZA, & SM given for 9 mos. were effective in a BMRC trial. However, extended use of an IA may not be feasible. It is not known if ETB would be as effective as SM in these regimens. An all-oral regimen x 12–18 mos. should be effective. But for more extensive disease &/or to shorten duration (e.g., 12 mos.), an IA may be added in the initial 2 mos. of rx.	
INH & RIF plus any FQ and at least one of 3 second-line drugs: capreomycin, kanamycin or amikacin	See comments	18–24	Therapy requires administration of 4-6 drugs to which infecting organism is susceptible, including multiple second-line drugs (*MMWR 56:250, 2007; CID 45:338, 2007*). Increased mortality in HIV+ patients. Successful culture conversion correlates with initial susceptibility to FQs and kanamycin (*CID 46:42, 2008*).	

NOTE: All dosage recommendations are for adults (unless otherwise indicated) & assume normal renal function.

TABLE 12 (6)

BACTERIAL INFECTIONS (continued)

	INITIAL & CONTINUATION THERAPY			ALT. REGIMEN	COMMENTS
Concomitant protease inhibitor (PI) therapy requires dose modification	INH 300 mg + RFB (see below for dose) + ETB 15 mg/kg q24h x 2 mos.; then INH + RFB x 4 mos. (up to 7 mos.)			INH + SM + PZA + ETB x 2 mos.; then INH + SM + PZA 2–3x/wk for 7 mos. May be prolonged to 12 mos. in pts with delayed response. May be used with any PI regimen.	Rifamycins induce cytochrome CYP450 enzymes (RIF > rifapentine > RFB) & reduce serum levels of concomitantly administered PIs. Conversely, PIs (ritonavir > amprenavir > indinavir = nelfinavir > saquinavir) inhibit CYP450 & cause ↑ in serum levels of RIF & RFB. If dose of RFB is not reduced, toxicity ↑. RFB/PI combinations are therapeutically effective. Based on new data, MMWR now recommends that RIF can be used for rx of active TB in pts on regimens containing efavirenz or ritonavir (CMR 24:351, 2011). **RIF should not be administered to pts on ritonavir + saquinavir because drug-induced hepatitis with marked transaminase elevations has been observed in healthy volunteers receiving this regimen** (www.fda.gov). RFB can also be used with efavirenz or ritonavir but dose should be ↑ to 450–600 mg/day with efavirenz &, ↓ to 150 2 or 3x/wk with ritonavir. (CID 41:1343, 2005) No dose modification of RFB with saquinavir (softgel) as single agent. RFB has no effect on nelfinavir levels at nelfinavir dose of 1250 mg po q12h. Monitor plasma levels of RFB when given with Lopinavir/ritonavir (CID 49:1305, 2009). Therapy for TB seems to increase stavudine toxicity (CID 48:1617, 2009). ART regimens containing efavirenz less compromised by concomitant RIF than nevirapine (CID 48:1752, 2009). RIF preferred rifamycin with efavirenz-based ART regimen (CMR 24:351, 2011).
	PI Regimen	**RFB Dose**	**PI Dose**		
	Nelfinavir, indinavir or amprenavir	150 mg q24h or 300 mg intermittently	Nelfinavir 1250 mg q12h Indinavir—consider ↑ to 1000 mg q8h. Amprenavir 1200 mg q12h.		
	Saquinavir	300 mg q24h or intermittently	No change		
	Ritonavir	150 mg 2x/wk	No change		
	Lopinavir/ritonavir	150 mg 2x/wk	No change		

FOOTNOTES: (in order of preference):

1 See page 132.

2 When DOT is used, drugs may be given 5 days/wk & the necessary number of doses adjusted accordingly. Although there are no studies that compare 5 with 7 daily doses, extensive experience indicates this would be an effective practice.

3 Patients with cavitation on initial chest x-ray & positive cultures at completion of 2 mos of rx should receive a 7-month (31 wk; either 217 doses [daily] or 62 doses [2x/wk] continuation phase.

4 5-days a wk regimen is always given by DOT.

5 Not recommended for HIV-infected pts with CD4 cell counts <100 cells/µl.

6 Options 4a & 4b should be considered only when options 1–3 cannot be given.

7 Alternative agents = ethionamide, cycloserine, p-aminosalicylic acid, clarithromycin, AM/CL, linezolid.

8 Modified from MMWR 52(RR-11):1, 2003. See also IDCP 11:329, 2002.

NOTE: All dosage recommendations are for adults (unless otherwise indicated) & assume normal renal function.

TABLE 12 (7)

CAUSATIVE AGENT/DISEASE	MODIFYING CIRCUMSTANCES	SUGGESTED REGIMENS		COMMENTS
		PRIMARY	ALTERNATIVE	
BACTERIAL INFECTIONS *(continued)*				
Mycobacterium avium-intracellulare complex (MAC or MAI) (CID 42:1756, 2006; AJRCCM 175:367, 2007).	**Primary prophylaxis:** Pt's CD4 count <50–100/mm³ NOTE: Prophylaxis in pts with sustained ↑ in CD4 cells of ≥100/mm³ on ART (AnIM 133:493, 2000; NEJM 342:1085, 2000)	**Azithro** 1200 mg po weekly OR **Clarithro** 500 mg po q12h	**RFB** 300 mg po q24h OR **Azithro** 1200 mg po weekly + RIF 300 mg po q24h	RFB reduces MAC infection rate by 55% (no survival benefit) (CID 26:611, 1998). Azithro by 68% (30% survival benefit); azithro by 59% (68% survival benefit) (CID 335:392, 1996). Azithro + RFB more effective than either alone but not as well tolerated (NEJM 335:392, 1996). Many drug-drug interactions, see Table 16A. RFB ↑ metabolism of ZDV with 32% ↓ in AUC. Clarithro ↑ blood levels of non-sedating antihistamines with attendant risk of arrhythmias. Drug-resistant MAI disease seen in 29–58% of pts in whom disease develops while taking clarithro prophylaxis & in 11% of those on azithro but has not been observed with RFB prophylaxis (J Inf 38:6, 1999). Clarithro resistance more likely to be seen in pts with extremely low CD4 counts at initiation (CID 27:807, 1998). Need to be sure no active M. tbc; RFB used for prophylaxis may promote selection of rifampin-resistant M. tbc. (NEJM 335:384 & 428, 1996).
	Treatment: Either presumptive dx or after positive culture of blood, bone marrow, or other usually sterile body fluids, e.g., liver. (CID 42:1756, 2006)	[**Clarithro** 500 mg* po q12h or **azithro** 600 mg po q24h] + **ETB** 15–25 mg/kg/day +/– **RFB** 300 mg po q24h * **Higher doses of clari (1000 mg q12h) may be associated with ↑ mortality** (CID 29:125, 1999)	[Clarithro or azithro + ETB +/– RFB + one or more of: **CIP** 750 mg po q12h **Oflox** 400 mg po q12h **Amikacin** 7.5–15 mg/kg IV q24h In pts receiving protease inhibitors can use [Clarithro 500 mg q12h (or azithro 600 mg po q24h) + ETB 15–25 mg/kg/day] if the pt has not had previous prophylaxis with a neomacrolide (Johns Hopkins AIDS Report 9:2, 1997). Moxifloxacin and gatifloxacin active in vitro and in vivo (AAC 51:4071, 2007).	Median time to neg blood culture: clarithro + ETB 4.4 wks vs. azithro + ETB >16 wks. At 16 wks, clearance of bacteremia seen in 37.5% of azithro- & 85.7% of clarithro-treated pts (CID 27:1278, 1998). More recent study suggests similar clearance rates for azithro (46%) vs. clarithro (56%) at 24 wks when combined with ETB (CID 31:1245, 2000). Azithro 250 mg q24h not effective but azithro 600 mg po q24h as effective as 1200 q24h & yields fewer adverse effects (AAC 43:2869, 1999). Addition of RFB to clarithro + ETB ↓ emergence of resistance to clari, ↓ relapse rate, & improves survival (CID 37:1234, 2003). Data on clofazimine difficult to assess. Earlier study suggested adding CLO of no value (CID 25:621, 1997). More recent study suggests it may be as effective as RFB in 3 drug regimens containing clari & ETB (CID 29:125, 1999) although it may not be as effective as RFB at preventing clari resistance (CID 28:136, 1999). Thus, pending more data, we still do not recommend CLO for MAI in HIV+ pts. Drug toxicity: With clarithro, 23% pts had to stop drug 2° to dose-limiting adverse reaction (AnIM 121:905, 1994). Combo of clarithro, ETB & RFB led to uveitis & pseudojaundice (NEJM 330:438, 1994); result is reduction in max. dose of RFB to 300 mg. Treatment failure rate is high. Reasons: drug toxicity, development of drug resistance, & inadequate serum levels. Serum levels of clarithro ↓ in pts also given RIF or RFB (JID 171: 747, 1995). If pt not responding to initial regimen after 2–4 wks, add 1 or more drugs. Several anecdotal reports of pts not responding to usual primary regimen who gained weight & became afebrile with dexamethasone 2–4 mg/day po (AAC 38: 2215, 1994; CID 26:682, 1999).
	Chronic post-treatment suppression—secondary prophylaxis	**Always necessary** (**Clarithro** or **azithro**) + **ETB** (lower dose than prophylaxis) (Dosage above)	**Clarithro** or **azithro** or **RFB** (dosage above)	Recurrences almost universal without chronic suppression. In pts with good response to ART (robust CD4 ↑) it is possible to discontinue chronic suppression (JID 178:1446, 1998; NEJM 340:1301, 1999) (see Table 11B).

NOTE: All dosage recommendations are for adults (unless otherwise indicated) & assume normal renal function.

TABLE 12 (8)

CAUSATIVE AGENT/DISEASE	MODIFYING CIRCUMSTANCES	SUGGESTED REGIMENS		COMMENTS
		PRIMARY	ALTERNATIVE	
BACTERIAL INFECTIONS (continued)				
Mycobacterium celatum	Treatment; optimal regimen not defined	Easily confused with M. xenopi & MAC. May be susceptible to clarithro, FQ (Clin Microbiol Inf 3:582, 1997). Suggested treatment like MAI but may be resistant to RIF (J Inf 38:157, 1999). Most reported cases received 3 or 4 drugs—usually **clari** + **ETB** + **CIP** ± **RFB** (EID 9:399, 2003).		Isolated from blood of patients with AIDS (CID 24:140 & 144, 1997). Usually resistant to INH, PZA, capreomycin (JCM 33:137, 1995; CID 24:140, 1997).
Mycobacterium chelonae, ssp. abscessus, chelonae	Treatment. Surgery is important adjunct to therapy (CID 24:1147, 1997). For role of surgery in M. abscessus pulmonary disease, see CID 52:565, 2011	**Clarithro** 500 mg po q12h x 6 mos. (AnIM 119:482, 1993; CID 24:1147, 1997; EJCMID 19:43, 2000). **Azithro** may also be effective. For serious, disseminated infections add **amikacin** + **IMP or cefoxitin** for first 2–6 wks (CMR 15:716, 2002; ARJCCM 175:367, 2007) **OR** add **Moxi** or **Levo** (CID 49:1365, 2009).		M. abscessus susceptible in vitro to clarithro (95%), clofazimine, cefmetazole, RFB, FQ, amikacin (70%), cefoxitin (70%), IMP, azithro, cipro, doxycycline, minocycline, tigecycline (CID42:1756, 2006; JIC 5:46, 2009). Clarithro-resistant strains described (JCM 39:2745, 2001). M. chelonae susceptible in vitro to clarithro, tobramycin (100%), amikacin (80%), IMP (60%), moxifloxacin, ciprofloxacin, minocycline, doxycycline, linezolid (94%) (AJRCCM 156:S1, 1997; AAC 46:3283, 2002; CID 42:1756, 2006). Tigecycline highly active in vitro (AAC 52:4184, 2008).
Mycobacterium fortuitum	Treatment	Optimal regimen not defined. **Amikacin** + **cefoxitin** + **probenecid** 2–6 wks, then po TMP/SMX, or doxycycline 2–6 mos (J Inf Dis 152:50, 1985). Surgical excision of infected areas. Nail salon-acquired skin infections in immunocompetent pts have responded to 4–6 mos. of minocycline or doxycycline or CIP (CID 38:38, 2004).		Resistant to all standard anti-TBc drugs. Sensitive in vitro to cefoxitin, doxycycline, minocycline, imipenem, amikacin, TMP/SMX, CIP, oflox. Some strains resistant to RFB, azithro, variably susceptible to clarithro, linezolid, tigecycline (JAC 39:567, 1997; CMR 15:716, 2007; AAC 52:4184, 2008). Usually responds to 4–6 mos. of oral rx with 2 drugs to which it is susceptible (AJRCCM 156:S1, 1997; AAC 46:3283, 2002; CMR 15:716, 2007). For M. fortuitum pulmonary disease: treat with at least 2 agents active in vitro until sputum cultures negative for 12 mos (ARJCCM 175:367, 2007).
Mycobacterium genavense	Treatment	Regimens used include ≥2 drugs: **ETB**, **RIF**, **RFB**, **clofazimine**, **clarithro**. In animal model, clarithro & RFB (& to lesser extent amikacin & ETB) shown effective in reducing bacterial counts; CIP not effective (JAC 42:483, 1998).		Clinical: CD4 <50. Symptoms of fever, weight loss, diarrhea. Lab: growth in BACTEC vials slow (mean 42 days). Subcultures grow only on Middlebrook 7H11 agar containing 2 mcg/mL mycobactin J—growth still insufficient for in vitro sensitivity testing (Lancet 340:76, 1992; AnIM 117:586, 1992). Survival ↑ from 81 to 263 days in pts rx for at least 1 month with ≥2 drugs (Arch Int Med 155:400, 1995).
Mycobacterium gordonae	Treatment	Regimen(s) not defined, but consider **RIF** + **ETB** + **kanamycin** or **CIP** (J Inf 38:157, 1999) or **linezolid** (ARJCCM 75:367, 2007).		In vitro: sensitive to ETB, RIF, amikacin, CIP, clarithro, linezolid (AAC 47:1736, 2003). Resistant to INH (CID 14:1229, 1992). Surgical excision.
Mycobacterium haemophilum	Treatment	Regimen(s) not defined. In animal model, **clarithro** + **RFB** effective (AAC 39:2316, 1995). Combo of **CIP** + **RFB** + **clari** reported effective but clinical experience limited (CMR 9:435, 1996; CID 52:488, 2011). Surgical debridement may be nec. (CID 26:505, 1998).		Clinical: Ulcerating skin lesions, synovitis, osteomyelitis, pneumonia, cervicofacial lymphadenitis in children (CID 39:1569, 2005). Associated with permanent eyebrow makeup (CID 52:488, 2011). Lab: Requires supplemented media to isolate. Sensitive in vitro to: CIP, cycloserine, RFB, moxifloxacin. Over 50% resistant to: INH, RIF, ETB, PZA (AnIM 120:118, 1994).

NOTE: All dosage recommendations are for adults (unless otherwise indicated) & assume normal renal function.

TABLE 12 (9)

CAUSATIVE AGENT/DISEASE	MODIFYING CIRCUMSTANCES	SUGGESTED REGIMENS		COMMENTS
		PRIMARY	ALTERNATIVE	
BACTERIAL INFECTIONS (continued)				
Mycobacterium kansasii	Treatment	**RIF** (600 mg po q24h) + **ETB** (25 mg/kg x 2 mos, then 15 mg/kg/day) + **INH** (300 mg po q24h) for 15-18 mos (AnIM 120:945, 1994)	If RIF-resistant, use **INH** 900 mg po q24h + **pyridoxine** 50 mg po q24h + **ETB** 25—15 mg/kg/day po x until culture negative x 12-15 mos. 1 gm po q8h. Rx until culture negative x 12-15 mos. **Clari + ETB + RIF** also effective in small study (CID 37: 1178, 2003).	If organism resistant to (≥1 mcg/mL) INH, discontinue (70-85% isolates resistant). **All isolates resistant to PZA.** Rifapentine, azithro, ETB effective alone or in combo in athymic mice (AAC 42:417, 2001). Highly susceptible to linezolid in vitro (AAC 47:1736, 2003) and to clari and moxifloxacin (AAC 55:950, 2005). If HIV+ pt taking protease inhibitor, substitute either clarithro (500 mg bid) or RFB (150 mg/d) for RIF (AJRCCM 156:S1, 1997). Because of variable susceptibility to INH, some substitute clarithro 500-750 mg q24h for INH. Resistance to clarithro reported (DMID 31:369, 1998), but most strains susceptible to clarithro as well as moxifloxacin (JAC 55:950, 2005) & levofloxacin (AAC 48:4562, 2004). Prog related to level of immunosuppression (CID 37:584, 2003).
Mycobacterium marinum	Treatment	(RIF + ETB) or doxycycline or minocycline or TMP/SMX or clarithro for at least 12 wks (Arch Int Med 147:817, 1986; AJRCCM 156:S1, 1997; Eur J Clin Micro ID 25:609, 2006). Surgical excision.		Sensitive in vitro to clarithro, reported effective in 2 pts (1 HIV+) who failed on other regimens) (CID 18:664, 1994). Resistant to INH & PZA (AJRCCM 156:S1, 1997). Susceptible in vitro to linezolid, CIP, moxifloxacin also show moderate in vitro activity (AAC 46:1114, 2002).
Mycobacterium scrofulaceum	Treatment	Although regimens not defined, clarithro + clofazimine with or without ETB. Surgical excision.		In vitro resistant to INH, RIF, ETB, PZA, amikacin, CIP (CID 20:549, 1995).
Mycobacterium simiae	Treatment	Regimen(s) not defined. If true infection, start 4 drugs as for disseminated MAI. Anecdotal reports of response in pts on ART who received clarithro, ETB & CIP (J Inf 41:143, 2000).		
Mycobacterium ulcerans (Buruli ulcer)	Treatment	WHO recommends RIF + SM for 8 weeks (Ln ID 6:288, 2006; Lancet 367:1849, 2006; AAC 51:645, 2007). RIF + SM resulted in 47% cure rate (AAC 51:4029, 2007). **RIF + CIP** recommended as alternative by WHO (CMN 31:119, 2009). Recent small studies document similar effectiveness of 4 wks RIF + SM followed by RIF + Clari (Lancet 375:664, 2010) and a regimen of 8 wks RIF + Clari (No relapse in 30 pts) (CID 52:94, 2011).		Susceptible in vitro to RIF, strep, CLO, clarithro, CIP, ofloxx, amikacin, moxifloxacin, linezolid (AAC 42:2070, 1998; JAC 45:231, 2000; AAC 46:3193, 2002; AAC 50:1921, 2006). Monotherapy with RIF selects resistant mutants in mice (AAC 47:1228, 2003). RIF + moxi; RIF + clarithro; moxi + clarithro similar to RIF + SM in mice (AAC 51:3737, 2007).
Mycobacterium xenopi	Treatment (NOTE: Recent study suggests no need to treat in most pts with HIV) (CID 37:1250, 2003)	Regimen(s) not defined (CID 24:226 & 233, 1997). INH + RIF + ETB suggested but no clinical trials available (Clin Chest Med 17:697, 1996). Not always susceptible to these agents in vitro (CID 25:206, 1997). Macrolide + (RIF or RFB) + ETB ± SM also recommended (AJRCCM 156:S1, 1997) or RIF + INH ± ETB (Resp Med 97:439, 2003), but recent study suggests no need to treat in most pts with HIV (CID 37:1250, 2003).		In vitro, sensitive to clarithro (ACC 36:2841, 1992) & RFB (JAC 39:567, 1997) & many standard antimycobacterial drugs. Clarithro-containing regimens more effective than RIF/INH/ETB in mice (AAC 45:3229, 2001). FQs, linezolid also active.

NOTE: All dosage recommendations are for adults (unless otherwise indicated) & assume normal renal function.

TABLE 12 (10)

CAUSATIVE AGENT/DISEASE	MODIFYING CIRCUMSTANCES	SUGGESTED REGIMENS		COMMENTS
		PRIMARY	ALTERNATIVE	
BACTERIAL INFECTIONS *(continued)*				
Mycobacterium leprae (leprosy) Refs: *LnID 11:464, 2011 (Overview); IDCP 18:235, 2010 (Mgmt); CID 44:1096, 2007 (Classification).*	Therapy of HIV may "uncover" underlying leprosy in previously infected patients. Frequency of this phenomenon not presently known. There are 2 sets of therapeutic recommendations here: one from USA (National Hansen's Disease Programs [NHDP], Baton Rouge, LA) and one from WHO. Both are based on expert recommendations and neither has been subjected to controlled clinical trial (M. P. Joyce & D. Scollard, Conns Current Therapy 2004; MP Joyce, Immigration Medicine, in press 2006; J Am Acad Dermatol 51:417, 2004).			
Type of Disease	NHDP Regimen	WHO Regimen	Comments	
Paucibacillary Forms: (Intermediate, Tuberculoid, Borderline tuberculoid)	**(Dapsone** 100 mg/day + **RIF** 600 mg po/day for 12 months	**(Dapsone** 100 mg/day (unsupervised) + **RIF** 600 mg 1x/mo (supervised) for 6 mo	Side effects overall 0.4%. In patients receiving protease inhibitors, authors suggest substituting RFB for RIF, but no clinical data exist to backup this recommendation.	
Single lesion paucibacillary	Treat as paucibacillary leprosy for 12 months	Single dose **ROM** therapy: **(RIF** 600 mg + **Oflox** 400 mg + **Mino** 100 mg) *(Ln 353:655, 1999).*		
Multibacillary forms: Borderline Borderline-lepromatous Lepromatous See Comment for erythema nodosum leprosum Rev: *Lancet 363:1209, 2004*	**(Dapsone** 100 mg/day + **CLO** 50 mg/day + **RIF** 600 mg/day) for 24 mo **Alternative regimen:** **(Dapsone** 100 mg/day + **RIF** 600 mg/day + **Minocycline** 100 mg/day) for 24 mo if **CLO** is refused or unavailable	**(Dapsone** 100 mg/day + **CLO** 50 mg/day (both unsupervised) + **(RIF** 600 mg + **CLO** 300 mg once monthly (supervised)). Continue regimen for 12 months.	Side effects overall ≤ 1%. For **erythema nodosum leprosum:** prednisone 60–80 mg/day or thalidomide 100–400 mg/day *(BMJ 44:775, 1988; AJM 108:487, 2000).* Thalidomide available in US at 1-800-4-CELGENE. Altho thalidomide effective, WHO no longer rec because of potential toxicity *(JID 193:1743, 2006)* however the majority of leprosy experts feel thalidomide remains drug of choice for ENL under strict supervision. CLO (Clofazimine) available from NHDP under IND protocol; contact at 1-800-642-2477. **Ethionamide** (250 mg q24h) or **prothionamide** (375 mg q24h) may be subbed for CLO. Etanercept effective in one case refractory to standard therapy *(CID 52:e133, 2011).* Oflox 400 mg po q24h, bactericidal and effective clinically with 4 log₁ in organisms in small trials *(AAC 38:662, 1994; AAC 38:61, 1994).* Clarithro also rapidly bactericidal *(AAC 38:515, 1994; Ln 345:4, 1995).* Regimens incorporating clarithro, minocycline, RIF, moxifloxacin, and/or oflox also show promise *(AAC 44:2919, 2000; AAC 50:1558, 2006).* High relapse rate in pts treated with q24h RIF + oflox for 4 wk *(AAC 41:1953, 1997).* Resistance to dapsone, RIF & oflox reported *(Ln 349:103, 1997).* Dapsone monotherapy has been abandoned due to emergence of resistance *(CID 52:e127, 2011),* but older patients previously treated with dapsone monotherapy may remain on lifelong maintenance therapy. Dapsone (or acedapsone⁽?⁾) effective for prophylaxis in one study *(J Inf 41:137, 2000).* **Moxifloxacin** highly active in vitro and produces rapid clinical response *(AAC 52:3113, 2008).*	
Neisseria gonorrhoeae (gonococcus) Ref: *MMWR 59(RR-12):1, 2010.* Do not use oral cephalosporins because of resistance *(MMWR 61:591, 2012)*	Gonorrhea, urethritis, conjunctivitis, proctitis; mucopurulent cervicitis; epididymoorchitis (sexually acquired); for disseminated disease, see *Sanford Guide to Antimicrobial Therapy*	**[Ceftriaxone** (250 mg IM x 1) **PLUS**—if **Chlamydia** infection not ruled out: **(Azithro** 1 gm po x 1) or **(doxy** 100 mg po x2/day x 7 d)] **Note:** Due to increasing resistance, **fluoroquinolones** no longer recommended *(MMWR 56:332, 2007).*	**Treat for both GC & C. trachomatis. Screen for syphilis.** Other alternatives for GC: Spectinomycin^NUS 2 gm IM x 1 Other single-dose cephalosporins: ceftizoxime 500 mg IM, cefotaxime 500 mg IM, cefotetan 1 gm IM, (cefoxitin 2 gm IM + probenecid 1 gm po). Azithro 1 gm po x 1 effective for chlamydia but need 2 gm po x 1 for GC; not recommended for GC due to GI side effects & expense. For severe Penicillin allergy: Azithromycin 2 gm po x 1.	

NOTE: All dosage recommendations are for adults (unless otherwise indicated) & assume normal renal function.

TABLE 12 (11)

CAUSATIVE AGENT/DISEASE	MODIFYING CIRCUMSTANCES	SUGGESTED REGIMENS		COMMENTS
		PRIMARY	ALTERNATIVE	
BACTERIAL INFECTIONS (continued)				
Nocardiosis N. asteroides complex, N. farcinica, & N. brasiliensis; numerous other species, varying in susceptibilities; susceptibility testing recommended for all clinically significant isolates (Clin Micro Rev 19:259, 2006). Reference labs: R.J. Wallace (903) 877-7680 or CDC (404) 639-3158				
Cutaneous & lymphocutaneous (sporotrichoid)	N. asteroides N. brasiliensis	**TMP/SMX:** 5–10 mg/kg/day TMP & 25–50 mg/kg/day SMX in 2–4 div. doses/day, po or IV	**Sulfisoxazole** 2 gm po q6h or **minocycline** 100–200 mg po q12h	**TMP/SMX** (or other sulfonamide) is drug of choice **Linezolid** 600 mg po bid for 1.5-12 mos an alternative for TMP/SMX intolerance or salvage: 9/11 non-HIV (5 disseminated, 4 CNS, 1 lung, 1 skin) cured with 1 possible relapse, 1 clinical failure; high adverse events rate with myelosuppression or peripheral neuropathy in 7 (Am Pharmacother 41:1694, 2007).
Pulmonary, disseminated, brain abscess Ref: Medicine 88:250, 2009	N. brasiliensis	**Triple drug regimen for empirical therapy of serious infection pending results of susceptibility testing: TMP/SMX** initially: 15 mg/kg/day of TMP & 75 mg/kg/day of SMX IV or po, div. in 2–4 doses + **IMP** 500 mg IV q6h + **Amikacin** 7.5 mg/kg IV q12h. After 3-4 wks, **TMP/SMX as** 10 mg/kg/day TMP in 2–4 doses po. Do serum level. (See Comment.)	**Ceftriaxone** 2 gm once or twice daily + **amikacin** 7.5 mg/kg IV + **TMP/SMX** (as primary regimen) q12h x 3-4 wks & then po regimen PO options: TMP/SMX, Minocycline, AM-CL	**Ceftriaxone** & other cephalosporins, minocycline, amoxicillin/clavulanate may also be active, depending on the species (Clin Micro Rev 19:259, 2006) Optimal therapy not established. Duration of therapy based on clinical response but generally 3 mos. for immunocompetent host & 6 mos. for immunocompromised (e.g. organ transplant, malignancy, chronic lung disease, diabetes, ETOH use, steroid rx, & AIDS).
Pelvic inflammatory disease (PID), salpingitis, tuboovarian abscess Etiology polymicrobic: gono-coccus, C. trachomatis, bac-teroides, enterobacteriaceae, streptococci, mycoplasma. Ref: MMWR 55(RR-11), 2006	Outpatient (limit to pts with temp <38 °C, WBC <11,000/mm³, minimal evidence of peritonitis, active bowel sounds & able to tolerate oral nourishment See www.cdc.gov/std/treatment	**Outpatient rx: (ceftriaxone** 250 mg IM x 1 + **doxy** 100 mg po q12h)± **metro** 500 mg po q12h) OR **(cefoxitin** 2 gm IM with **probenecid** 1 gm po–both as single dose)± (**doxy** 100 mg po bid with **metro** 500 mg po bid). Treat for 14 days.	**Inpatient regimens:** [**Cefotetan** 2 gm IV q12h or **cefoxitin** 2 gm IV q6h) + (**doxy** 100 mg IV/po q12h)] ------ [**Clinda** 900 mg IV q8h] + **gentamicin** 2 mg/kg loading dose, then 1.5 mg/kg q8h or single daily dosing), then **doxy** 100 mg po q12h x 14 d	Alternative parenteral regimen: **AM-SB** 3 gm IV q6h + **doxy** 100 mg IV/po q12h FQs not recommended due to increasing resistance (MMWR 56:332, 2007). **Remember: Evaluate & treat sex partner.**

NOTE: All dosage recommendations are for adults (unless otherwise indicated) & assume normal renal function.

TABLE 12 (12)

CAUSATIVE AGENT/DISEASE	MODIFYING CIRCUMSTANCES	SUGGESTED REGIMENS		COMMENTS
		PRIMARY	ALTERNATIVE	
BACTERIAL INFECTIONS (continued)				
Prostatitis—Review: AJM 106:327, 1999				
Acute	N. gonorrhoeae, C. trachomatis	(**ceftriaxone** 250 mg IM x 1, then **doxy** 100 mg po q12h x 10 d)		In AIDS pts, prostate may be focus of Cryptococcus neoformans. **FQs** no longer recommended for gonococcal infections.
≤35 years of age		**FQ: CIP-ER** 500 mg po 1x/day or **CIP** 400 mg IV bid or **levo** 750 mg IV/po 1x/day. See comment.	**TMP/SMX-DS** 1 tab po bid x 3-4 wks. See comment.	Treat as acute urinary infection, 14 d (not single dose regimen). **Some authorities recommend 3–4 wk therapy.** If uncertain, do urine NAAT for C. trachomatis & N. gonorrhoeae.
>35 years of age	Enterobacteriaceae (coliforms)			
Chronic bacterial	Enterobacteriaceae (80%), enterococci (15%), P. aeruginosa	**FQ (CIP** 500 mg po q12h x 4 wks, OR **levo** 750 mg po q24h x 4 wks)—see Comment	**TMP/SMX-DS** 1 tab po q12h x 1–3 mos.	With rx failures, consider infected prostatic calculi. FDA-approved dose of levo is 500 mg, editors prefer higher 750 mg dose.
Chronic prostatitis/chronic pain syndrome (NIH classification, JAMA 282: 236, 1999)	The most common prostatitis syndrome, etiology is unknown; molecular probe data suggest infectious etiology (Clin Micro Rev 11:604, 1998)	**α-adrenergic blocking agents are controversial** (AnIM 133:367, 2000).		Definition of chronic prostatitis: pt. has sx of prostatitis, cells in prostatic secretions, but routine cultures negative. Chlamydia, ureaplasma suspected. Definition of chronic pain: pt. has sx of prostatitis but negative cultures & no cells in prostatic secretions. Review: JAC 46:157, 2000. In randomized double-blind study, CIP and alpha blocker were of no benefit (AnIM 141:581 & 639, 2004).
Rhodococcus equi (Corynebacterium equi)	Pulmonary infection	(**Erythro** (0.5 gm IV q6h) or **IMP** (0.5 gm IV q6h)) + **RIF** 600 mg po q24h for at least 2 wks	**CIP** 750 mg po q12h ≥2 wks. CIP-resistant strains SE Asia (CID 27:370, 1998)	¾ pts have positive blood cultures. Prolonged oral suppressive therapy (macrolide + RIF) indicated since relapses are frequent. Vancomycin active in vitro & rx success in pt who relapsed after erythro + RIF (IDCP 7:480, 1998). Linezolid active in vitro.
Salmonella sp., bacteremia Fever in 71-91% Bloody stool 34%	**Bacteremia, AIDS patient** For typhoid fever, see Sanford Guide to Antimicrobial Therapy	**1st episode:** CIP 400 mg IV bid until afebrile, then 500-750 mg po bid x 7-14 d if CD4 ≥200 or 2-6 wks if CD4 <200	**Pt who relapses:** Assuming in vitro susceptibility, long term suppression with **CIP** 500 mg po bid or **TMP/SMX-DS** tab po bid	**Primary therapy: fluid & electrolyte replacement.** Note: Long duration of primary therapy is for an AIDS pt. Immunocompetent host initial therapy is 5-7 days. **Azithro** 1 gm po x 1, then 500 mg po q24h x 7-14 days.
Shigellosis Fever in 58% Bloody stool 51%	Treatment Acute	CIP 750 mg po once daily x 3 days	**Azithro** 500 mg po once daily x3 days	Treatment shortens illness & prevents spread of disease. If bacteremic, treat for 14 days.
	Recurrent in AIDS pts	CIP 500 mg po q12h (perhaps indefinitely)	750 mg po q24h indefinitely	
Staphylococcus aureus: methicillin/oxacillin susceptible (MSSA)	Treatment: Folliculitis/furunculosis/ subcutaneous abscess in "skin poppers"	Dicloxacillin 500 mg po q6h for 7-14 days. **Need hot packs and I&D**	Mupirocin (Bactroban) apply to affected area q8h for 5 days (if infection not disseminated)	**Hot packs & drainage are equal in effectiveness to antimicrobic therapy.**
Culture furuncles if possible	Bacteremia &/or endocarditis	**PRSP (nafcillin** or **oxacillin** 2 gm IV q4h x 4 wks)	**Cefazolin** 2 gm IV q8h x 4-6 wks)	Vancomycin should be used only in patients intolerant of beta-lactams or with severe allergy.

NOTE: All dosage recommendations are for adults (unless otherwise indicated) & assume normal renal function.

TABLE 12 (13)

CAUSATIVE AGENT/DISEASE	MODIFYING CIRCUMSTANCES	SUGGESTED REGIMENS		COMMENTS
		PRIMARY	ALTERNATIVE	
BACTERIAL INFECTIONS *(continued)*				
Staphylococcus aureus: Methicillin resistant (MRSA) *(see Sanford Guide to Antimicrobial Therapy for details)*				
			If CA-MRSA:	
Possible community-acquired MRSA Incidence of CA-MRSA SSTIs ↑ in HIV+ patients *(CID 50:979, 2010)*	Furuncles (boils) and carbuncles **EMPIRIC THERAPY**	Hot packs, **incision & drainage** (with culture and sensitivities if possible), most important part of therapy **TMP/SMX-DS** 1 tab po q12h *(AAC 55:5430, 2011)*	**Doxy** or **minocycline** 100 mg po bid x 7-10 days or **Clindamycin** 300 mg po tid x 7-10 days	Simple abscesses usually respond to incision and drainage alone.
Could be MSSA or MRSA; (usually MRSA)	Ventilator (hospital)-associated pneumonia. Document with quantitative cultures of lower airway.	**EMPIRIC THERAPY: Vanco** 30-60 mg/kg/day in 2-3 divided doses (monitor trough serum concentrations) or **linezolid** 600 mg IV/po q12h	**SPECIFIC THERAPY for:** 1) **MSSA: nafcillin** or **oxacillin** 2 gm IV q4h. Simple abscesses usually respond to incision and drainage alone. 2) **MRSA: vanco** 1 gm IV q12h or **linezolid** 600 mg IV/po q12h	Target trough serum concentrations of Vancomycin to achieve 15-20 mcg/mL. Check CBC at least once weekly while taking linezolid.
Could be MSSA or MRSA (usually MRSA)	Bacteremia and possible endocarditis	**EMPIRIC THERAPY: vanco** 30-60 mg/kg/day in 2-3 divided doses to achieve trough serum concentration of 15-20 mcg/mL. Do not combine vanco with nafcillin or oxacillin.	1) **MSSA: nafcillin** or **oxacillin** 2 gm IV q4h or **vanco alone** if pen allergic or intolerant 2) **MRSA: vanco** or **dapto** 6 mg/kg IV q24h	
Streptococcus pneumoniae **Pneumonia—culture & in vitro susceptibility results available.** Assumes no meningitis.	Susceptible or intermediate resistance to pen G in vitro	**Ceftriaxone** 1 gm IV q24h OR **Penicillin G** 2 million units IV q4h OR **Amox** 1 gm po tid OR **Ampicillin:** 2 gm IV q6h	**Erythro** 500 mg IV q6h OR **Azithro** 500 mg IV/day OR **Clindamycin** 600 mg IV q8h	Prevalence of high-level pen G-resistance decreased as in vitro "cut-off" for resistance was increased. Macrolide resistance still a problem. U.S. isolates may or may not be clindamycin-susceptible. β-lactam/β-lactamase inhibitor combinations are not effective vs. resistant strains, as mechanism of resistance is target change, not β-lactamase production.
	High-level resistance to pen G in vitro	**Levo** 750 mg IV q24h or **Moxi** 400 mg IV q24h **If oral therapy:** **Levo** 750 mg po q24h or **Moxi** 400 mg po q24h	**Vancomycin** 1 gm IV q12h	In animal model of post-influenza pneumococcal pneumonia, combination of ceftriaxone and azithro highly efficacious *(JID 199:311, 2009).*

NOTE: All dosage recommendations are for adults (unless otherwise indicated) & assume normal renal function.

TABLE 12 (14)

CAUSATIVE AGENT/DISEASE	MODIFYING CIRCUMSTANCES	SUGGESTED REGIMENS		COMMENTS
		PRIMARY	ALTERNATIVE	
BACTERIAL INFECTIONS/Streptococcus pneumoniae (continued)				
Meningitis—culture & in vitro susceptibility results available	Susceptible to pen G in vitro	**(Aq. pen G** 4 million units IV q4h OR **ceftriaxone** 2 gm IV q12h OR **ampicillin** 2 gm IV q4h) + **dexamethasone—**See Comment	For severe penicillin allergy (IgE-mediated anaphylaxis, angioneurotic edema): **Vanco** 15 mg/kg IV q8h (target trough 15-20 mcg/mL)	**Adjunctive dexamethasone, 1st dose 15-20 min. prior to, or concomitant with, 1st dose of antibiotic.** Dose 0.4 mg/kg IV q12h x 2 d. (1) In children, steroids do **not** reduce CSF penetration of vanco. (2) In adults, unclear if steroids ↓ vanco CSF penetration. **Vanco dosage:** Due to low/erratic CSF penetration, recommended dosage in children of 15 mg/kg q6h is double usual dose; in adults a max. dose of 2-3 gm of vanco/day suggested, i.e. 15 mg/kg IV q8h.
	High-level resistance to pen G in vitro	(**Vancomycin** 500-750 mg IV q6 (see Comment) + **ceftriaxone** 2 gm IV q12h) + **dexamethasone** —See Comment	**Meropenem** may work— 2 gm IV q8h. Severe penicillin allergy: **Vanco** 15 mg/kg IV q8h + **RIF** 600 mg po/IV q24h	If MIC to ceftriaxone >2 mcg/mL, add Rifampin 600 mg po/IV once daily. Vancomycin target trough levels: 15-20 mcg/mL.
Syphilis (Treponema pallidum) Recommendations are for pts with normal CD4. T-lymphocyte counts in AIDS pts, clinical course may be atypical. Higher doses/longer periods of rx may be required— MMWR 59 (RR-12) 26, 2010.	Primary (chancre), secondary (rash, mucositis, lymphadenopathy), & early latent (<1 year)	**Benzathine penicillin G (Bicillin L-A)** 2.4 mUnits IM x 1. Dose for children: 50,000 units/kg IM up to max. of 2.4 mUnits.	**Doxycycline** 100 mg po q12h x 14 d or **Tetracycline** 500 mg po q6h x 14 d or **Ceftriaxone** 1 gm IM/IV q24h x 8-10 d For failures of initial rx, re-treat with benzathine penicillin G 2.4 mUnits IM weekly x 3.	For all stages, penicillin best drug. If penicillin allergy, skin test if available or desensitize & treat with penicillin. Erythro not acceptable alternative agent; use doxycycline if unable to desensitize. Limited data on efficacy of alternative regimens. Need baseline titered VDRL (RPR) & repeat titered serology at 3, 6, 12, 24 mos. Repeat rx if (1) persistent clinical signs, (2) titer of VDRL increases 4-fold or fails to decrease 4-fold after 3-6 mos. Even with recommended rx, serologic relapse frequent. **CSF examination indicated if neurologic signs or symptoms are present.**
Azithro resistance in California, Ireland, & elsewhere (CID 44:S130, 2007; AAC 54:583, 2010)	Late latent: >1 year duration & neg. CSF exam	**Benzathine penicillin G (Bicillin L-A)** 2.4 mUnits IM q wkly x 3 wks	**Doxycycline** 100 mg po q12h; 28 d or **Tetracycline** 500 mg po q6h x 28 d	**Azithromycin resistance in California, Ireland, & elsewhere. Do not use. In pregnancy or MSM (MMWR 59 (RR-12); 26, 2010.) Azithro:** single 2 gm po dose effective for early syphilis in pts with severe pen allergy.
	Neurosyphilis or optic neuritis	**Pen G** 3-4 mUnits IV q4h IV x 10-14 d	**Procaine pen G** 2.4 mUnits IM q24h + **probenecid** 0.5 gm po q6h) both x 10-14 d—See Comment	**Ceftriaxone** 2 gm IV q24h (IV or IM) x 14 d: 23% failure rate reported (AJM 93:481, 1992). If pen. penicillin allergy: either desensitize to penicillin or obtain infectious diseases consultation. **Serologic criteria for response to rx: 4-fold or greater ↓ in VDRL titer over 6-12 mos.** [CID 28(Suppl.1):S21, 1999]

NOTE: All dosage recommendations are for adults (unless otherwise indicated) & assume normal renal function.

TABLE 12 (15)

FIGURE 15 Activity of Selected Antifungal Drugs Against Pathogenic Fungi

Microorganism	Antifungal[1-4]					
	Fluconazole[5]	Itraconazole	Voriconazole	Posaconazole	Echinocandin	Polyenes (Amphotericin)
Candida albicans	+++	+++	+++	+++	+++	+++
Candida dubliniensis	+++	+++	+++	+++	+++	+++
Candida glabrata	±	±	+	++	+++	+++
Candida tropicalis	+++	+++	+++	+++	+++	+++
Candida parapsilosis[6]	+++	+++	+++	+++	++ (higher MIC)	+++
Candida krusei	-	+	+++	++	+++	++
Candida guilliermondii	+++	+++	+++	+++	++ (higher MIC)	++
Candida lusitaniae	+	+	++	++	+	±
Cryptococcus neoformans	+++	+	+++	+++	-	+++
Aspergillus fumigatus[7]	-	++	+++	+++	++	++
Aspergillus flavus	-	++	+++	+++	++	++ (higher MIC)
Aspergillus terreus	-	++	+++	+++	++	-
Fusarium sp.	-	±	++	++	-	++ (lipid formulations)
Scedosporium apiospermum (*Pseudallescheria boydii*)	-	-	+++	+++	-	-
Scedosporium prolificans[8]	-	-	±	±	-	-
Trichosporon spp.	±	-	++	++	-	+
Zygomycetes (e.g., *Absidia, Mucor, Rhizopus*)	-	-	-	+++	-	+++ (lipid formulations)
Dematiaceous molds[9] (e.g., *Alternaria, Bipolaris, Curvularia, Exophiala*)	-	++	+++	+++	+	+
Dimorphic Fungi[10]						
Blastomyces dermatitidis	++	+++	++	++		+++
Coccidioides immitis/posadasi	+++	+++	++	++		+++
Histoplasma capsulatum	+	+++	++	+		+++
Sporothrix schenckii		++				+

- = no activity; ± = possibly active; + = active; ++ = Active (less active clinically); +++ = Active, 1st line therapy (usually active clinically)

1. Minimum inhibitory concentration values do not always predict clinical outcome.
2. Echinocandins, voriconazole, posaconazole and polyenes have poor urine penetration.
3. During severe immune suppression, success requires immune reconstitution.
4. Flucytosine has activity against *Candida* sp. *Cryptococcus* sp., and dematiaceous molds, but is primarily used in combination therapy.
5. For candidal infections, patients with prior triazole therapy have higher likelihood of triazole resistance.
6. Successful treatment of infections from *Candida parapsilosis* requires removal of foreign body or intravascular device.
7. Lipid formulations of amphotericin may have greater activity against *A. fumigatus* and *A. flavus* (+++).
8. *Scedosporium prolificans* is poorly susceptible to single agents and may require combination therapy (e.g., addition of terbinafine).
9. Infections from zygomycetes, some *Aspergillus* spp. and dematiaceous molds often require surgical debridement.
10. For infections (other than cocci meningitis) caused by dimorphic fungi, itraconazole is first-line therapy and active clinically (+++).

NOTE: All dosage recommendations are for adults (unless otherwise indicated) & assume normal renal function.

TABLE 12 (16)

TYPE OF INFECTION/ORGANISM/ SITE OF INFECTION	SUGGESTED REGIMENS		COMMENTS
	PRIMARY	ALTERNATIVE	
FUNGAL INFECTIONS			
Aspergillosis **Invasive, pulmonary (IPA) or extrapulmonary:** Post-chemotherapy in neutropenic pts (PMN <500 per mm³) but may also present with neutrophil recovery. **Typical x-ray/CT lung lesions** (halo sign, cavitation, or macronodules (*CID 44:373, 2007*). Initiation of antifungal Rx based on halo signs on CT associated with better response to Rx & improved. Immunologic assay of galactomannan in serum has a sensitivity of 78% (95% CI of 61-89%) and specificity of 81% (95% CI, 72-88%) for invasive aspergillosis in immunocompromised patients (*Cochrane Database Syst Rev 2008:CD007394*). Sensitivity better with forming the test on BAL fluid (*Curr Opin Pulm Med 17:167, 2011; Chest 138:817, 2010*). Beta-D-glucan has similar sensitivity and specificity for invasive fungal infection (*J Clin Micro 50:7, 2012*), but lacks specificity for specific pathogens because beta-D-glucan is a major cell wall component of several fungal pathogens, including Pneumocystis jiroveci (PJ): sensitivity of 96% for PJ pneumonia (versus 80% for other invasive fungal infection) makes it excellent screening tool for PJ pneumonia (*J Clin Micro 50:7, 2012*).	**Primary therapy** (See *CID 46:327, 2008; MMWR 58 (RR-1):1, 2009*): **Voriconazole** 6 mg/kg IV q12h on day 1; then either (4 mg/kg/day IV q12h) or (200 mg po q12h for body weight ≥40 Kg, but 100 mg po q12h for body weight <40 kg) **Alternative therapies:** **Liposomal ampho B** (L-AMB) 3-5 mg/kg/day IV **OR** **Ampho B lipid complex** (ABLC) 5 mg/kg/d IV **OR** **Caspofungin** 70 mg/day then 50 mg/day thereafter **OR** **Micafungin** ᴺᴬᴵ 100-150 mg/day **OR** **Posaconazole** ᴺᴬᴵ 200 mg qid, then 400 mg bid after stabilization of disease		**Voriconazole** more effective than ampho B. Vori, both a substrate and an inhibitor of CYP2C19, CYP2C9, and CYP3A4, has potential for deleterious drug interactions (e.g. with protease inhibitors) and careful review of concomitant medications is mandatory. In patients with ClCr < 50 mL/min, the drug should be given orally, not IV, since the intravenous vehicle (SBECD-sulfobutylether-B cyclodextrin) may accumulate. **Ampho B: not recommended except as a lipid formulation, either L-AMB or ABLC.** 10 mg/kg and 3 mg/kg doses of L-AMB are equally efficacious with greater toxicity of higher dose (*CID 2007; 44:1289-97*). One comparative trial found much greater toxicity with ABLC than with L-AMB: 34.6% vs. 9.4% adverse events and 21.2% vs. 2.8% nephrotoxicity. Vori preferred as primary therapy. **Caspo:** ~50% response rate in IPA. Licensed for salvage therapy. Efavirenz, nelfinavir, nevirapine, phenytoin, rifampin, dexamethasone, and carbamazepine, may reduce caspofungin concentrations. **Micafungin:** Favorable responses to micafungin as a single agent in 6/12 patients in primary therapy group and 9/22 in the salvage therapy group of an open-label, non-comparative trial (*J Infect 53: 337, 2006*). Outcomes no better with combination therapy. No significant drug interactions identified for micafungin. **Posaconazole:** In a prospective controlled trial of IPA immunocompromised pts refractory or intolerant to other agents, 42% of 107 pts receiving posa vs. 26% controls (p.006) were successful (*CID 44:2, 2007*). Posa inhibits CYP3A with potential for drug-drug interactions. Do not use for treatment of azole-non-responders as there is a potential for cross-resistance. **Combo therapy:** Uncertain role and not routinely recommended for primary therapy; consider for treatment of refractory disease, although benefit unproven. A typical combo regimen would be an echinocandin in combination with either an azole or a lipid formulation of ampho B.
Blastomycosis (*IDSA Treatment Guidelines:* *Clin Infect Dis 46:1801, 2008*).	(Liposomal Ampho B 3-5 mg/kg/day or **Ampho B** 0.7 mg/kg/day) x 1-2 weeks or until clinical response, then **Itra** 200 mg tid x 3 days, followed by **Itra** 200 mg bid.	Mild or moderate disease: **Itra** 200 200 mg tid x 3 days, then 200 mg bid or **Fluconazole** 400-800 mg/day	**Itraconazole** is drug of choice. In HIV+ pts, because of potential for drug/drug interactions, fluconazole 400-800 mg/day may be used instead of itraconazole. Duration of therapy: 6-12 months in non-HIV but consider chronic suppressive therapy for patients not on ART and with low CD4 count.

TABLE 12 (17)

TYPE OF INFECTION/ORGANISM/ SITE OF INFECTION	SUGGESTED REGIMENS		COMMENTS
	PRIMARY	SECONDARY	

FUNGAL INFECTIONS *(continued)*

Candidiasis: Oral, esophageal, or vaginal candidiasis is a major manifestation of advanced HIV & represents one of the most common AIDS-defining diagnoses. Candida is also a common cause of nosocomial bloodstream infection. A decrease in C. albicans & increase in non-albicans species show ↓ susceptibility among candida species to antifungal agents (esp. fluconazole). These changes have predominantly affected immunocompromised pts in environments where antifungal prophylaxis (esp. fluconazole) is widely used. *See Figure 14, page 91. See CID 48:503, 2009 for updated IDSA Guidelines and MMWR 58 (RR-1):1, 2009 for recommendations in HIV.*

Bloodstream: non-neutropenic patient Remove all intravascular catheters if possible; replace catheters at a new site (not over a wire). Higher mortality associated with delay in therapy *(CID 43:25, 2006).*	**Caspofungin** 70 mg IV loading dose, then 50 mg IV daily –35 mg for moderate hepatic insufficiency **OR** **Micafungin** 100 mg IV daily **OR** **Anidulafungin** 200 mg IV loading dose then 100 mg IV daily	**Ampho B** 0.7 mg/kg IV daily **OR** **Lipid-based ampho** 3-5 mg/kg IV daily **OR** **Voriconazole:** 400 mg twice daily for 2 doses then 200 mg bid **OR** **Fluconazole** 800 mg (12 mg/kg) loading dose; then 400 mg once daily	**Echinocandin** (Caspofungin, Micafungin, Anidulafungin) preferred for initial therapy based on analysis of data compiled from 7 clinical trials of invasive candidiasis found that treatment with an echinocandin compared to polyenes or an azole was associated with better survival and is considered the first-line drug of choice by some *(Clin Infect Dis 54:1110, 2012).* An echinocandin should be used for treatment of C. glabrata unless susceptibility to Fluconazole or Voriconazole has been confirmed. **Fluconazole** 400 mg IV no longer preferred for initial therapy: may be used as step-down therapy from an echinocandin for stable patients with Candida albicans or other azole-susceptible species. **Voriconazole** with little advantage over fluconazole (more drug-drug interactions) except for oral step-down therapy of Candida krusei or voriconazole-susceptible Candida glabrata. Recommended **duration of therapy** is 14 days after last positive blood culture. Duration of systemic therapy should be extended to 4-6 weeks for eye involvement. **Funduscopic examination** within first week of therapy to exclude ophthalmic involvement. Intraocular injections of ampho B may be required for endophthalmitis; echinocandins have poor penetration into the eye.
Bloodstream: neutropenic patient Remove all intravascular catheters if possible; replace catheters at a new site (not over a wire).	**Caspofungin** 70 mg IV loading dose, then 50 mg IV daily –35 mg for moderate hepatic insufficiency **OR** **Micafungin** 100 mg IV daily **OR** **Anidulafungin** 200 mg IV loading dose then 100 mg IV daily **OR** **Lipid-based ampho** 3-5 mg/kg IV daily	**Fluconazole** 800 mg (12 mg/kg) loading dose; then 400 mg daily **OR** Lipid-based Ampho B 3-5 mg/kg daily	Fluconazole no longer preferred initial therapy *(see Comments above).* Duration of therapy in absence of metastatic complications is for 2 weeks after last positive blood culture, resolution of signs, and resolution of neutropenia. Perform funduscopic examination after recovery of white count as signs of ophthalmic involvement may not be seen during neutropenia. *See comments above for recommendations concerning choice of specific agents.*

NOTE: All dosage recommendations are for adults (unless otherwise indicated) & assume normal renal function.

TABLE 12 (18)

TYPE OF INFECTION/ORGANISM/ SITE OF INFECTION	SUGGESTED REGIMENS		COMMENTS
	PRIMARY	SECONDARY	
FUNGAL INFECTIONS/Candidiasis *(continued)*			
Oropharyngeal candidiasis	**Fluconazole** 100-200 mg daily for 7-14 days	Itraconazole solution 200 mg daily **OR** Posaconazole suspension 400 mg bid for 3 days then 400 mg daily **OR** **Voriconazole** 200 mg bid	ART recommended to prevent recurrent disease. Suppressive therapy not necessary, especially with ART and CD4 > 200/mm³; but if required to prevent recurrences Fluconazole 200 mg once daily recommended. Itra, posa, or vori for 28 days for fluconazole-refractory disease. IV echinocandin also an option.
Candida esophagitis	**Fluconazole** 200-400 mg daily	An **azole** (itraconazole solution 200 mg daily, or posaconazole suspension 400 mg bid for 3 days then 400 mg daily or voriconazole 200 mg bid) **OR** An **echinocandin** (capsofungin 50 mg IV daily, or micafungin 150 mg IV daily, or anidulafungin 200 mg IV loading dose then 100 mg IV daily) **OR** **Ampho B** (0.3-0.7 mg/kg daily	Dysphagia or odynophagia predictive of esophageal candidiasis. **Duration of therapy** 14-21 days. IV echinocandin or ampho B for patients unable to tolerate oral therapy. For fluconazole refractory disease, itra (80% will respond), posa, vori, an echinocandin, or ampho B. Echinocandins associated with higher relapse rate than fluconazole. ART recommended. Suppressive therapy with fluconazole 200 mg once daily for recurrent infections. Suppressive therapy may be discontinued once CD4 > 200/mm³.
Vulvovaginitis, Candida Common among healthy young females & unrelated to HIV status.	Topical **azoles** (clotrimazole, buto, tico, mico, tercon) x 3-7 days; OR Topical **nystatin** 100,000 units/day as vaginal tablet x 14 days; OR Oral **flu** 150 mg x 1 dose		For recurrent disease 10-14 days of topical azole or oral fluconazole 150 mg, then fluc 150 mg weekly for 6 mo
Coccidioidomycosis *(See IDSA guidelines: CID 41:1217, 2005)*	**Primary prophylaxis:** Not recommended.		
Pulmonary & extrapulmonary (not meningitis). Usually seen in pts with <250 CD4/mm³. Usually involves generalized lymphadenopathy, skin nodules or ulcers, peritonitis, liver abnormalities, & bone/joint involvement.	**Acute phase (milder disease):** • **Flu** 400-800 mg po q24h; or **itra** 200 mg po q12h **Acute phase (diffuse pulmonary disease):** • **Ampho B** 0.5-1 mg/kg IV q24h, continue until clinical improvement, usually 500-1000 mg total dose **Disseminated disease:** • **Ampho B** 0.5-1 mg/kg IV q24h, continue until clinical improvement, usually 500-1000 mg total dose • **Flu** 400 mg/d (up to 2g/d recommended by some) • **Itra** up to 800 mg/d as 200 mg doses **Suppression:** • **Flu** 400 mg/d (preferred) • **Itra** 200 mg po q12h	Acute phase (diffuse pulmonary or disseminated disease): Some specialists add azole to ampho B therapy.	Lung infection in approx. 80% of pts. Despite rx with ampho B ± subsequent po azole, mortality reported as 60%. Posaconazole 400 mg twice daily per day effective in 11/15 patients with refractory non-meningeal cocci (*Chest 132:952, 2007*); 400 mg per day effective in 17/20 patients with chronic or disseminated without meningeal disease (*CID 45:562, 2007*). In those patients with CD4+ cell counts > 250 µL, dc of suppression may be considered if there is clinical evidence of control of infection.

NOTE: All dosage recommendations are for adults (unless otherwise indicated) & assume normal renal function.

TABLE 12 (19)

TYPE OF INFECTION/ORGANISM/ SITE OF INFECTION	SUGGESTED REGIMENS		COMMENTS
	PRIMARY	SECONDARY	

FUNGAL INFECTIONS/Coccidiomycosis *(continued)*

TYPE OF INFECTION/ORGANISM/ SITE OF INFECTION	PRIMARY	SECONDARY	COMMENTS
Meningitis **Occurs in 1/10 to 1/3 of pts with disseminated cocci** CSF demonstrates lymphocytic pleocytosis. CSF glucose <50 mg/day & normal to mildly ↑ protein.	**Treatment: Fluconazole** 400–1000 mg po q24h	IV amphotericin B as for pulmonary + 0.2–0.5 mg intrathecal (intraventricular via reservoir device) 2–3x/wk	Flu effective in up to 80% of cases. Vori successful in high doses (6 mg/kg IV q12h) followed by oral suppression (400 mg po q12h). Itra should not be used for treatment or suppression of meningitis, as it does not penetrate into CSF.
	Suppression: Do not dc for patients with meningitis even with robust response to ART. **Fluconazole** 400 mg/day po as single dose or 200 mg po q12h	**Amphotericin B** 1 mg/kg IV once	Relapses are common in both HIV+ & HIV– pts. Lifelong suppression indicated for patients with meningitis.

Cryptococcosis
IDSA Treatment Guidelines: *Clin Infect Dis 50:291, 2010.*

Cryptococcemia &/or Meningitis *(MMWR 58 (RR-1):1, 2009)*

Treatment *(also see Table 11A)*
↓ in era of ART but still common presenting OI in newly diagnosed AIDS pts. Cryptococcal infection may be manifested by positive blood culture or positive test of serum for cryptococcal antigen (CRAG, >96% sens). CRAG no help in monitoring response to therapy.

With ART, symptoms of acute meningitis may return: immune reconstitution inflammatory syndrome (IRIS). ↑ CSF pressure associated with high mortality; lower with CSF removal.
If frequent LPs not possible, ventriculoperitoneal shunts an option.

In African study, early ART increased mortality (*CID 50:1532, 2010*); similar results in cryptococcal optimal timing (COAT) study.

PRIMARY	SECONDARY	COMMENTS
Primary prophylaxis: Not recommended. *See MMWR 58 (RR-1):1, 2009.*		
Ampho B 0.7 mg/kg IV q24h **+ flucytosine¹** 25 mg/kg po q6h x 2 wks **OR** **Liposomal amphotericin B** 4 mg/kg IV q24h **+ flucytosine¹** 25 mg/kg po q6h x 2 wks **OR** (Ampho B or Liposomal Ampho B) + Fluconazole 800–1200 mg/day	(**Liposomal Ampho B** 4 mg/kg IV **or Ampho B** 0.7 mg/kg IV) x 2 weeks if Flucytosine not tolerated **OR** **Fluconazole** 400–800 mg/day po or IV + **flucytosine** 25 mg/kg po q6h x 4–6 wks (only if Amphotericin-based therapy not tolerated). Note: Fluconazole 400–800 mg/day only for less severe disease and when Ampho B not tolerated.	Outcome of treatment: failure associated with dissemination of infection & high serum antigen titer, indicative of ↑ burden of organisms and lack of 5FC use during inductive Rx, abnormal neurological evaluation & underlying hematological malignancy. Mortality rates still 12% at 3 mos. Early Dx essential for improved outcome *(PLOS Medicine 4:e47, 2007)*. Ampho B + 5FC treatment ↓ crypto CFUs more rapidly than ampho + flu or ampho + 5FC + flu. Ampho B 1 mg/kg/d alone much more rapidly fungical in vivo than flu 400 mg/d *(CID 45:76&81, 2007)*. Ampho B + 5FC and Ampho B + Fluconazole 800–1200 mg/day had similar rates of clearance of crypto from CSF *(CID 54:121, 2012)*; Fluconazole may be an acceptable alternative to 5FC in combo with Ampho B. Monitor 5-FC levels: peak 70–80 mg/L, trough 30–40 mg/L. Higher levels assoc with bone marrow toxicity. No difference in outcome if given IV or po. If normal mental status, >20 cells/mm³ CSF, & CSF CRAG <1:1024, flu alone may be reasonable. Although less well studies, posaconazole or voriconazole may be effective. Survival improved with ART, but IRIS may complicate its use in up to 1/3 or more of treatment courses *(Lancet Infect Dis 10:791, 2010)*; onset may be up to one year after initiation or change in ART. Presentation: aseptic meningitis, high CSF opening pressure, positive CSF CRAG, negative culture; prognosis good. Short course corticosteroids may be beneficial in severe disease.
Consolidation therapy: CSF should be sterile before initiation of consolidation therapy, then **Fluconazole** 400 mg po q24h to complete a 10-wk course, then suppression (see below). **Then** Start ART if possible: generally after 5 weeks of antifungal therapy.		

---

¹ Flucytosine = 5-FC

NOTE: All dosage recommendations are for adults (unless otherwise indicated) & assume normal renal function.

TABLE 12 (20)

TYPE OF INFECTION/ORGANISM/ SITE OF INFECTION	SUGGESTED REGIMENS		COMMENTS
	PRIMARY	SECONDARY	
FUNGAL INFECTIONS: Cryptococcus/Cryptococcosis/Cryptococcemia &/or Meningitis *(continued)*			
Suppression (chronic maintenance therapy). Discontinuation of antifungal Rx can be considered among pts who remain asymptomatic with CD4 ≥ 200 for at least 6 months; completed ≥ 6 months of ART; resolution of signs and symptoms.	Fluconazole 200 mg/day po. If CD4 count rises to >100/mm³ with effective antiretroviral rx and is sustained for 6 mo, suppressive rx can be discontinued. Some might consider performing a lumbar puncture before discontinuation of maintenance rx.	Itraconazole 200 mg po q12h If flu intolerant or failure.	Itraconazole less effective than fluconazole & not recommended because of higher relapse rate (23% vs. 4%). Recurrence rate (95% CI) of 0.4 to 3.9 per 100 patient-years with discontinuation of suppressive therapy in 100 patients on ART with CD4 >100 cells/mm³
Histoplasmosis (IDSA treatment guidelines in *CID 45:807, 2007*)	**Primary prophylaxis:** itraconazole (200 mg daily) for patients with CD4 cell counts <150 cells/mm³ in endemic areas where the incidence of histoplasmosis is ≥10 cases per 100 patient-years.		
In a Colombian study comparing 30 pts with AIDS with 20 pts without HIV infection with disseminated histo, the AIDS pts had ↑ numbers of skin lesions, ↑ sed rate, anemia, leucopenia, fungal isolated from multiple sites, had ↓ response to itra which ↑ with ART to non-AIDS levels. Best diagnostic test is urinary histoplasma antigen (90% sensitivity) (*Curr Opin Infect Dis 21:421, 2008*); MiraVista Diagnostics (1-866-647-2847).	**Severe disseminated:** Acute phase (1-2 wks): • Liposomal ampho B 3 mg/kg/d IV, or • ABLC 5 mg/kg/d IV		Institute ART as early as possible. ART improves outcome and although immune response inflammatory syndrome occurs, it is rare, usually not severe and easily managed. L-AMB less toxic and more effective than ampho B: higher response rate, lower mortality.
	Continuation phase (12 mos): Itra 200 mg po q12h		Itra is the preferred azole; flu less effective, keto less expensive but has more adverse effects; vori and posa anecdotally effective, but too few patients to recommend. All are second-line agents and if any of these instead of itra is used, reasons for doing so should be documented in the medical record.
	Less severe disseminated: Itra 200 mg po twice daily for 12 mos		Blood levels should be documented during the first month of itra Rx.
Risk factors for death: dyspnea, platelet count <100,000/mm³, & LDH >2x upper limit normal.	**Meningitis:** Liposomal ampho B 5 mg/kg IV for 4-6 wks; Itra 200 mg 2-3 times a day for 12 mos.	Fluconazole 800-1200 mg/day for 12 mos	**Itra is a potent CYP3A4 inhibitor: contraindicated drugs include efavirenz, statins, rifamycins, midazolam, triazolam, cisapride, pimozide, quinidine, dofetilide, or levacetylmethadol. Important drug interactions with antiretroviral agents, PIs in particular.**
In 1 study suppression was safely dc after 12 mos. of antifungal rx & 6 mos. of ART with CD4 >150: 0 relapses after 2 yrs follow-up in 32 pts.		Suppression: Itra 200 mg po q24h. Suppressive therapy may be discontinued in pts who have completed 1 yr of therapy, neg. blood cultures, a serum and urinary histo antigen < 2 ng/mL, CD4 > 150 cells/mm³, and who are on ART for ≥ 6 mos	Itraconazole relapse rate is approx 5%: 5% relapse rate; 10-20% relapses with ampho B
	Fluconazole 200 mg daily or Amphotericin B 1 mg/kg IV weekly or biweekly		

NOTE: All dosage recommendations are for adults (unless otherwise indicated) & assume normal renal function.

TABLE 12 (21)

TYPE OF INFECTION/ORGANISM/ SITE OF INFECTION	SUGGESTED REGIMENS		COMMENTS
	PRIMARY	SECONDARY	
FUNGAL INFECTIONS (continued)			
Paracoccidioidomycosis (South American blastomycosis)/*P. brasiliensis* (*Dermatol Clin 26:257, 2008; Expert Rev Anti Infect Ther 6:251, 2008*)	**TMP/SMX** 800/160 mg every bid or tid for 30 days then 400/80 mg indefinitely (24 months or longer) or **Itraconazole** 200 mg daily (indefinitely)	**Ketoconazole** 200–400 mg daily for 6–18 mos. **Ampho B** total dose > 30 mg/kg.	Improvement in >90% pts on Itra or keto[NFDA]. Sulfa: 4–6 gm/day for several weeks, then 500 mg/day for 3–5 yrs also used. (*J Infect 51: 248, 2005*). **TMP/SMX ± ampho B** used successfully in AIDS patients. Low-dose Itra (50–100 mg/day), keto (200–400 mg/day) & sulfadiazine (up to 6 mg/day) showed similar clinical responses in 4–6 mos. in a randomized study (*Cochrane Database Syst Rev. 2006 Apr 19:CD004967, 2006*). **HIV+: TMP/SMX suppressive rx.**
Penicilliosis (*Penicillium marneffei*) Common disseminated fungal infection in AIDS pts in SE Asia (esp. Thailand & Vietnam). Most occur when CD4 <50/mm³	**Ampho B** 0.5–1 mg/kg/day x 2 wks followed by **Itraconazole** 400 mg/day for 10 wks Then **suppressive therapy** 200 mg/day po for HIV-infected pts.	For less sick pts. **Itra** 200 mg po q8h x 3 days, then 200 mg q12h po x 12 wks. then 200 mg po q24h (IV if unable to take po). continue as suppressive therapy for HIV-infected pts.	3rd most common OI in AIDS pts in SE Asia following TB & cryptococcal meningitis. May resemble histoplasmosis or TB. Skin nodules are umbilicated (mimic cryptococcal infection or molluscum contagiosum). In AIDS pts. suppression with Itra effective in **preventing relapses**. One retrospective study of 33 patients on ART and > 6 mos of CD4 > 100 cells/mm³ in whom suppressive therapy was stopped found zero cases of recurrence per 641 person-months (95% confidence interval 0–0.6 cases per person-month) after a median follow-up of 18 months (range 6–45) (*AIDS 21:365, 2007*).
Pneumocystis pneumonia (PCP) Etiology: Pneumocystis jiroveci Beta-D-glucan with a sensitivity of 96% is an excellent screening tool for PjP (*J Clin Micro 50:7, 2012*)	**Not acutely ill**, able to take po meds, PaO₂ >70 mmHg on room air.	**Clinda** (600 mg IV or 300–450 mg po) q6h + **primaquine** 15 mg po 30 mg base po q24h) x 21 d **OR atovaquone suspension** 750 mg po bid with food x 21 d or (Dapsone 100 mg/day + TMP 15 mg/kg/day po in 3 divided doses)	**After 21 days of therapy, then chronic suppression in AIDS pts**
	(TMP/SMX-DS, 2 tabs po q8h x 21 d) OR **(Dapsone** 100 mg po q24h + **TMP** 5 mg/kg po q8h x 21 d)		
	NOTE: Concomitant use of corticosteroids usually reserved for sicker pts with PaO₂ <70		
	Acutely ill, po therapy not possible, PaO₂ < 70 mmHg. Unclear whether anti-HIV therapy should start during or after treatment of PjP (*CID 46:625 & 635, 2008*).	**Clinda** (600 mg IV or 300–450 mg po) q6h + **primaquine** 15 mg po 30 mg base po q24h) x 21 d **OR atovaquone suspension** 750 mg po bid with food x 21 d or (Dapsone 100 mg/day + TMP 15 mg/kg/day po in 3 divided doses)	After 21 days of therapy, then chronic suppression. Clinical failure defined as absence of clinical response after 7 days; then switch to **Clinda + primaquine** or **pentamidine** (*JAIDS 48:63, 2008*) or maybe add **caspofungin** (*Transplant 84:685, 2007*). **Caspofungin** active in animal models: *CID 36:1445, 2003*.
	[Prednisone 15–30 min. before TMP/ SMX—start with 40 mg po q12h x 5 d, then 40 mg po q24h x 5 d, then 20 mg po q24h x 11 d] + **[TMP/SMX** (15–20 mg of TMP component/kg/day) IV div. q6-8h x 21 d].	**[Pentamidine** 300 mg in 6 mL sterile water by aerosol q4 wks) OR **(dapsone** 200 mg po + **pyrimethamine** 75 mg po + **folinic acid** 25 mg po—all once a week); OR **atovaquone** 1500 mg po q24h with food.	
	Can substitute IV prednisolone (reduce dose 25%) for po prednisone		
Primary prophylaxis & post-treatment suppression	**(TMP/SMX-DS**, 1 tab po q24h) or 3x/wk) OR **(dapsone** 100 mg po q24h) OR **TMP/SMX-SS**, 1 tab po q24h). DC when CD4 >200 x 3 mos.		**TMP/SMX-DS** regimen also provides cross-protection vs. toxo & other bacterial infections. Dapsone + pyrimethamine protects vs. toxo.

NOTE: All dosage recommendations are for adults (unless otherwise indicated) & assume normal renal function.

TABLE 12 (22)

TYPE OF INFECTION/ORGANISM/ SITE OF INFECTION	SUGGESTED REGIMENS		COMMENTS
	PRIMARY	SECONDARY	
FUNGAL INFECTIONS (continued)			
Sporotrichosis (See IDSA treatment guidelines: CID 45:1255, 2007)			
Cutaneous/Lymphonodular Dissemination is uncommon in immunocompetent pts, but tends to occur in AIDS.	**Itraconazole** 200 mg/day po x 3-6 mos. For non-responders, use itra 200 mg twice daily, or terbinafine 500 mg twice daily, or saturated solution of potassium iodide (SSKI) 5 drops 3x a day, increasing to 40-50 drops 3x a day as tolerated	**Fluconazole** 400-800 mg po q24h. Only in those unable to tolerate other agents.	SSKI side effects: nausea, rash, fever, metallic taste, salivary gland swelling. Duration of itra suppressive therapy is indefinite. Based on experience with other fungal infections, it seems reasonable to discontinue suppressive therapy in those treated with itra for at least 1 year and whose CD4+ cell counts have remained > 200 cells/mm³ for >1 year.
Osteoarticular	**Itraconazole** 200 mg po q12h for 12 mos. (IV if unable to take po)	**Lipid-based ampho B** 3-5 mg/kg/d or ampho B 0.7-1.0 mg/kg/d for initial therapy; then after a favorable response **itra** 200 mg q12h to complete 12 mos of therapy.	Determine itra serum concentrations at two weeks of therapy to document adequate levels.
Pulmonary	**For more severe disease: Lipid-based ampho B** 3-5 mg/kg/d OR **Ampho B** 0.7-1.0 mg/kg/d for initial therapy then after a favorable response **itra** 200 mg q12h to complete 12 mos of therapy	**For less severe disease itra** 200 mg q12h for 12 mos. (IV if unable to take po).	Determine itra serum concentrations at two weeks of therapy to document adequate levels. Surgery is recommended for resection of localized disease.
Disseminated	**Lipid-based ampho B** 3-5 mg/kg/d for initial therapy then after a favorable response **itra** 200 mg q12h to complete 12 mos of therapy		Determine itra serum concentrations at two weeks of therapy.
Meningeal	**Lipid-based ampho B** 5 mg/kg/d for 4-6 weeks then **itra** 200 mg q12h to complete 12 mos of therapy		Determine itra serum concentrations at two weeks of therapy.

NOTE: All dosage recommendations are for adults (unless otherwise indicated) & assume normal renal function.

TABLE 12 (23)

TYPE OF INFECTION/ORGANISM/ SITE OF INFECTION	SUGGESTED REGIMENS		COMMENTS
	PRIMARY	SECONDARY	
FUNGAL INFECTIONS/Sporotrichosis (continued)			
Suppressive therapy	Itra 200 mg once daily		Suppressive therapy is recommended for AIDS and other immunocompromised pts to prevent relapse of meningeal and disseminated disease and, because of propensity for dissemination in AIDS, should be considered for cutaneous, osteoarticular, and pulmonary disease. Duration of suppression is not defined, but may be lifelong in meningeal disease. In disseminated and localized disease discontinuation of itra may be reasonable in the patient treated with itra for at least 1 yr and whose CD4 counts are >100 cells/mm³ for ≥1 yr.
Mucormycosis—Rhizopus, Rhizomucor, Absidia, Mucor, Cunninghamella spp. Rhinocerebral, pulmonary, pulmonary, gastrointestinal forms; invasive. Key to successful rx: early dx with symptoms suggestive of sinusitis (or lateral facial pain or numbness): think mucor with palatal ulcers, &/or black eschars, onset unilateral blindness in immunocompromised or diabetic p. Rapidly fatal without rx. Dx by culture of tissue or stain: wide ribbon-like, non-septated with variation in diameter & right angle branching.	**Liposomal Ampho B 5-10 mg/kg/day (optimal dose not defined)**	**Posaconazole** 400 mg po bid with meals (if not taking meals, 200 mg po qid).	Cure dependent on: (1) surgical debridement, (2) rx of hyperglycemia, correction of neutropenia, or reduction in immunosuppression; (3) antifungal rx: liposomal amphotericin longterm or **posaconazole.** Complete or partial response rates of 60-80% in posaconazole salvage protocols (JAC 61, Suppl. 1, i35, 2008). Adjunctive Echinocandin to Liposomal Amphotericin B is promising given safety profile, synergy in murine models, and observational clinical data (Clin Infect Dis 54(S1):S73, 2012)

PARASITIC INFECTIONS. Reference with pediatric dosages: Medical Letter online version: Drugs for Parasitic Infections (Suppl.), 2007

Protozoan—Intestinal			
Blastocystis hominis Need to treat is dubious.	Role as pathogen supported by one controlled rx trial: metro vs. placebo (J Travel Med 10:128, 2003)		Perhaps best viewed as marker of fecal-oral contamination, e.g., if blastocystis present, look harder for Giardia—if history & symptoms suggestive. Ref: J Clin Gastro 44:855, 2010.
Cryptosporidium parvum & C. hominis Ref: CID 39:504, 2004 Treatment unsatisfactory.	Immunocompetent —no HIV: **Nitazoxanide** 500 mg po q12h x 3 days (expensive) Effective ART best therapy	**HIV with immunodeficiency—ART best treatment. Nitazoxanide** is not licensed for immunocompromised pts: no clinical or parasite response compared to placebo.	**Nitazoxanide.** Approved for immunocompetent pts: liquid formulation for rx of children & 500 mg tabs for adults. Ref: CID 40:1173, 2005. In AIDS pts, infection of respiratory and biliary tracts recognized. Post **C. hominis** syndrome: eye/joint pain, headache, dizziness (CID 39:504, 2004).
Cyclospora cayetanensis	Immunocompetent pts: TMP-SMX-DS 1 tab bid x 7-10 days	AIDS pts: TMP/SMX-DS 1 po q6h for up to 3-4 wks.	If sulfa-allergic: **CIP** 500 mg po q12h x 7 d (inconsistent results). Ref: J Clin Gastro 23:218, 2010. Anecdotal success with Nitazoxanide.

NOTE: All dosage recommendations are for adults (unless otherwise indicated) & assume normal renal function.

TABLE 12 (24)

CAUSATIVE AGENT/DISEASE	MODIFYING CIRCUMSTANCES	SUGGESTED REGIMENS		COMMENTS
		PRIMARY	ALTERNATIVE	
PARASITIC INFECTIONS/Protozoan—Intestinal (continued)				
Entamoeba histolytica Refs: *Ln 361:1025, 2003; NEJM 348:1563, 2003*	Asymptomatic cyst passer	**Paromomycin**[NUS] (aminosidine in U.K.) 500 mg po q8h x 7 d **OR iodoquinol** (Yodoxin) 650 mg po q8h x 20 days	**Diloxanide furoate**[NUS] (Furamide) 500 mg po q8h x 10 days (Source: Panorama Compound Pharm, 800-247-9767)	Metronidazole not effective vs. cysts.
	Patient with diarrhea/ dysentery; mild/moderate disease. Oral therapy possible	**Metronidazole** 500-750 mg po q8h x 10 d or **tinidazole** 2 gm po q24h x 3 days, followed by: Either **[iodoquinol** (was diiodohydroxyquin) 650 mg po q8h x 20 d] or **[paromomycin**[NUS] 500 mg po q8h x 7 d] to clear intestinal cysts.	**Ornidazole**[NUS] 500 mg po q12h x 5 days followed by:	Colitis can mimic ulcerative colitis; ameboma can mimic adenocarcinoma of colon. **Dx:** Antigen detection and PCR better than O&P. Watch out for non-pathogenic but morphologically identical *E. dispar* (*CID 29:1117, 1999*). Another alternative **nitazoxanide** 500 mg po bid x 3 days (*Trans R Soc Trop Med & Hyg 101:1025, 2007*).
	Extraintestinal infection, e.g., hepatic abscess	**(Metronidazole** 750 mg IV/po q8h x 10 d **OR tinidazole** 800 mg po q8h x 20 d) followed by **paromomycin** 500 mg po q8h x 7 days **OR iodoquinol** 650 mg po tid x 20 days		**Serology positive with extraintestinal disease.**
Giardia lamblia Ref: *J Infection 56:268, 2008*	Epigastric-ulcer-like symptoms	**Tinidazole** 2 gm po x 1 **OR Nitazoxanide** 500 mg po q12h x 3 days **OR Albendazole** 400 mg po once daily with food x 5 days	**Metronidazole** 250 mg po q8h x 5 days (high frequency of GI side effects). See Comment. Rx if pregnant: **Paromomycin**[NUS] 25-35 mg/kg/day po in 3 divided doses x 5-10 days	**Refractory pts: (Metro** 750 mg po + **quinacrine** 100 mg po)—both 3x/day x 3 wks. (Quinacrine from Panorama Compounding Pharm, Tel 800-247-9767). Ref: *CID 33:22, 2001.* Nitazoxanide Ref: *CID 40:1173, 2005.*
Isosporiasis: **Cystoisospora belli** (formerly *Isospora belli*) (*MMWR 58 (RR-4):1, 2009*)	Immunocompetent:	**TMP/SMX-DS** tab 1 po bid x 7-10 d; if AIDS pt, then **TMP/SMX-DS** 1 tab qid for up to 4 weeks	**CIP** 500 mg po q12h x 7 d (*AnIM 132:885, 2000*) or Pyrimethamine 50-75 mg/day po + folinic acid 10-25 mg/day po	Chronic suppression in AIDS pts: either **TMP/SMX-DS** 1 tab daily or 3x/wk OR both daily **(pyrimethamine** 25 mg/day po + **folinic acid** 5 mg/day po). 2nd line alternative: **CIP** 500 mg po 3x/week.
Microsporidiosis (Ref: *Curr Opin Infect Dis 19:485, 2006*)	**Effective ART is main therapy.**			
Ocular (Keratoconjunctivitis): Encephalitozoon hellum or cuniculi, Vittaforma (Nosema) corneae or Nosema ocularum.	If corneal infection and disseminated disease, use Fumagillin eyedrops + **Albendazole** 400 mg po bid x 3 weeks	If no disseminated infection: **fumagillin** eyedrops. For V. corneae, may need keratoplasty	**To obtain fumagillin (Fumidil B):** 1-800-292-6773 or *www.leiters.com.* Neutropenia/thrombocytopenia serious side effects. **Dx:** Most labs use modified trichrome stain. Need electron micrographs for species identification. FA & PCR methods in development. Peds does ref: *PIDJ 23:915, 2004.*	
Intestinal (diarrhea): Enterocytozoon bieneusi, Encephalitozoon (Septata) intestinalis		**Albendazole** 400 mg po bid x 3-4 wks. Peds dose: 15 mg/kg per day divided bid x 7 d (*PIDJ 23:915, 2004*) for E. intestinales	**Fumagillin** 20 mg po tid reported effective for E. bieneusi (*NEJM 346:1963, 2002*). Oral prep is available internationally, but not in the U.S.	Oral fumagillin causes Neutropenia/thrombocytopenia.
Disseminated: E. hellum, cuniculi or intestinalis; Pleistophora sp.		**Albendazole** 400 mg po q12h x 2-4 wks		

NOTE: All dosage recommendations are for adults (unless otherwise indicated) & assume normal renal function.

TABLE 12 (25)

CAUSATIVE AGENT/DISEASE	MODIFYING CIRCUMSTANCES	SUGGESTED REGIMENS PRIMARY	SUGGESTED REGIMENS ALTERNATIVE	COMMENTS
PARASITIC INFECTIONS (continued)				
Protozoan—Extraintestinal				
Babesiosis (B. microti) Ref: *NEJM 366:2397, 2012*	Exchange transfusion indicated if > 10% parasitemia & hemolysis.	For mild/moderate disease: (**Atovaquone** 750 mg po bid + **azithro** 600 mg po on day 1, then 250-1000 mg/day) x 7-10 days. See *Comment*	For severe disease: (**Clinda** 600 mg IV/po tid) + exchange transfusion + (**quinine** 650 mg po tid) x 7-10 days. For adults, can give **clinda** IV as 1.2 gm q12h.	If relapse treat for 6 or more weeks and 2 weeks beyond clearance of organisms from blood smear. *(CID 46:370, 2008).* If ≥10% parasitemia, consider exchange transfusion.
Toxoplasma gondii (AIDS)				
Cerebral toxoplasmosis (Toxoplasma encephalitis) Ref: *MMWR 58(RR-4):1, 2009* IgG toxo antibody positive in approx. 84% of pts with cerebral toxoplasmosis. **Note: Leucovorin = folinic acid**		**Pyrimethamine** (pyri) 200 mg po x 1 dose then (75 mg/day po) + **sulfadiazine** (wt-based dose): < 60 kg, 1.5 gm if ≥60 kg) po q6h) + (**folinic acid** 10-25 mg/day po) x 6 wks after resolution of signs/symptoms, & then suppressive rx (see below) **OR** **TMP/SMX** 10/50 mg/kg/day po or IV div q12h x 6 wks)	**Pyri + folinic acid** (as in primary regimen) plus: (1) **Clinda** 600 mg po/IV q6h or (2) **Atovaquone** 750 mg po q6h **or** (3) **Azithro** 900-1200 mg po once daily All above for 4-6 weeks after resolution of signs & symptoms, then suppression.	Use alternative regimen for pts with severe sulfa allergy. If multiple ring-enhancing brain lesions (CT or MRI), >85% of pts respond to 7-10 days of empiric rx. If no response, suggest brain biopsy. **Dexamethasone:** 4 mg po/IV q6h if evidence of increased cranial pressure.
Primary prophylaxis. AIDS pts—IgG toxo antibody present + CD4 count <100/µl		(**TMP/SMX-DS**, 1 tab po q24h) or (**TMP/SMX-SS**, 1 tab po q24h)	(**Dapsone** 50 mg po q24h) + (**pyri** 50 mg po q week) + (**folinic acid** 25 mg po q week) or (**atovaquone** 1500 mg po q24h)	Prophylaxis for pneumocystis with TMP/SMX also effective vs. toxo. Ref: *MMWR 58(RR-4):1, 2009.* Another alternative: (**Dapsone** 200 mg po + **Pyri** 75 mg po + **Folinic acid** 25 mg po weekly).
Suppression. Secondary prophylaxis after treatment of cerebral toxo. Ref: *CID 40 (Suppl. 3), 2005*		(**Sulfadiazine** 500-1000 mg po 4x/day) + (**pyri** 25-50 mg po q24h) + (**folinic acid** 10-25 mg po q24h)	(**pyri** 25-50 mg po q24h) + (**folinic acid** 10-25 mg po q24h) or (**atovaquone** 750 mg po q6-12h)	(**pyri + sulfa**) prevents PJP & toxo; (**clinda + pyri**) prevents toxo only. Discontinue suppression when CD4 > 200 for 3 months.
Vaginitis— *MMWR 59 (RR-12):56, 2010*				
Bacterial vaginosis Malodorous vaginal discharge, pH >4.5 Polymicrobic: associated with Gardnerella vaginalis, Mobiluncus, Mycoplasma hominis, Prevotella sp., Atopobium sp., et al. Etiology unclear. Ref: *JID 193:1475, 2006*		**Metronidazole** (0.5 gm bid po x 7 d) OR **metronidazole vaginal gel**[1] (1 applicator intravaginally) once daily x 5 d (avoid in 1st trimester pregnancy) OR **tinidazole** (2 gm po once daily x 2 days) **OR** (1 gm po once daily x 5 days)	**Clinda** (0.3 gm bid po x 7 d) or **2% clinda vaginal cream** 5 gm intravaginally at bedtime x 7 d OR **clinda ovules** 100 mg intravaginally at bedtime x 3 d	50% increase in cure rate with condoms or if abstain from sex *(CID 44:213 & 20, 2007).* **Rx of male sex partner not indicated unless balanitis present. Metro-ER** 750 mg po once daily available, efficacy unclear. **In pregnancy:** Rx same as non-pregnancy, except avoid clindamycin cream (↑ risk premature birth). Atopobium resistant to **metro** in vitro; susceptible to **clinda** *(BMC Inf Dis 6:51, 2006).*
Candidiasis vulvovaginal. Pruritus, thick cheesy discharge, pH <4.5	Candida albicans 80-90%. C. glabrata, C. tropicalis may be increasing—less suscept. to azoles.	**Fluconazole** 150 mg single dose po or **Itraconazole** 200 mg po q12h x 1 d	**Intravaginal azoles:** Variety of strengths. Regimens vary from 1 dose to 7-14 d. Examples (all end in -azole): butocon, clotrim, micon, tiocon, tercon	**Intravaginal azoles available OTC & by prescription.** Nystatin vaginal tabs x 14 days less effective than azoles. Other therapies for azole-resistant strains: gentian violet, boric acid. With normal CD4 lymphocyte count, usual duration of rx: If AIDS pt, treat for 10-14 d. If 4 or more episodes/year: 6 mos suppression with fluconazole 150 mg once weekly.

[1] 1 applicator contains 5 gm of gel with 37.5 mg metronidazole
NOTE: All dosage recommendations are for adults (unless otherwise indicated) & assume normal renal function.

TABLE 12 (26)

CAUSATIVE AGENT/DISEASE	MODIFYING CIRCUMSTANCES	SUGGESTED REGIMENS		COMMENTS
		PRIMARY	ALTERNATIVE	

PARASITIC INFECTIONS/Protozoan—Extraintestinal/Vaginitis *(continued)*

CAUSATIVE AGENT/DISEASE	MODIFYING CIRCUMSTANCES	PRIMARY	ALTERNATIVE	COMMENTS
Trichomoniasis Copious foamy discharge, pH >4.5	Trichomonas vaginalis	**Metronidazole** (2 gm as single dose) (contraindicated in 1st trimester of pregnancy) **OR** **Tinidazole** 2 gm po x 1 dose **Pregnancy:** See Comment	**For rx failure:** Re-treat with metro 500 mg po q12h x 7 d; if 2nd failure: metro 2 gm po q24h x 3–5 d. If still failure, suggest ID consultation &/or contact CDC: 770-488-4115 or www.cdc.gov/std.	Treat male sexual partners **(2 gm metronidazole po as single dose).** Nearly 20% of men with NGU infected with trichomonas *(JID 188:465, 2003).* **Pregnancy: Metro is not mutagenic or teratogenic.** Ref: *CID 44:S123, 2007.*
Nematode infections Strongyloides stercoralis (strongyloidiasis)	Risk of hyperinfection in AIDS pts	**Ivermectin** 200 mcg/kg po q24h x 2 d	**Albendazole** 400 mg po bid x 7 days	For hyperinfection: repeat rx at 15 days; can use veterinary ivermectin (IV or rectally) *(CID 49:1411, 2009).*

Ectoparasites. NOTE: Due to potential neurotoxicity, use lindane products only as last resort.

CAUSATIVE AGENT/DISEASE	MODIFYING CIRCUMSTANCES	PRIMARY	ALTERNATIVE	COMMENTS
Pediculus humanus corporis **(body lice)** For use of ivermectin in outbreak see *JID 193:474, 2006.*		For clothing: either hot wash (149 °F), dry clean or discard. If washed, use hot iron, especially on seams. If nits on body hair (rare) 5% permethrin cream to entire skin x 1. Leave cream on for 6-8 hrs		Organism lives, and deposits eggs, in clothing seams. Body louse leaves clothing only for blood meal. Nits in clothing viable for 1 month. See *Cutis 80:397, 2007.*
P. humanus var. capitis **(head louse,** nits) Refs: *NEJM 362:896, 2010; Pediatrics 126:392, 2010.*		**Permethrin.** 1% generic lotion or cream rinse (RID, Pronto, others): Apply to shampooed dry hair for 10 min; repeat in one week **OR** **Ivermectin** 200-400 mcg/kg po once (report that 3 doses at 7 day intervals works *(JID 193:474, 2006)*); does not affect nits **OR** **Malathion 0.5% lotion** (Ovide). Apply to dry hair for 8–12 hrs, then shampoo. Repeat in 7 days.		**Permethrin:** Success in 78%. Extra nit combing of no benefit. Resistance increasing. No advantage to 5% permethrin. **Malathion:** 98% effective. In alcohol—potentially flammable. Ref: *Ped Dermatol 24:405, 2007; NEJM 362:896, 2010; Ped Infect Dis J 29:991, 2010.*
Phthirus pubis (Crab louse) Eyelash infection: see Comment		**Topical: Permethrin** 1% cream to pubic & perianal skin, thighs, trunk & axillae. Wash off after 10 minutes. May need retreatment in 7 days **OR** **Malathion** 0.5% lotion. Apply as above; leave on for 8-12 hrs before washing off.	Oral therapy (if refractory to topical): **Ivermectin** 250 mcg/kg po x 1 dose; repeat in one week. DO not use in pregnancy or in children if wt < 15 kg.	Pediculosis ciliaris (eyelash involvement) treatment: Occlusive petroleum jelly or yellow oxide of mercury to lid margin bid x 8-10 days then mechanical removal of lice and nits. For failures: oral **Ivermectin.** Ref: *MMWR 59 (RR-12):88, 2010.*
Sarcoptes scabiei **(scabies)** (mites) Ref: *NEJM 362:717, 2010*	Immunocompetent patients	**Primary: Permethrin** 5% cream (ELIMITE). Apply entire skin except around eyes. Leave on 8–10 hrs. Repeat in 1 wk. Safe for children > 2 mos. old. **Alternatives: Ivermectin** 200 mcg/kg po, repeat in 14 days **OR crotamiton** 10% cream topically q24h x 2 d (less effective).		Trim fingernails. Reapply cream to hands after handwashing. Pruritus may persist x 2 wks after mites gone. **Do not use lindane in pregnancy or in young children**—absorbed through skin; can use 6–10% precipitated sulfur in petrolatum q24h x 3 d.
	AIDS patients, CD4 <150/mm3, lymphoma **(Norwegian scabies—"Crusted" scabies)**	For Norwegian scabies: **(Permethrin** 5 daily x 7 days, then 2x/week until cured + **Ivermectin** 200 mcg/kg po with food on days 1, 2, 8, 9, 15 (and maybe 22 & 29)).		Norwegian scabies in AIDS pts: Extensive, crusted. Can mimic psoriasis. Not pruritic. **Highly contagious—isolate!**

NOTE: All dosage recommendations are for adults (unless otherwise indicated) & assume normal renal function.

TABLE 12 (27)

FIGURE 16 Activity Of Antiviral Agents Against Treatable Pathogenic Viruses

ANTIVIRAL AGENT

Virus	Acyclovir	Amantadine	Adefovir Entecavir Lamivudine	Cidofovir	Famciclovir	Foscarnet	Ganciclovir	αInterferon Or PEG INF + DAA (if HCV genotype 1)	Oseltamivir	Ribavirin	Rimantidine	Valacyclovir	Valganciclovir	Zanamivir
Adenovirus	·	·	·	+	·	·	±	·	·	·	·	·	±	·
BK virus	·	·	·	+	·	·	·	·	·	·	·	·	·	·
Cytomegalovirus	±	·	·	+++	±	+++	+++	·	·	·	·	±	+++	·
Hepatitis B	·	·	+++	·	·	·	·	+++	·	·	·	·	·	·
Hepatitis C	·	·	·	·	·	·	·	+++[1]	·	+++[1]	·	·	·	·
Herpes simplex virus	+++	·	·	++	+++	++	++	·	·	·	·	+++	++	·
Influenza A	·	±[2]	·	·	·	·	·	·	+++[3]	·	±[2]	·	·	+++
Influenza B	·	·	·	·	·	·	·	·	++	·	·	·	·	++
JC virus	·	·	·	+	·	·	·	·	·	·	·	·	·	·
Respiratory Syncytial Virus	·	·	·	·	·	·	·	·	·	+	·	·	·	·
Varicella zoster virus	+	·	·	+	++	++	·	·	·	·	·	+++	+	·

[1] 1st line rx = an IFN + Ribavirin + (Boceprevir or Telaprevir (for genotype 1 infection)
[2] not CDC recommended
[3] High level resistance H1N1 (2009)

- = no activity; ± = possible activity; + = active, 3rd line therapy (least active clinically)
++ = Active, 2nd line therapy (less active clinically); +++ = Active, 1st line therapy (usually active clinically)

NOTE: All dosage recommendations are for adults (unless otherwise indicated) & assume normal renal function.

TABLE 12 (28)

TYPE OF INFECTION/ORGANISM/ SITE OF INFECTION	SUGGESTED REGIMENS		COMMENTS
	PRIMARY	ALTERNATIVE	
VIRAL INFECTIONS			
Cytomegalovirus (CMV) Marked ↓ in CMV infections & death from CMV with Highly Active Antiretroviral Rx: there is a progressive ↓ in CMV DNA & most pts actually become neg. after a median time of 3 mos (JID 180:847, 1999; JAC 54:582, 2004; EJCMID 23:550, 2004). Initial rx for CMV infections should include optimization of ART.	**Primary prophylaxis** not generally recommended; preemptive rx in pts with ↑ CMV DNA titers in plasma & CD4 <100/mm³. Recommended by some: **valganciclovir** 900 mg po q24h (CID 32: 783, 2001). Authors rec. primary prophylaxis be dc if response to ART ↑ CD4 >100 for 6 mos. (MMWR 53:98, 2004).		Risk for developing CMV disease correlates with quantity of CMV DNA in plasma: +DNAu ↑ 3.4-fold & each log₁₀ ↑ associated with 3.1-fold ↑ in disease (JCI 101:497, 1998; CID 28:758, 1999).
Colitis, esophagitis Dx best by biopsy of ulcer base/edge (Clin Gastro Hepatol 2:564, 2004). Multiple biopsies (6 -10) required.	**Ganciclovir** as with retinitis except induction period extended for 3-6 wks. No agreement on use of maintenance; may not be necessary except after relapse (AJM 158:957, 1998). Responses less predictable than for retinitis (AJM 98:109, 1995). **Foscarnet** 90 mg/kg q12h effective in 9/10 pts (AAC 41:1226, 1997). **Valganciclovir also likely effective.** Switch to oral valganciclovir when po tolerated & when symptoms not severe enough to interfere with absorption.		
CMV of the nervous system: Encephalitis & ventriculitis, lesions usually periventricular. Treatment not defined, but should be considered the same as retinitis. Disease may develop while taking ganciclovir as suppressive therapy. (See Herpes 11(Suppl.12):95A, 2004.) **Optimize ART!** Most would use combination of ganciclovir & foscarnet, but high dose valganciclovir (900 mg po bid) successful in single case (AIDS Reader 17:133, 2007).			
Lumbosacral polyradiculopathy	**Ganciclovir** as with retinitis. Consider combination of ganciclovir & foscarnet, esp. if prior CMV rx used. Switch to **valganciclovir** when possible. Suppression continued until CD4 remains >100/mm³ for 6 mos.	**Cidofovir** 5 mg/kg IV, once weekly for 2 weeks followed by administration q2 weeks. MUST be administered with probenecid 2 gm po 3 hrs before each dose and further 1 gm doses 2 hours and 8 hours after completion of the cidofovir infusion. IV saline hydration is essential.	About 50% will respond (CID 20:747, 1995); survival ↑ (5.4 wks to 14.6 wks) (CID 27:345, 1998).
Mononeuritis multiplex	Not defined		Due to vasculitis & may not be responsive to antiviral rx (AnNeurol 29:139, 1991).
CMV pneumonia—seen predominantly in transplants (esp. bone marrow), rare in HIV Rx only when histological evidence present in AIDS pts & other pathogens not identified. High rate of CMV reactivation in immunocompetent ICU patients; prolonged hospitalizations and increased mortality (JAMA 300:413, 2008).	**Ganciclovir/valganciclovir**, as with retinitis. Many transplant units also use IVIG or CMV specific immune globulin as adjunctive Rx (no studies).		In BMT recipients, serial measure of pp65 antigen was useful in establishing early dx of CMV interstitial pneumonia with good results if GCV was initiated within 6 days of antigen positivity (Bone Marrow Transplant 26:413, 2000). For preventive therapy, see Table 10.

TABLE 12 (29)

TYPE OF INFECTION/ORGANISM/ SITE OF INFECTION	SUGGESTED REGIMENS		COMMENTS
	PRIMARY	ALTERNATIVE	
VIRAL INFECTIONS/Cytomegalovirus (CMV) *(continued)*			
CMV Retinitis (most common in AIDS) Still the most common cause of blindness in AIDS patients with <50/mm³ CD4 counts. Differential dx: HIV retinopathy, herpes simplex retinitis (*Arch Ophthal 114: 834, 1996*), varicella zoster retinitis (rare, hard to diagnose). 11.6% of 374 pts followed with CMV retinitis who responded to ART (↑ of ≥50 CD4 cells/mL) developed immune recovery vitreitis (vision ↓) & floaters with posterior segment inflammation →vitreitis, papillitis & macular changes) (*Ophthal 113:684, 2006*). Risks for IRV were large CMV retinitis lesions and use of intravitreous cidofovir. Another reported 8/21 pts receiving ART had inflammatory complications (*AIDS 14: 1163, 2000*). Corticosteroid rx ↓ inflammatory reaction of immune recovery vitreitis without reactivation of CMV retinitis, either periocular corticosteroids or short course of systemic steroid.	**Treatment:** • **For immediate sight-threatening lesions:** Ganciclovir intraocular implant & **Valganciclovir** 900 mg po q12h. • **For peripheral lesions:** **Ganciclovir** 900 mg po q12h x 14–21 d, then 900 mg po q24h **Suppression:** • **Chronic maintenance Rx or secondary prophylaxis:** **Valganciclovir** 900 mg po q24h OR **Foscarnet** 90 mg/kg IV q24h Dc with CD4 >100 x 6 mos.	**Ganciclovir** 200 to 400 μgm/0.1 mL (of 4 mgm/mL solution) by intravitreal injection every other wk until retinitis inactive: ↓ cost and useful in resource restricted regions (*J Med Assoc Thai 88: Suppl. 9:S63, 2005*). **Ganciclovir** 5 mg/kg IV q12h x 14–21 d, then **valganciclovir** 900 mg po q24h OR **Foscarnet** 60 mg/kg IV q8h or 90 mg/kg IV q12h x 14–21 d, then 90–120 mg/kg IV q24h OR **Cidofovir** 5 mg/kg IV x 2 wks, then 5 mg/kg every other wk; each dose should be administered with IV saline hydration & oral probenecid OR Repeated intravitreal injections with **fomivirsen** (for relapses only, not as initial therapy, active against resistant strains) **Suppression, 2°:** Intravitreal maintenance therapy. **Cidofovir** 5 mg/kg IV every other week with **probenecid** 2 gm po 3 hrs before the dose followed by 1 gm po 2 hrs after the dose, & 1 gm by mouth 8 hrs after the dose (total of 4 gm); OR **fomivirsen** 1 vial (330 mg) injected into the vitreous, then repeated every 2–4 wks	Valganciclovir po equal to GCV IV in induction of remission: 7/71 progressed on Val & 7/70 on GCV during 1st 4 wks & 72% of Val- & 77% of GCV-treated pts had satisfactory responses to induction rx. (*NEJM 346:1119, 2002*). Valganciclovir 900 mg q24h has similar efficacy (17% progressed over 1 year) & toxicity profile as IV ganciclovir but with fewer IV-related events (*J AIDS 30:392, 2002*). There is also a significant ↓ in cost vs IV rx (*J AIDS 36:972, 2004*). Cannot clear GCV ocular implant alone as approx. 50% risk of CMV retinitis other eye at 6 mos. & 31% risk visceral disease. When contralateral retinitis does occur, ganciclovir-resistant mutation often present (*JID 189:611, 2004*). **Concurrent systemic rx recommended which reduce risk.** Complications related to implant occurred at rate of 0.064 events per pt yr and ↓ with time (*Ophthal 113:683e1-8, 2006*). Intravitreal ganciclovir qpw effective in 8/27 pts with active retinitis also receiving ART in Thailand. A mean of 5 cc injections necessary and no relapses but follow up only 5 mos. Complications in 7 of 51 eyes (14%) included vitreous haze, retinal detachment, endophthalmitis & immune recovery vitreitis (*J Med Assoc Thai 88: Suppl. 9:S63, 2005*). Retinal detachments 50–60% within 1 yr of dx of retinitis. In 271 AIDS pts with CMV retinitis, both 2° eye involvement & retinal detachment markedly ↓ with ART but only if good CD4 cell response (*Ophthal 111:2232, 2004*). Equal efficacy of IV GCV & FOS-APV. GCV avoids nephrotoxicity of FOS-APV. FOS-APV avoids bone marrow suppression of GCV. (**Oral valganciclovir should replace both**) although bone marrow toxicity may be similar to ganciclovir. A single report indicates success of combination rx with GCV at ½ dose 5 mg/kg/day q24h & FOS at ½ to 125 mg/kg/day for GCV-resistant isolates in solid organ transplants (*CID 34:1337, 2002*). Hypomagnesemia common complication.

NOTE: All dosage recommendations are for adults (unless otherwise indicated) & assume normal renal function.

TABLE 12 (30)

TYPE OF INFECTION/ORGANISM/ SITE OF INFECTION	SUGGESTED REGIMENS		COMMENTS
	PRIMARY	ALTERNATIVE	
VIRAL INFECTIONS/CMV Retinitis *(continued)*			
Maintenance can be discontinued if CD4 >100/mm³ x 6 mos. Pts who discontinue maintenance rx should undergo regular eye examination for early detection of relapses! Risk for reactivation very low 0.016 per person yr of follow up *(HIV Clin Trials 7:1, 2006)*.			Potential emergence of resistant CMV. 27.5% pts treated 9 mos developed CMV isolates resistant to GCV *(JID 177:770, 1998)*, hence may be reason for clinical failure.
Hairy leukoplakia (Epstein Barr virus, EBV)	Usually asymptomatic & no treatment indicated	Acyclovir (800 mg po 5x/day) or topical podophyllin resin (one application) (not currently FDA-approved for this indication)	Patients usually asymptomatic, lesions respond to rx but recur.
Hepatitis A *(Ln 351:1643, 1998)*	No therapy recommended. If within 2 wks of exposure, gamma globulin 0.02 mL/kg IM injection x 1 is protective. Hep A vaccine equally effective as IVIG in randomized trial and is emerging as preferred Rx. *(NEJM 357:1685, 2007)*		For vaccine recommendations, see *Table 19 (MMWR 48:RR-12, 1999)*. Based on increased severity of acute hepatitis A superimposed on chronic liver disease, HAV vaccine recommended for all patients with chronic liver disease *(Am J Med 118:21S, 2005)*. Up to 20% of pts require hospitalization *(NEJM 353: 890, 2005)*.

Hepatitis B *(see Ln 362:2089, 2003). For treatment recommendations, see Table 9J, page 91.*

Hepatitis C. For treatment recommendations, see *Table 9E, page 86.*

Herpes simplex virus (HSV)
Genital herpes ↑ transmission and acquisition of HIV *(See JAIDS 35:435, 2004; Ln 357:1149, 2001)*

Mucocutaneous (oral, anal, genital, skin) **Treatment** **Mild**	Acyclovir 400 mg po q8h x 7–14 d **OR** Famciclovir 500 mg po q12h x 7–14 d **OR** Valacyclovir 1000 mg po q12h x 7–14 d[HSV-A] No data on treating recurrences in HIV+ pts—use recommendations for treating HIV–.	Chronic suppression indicated if frequent recurrences &/or extensive disease. 1% foscarnet cream applied 5x/day in acyclovir-unresponsive ulcers had 65–90% partial to complete response *(JID 21:301, 1999)*. Famciclovir approved for "fever blister" at 1500 mg po x 1 dose and for acute exacerbations of genital lesions at 1000 mg bid x one day for normal hosts. Not yet approved for HIV-infected persons at these doses.	
Severe—extensive disease, systemic toxicity	Acyclovir 5 mg/kg q8h IV x 5–10 d [For encephalitis 10 to 14 mg/kg IV q8h x 10 d] After lesions begin to heal, switch to famciclovir 500 mg po q12h or valacyclovir 1000 mg po q12h, or acyclovir 400 mg po q8h. Continue rx until lesions have completely healed.	If acyclovir-resistant: Foscarnet 40–60 mg/kg IV q8h IV **OR** Cidofovir 5 mg/kg IV q wk until clinical response	Severe disease not responding to acyclovir may represent resistant virus. Acyclovir-resistant HSV occurs, esp. in large ulcers. Most will respond to IV foscarnet or cidofovir, but recur after drug discontinued [median 6 wks *(NEJM 325:551, 1991)*]. HSV that becomes resistant to both acyclovir & foscarnet will usually remain sensitive to cidofovir *(JID 180:487, 1999)*.

NOTE: All dosage recommendations are for adults (unless otherwise indicated) & assume normal renal function.

TABLE 12 (31)

TYPE OF INFECTION/ORGANISM/ SITE OF INFECTION	SUGGESTED REGIMENS		COMMENTS
	PRIMARY	ALTERNATIVE	

VIRAL INFECTIONS/Herpes simplex virus (HSV) *(continued)*

Suppression, post-treatment, only if recurrences are frequent or severe *See CID 39 (Suppl. 5):S237, 2004*	**Acyclovir** 400 mg po q12h or 200 mg po q8h indefinitely. 4x/d more effective in 1 study *(5th CRV, Abst. 499)* **OR** **Famciclovir** 250–500 mg po q12h **OR** **Valacyclovir** 500 mg po q12h approved for HIV-infected pts with CD4 count ≥100. If acyclovir-resistant: **Foscarnet** 40 mg/kg IV q24h indefinitely	[Higher doses 800 mg]	NOTE: For pts taking acyclovir for chronic suppression who then develop CMV retinitis, stop acyclovir when ganciclovir started—GCV active vs. H. simplex. Suppressive rx with famciclovir (500 mg po q12h) reduced viral shedding & clinical recurrences (total days with lesions 18% vs. 5%) in HIV-infected pts *(AnIM 128:21, 1998)*, similar to findings with acyclovir. Valacyclovir (500 mg po q12h) rx of HIV-infected pt: at 6 mos, 65% were recurrence-free vs. 26% receiving placebo *(package insert, Valtrex)*. Effective suppression with valacyclovir decreased genital HSV and HIV shedding while also reducing plasma HIV RNA levels. *Will it also reduce HIV transmission? (NEJM 356:790, 2007)*

Human herpesvirus 8 (Kaposi's sarcoma-associated herpesvirus) *See JCI 113:21, 2004*

	See Table 18, Treatment of HIV-Associated Malignancies. Effective suppression of HHV-1 replication with ART has best chance of preventing progression of KS or occurrence of new lesions. Castleman's disease responded to ganciclovir *(JID 2006)*		Virus appears to be spread by saliva *(JID 190:199, 2004)*. HHV8-associated Castleman disease responds to ART with immune reconstitution, but relapse of disease still occurred. Survival was 48 mos. *(CID 35:880, 2002)* Associated with diabetes in sub-Saharan Africa *(JAMA 299:2770, 2008)*.

Human papillomavirus (HPV): Condyloma acuminatum (CA) (anogenital warts) *(MMWR 53:46, 2004)* Progression of disease correlates with ↑ HIV RNA in plasma *(JID 179:1405, 1999)*. Rate of recurrence is high, esp. in HIV+ pts, despite rx. For rx of cervical or anal intraepithelial neoplasia (CIN & AIN), see *MMWR 53 (RR-15):46 & 91, 2004*.

	Patient-applied: **Podofilox** 0.5% solution or 0.5% gel. Apply to all lesions q12h x 3 consecutive days. Repeat weekly for up to 4 wks **OR** **Imiquimod** 5% cream: apply to lesions at bedtime & remove in morning on 3 consecutive nights, weekly for up to 16 wks.	**Provider-applied:** Liquid nitrogen cryotherapy— apply until each lesion is thoroughly frozen; repeat every 1–2 wks x 3–4 times. **or Trichloroacetic acid or bichloroacetic acid cauterization 80–95% aqueous solution—apply to each lesion; repeat weekly for 3–6 wks.** Surgical excision or laser surgery Podophyllin resin 10–25% suspension in tincture of benzoin—apply to area & wash off in a few hrs; repeat weekly for up to 3–6 wks.	Do not use cervical warts until results of Pap smear known. Avoid podophyllin & podofilox in pregnant women. Alternatives: cryotherapy with liquid nitrogen, electrocautery. Cidofovir topical gel + surgical excision 100% effective in achieving complete response in 19 pts but 27% relapsed *(AIDS 16:447, 2002)*. Common Side Effects: • **Podofilox**: inexpensive and safe (pregnancy safety not established). Mild irritation after treatment. • **Imiquimod**: Mild to moderate redness & irritation. Topical imiquimod effective for treatment of vulvar intraepithelial neoplasms *(NEJM 358:1465, 2008)*. Safety in pregnancy not established. • **Cryotherapy**: blistering and skin necrosis common. • **Podophyllin resin**: Must air dry before treated area contacts clothing. Can irritate adjacent skin. • **TCA**: caustic. Can cause severe pain on adjacent normal skin. Neutralize with soap or sodium bicarbonate

Molluscum contagiosum virus *(See Curr Opin Inf Dis 12:185, 1999)*

	Treatment: Usually rx with destructive modalities: cryotherapy with liquid nitrogen, light electrocautery, or curettage	3 pts also responded to either IV or topical cidofovir (1% cream) *(5th CRV, Abst. 504; Ln:353:2042, 1999)*.	Interferon alfa is not effective. Spontaneous resolution observed in pts with good response to antiretroviral therapy.
	Suppression: Retinoic acid (Retin A) applied once nightly to face may ↓ rate of appearance but does not affect already established lesions.		Retinoic acid cannot be used on eyelids or genitalia. Lesions in disseminated cryptococcosis, histoplasmosis may resemble molluscum contagiosum.

NOTE: All dosage recommendations are for adults (unless otherwise indicated) & assume normal renal function.

TABLE 12 (32)

TYPE OF INFECTION/ORGANISM/ SITE OF INFECTION	SUGGESTED REGIMENS		COMMENTS
	PRIMARY	ALTERNATIVE	
VIRAL INFECTIONS (continued)			
Parvovirus B-19 "Pure red cell aplasia"	**Immunoglobulin G:** 2 gm/kg IVIG given over 2 days. Most pts with <80 CD4/mm³ suffer relapse within 6 mos. & require re-rx with IVIG. Maintenance rx with IVIG 0.4 gm/kg q4 wks effective in preventing relapses; probably not necessary if CD4 count >300/mm³ (Am J Hematol 61:16, 1999).		Persistent parvovirus B-19 infection is a cause of anemia in HIV+ pts. Found in 1/3 HIV+ pts (J Invest Med 45:65A, 1997). Essentially all pts (27) reported have responded to IVIG.
Progressive multifocal leukoencephalopathy (PML) (JC virus) Usually in pts with advanced HIV disease (see Table 11A, page 98)	**ART** ↑ survival (545 days vs. 60 days, p < 0.0001) & either improved (50%) or stabilized (50%) neurological deficits in 12 pts (AIDS 12:2467, 1999). Pts have experienced ↑ neurological manifestations (including death) after initiating ART—possibly due to IRIS. **Watch for IRIS!**		Cytarabine of no value in controlled trial (NEJM 338:1345, 1998). Cidofovir effective in some patients. Should be used in conjunction with ART. Cidofovir dose same as for CMV disease (5 mg/kg weekly for 2 weeks, then 5 mg/kg every other week). Must be administered with IV saline hydration and probenecid. Follow renal function.
Varicella zoster virus (VZV) ↑ frequency of zoster reported within 2 mos. of starting ART (7% of 193 pts) (5th CRV, Abst. 501). PCR for VZV DNA in CSF for CNS infection helpful for dx (J Neurovirol 15:172, 1999).			Treatment must be begun within 72 hrs of onset of vesicles. Chronic post-treatment suppression not required. Acyclovir: adjust dose if renal function ↓. Acyclovir-resistant VZV occurs in HIV pts previously
Herpes zoster (shingles) (CID 44: Suppl: 51, 2007). Not severe (local dermatomal zoster)	**Acyclovir** 800 mg po 5 x/day OR **Famciclovir** 500 mg po tid OR **Valacyclovir** 1 gm po tid[NEW] All for 7–10 days.		rx with acyclovir, only 3 had in vitro resistance (mutation of thymidine kinase gene) & no resistance developed on rx. Authors recommend 21 days of rx in such cases (CID 33:2061, 2001). Foscarnet: 4/5 pts rx responded, although 2 relapsed within 14 days. (Ann M 115:19, 1991; J AIDS 7:254, 1994).
Severe (extensive cutaneous, >1 dermatome, trigeminal nerve or visceral involvement)	**Acyclovir** (Zovirax) 10 mg/kg IV (infuse over 1 hr) q8h. Continue until cutaneous & visceral disease clearly resolved.	**Foscarnet** 40 mg/kg IV (infuse over 2 hrs) q8h or 60 mg IV q12h for 14–26 days. *Especially if previous Rx with acyclovir documented acyclovir resistance.*	
Varicella (chickenpox) Mortality high (43%) in AIDS pts (Int J Inf Dis 6:6, 2002)	**Acyclovir** 10 mg/kg IV (infuse over 1 hr) q8h x 7 d.	Switch to oral rx (acyclovir 800 mg po 5x/day or famciclovir 500 mg po q8h or valacyclovir 1 gm po q8h) after defervescence if no evidence for visceral involvement (MMWR 53:99, 2004).	Adjust dosage if renal function ↓.

NOTE: All dosage recommendations are for adults (unless otherwise indicated) & assume normal renal function.

TABLE 12 (33)

TYPE OF INFECTION/ORGANISM/ SITE OF INFECTION	SUGGESTED REGIMENS		COMMENTS
	PRIMARY	ALTERNATIVE	
MISCELLANEOUS CONDITIONS			
Aphthous ulcers, recurrent (RAU)		Topical corticosteroids in 60% Orabase may decrease pain and swelling. **Thalidomide** 200 mg po q24h x 14–28 d or 400 mg po q24h x 7 d followed by 200 mg q24h x 7 wks. **CAUTION: Severe teratogenicity—pregnancy category X!** Contraindicated in women who are or have potential to become pregnant. Men must use condoms because drug appears in semen. *Restricted distribution; prescribers must be registered.* Teratogenicity may occur after a single dose. Not an approved indication. Numerous adverse effects including: somnolence, rash (incl. Stevens-Johnson), photosensitivity, neuropathy, ↓ WBC, venous thrombosis.	16/29 pts responded to 200 mg q24h vs. 2/28 placebo. Side effects: somnolence 7/29 & rash 6/29 *(NEJM 336;1487, 1997).* In another study, 8/11 responded to 200 mg q24h; 4 had somnolence. 2 rash *(JID 180:61, 1999).* 9/10 responded to high-dose (400 mg q24h) but 8/10 developed rash *(CID 28;892, 1999).*
Psoriasis Mild to moderate	Topical therapy: emollients, steroids + tar products or equivalent. Skin lesions may improve with initiation of ART *(Lancet ID 7:496, 2007; Skin Ther Lett 12: 1, 2007).*		Methotrexate rx has been associated with rapid immune suppression & death *(AnIM 106:19, 1987).* Phototherapy often is effective. Calcineurin inhibitors (tacrolimus and pimecrolimus) may have a role in severe cases of psoriasis. Other biologics; alefacept (Amevive), etanercept (Enbrel), infliximab (Remicade) and ustekinumab (Stelara) are approved for use in non-HIV infected pts with difficult to treat psoriasis. Limited data in HIV pts.
Severe			
Seborrheic dermatitis Scalp, mild-moderate	Regular use of dandruff shampoo containing selenium sulfide (Selsun), zinc pyrithione (Head & Shoulders, Danex, Zincon) or sulfur/salicylic acid (Vanseb, Sebulex), or anti-fungal (e.g., 2% ketoconazole) shampoo. Medium potency steroid for short-term may reduce sx. but risk of skin atrophy.		Extremely common in HIV+ patients. Involves hairy areas of scalp, face, chest, back & groin. *(See NEJM 360:387, 2009 for review of seborrheic dermatitis).*
Facial, trunk, &/or groin	Topical imidazole cream (ketoconazole 2%, clotrimazole 1%) + low potency topical steroid (hydrocortisone 1–2.5%, desonide 0.05%) applied 2x q24h.		Topical rx may cause skin irritation.
Wasting Syndrome	rhGH 3–6 mg SQ daily. Antiretroviral therapy often sufficient to reverse wasting syndrome in those with advanced HIV disease.	rhGHRF (tesamorelin) 2 mg SQ daily	Modest effects on reduction in VAT (visceral adipose tissue) and increase in lean body mass. AEs consist of metabolic complications (DM; increase in IGF-1) swollen hands, soft tissue swelling, and injection site reactions. Effect is lost once drug discontinued. Expensive.

NOTE: All dosage recommendations are for adults (unless otherwise indicated) & assume normal renal function.

TABLE 13: DRUGS USED IN TREATMENT &/OR CHRONIC SUPPRESSION OF AIDS-RELATED INFECTIONS: ADVERSE EFFECTS, COMMENTS

DRUG NAME, GENERIC (TRADE)/ USUAL DOSAGE	ADVERSE EFFECTS/COMMENTS
ANTIFUNGAL DRUGS	
Non-lipid amphotericin B deoxycholate (Fungizone): 0.3–1 mg/kg/day as single infusion 50 mg Mixing ampho B with lipid emulsion results in precipitation & is discouraged.	**Admin:** Ampho B is a colloidal suspension that must be prepared in electrolyte-free D5W at 0.1 mg/mL to avoid precipitation. No need to protect drug suspensions from light. Ampho B infusions cause chills/fever, myalgia, anorexia, nausea, rarely hemodynamic collapse/hypotension. Postulated due to proinflammatory cytokines but does not appear to be histamine release. Manufacturer recommends a test dose of 1 mg, but often not done (1st few mL of 1st dose is a test dose). Duration of infusion usually 4 or more hrs. No difference found in 1- vs. 4-hr infusions except chills/fever occurred sooner with 1-hr. infusion. Febrile reactions decrease with repeated doses. Rare pulmonary reactions (severe dyspnea & focal infiltrates suggesting pulmonary edema) associated with rapid infusion. Severe rigors respond to meperidine (25–50 mg IV). Premedication with acetaminophen, diphenhydramine, hydrocortisone (25–50 mg) & heparin (1000 units) had no influence on rigors/fever. If cytokine postulate correct, NSAIDs or high-dose steroids may prove efficacious but their use may risk worsening infection under rx or increased risk of nephrotoxicity (i.e., NSAIDs). Clinical side effects ↓ with ↑ age. **Toxicity:** Major concern is nephrotoxicity (15% of 102 pts surveyed). Manifest initially by kaliuresis & hypokalemia, then fall in serum bicarbonate (may proceed to renal tubular acidosis), ↓ in renal erythropoietin & anemia, & rising BUN/serum creatinine. Hypomagnesemia may occur. Can reduce risk of renal injury by **(a) pre- & post-infusion hydration with 500 mL saline (if clinical status will allow salt load), (b)** avoidance of other nephrotoxins, e.g. radiocontrast, aminoglycosides, cisplatinum, (c) use of lipid prep of ampho B. Use of low-dose dopamine did not significantly reduce renal toxicity. **Toxicity:** Fever & chills in 14–18%; nausea 9%, vomiting 8%; serum creatinine ↑ in 11%; renal failure 5%; anemia 4%; ↓ K 5%; rash 4%.
Lipid-based amphoB products:[1,2] Amphotericin B lipid complex (ABLC) (Abelcet): 5 mg/kg/day as single infusion	**Admin:** Consists of ampho B complexed with 2 lipid bilayer ribbons. Compared to standard ampho B, larger volume of distribution, rapid blood clearance & high tissue concentrations (liver, spleen, lung). Dosage: **5 mg/kg q24hr;** infuse at 2.5 mg/kg/hr; adult & ped. dose the same. DO NOT use an in-line filter. Do not dilute with saline or mix with other drugs or electrolytes. **Toxicity:** Fever & chills in 14–18%; nausea 9%, vomiting 8%; serum creatinine ↑ in 11%; renal failure 5%; anemia 4%; ↓ K 5%; rash 4%.
Liposomal amphotericin B (L-AMB, AmBisome): 1–5 mg/kg/day as single infusion.	**Admin:** Consists of vesicular bilayer liposome with ampho B intercalated within the membrane. Dosage: **3–5 mg/kg/day** IV as single dose infused over a period of approx. 120 min. 10 mg/kg/d no more efficacious but more toxic than 3 mg/kg/d in a double-blind trials of patients with invasive mold infection (CID 44:1289, 2007). If infusion is well tolerated, infusion time can be reduced to 60min.[1] 1 mg/kg/day was as effective as 4 mg/kg/day (6 mo. survival rates 43% vs 37%, respectively) in pts with invasive aspergillosis complicating bone marrow transplant &/or neutropenia &/or malignancy. **Major toxicity:** Generally less than ampho B. Nephrotoxicity 18.7% vs 33.7% for ampho B; chills 47% vs. 75%, nausea 39.7% vs. 38.7%, vomiting 31.8% vs. 43.9%, rash 24% for both. ↓ Ca 18.4% vs. 20.9%; ↓ K 20.4% vs. 25.6%; ↓ Mg 20.4% vs. 25.6%. Acute infusion-related reactions are common with liposomal ampho B. 20–40%: 86% occurred within 5 min. of infusion, including chest pain, dyspnea & hypoxia or severe abdominal, flank or leg pain; 14% developed flushing & urticaria near the end of 4-hr infusion. All responded to diphenhydramine (1 mg/kg) & interruption of L-AMB infusion. These reactions may be due to complement activation by the liposome.
Caspofungin (Cancidas) 70 mg IV on day 1 followed by 50 mg IV q24h (reduce to 35 mg IV q24h with moderate hepatic insufficiency) Ref: Ln 362:1142, 2003	An echinocandin which inhibits synthesis of β-(1, 3)-D-glucan, a critical component of fungal cell walls. Fungicidal against candida (MIC <2 mcg/mL) including those resistant to other antifungals & active against aspergillus (MIC 0.4–2.7 mcg/mL). Serum levels on rec. dosages = peak 12, trough 1.3 (24 hrs) mcg/mL. Approved for rx of candidemia & other candida infections (intra-abdominal abscess, esophageal peritonitis, pleural sponge infection) & refractory aspergillus infections & was successful as salvage Rx in approx half of pts with invasive aspergillosis in severely impaired hosts. Only 2% of 263 pts in double-blind trial dc drug due to drug-related adverse event. 14% had ↑ transaminases (similar to triazoles). Most common adverse effect: pruritus at infusion site & headache. Fever, chills, vomiting, & diarrhea associated with infusion. Drug metabolized in liver & dosage ↓ to 35 mg in moderate to severe hepatic failure. Class C for pregnancy (embryotoxic in rats & rabbits), so only use if potential benefits outweigh risks. See Table 16A for drug-drug interactions, esp. cyclosporine (hepatic toxicity) & tacrolimus (drug level monitoring recommended). **No drug in CSF or urine.**

[1] Published data from patients intolerant of or refractory to conventional ampho B deoxycholate (Amp B). **In general ampho B lipid formulations are not superior to ampho B in efficacy in prospective trials although they are less nephrotoxic.**

[2] Comparisons between Abelcet & AmBisome suggest higher infusion-assoc. toxicity (70% vs 36%) & febrile episodes with Abelcet (70% vs 36%) but a higher frequency of mild hepatic toxicity with AmBisome (59% vs 38%, p=0.05). Mild elevations in serum creatinine were observed in 1/3 of both.

TABLE 13 (2)

DRUG NAME, GENERIC (TRADE)/ USUAL DOSAGE	ADVERSE EFFECTS/COMMENTS
ANTIFUNGAL DRUGS *(continued)*	
Micafungin (Mycamine) 150 mg/day IV for esophageal candidiasis; 100 mg/day IV for candidemia; 50 mg per day for prophylaxis post-bone marrow stem cell transplant	Echinocandin approved by the FDA for rx of esophageal candidiasis & for prophylaxis against candida infections in HSCT recipients. Active against most strains of candida sp. & aspergillus sp., including those resistant to fluconazole such as *C. glabrata* & *C. krusei*. No antagonism seen when combined with other antifungal drugs & occ. synergism with ampho B. No dosage adjustment for severe renal failure or moderate hepatic impairment. Low potential for drug interactions. Micafungin is well tolerated & common adverse events include nausea 7.8%, vomiting 2.4%, & headache 2.4%. Transient ↑ LFTs, BUN, creatinine reported; rare cases of significant hepatitis & renal insufficiency. Few drug-drug interactions. **No drug in CSF or urine.**
Anidulafungin (Eraxis) 200 mg IV on day 1 followed by 100 mg/day IV; for esophageal candidiasis 100 mg IV times 1, then 50 mg IV q24h	An echinocandin with antifungal activity (cidal) against candida sp. & aspergillus sp. including ampho B- & triazole-resistant strains. Effective in clinical trials of esophageal candidiasis & in 1 trial was superior to fluconazole in rx of invasive candidemia, remarkably non-toxic; most common side effects: nausea, vomiting, ↓ Mg, ↓ K & headache in 11–13% of pts. No dose adjustments for renal or hepatic insufficiency. Few drug-drug interactions. **No drug in CSF or urine.**
Fluconazole (Diflucan) (available generically) 100 mg tabs 150 mg tabs 200 mg tabs 400 mg IV Oral suspension: 50 mg/5 mL	IV–oral dose because of excellent bioavailability. Pharmacology: absorbed po, water solubility enables IV. Peak serum levels (*see Table 14A*). T½ 30 hrs (range 20–50 hrs). 12% protein bound. **CSF levels 50–90% of serum in normal,** ↑ in meningitis. No effect on mammalian steroid metabolism. **Drug-drug interactions common, see Table 16A.** Side effects overall 16% [more common in HIV+ pts (21%)]. Nausea 3.7%, headache 1.9%, skin rash 1.8%, abdominal pain 1.7%, vomiting 1.7%, diarrhea 1.5%, ↑ SGOT 20%. Alopecia (scalp, pubic crest) in 12–20% pts on ≥400 mg po q24h after median of 3 mos (reversible in approx. 6 mos). Rare: severe hepatotoxicity, exfoliative dermatitis. Anaphylaxis, thrombocytopenia, leukopenia.
Flucytosine (Ancobon) 500 mg cap	AEs: Overall 30%. GI 6% (diarrhea, anorexia, nausea, vomiting); hematologic 22% [leukopenia, thrombocytopenia when serum level > 100 mcg/mL, esp. in azotemic pts)]; hepatotoxicity (asymptomatic; ↑ SGOT, reversible); skin rash 7%; aplastic anemia (rare—2 or 3 cases). False ↑ in serum creatinine on EKTACHEM analyzer.
Griseofulvin (Fulvicin, Grifulvin, Grisactin) 500 mg tab Susp 125 mg/mL	Photosensitivity, urticaria, GI upset, fatigue, leukopenia (rare). Interferes with warfarin drugs. Increases blood & urine porphyrins, should not be used in patients with porphyria. Minor disulfiram-like reactions. Exacerbation of systemic lupus erythematosus.
Imidazoles, topical For vaginal &/or skin use	Not recommended in 1st trimester of pregnancy. Local reactions: 0.5–1.5% dyspareunia, mild vaginal or vulvar erythema, burning, pruritus, pruritus, urticaria, rash. Rarely similar symptoms in sexual partner.
Itraconazole (Sporanox) 100 mg cap 10 mg/mL oral solution (fasting state)	**Itraconazole tablet & solution forms are not interchangeable, solution preferred.** Many authorities recommend measuring drug serum concentration after 2 wks on prolonged rx to ensured satisfactory absorption. To obtain the highest plasma concentration, the tablet is given with food & acidic drinks (e.g. cola) while the solution is taken in the fasted state; under these conditions, the peak conc. of the capsule is approx. 3 μg/mL & of the solution 5.4 mcg/mL. Peak levels are reached faster (2.2 vs. 5 hrs) with the solution. **Peak plasma concentrations after IV injection (200 mg) compared to oral capsule (200 mg): 2.8 μg/mL (on day 7 of rx) vs. 2 μg/mL (on day 36 of rx).** Protein-binding for both preparations is over 99%, which explains the virtual absence of penetration into the CSF (**do not use to treat meningitis**). Most common adverse effects are dose-related nausea 10%, diarrhea 8%, vomiting 6%, & abdominal discomfort 5.7%. Allergic rash 8.6%, ↑ bilirubin 6%, edema 3.5%, & hepatitis 2.7% reported. ↑ doses may produce hypokalemia 8% & ↑ blood pressure 3.2%. Thrombocytopenia & leukopenia reported. Delirium reported (*Psychosomatics 44:260, 2003*). Hypokalemia & rhabdomyolysis reported. **Reported to produce impairment in cardiac function.** Potential for significant **drug-drug interactions (see Table 16A) which can be life-threatening.**
Ketoconazole (Nizoral) 200 mg tab	Gastric acid required for absorption—cimetidine, omeprazole, antacids block absorption in achlorhydria, dissolve tablet in 4 mL 0.2N HCl, drink with a straw. Coca-Cola ↑ absorption by 65% (*AAC 39:1671, 1995*). CSF levels 'none.' **Drug-drug interactions important, see Table 16A.** Some interactions can be life-threatening. Dose–dependent nausea & vomiting. Liver toxicity of hepatocellular type reported in about 1:10,000 exposed pts—usually after several days to weeks of exposure. At doses of ≥800 mg/day serum testosterone & plasma cortisol levels fall. With high doses, adrenal (Addisonian) crisis reported.

NOTE: All dosage recommendations are for adults (unless otherwise indicated) & assume normal renal function.

TABLE 13 (3)

DRUG NAME, GENERIC (TRADE)/ USUAL DOSAGE	ADVERSE EFFECTS/COMMENTS
ANTIFUNGAL DRUGS *(continued)*	
Miconazole (Monistat IV) 200 mg—*not available in U.S.*	IV miconazole indicated in patient critically ill with Pseudallescheria boydii. Very toxic due to vehicle needed to get drug into solution.
Nystatin (Mycostatin) 30 gm cream 500,000 units oral tab	Topical: virtually no adverse effects. Less effective than imidazoles & triazoles. PO: large doses give occasional GI distress & diarrhea.
Posaconazole (Noxafil) 400 mg bid with meals (if not taking meals, 200 mg qid). No cost data available. (See *Drugs* 65:1552, 2005) 200 mg po tid (with food) for prophylaxis	An oral triazole with activity against a wide range of fungi refractory to other antifungal rx including: aspergillosis, zygomycosis, fusariosis, Scedosporium (Pseudallescheria), phaeohyphomycosis, histoplasmosis, refractory coccidioidomycosis, refractory cryptococcosis, & refractory chromoblastomycosis. Approved for prophylaxis. Posaconazole has similar toxicities as other triazoles: nausea 9%, vomiting 6%, abd. pain 5%, headache 5%, diarrhea, ↑ ALT, AST, & rash (3% each). In pts k for >6 mos, elevation of serum concentrations recommended for patients undergoing prolonged prolongation. Significant drug-drug interactions; inhibits CYP3A4. Measurement of serum concentrations recommended for patients undergoing prolonged courses of therapy; target trough >0.5 to 1.5 mcg/mL.
Terbinafine (Lamisil) 250 mg tab	Rare cases (8) of idiosyncratic & symptomatic hepatic injury & more rarely liver failure leading to death or liver transplantation reported in pts receiving terbinafine for onychomycosis. Therefore, the drug is **not recommended** for pts **with chronic or active liver disease** although hepatotoxicity may occur in pts with or without pre-existing disease. Pretreatment screening of serum transaminases (ALT & AST) is advised & alternate rx used for those with abnormal levels. Pts started on terbinafine should be warned about symptoms suggesting liver dysfunction (persistent nausea, anorexia, fatigue, vomiting, RUQ pain, jaundice, dark urine or pale stools). If symptoms develop, drug should be discontinued & liver function immediately evaluated. In controlled trials, changes in ocular lens & retina reported—clinical significance unknown. Major drug-drug interaction is 100% ↑ in rate of clearance by rifampin. AEs: usually mild, transient & rarely caused discontinuation of rx. % with AE: terbinafine vs. placebo: nausea/diarrhea 2.6–5.6 vs. 2.9; rash 5.6 vs. 2.2; taste abnormality 2.8 vs. 0.7. Inhibits CYP2 d6 enzymes.
Voriconazole (Vfend) IV: Loading dose 6 mg/kg q12h x 1 day, then 4 mg/kg q12h IV for invasive aspergillus & serious mold infections; 3 mg/kg q12h IV for serious candida infections **Oral:>40 kg body weight:** 400 mg po q12h x 1 day, then 200 mg po q12h; **<40 kg body weight:** 200 mg po q12h x 1 day, then 100 mg po q12h **Take oral dose 1 hr before or 1 hr after eating.** Oral suspension (40 mg/mL) Oral suspension dosing: Same as for oral tabs. Reduce to ½ maintenance dose for moderate hepatic insufficiency.	A triazole with activity against Aspergillus sp., including Ampho resistant strains of A. terreus. Active vs. Candida sp. (including krusei), Fusarium sp., & various molds. Toxicity similar to other azoles/triazoles including uncommon serious hepatic toxicity (hepatitis, cholestasis & fulminant hepatic failure. Liver function tests should be monitored during rx & drug dc: if abnormalities develop. Rash reported in up to 20%; occ. photosensitivity & rare Stevens-Johnson. Hallucinations. & anaphylactoid infusion reactions with fever & hypertension. 1 case of QT prolongation with ventricular tachycardia in a 15 y/o pt with ALL reported. **Approx. 30% experience a transient visual disturbance** following IV or po ("altered/enhanced visual perception", blurred or colored visual change or photophobia) within 30–60 minutes. Visual changes resolve within 30–60min. after administration & are attenuated with repeated doses (**do not drive at night for outpatient rx**). No persistence of effect reported. Cause unknown. In patients with ClCr <50 mL/min, the drug should be given orally, not IV, since the intravenous vehicle (SBECD-sulfobutylether-B cyclodextrin) may accumulate. Potential for drug-drug interactions high—see *Table 16A*. **NOTE:** Not in urine in active form. **Pediatric Dosing** (*Antimicrob Agents* 56:3032, 2012): **IV DOSING: Age < 12 years or age 12-14 year old, weighing < 50 kg:** 9 mg/kg q12h x 2 doses, then 4-8 mg/kg q12h (higher dose invasive molds and more serious infections); **Age 12-14 year old weighing > 50 kg or age > 15 years old:** adult dose. **PO DOSING: Age < 12 years or age 12-14 year old, weighing < 50 kg:** 9 mg/kg (max 350 mg) q12h; **Age 12-14 year old weighing > 50 kg or age > 15 years old:** adult dose.

NOTE: All dosage recommendations are for adults (unless otherwise indicated) & assume normal renal function.

TABLE 13 (4)

DRUG NAME, GENERIC (TRADE)/ USUAL DOSAGE	ADVERSE EFFECTS/COMMENTS
ANTIMYCOBACTERIAL DRUGS	
FIRST LINE DRUGS	
Isoniazid (INH) (Nydrazid, Laniazid, Teebaconin) 300 mg/day po 300 mg tab 100 mg/mL in 10 mL vials (IM) (Nydrazid, Apothecon)	**Adverse effects:** Overall ~1%. **Peripheral neuropathy** (<1.0%); pyridoxine 25 mg q24h will ↓ incidence; other neurologic sequelae, convulsions, optic neuritis, toxic encephalopathy, psychosis, muscle twitching, dizziness & alterations of sensorium, coma (all rare); allergic skin rashes, lymphadenopathy & vasculitis (SLE-like reaction), fever, minor disulfiram-like reaction, flushing after Swiss cheese, constipation, **hepatitis** (children 10% mild ↑ SGOT, normalizes with continued rx, age <20 yrs rare, 20–34 yrs 0.3%, 35–40 yrs 1.2%, ≥50 yrs 2.3%) (also ↑ with daily alcohol); acute liver failure (fatal or requiring transplantation) (*Lancet* 345:555, 1995); blood dyscrasias (rare); + antinuclear antibody 20%.
Rifampin (Rifadin, Rimactane, Rifocin) 600 mg/day po 300 mg cap (IV available, Aventis, 600 mg)	**Adverse effects:** Produces an orange-brown discoloration of urine, tears (can stain contact lens), semen & sweat. Can falsely elevate lab measurements of bilirubin. **Drug-drug interactions:** Many (see *Table 16A*); induces liver cytochrome P450 system (CYP3A) to ↑ drug metabolism, e.g., ↑ Coumadin requirement, ↑ steroid dosage in pts with Addison's disease or asthmatics, ↓ effectiveness of oral contraceptives (uterine bleeding, pregnancies), methadone less effective, reduced levels of azole antifungals, e.g., fluconazole. "Flu syndrome" Manifest as fever/chills, headache, bone pain, dyspnea if rifampin ingestion irregular. Hepatotoxicity: 16 deaths reported in 500,000 recipients. Minor enzyme changes common & resolve while continuing the drug. Alcoholics with preexisting liver disease prone to rifampin-induced toxicity. Interstitial nephritis reported.
Ethambutol (Myambutol) 15–25 mg/kg/day po 400 mg tab	**Adverse effects: Optic neuritis** with decreased visual acuity, central scotomata, & loss of green & red perception at 25 mg/kg/day, not at 15 mg/kg/day; peripheral neuropathy & headache (~1%), rashes (rare), arthralgia (rare), hyperuricemia (rare). Monthly evaluation of visual acuity (>10% loss considered significant), red/green color discrimination; usually reversible if drug discontinued. Anaphylactoid reaction. **Comment:** Disrupts outer cell membrane in M. avium with ↑ activity of other drugs.
Pyrazinamide (PZA) 25 mg/kg/day po 500 mg tab	**Adverse effects: Arthralgia; hyperuricemia** (with or without symptoms); hepatitis (not over 2% if recommended dose not exceeded); gastric irritation; photosensitivity (rare). Serum uric acid if symptomatic gouty attack occurs. **Comment:** Maximum dose 2 gm/day.
Streptomycin 0.75–1 gm/day IM (or IV) 1 gm	**Adverse effects:** Overall 8%. Ototoxicity, vestibular dysfunction (vertigo); paresthesias; dizziness & nausea (all less in pts receiving 2–3 doses/wk); tinnitus & high frequency loss 1%; nephrotoxicity (rare); allergic skin rashes 4–5%; drug fever. Available from Pfizer/Roerig 1-800-254-4445. Reference for IV use: *CID* 19:1150, 1994.
Rifamate® (see *Comment for content*) 2 tablets single dose po q24h (1 hr before meal). 1 tab	**Adverse effects:** Same as individual components. **Comments:** 1 tablet contains 150 mg INH, 300 mg RIF.
Rifater® (See *Comment for content*) If pt not >55 kg: 6 tablets single dose po q24h (1 hr before meal). 1 tab	**Adverse effects:** Same as individual components. **Comments:** 1 tablet contains 50 mg INH, 120 mg RIF, 300 mg PZA. Used in 1st 2 mos of rx (PZA 25 mg/kg). Purpose is convenience in dosing. ↑ compliance (*AnIM* 122:951, 1995) but costs 1.5x more.
SECOND LINE DRUGS	
Para-aminosalicylic acid (PAS) (Na⁺ or K⁺ salt) (Paser) 4–6 gm po q12h (200 mg/kg/day) 450 mg tab	**Adverse effects: Gastrointestinal irritation** 10–15%; goitrogenic action (rare); depressed prothrombin activity (rare); G6PD-mediated hemolytic anemia (rare), drug fever, rashes, hepatitis, myalgia, arthralgia. Retards hepatic enzyme induction, may ↓ INH hepatotoxicity. Available from *Jacobus Pharm. Co.* (609) 921-7447; CDC (404) 639-3670.
Ethionamide (Trecator-SC) 500–1000 mg/day (15–20 mg/kg/day) po as 1–3 doses. 250 mg tab	**Adverse effects: Gastrointestinal irritation** (up to 50% on large dose); goiter; peripheral neuropathy (rare); convulsions (rare); changes in affect (rare); difficulty in diabetes control; rashes; hepatitis; purpura; stomatitis; gynecomastia; menstrual irregularity. Give drug with meals or antacids; 50–100 mg pyridoxine per day concomitantly; SGOT monthly. Possibly teratogenic.

NOTE: All dosage recommendations are for adults (unless otherwise indicated) & assume normal renal function.

TABLE 13 (5)

DRUG NAME, GENERIC (TRADE)/ USUAL DOSAGE	ADVERSE EFFECTS/COMMENTS
ANTIMYCOBACTERIAL DRUGS/Second Line Drugs (continued)	
Cycloserine (Seromycin) 750–1000 mg/day (15 mg/kg/day) po as 2–4 doses. 250 mg cap.	**Adverse effects:** Convulsions, **psychoses** (5–10% of those receiving 1 gm/day); headache; somnolence; hyperreflexia; increased CSF protein & pressure, peripheral neuropathy; contraindicated in epileptics & active alcoholics: 50 mg pyridoxine for every 250 mg cycloserine should be given concomitantly.
Amikacin (Amikin) 7.5–10 mg/kg/day IV or IM 500 mg vial	**Adverse effects:** Nephrotoxicity, **ototoxicity** (usually high frequency loss—especially with larger total dose (>10 gm), longer duration (>10 days), prior aminoglycosides, pos. family history, assoc. renal impairment & rising trough level (>10 μg/mL). All aminoglycosides may cause or ↑ neuromuscular blockade. Use with caution in pts with myasthenia gravis, Parkinsonism, botulism, with neuromuscular blocking drugs (Table 16A), or with massive transfusion of citrated blood. Avoid concurrent use with ethacrynic acid, furosemide or methoxyflurane. ↑ risk of nephrotoxicity with cis platinum, vancomycin, radiocontrast agents. **Comments:** With edema, ascites, &/or obesity, base calculation of est. creatinine clearance on lean body mass & ideal body weight. For dosing with renal impairment, see Table 75A.
Capreomycin sulfate (Capastat sulfate) 1 gm/day (15 mg/kg/day) as 1 dose IM.	**Adverse effects: Nephrotoxicity** 36%, **ototoxicity** (auditory 11%), eosinophilia, leucopenia, skin rash, fever, hypokalemia, neuromuscular blockade. Abnormal liver function tests.
Amithiozone (Thiacetazone, Tibione. Thioparamizone) (NOT MARKETED IN U.S.) 150 mg/day po	**Adverse effects:** Common: nausea, vomiting, skin rash, dizziness. Uncommon: bone marrow depression, jaundice 0.2%, & renal toxicity. Marked differences in frequency of side effects between racial groups noted, Asia > Africa. Total incidence 21–38%, ½ in 1st 4 weeks, ½ lasted 6 days or less. ½ mild. **Comments: Skin reactions** reported in 20% of HIV+ pts. Felt to be responsible for a 3% **mortality** (Lancet 1:627, 1991). In trial comparing RIF/INH/PZA (RHZ) with SM/thiacetazone/INH (STH), relative risk of death with STH 1.6, drug reactions 11.7 & sputum negative at 2 mos RHZ 74% vs. 37% in STH (Lancet 344:323, 1994; Lancet 345:62, 1995).
Clofazimine (Lamprene) 50 mg po (with meals) 50 mg	**Adverse effects:** Skin: **pigmentation (pink-brownish black)** 75–100%; dryness 20%, pruritus 5%. GI: abdominal pain 50% (rarely severe leading to exploratory laparoscopy), splenic infarction (very rare), bowel obstruction (very rare). Eye: conjunctival irritation, retinal crystal deposition.
Rifabutin (Mycobutin) 300 mg/day po (prophylaxis or treatment) 150 mg	**Adverse effects:** In an anti-MAI trial, rifabutin-related adverse effects occurred in 77% of pts receiving 600 mg (high dose) rifabutin with either clarithro or azithro. Most common was a fall in WBC, then nausea/vomiting/diarrhea in 42%, diffuse polyarthralgia in 19%, & anterior uveitis in 8% (CID 21:594, 1995). Uveitis responds to topical steroids & cycloplegics (CID 22[Suppl. 1]:S43, 1996). Subsequently, max. dose of rifabutin reduced to 300 mg. Other adverse effects similar to rifampin: skin rash 11%, orange-tan to brown skin pigmentation (CID 21:1515, 1995). Discolored (reddish) urine 30%. Lab: ↑ SGOT/SGPT 8%.
Rifapentine (Priftin) 600 mg po twice weekly for first 2 mos., then 600 mg po q week 150 mg tabs	**Adverse effects:** Similar to other rifamycins (see RIF, RFB). Hyperuricemia seen in 21%. Causes red-orange discoloration of body fluids. Note ↑ prevalence of RIF resistance in pts on weekly rx (Ln 353:1843, 1999).

NOTE: All dosage recommendations are for adults (unless otherwise indicated) & assume normal renal function.

TABLE 13 (6)

DRUG NAME, GENERIC (TRADE)/ USUAL DOSAGE	ADVERSE EFFECTS/COMMENTS
ANTIMYCOBACTERIAL DRUGS/SECOND LINE DRUGS (continued)	
Fluoroquinolones	**Review drug-drug interactions.**
Ciprofloxacin (Cipro) & **Ciprofloxacin-extended release** (Cipro XR) **500–750 mg po q12h.** **Urinary tract infection: 250 mg po q12h or Cipro XR 500 mg q24h.** Parenteral rx 200–400 mg IV q12h. 500 mg po, Cipro XR 500 mg. 400 mg IV.	**Children:** No FQ approved for use under age 16 based on joint cartilage injury in immature animals. Articular SEs in children est. at 2–3% (*Ln ID 3:537, 2003*). **CNS toxicity:** Poorly understood. Varies from mild (lightheadedness) to moderate (confusion) to severe (seizures). May be aggravated by NSAIDs. **Gatifloxacin:** Due to documented hypo- and hyperglycemic reactions (*NEJM 354:1352, 2006*), U.S. distribution of gati ceased in Jun 2006. Gati ophthalmic solution remains available. **Opiate screen false-positives:** FQs can cause **false-positive urine assay for opiates** (*JAMA 286:3115, 2001*). **Photosensitivity**
Gemifloxacin (Factive) 320 mg po q24h. 320 mg	QT_c **(corrected QT) interval prolongation:** ↑ QT_c (>500 msec or > 60 msec from baseline) is considered possible with any FQ. ↑ QT_c can lead to torsades de pointes & ventricular fibrillation. Risk low with current marketed drugs. Risk ↑ women, ↓ K+, ↓ Mg++, bradycardia. (Refs: *NEJM 351:1053 & 1089, 2004*). **Avoid concomitant drugs with potential to prolong QTc:** *For list of such drugs, see SANFORD GUIDE TO ANTIMICROBIAL THERAPY, Table 10C, fluoroquinolones, or www.qtdrugs.org.*
Levofloxacin (Levaquin) 250–750 mg po/IV q24h. 750 mg po, 750 mg IV.	**Skin rash with gemifloxacin:** Macular rash after 8–10 d of Rx. Highest frequency in females <age 40 treated for 14 d (22.6%). Mechanism unclear. Self-limited. No known cross-reactivity with other FQs. **Tendinopathy:** Over age 60, approx. 2–6% of all Achilles tendon ruptures attributable to use of FQ (*AIM 163:1801, 2003*). ↑ risk with concomitant steroid or renal disease (*CID 36:1404, 2003*).
Moxifloxacin (Avelox) 400 mg po/IV q24h 400 mg po/IV.	
Ofloxacin (Floxin) 200–400 mg po q12h, 400 mg po.	
Clarithromycin (Biaxin) 500 mg po q12h or extended release (Biaxin XL) 2 x 500 mg q24hr 500 mg po, 500 mg ER *(FDA approved for MAC, investigational for other atypical mycobacteria, not effective vs. M. tuberculosis)*	**Adverse effects:** Overall ~13%, ~3% discontinued drug secondary to side effects. GI ~13%: diarrhea 3%, nausea 3%, abnormal taste 3%, abdominal pain 2%, dyspepsia 2%. CNS: headache 2%. Lab (each < 1%): ↑ SGOT, alk p'tase, ↑ WBC, ↑ prothrombin time 1%, ↑ BUN 4%, ↑ creatinine <1%. Should not be used in pregnant women, has demonstrated adverse effects in animals at blood levels 2–17x higher than achieved in humans. **Check drug-drug interactions. Table 16A.** Remember potential prolongation of QTc interval by clarithro, erythro & other macrolides, esp. in combination with other drugs capable of prolonged QTc (*NEJM 312:301, 2005*). *For list of worrisome drugs: www.qtdrugs.org*
Azithromycin (Zithromax) 250–500 mg po q24h; 1200 mg po once weekly 250 mg. 600 mg *(investigational in T. gondii, not effective vs. M. tuberculosis)*	**Adverse effects:** Overall 12%, 0.7% discontinued drug secondary to side effects. GI 12.8%: diarrhea 4%, nausea 3%, abdominal pain 2%, vomiting 1%. CNS 1% ototoxicity (3/21 pts 3d for 500 mg/day. *Lancet 343:241, 1994*). Lab: ↑ SGOT 1.5%, WBC ↓ or ↑ 1%, others <1%. Has not been studied in pregnant women. In rats no embryotoxicity at dose of 60x human total dose.
Imipenem-cilastatin (Primaxin) 500 mg q6h IV 500 mg	Active in vitro vs. M. tuberculosis. Being used in some trials. **Adverse effects:** Local: phlebitis 3%. Hypersensitivity 2.5%: rash, pruritus, eosinophilia <1% Blood: ↑ Coombs <1%, neutropenia <1%. Renal: oliguria <0.2%. Hepatic: ↑ SGOT, SGPT, alk p'tase <1%, CNS (0.2%): confusion, seizures (with 0.5 gm q6h 0.5–1.0% but with 1 gm q6h ~10%). GI: nausea 2%, vomiting 2% especially with too rapid IV, diarrhea 3%. **Comment:** Tbc treatment is not an FDA-approved indication, i.e., use is investigational.

NOTE: All dosage recommendations are for adults (unless otherwise indicated) & assume normal renal function.

TABLE 13 (7)

DRUG NAME, GENERIC (TRADE)/ USUAL DOSAGE	ADVERSE EFFECTS/COMMENTS
ANTIPARASITIC DRUGS	
Albendazole (Albenza) Doses vary with indication, 200–400 mg po q12h 200 mg tab	**Adverse effects: Teratogenic. Pregnancy Cat. C.** Give after negative pregnancy test. Abdominal pain, nausea/vomiting, alopecia, ↑ serum transaminase. Rare reports of bone marrow suppression. Take with fatty meal–increases absorption 5-fold.
Atovaquone (Mepron) (Suspension) 750 mg po q12h x 21 days for PJP rx; 1500 mg po q24h for PJP prophylaxis; 750 mg/5 mL suspension, cost 210 mL. Ref: AAC 46:1163, 2002	**Adverse effects:** Discontinuation rate 9%. Skin rash 23%, only 4% required discontinuation of rx, pruritus 5%. GI: nausea 21%, diarrhea 19%, vomiting 14%, abdominal pain 4%. CNS: headache 16%, insomnia 10%, dizziness 3%. General: fever 14%. Lab: anemia (Hgb <8.0 gm/dly, 6%), neutropenia (<750/mm³, 3%), ↑ AST 4%, ↑ amylase 7%. **Comments:** Has not been evaluated in severe PJP. Better absorbed with meals. Plasma concentration 3x higher when taken with fatty (>23 gm) meal.
Clindamycin (Cleocin) Dose & route varies with indication. 75, 150, 300 mg caps; oral solution 75 mg/5 mL; IV soln.	**Adverse effects:** Most serious is C. difficile toxin-mediated diarrhea, can cause non-toxin mediated diarrhea as well. **Allergic reactions:** Fever, rash, erythema multiforme & even anaphylaxis. Reversible neutropenia, thrombocytopenia & eosinophilia. Liver injury can range from minor to severe.
Dapsone (Dapsone USP, Aczone) 100 mg q24h or 2x weekly 100 mg tabs	Dose-dependent hemolysis of no consequence at usual doses. Hemolysis enhanced greatly in pts with G6PD deficiency. G-I irritation: anorexia, nausea, vomiting. Dapsone converts 20% of RBC hemoglobin to methemoglobin: only a problem if concomitant pneumonia. High incidence of concomitant rash. Acute poisoning if >1.5 gm po: hemolysis, methemoglobinemia, jaundice, coma (NEJM 364:957, 2011). **Comment:** Usually tolerated even if rash after TMP/SMX.
Iodoquinol (Yodoxin) 650 mg tabs	**Adverse effects:** CNS: fever, agitation, retrograde amnesia, iodine hypersensitivity rash (iododermal)-papular or pustules. Thyroid enlargement. Most serious: optic neuritis, peripheral neuropathy-usually with protracted therapy.
Ivermectin (Stromectol) Strongyloidiasis: 200 mcg/kg x 1 dose po Onchocerciasis: 150 mcg/kg x 1 po Scabies: 200 mcg/kg x 1 po 3 mg tabs	**Adverse effects:** Post-treatment reaction of pt with onchocerciasis (reaction to dying microfilaria) called Mazzotti-type reaction: pruritus (28%), fever (23%), skin urticaria (23%, tender lymph nodes (10%), arthralgia (9%).
Metronidazole (Flagyl) 500–750 mg po q12h–q8h 500 mg	**Adverse effects: GI:** nausea, vomiting, metallic taste. **Neuro:** headache, paresthesias. Avoid alcohol during & 48 hours post-rx or risk of disulfiram-like reaction: nausea, vomiting, flushing, tachycardia, dyspnea. Peripheral neuropathy possible.
Nitazoxanide (Alinia) Ages 1–4: 100 mg po q12h x 3 days Ages 4–11: 200 mg po q12h x 3 days Adults: 500 mg po q12h 500 mg tabs, peds suspn	**Adverse effects:** Dose dependent, mild and transient G-I disturbance. FDA-approved for otherwise healthy children with infection due to Giardia lamblia or Cryptosporidium parvum. Caution in diabetics: 5 mL suspension contains 1.5 gm sucrose. AEs in <1%. Discolored eyes & urine. Ref: CID 40:1173, 2005.
Paromomycin (Humatin, Aminosidine) Dose as 25–35 mg/kg/day po div tid 250 mg caps	**Adverse effects:** GI: doses of >3 gm, nausea, abdominal cramps, diarrhea. CNS: vertigo, headache. Skin: rash. **Comment:** This is an aminoglycoside similar to neomycin ("non-absorbed," ~3% of dose is absorbed). Discontinue promptly if patient complains of tinnitus, ↓ in hearing, or vertigo. Risk of oto-nephrotoxicity if oral drug adsorbed due to concomitant inflammatory bowel disease.
Pentamidine isethionate (IV) (Pentam 300) 4 mg/kg/day IV 300 mg powder	**Adverse effects:** Hypotension with rapid IV administration, rash, nausea, vomiting, nephrotoxicity, hepatotoxicity, pancreatitis, hypocalcemia, hypoglycemia followed by hyperglycemia. Sterile abscesses after IM administration. de pointes), neutropenia (15%), thrombocytopenia, cardiac arrhythmia (ventricular tachycardias including torsade **Comments:** Pentamidine inhibits distal nephron absorption of Na⁺ with resultant hyperkalemia similar to K-sparing diuretics.

NOTE: All dosage recommendations are for adults (unless otherwise indicated) & assume normal renal function.

TABLE 13 (8)

DRUG NAME, GENERIC (TRADE)/ USUAL DOSAGE	ADVERSE EFFECTS/COMMENTS
ANTIPARASITIC DRUGS (continued)	
Pentamidine (aerosol) (NebuPent) 300 mg/month (prophylaxis) 300 mg powder	**Adverse effects:** Cough may respond to bronchodilator, upper lobe pneumocystis may occur if given with patient sitting. **Comment:** Risk of extrapulmonary pneumocystis & pneumothorax greater than with systemic chemotherapy. Use aerosol only in patients intolerant of oral drugs.
Praziquantel (Biltricide) 600 mg tabs	**Adverse effects:** Mild and transient: abdominal pain, nausea. Headache. Dizziness. **Contraindications:** presence of ocular cysticercosis. Use in pts taking strong inducer of CYP3A4 enzymes, e.g., rifampin, anticonvulsants.
Primaquine: Primaquine phosphate 26.3 mg = 15 mg of base 15 mg to 30 mg (base) po q24h 26.3 mg	**Adverse effects:** Hemolytic anemia if G6PD deficient; may cause clinically significant methemoglobinemia; nausea/abdominal pain if taken on empty stomach.
Pyrimethamine (Daraprim, Malocide) 50–75 mg po q24h; 25 mg with Leucovorin, tablet 5 mg —see Comments) 100 mg tabs	**Adverse effects:** Pyrimethamine-induced folate deficiency can cause megaloblastic anemia, ↓WBC, ↓ platelets, glossitis, stomatitis & exfoliative dermatitis. PO folinic acid, 5 mg/day, will ↓ heme adverse effects & not interfere with efficacy of rx. If high-dose pyrimethamine, ↑ folinic acid to 10–50 mg/day. Pyri + sulfadazine can cause mental changes due to carnitine deficiency (AJM 95:112, 1993). Other: vomiting, diarrhea, xerostomia
Sulfadiazine 1–1.5 gm po q6h 500 mg tablet	**Adverse effects:** Compared to non-HIV pts, HIV pts have dramatic ↑ in incidence of pruritus, rash, Stevens-Johnson syndrome, myalgia/arthralgia in AIDS pts. Traditionally thought on hypersensitivity basis. Data supports postulate of dose-dependent accumulation of toxic sulfonamide metabolites that fail to clear due to concomitant glutathione deficiency in the AIDS pt (Brit J Pharm 39:621, 1995; JAC 34:1, 1994). In addition, can cause hemolytic anemia in G6PD-def. pts. All sulfonamides can cause crystalluria. Do not use in newborns or late stages of pregnancy as increases risk of kernicterus.
Trimethoprim (Proloprim) 5 mg/kg po q6h 100 mg tabs	**Adverse effects:** Rash, pruritus, marrow suppression rare. Rare cases of aseptic meningitis [fever, headache, CSF ↑ cells (monos), ↑ protein] reported (CID 19:431, 1994). **Comment:** Fewer reactions than TMP/SMX.
Trimethoprim (TMP)-sulfamethoxazole (SMX) (Cotrim, Bactrim, Septra) (Dosage depends on indication) 1 double-strength tab (160 TMP/800 mg SMX); 160/800 mg IV	**Adverse effects:** Compared to non-AIDS pts, AIDS pts have dramatic dose-dependent ↑ in pruritus, skin rash, Stevens-Johnson syndrome. In pts given TMP/SMX + steroids for PJP, % skin reactions ↓ from 47 to 13 (CID 18:319, 1994). Initially thought hypersensitivity was reason; accumulating data support hypothesis of dose-dependent accumulation of toxic sulfonamide metabolites (hydroxylamine). Clearance of metabolites requires glutathione & AIDS pts are deficient (Brit J Pharm 39:621, 1995; JAC 34:1, 1994). Reversible ability 2/3 of time to rx through rash (Arch Derm 130:1383, 1994). Beware progressive exanthem— some pts progress to exfoliation &/or Stevens-Johnson syndrome. Tremors associated with high dose (CID 22:598, 1996). **TMP** competes with creatinine for tubular secretion & can ↑ serum creatinine (reversible); **TMP** also blocks distal renal tubular reabsorption of Na+ & secretion of K+: ↑ serum K+ in 21% of pts (AnIM 124:316, 1996).

DRUG NAME(S), GENERIC (TRADE)	DOSAGE/ROUTE	COMMENTS/ADVERSE EFFECTS
ANTIVIRAL DRUGS (other than retroviral)		
CMV		
Cidofovir (Vistide)	5 mg/kg IV q week x 2 weeks, then once weekly every 2 wks. Properly timed IV prehydration with normal saline & oral probenecid **must be used with each cidofovir infusion** (see pkg insert for details). Renal function (serum creatinine & urine protein) must be monitored prior to each dose (see pkg insert for details).	**Adverse effects: Nephrotoxicity:** dose-dependent proximal tubular injury (Fanconi-like syndrome): proteinuria, glycosuria, bicarbonaturia, phosphaturia, polyuria (nephrogenic diabetic insipidus now reported, Ln 350:413, 1997), ↑ creatinine. Concomitant saline prehydration, probenecid, & extended dosing intervals allowed use. 25% of pts dc IV cidofovir due to nephrotoxicity. Other toxicities: nausea 48%, fever 31%, alopecia 16%, myalgia 16%, probenecid hypersensitivity 16%, neutropenia 29%. No effect on hematocrit, platelets, LFTs. Other **Black Box** warnings: contraindicated with concomitant nephrotoxic agents, ↓WBC, carcinogenic/teratogenic & ↓ sperm in animals, only indicated for rx of CMV retinitis. Contraindicated with serum creatinine > 1.5 mg/dL, or urine protein ≥ 100 mg/dL. **Comment:** Recommended dose, frequency or infusion rate of cidofovir must not be exceeded. Dose must be reduced or discontinued if changes in renal function occur during rx. For ↑ of 0.3–0.4 mg/dl in serum creatinine, cidofovir dose must be ↓ from 5 to 3 mg/kg; discontinue cidofovir if ↑ of 0.5 mg/dl above baseline or 3+ proteinuria develops (for 2+ proteinuria develops, observe pts carefully & consider discontinuation).

NOTE: All dosage recommendations are for adults (unless otherwise indicated) & assume normal renal function.

TABLE 13 (9)

DRUG NAME(S) GENERIC (TRADE)	DOSAGE/ROUTE	COMMENTS/ADVERSE EFFECTS
ANTIVIRAL DRUGS (other than retroviral)/CMV *(continued)*		
Foscarnet (Foscavir)	90 mg/kg q12h IV (induction) 90 mg/kg q24h IV (maintenance) Dosage adjustment with renal dysfunction *(see Table 15A)*	**Adverse effects: Major clinical toxicity is renal impairment (1/3 of patients)**—↑ creatinine, proteinuria, nephrogenic diabetes insipidus; ↓ K⁺, ↓ Ca²⁺, ↓ Mg²⁺, ↓ or ↑ phosphate. Other Black Box warnings: hydration & frequent monitoring imperative; dose adjustment with renal function *(see label and Table 15A)*; **seizures** related to electrolyte/mineral abnormalities. Infusion rate must be controlled; administer by infusion pump over 1.5 to 2 hrs. Prehydrate to establish diuresis before first dose and hydrate concomitantly with subsequent doses. Toxicity ↑ with other nephrotoxic drugs (amphotericin B, aminoglycosides or pentamidine (especially severe ↓ Ca²⁺]). Other: headache, mild (100%); fatigue (100%); nausea (80%), fever (25%) CNS: seizures. Hematol: ↓ WBC, ↓ High. Hepatic: liver function tests ↑. Neuropathy. Penile ulcers.
Ganciclovir (Cytovene)	IV: 5 mg/kg q12h x 14 days (induction) 5 mg/kg IV q24h daily or 6 mg/kg q24h 5 days per/wk (maintenance) Dosage adjustment with renal dysfunction *(see Table 15A)*	**Adverse effects: Black Box** warnings: cytopenias, carcinogenicity/teratogenicity & aspermia in animals. Absolute neutrophil count dropped below 500/mm³ in 15%, thrombocytopenia 21%, anemia 6%. Fever 48%. GI 50%, nausea, vomiting, diarrhea, abdominal pain 19%, rash 10%. Retinal detachment 11%. (Likely related to underlying disease, not drug). Confusion, headache, psychiatric disturbances & seizures. Neutropenia may respond to granulocyte colony stimulating factor (G-CSF or GM-CSF). Severe myelosuppression may be ↑ with coadministration of zidovudine or azathioprine. 32% dc/interrupted rx, principally for neutropenia. Avoid extravasation.
	Oral: 1 gm q8h with food (fatty meal)	Hematologic less frequent than with IV. Granulocytopenia 18%, anemia 12%, thrombocytopenia 6%. GI, skin same as with IV. Retinal detachment 8%.
Ganciclovir (Vitrasert)	Intraocular implant (~$5000/device + cost of surgery)	**Adverse effects:** Late retinal detachment (7/30 eyes). Does not prevent CMV retinitis in good eye or visceral dissemination. **Comment:** Replacement every 6 mos recommended.
Valganciclovir (Valcyte)	900 mg (two 450 mg tabs) po q12h x 21 days for induction, followed by 900 mg po q24h for maintenance. Take with food. Dosage adjustment with renal dysfunction *(see Table 15A)*	A prodrug of ganciclovir with better bioavailability than oral ganciclovir. 60% with food. **Adverse effects:** Similar to ganciclovir.
Herpesvirus (Non-CMV)		
Acyclovir (Zovirax)	Doses: see *Table 12* 200 mg caps, 400 mg and 800 mg tabs IV injection (multiple) Oral suspension 200 mg/5 mL Topical: 5% cream and 5% ointment Dosage adjustment with renal dysfunction *(see Table 15A)*.	**Oral:** Generally well-tolerated with occ. diarrhea, vertigo, arthralgia. Less frequent rash, fatigue, insomnia, fever, menstrual abnormalities, acne, sore throat, muscle cramps, lymphadenopathy. **IV:** Phlebitis, caustic with vesicular lesions with IV infiltration. CNS (1%): lethargy, tremors, confusion, hallucinations, delirium, seizures, coma *(CID 21:435, 1995)*. Improve 1–2 wks after rx stopped. Renal (5%): ↑ creatinine, hematuria. With high doses may crystalize in renal tubules → obstructive uropathy (rapid infusion, dehydration, renal insufficiency & ↑ dose ↑ risk). Adequate pre-hydration may prevent such nephrotoxicity. Hepatic: ↑ ALT, AST. Uncommon: neutropenia *(CID 20: 1557, 1995)*, rash, diaphoresis, hypotension, headache, nausea.
Famciclovir (Famvir)	Doses: see *Table 12* Tabs: 125 mg, 250 mg, 500 mg.	Pro-drug of penciclovir. **Adverse effects:** similar to acyclovir, included headache, nausea, diarrhea, & dizziness but incidence did not differ from placebo *(JAMA 276:47, 1996)*. May be taken without regard to meals. Dose should be reduced if CrCl <60 mL/min *(see package insert & Table 12, page 160 & Table 15A, page 192)*.
Penciclovir (Denavir)	Topical 1% cream (1.5 gm tubes)	Apply to area of recurrence of herpes labialis with start of sx, then q2h while awake x 4 days. Well tolerated.
Trifluridine (Viroptic)	Topical 1% solution: 1 drop q2h (max 9 drops/day) until corneal re-epithelialization, then dose is reduced for 7 additional days (one drop q4h for at least 5 drops/day), not to exceed 21 days total rx.	For HSV keratoconjunctivitis or recurrent epithelial keratitis. **Adverse effects:** Mild burning (5%), palpebral edema (3%), punctate keratopathy, stromal edema

NOTE: All dosage recommendations are for adults (unless otherwise indicated) & assume normal renal function.

TABLE 13 (10)

DRUG NAME(S) GENERIC (TRADE)	DOSAGE/ROUTE	COMMENTS/ADVERSE EFFECTS
ANTIVIRAL DRUGS (other than retroviral)/Herpesvirus (Non-CMV) *(continued)*		
Valacyclovir (Valtrex)	Doses: see *Table 12.* 500 mg tabs and 1 gm caplets. Dosage adjustment with renal dysfunction *(see Table 15A).*	An ester pro-drug of acyclovir that is well-absorbed, bioavailability 3–5x greater than acyclovir. Can take without regard to meals. **Adverse effects** similar to acyclovir *(see JID 186:S40, 2002).* Thrombotic thrombocytopenic purpura/hemolytic uremic syndrome reported in pts with advanced HIV disease & transplant recipients participating in clinical trials at doses of 8 gm/day.
Hepatitis		
Adefovir dipivoxil (Hepsera)	10 mg po q24h (with normal CrCl) 20-49 CrCl: 10 mg q48h 10-19 CrCl: 10 mg q72h Hemodialysis: 10 mg q7 days following dialysis. Each tab contains 10 mg	Adefovir dipivoxil is a prodrug of the active moiety adefovir. It is an acyclic nucleotide analog with activity against hepatitis B (HBV) at 0.2-2.5mM (IC₅₀). Peak plasma concentration after 10 mg po was 18.4 ± 6.26 ng/mL, 1–4 hrs after dose. Terminal elimination t½ was 7.48 ± 1.65 hrs. Primarily renal excretion: adjust dose with renal dysfunction. Remarkably few side effects. Nephrotoxicity found in early studies with 30 mg/d: at 10 mg/d there is potential for delayed nephrotoxicity. Monitor renal function, esp. with pts with pre-existing or other risks for renal impairment. Lactic acidosis reported with nucleoside analogs, esp. in women. Pregnancy Category C. Hepatitis may exacerbate when rx dc. 6–25% of pts developed ALT ↑ 10x normal within 12 wks, usually responds to re-treatment or self-limited, but hepatic decompensation has occurred.
Boceprevir (Victrelis)	800 mg tid in combination with PegIFN + RBV	Most common AEs: Fatigue, anemia, nausea, headache, and dysgeusia. Difficult to distinguish between AEs caused by pegIFN or RBV
Emtricitabine/ tenofovir disoproxil fumarate (Truvada)	See *Table 6B*	Treatment of choice for Hep B/HIV co-infected patients, despite **Black Box** warning regarding discontinuation of therapy leading to a potential flare in liver enzymes.
Entecavir (Baraclude)	0.5 mg q24h. If refractory to lamivudine: 1 mg per day Tabs: 0.5 mg and 1 mg Oral solution: 0.05 mg/mL	A nucleoside analog active against HBV including some lamivudine-resistant mutants. Minimal adverse effects reported: headache, fatigue, dizziness, & nausea reported in 22% of pts. Potential for lactic acidosis, exacerbation of hepB at discontinuation, and HIV resistance *(see Black Box warning).* Adjust dosage in renal impairment *(see Table 15A).* Do not use as single anti-retroviral agent in co-infected pts. HIV resistant mutation M134V will emerge *(NEJM 356:2614, 2007).*
PEG interferon alfa-2b (PEG-Intron)	0.5-1.5 mcg/kg subQ q wk	
Pegylated-2b interferon alfa-2a (Pegasys)	180 mcg subQ q wk	Attachment of INF to polyethylene glycol (PEG) prolongs half-life & allows weekly dosing. Better efficacy data with similar adverse effects profile compared to regular formulation. Doses may require adjustment (or dc) based on individual response or adverse events, and can vary by product. Indication (eg, HCV or HBV) and mode of use (mono- or combination-rx). *(Refer to labels of individual products.)*
Telaprevir (Incivek)	For Hep C: 750 mg q12h in combination with Peg INF + ribavirin	**Most common adverse effects:** Rash (inc rare Stevens Johnson reaction), pruritus, nausea, anorexia, headache, fatigue, anemia, insomnia, and depression. Difficult to dissect telaprevir AEs from IFN/ribavirin.
Lamivudine (3TC) (Epivir-HBV)	Hepatitis B dose: 100 mg po q24h Dosage adjustment with renal dysfunction (see label). Tabs 100 mg and oral solution 5 mg/mL	**Black Box warnings:** caution that this dose is lower than HIV dose; so must exclude co-infection with HIV before using this formulation; lactic acidosis/hepatic steatosis; severe exacerbation of liver disease can occur on dc; YMDD-mutants resistant to lamivudine may emerge on treatment. **Adverse effects:** See *Table 6B.*
Simeprevir (Olysio)	One 150 mg cap po once daily with food + (RBV + IFN)	**Warning:** combination (with RBV) is contraindicated in pregnancy. AEs: photosensitivity; rash; pruritus; nausea
Sofosbuvir (Sovaldi)	One 400 mg tab once daily with or without food + (RBV + IFN)	**Warning:** combination (with RBV) is contraindicated in pregnancy. AEs: fatigue; headache; nausea, insomnia; anemia

NOTE: All dosage recommendations are for adults (unless otherwise indicated) & assume normal renal function.

TABLE 13 (11)

DRUG NAME(S) GENERIC (TRADE)	DOSAGE/ROUTE	COMMENTS/ADVERSE EFFECTS
ANTIVIRAL DRUGS (other than retroviral)/Hepatitis (continued)		
Ribavirin (Rebetol, Copegus)	For use with an interferon for hepatitis C. Available as 200 mg caps and 40 mg/mL oral solution (Rebetol) or 200 mg tabs (Copegus) (See Comments regarding dosage)	**Black Box warnings:** ribavirin monotherapy of HCV is ineffective; hemolytic anemia may precipitate cardiac events—use with caution; teratogenic/embryocidal **(Preg Category X).** Drug may persist for 6 mos, avoid pregnancy for at least 6 mos after end of rx of women or their partners. Only approved for pts with Ccr > 50 mL/min. Also should not be used in pts with severe heart disease or some hemoglobinopathies. ARDS reported (Chest 124:406, 2003). **Adverse effects:** hemolytic anemia (may require dose reduction or dc); dental/periodontal disorders, and all adverse effects of concomitant interferon used (see above). See Table 12 for specific regimens, but dose depends on: interferon used, weight, HCV genotype, and is modified (or stopped) based on side effects (especially degree of hemolysis, with different criteria in those with/without cardiac disease). For example, initial Rebetol dose with Intron A (interferon alfa-2b) is wt-based: 400 mg am & 600 mg pm for wt < 75 kg, and 600 mg pm for wt > 75 kg, but with Pegintron approved dose is 400 mg am & 400 mg pm with meals. Doses and duration of Copegus with peg-interferon alfa-2a are less in pts with genotype 2 or 3 (800 mg per day divided into 2 doses, for 24 wks) than with genotypes 1 or 4 (1000 mg per day divided into 2 doses for wt < 75 kg and 1200 mg per day divided into 2 doses for wt ≥ 75 kg for 48 wks). (See individual labels for details, including initial dosing and criteria for dose modification in those with/without cardiac disease.)
Telbivudine (Tyzeka)	One 600 mg tab orally q24h, without regard to food. Dosage adjustment with renal dysfunction, Ccr < 50 mL/min (see label).	An oral nucleoside analog approved for Rx of Hep B. It has demonstrated higher rates of response and superior viral suppression than lamivudine. **Black Box** warnings regarding lactic acidosis/hepatic steatosis with nucleosides and potential for severe exacerbation of HepB on dc. Generally well-tolerated with reduced mitochondrial toxicity vs. other nucleosides and no dose limiting toxicity observed (Ann Pharmacother 40:472, 2006; Medical Letter 49:11, 2007). Myalgias and myopathy reported. The genotype resistance rate was 4.7 by one yr increasing to 21.5% by 2 yrs of treatment. It selects for YMDD mutation like lamivudine. Combination with lamivudine was inferior to monotherapy (Hepatology 45:507, 2007).
Tenofovir (TDF) (Viread)	See Table 6B	Treatment of hepB is not an FDA approved indication, but drug is treatment of choice in HIV/HBV co-infected patients requiring therapy for both.
Warts (See CID 28:S37, 1999) Regimens are from drug labels specific for external genital and/or perianal condylomata acuminata only (see specific labels for indications, regimens, age limits).		
Interferon alfa-2b (IntronA)	Injection of 1 million international units into base of lesion, thrice weekly on alternate days for up to 3 wks. Maximum 5 lesions per course.	Interferons may cause "flu-like" illness and other systemic effects. 88% had at least one adverse effect.
Interferon alfa-N3 (Alferon N)	Injection of 0.05 mL into base of each wart, up to 0.5 mL total per session, twice weekly for up to 8 weeks.	Flu-like syndrome and hypersensitivity reactions. Contraindicated with allergy to mouse IgG, egg proteins, or neomycin.
Imiquimod (Aldara)	5% cream. Thin layer applied at bedtime, washing off after 6-10 hr, thrice weekly to maximum of 16 weeks.	Erythema, itching & burning, erosions. Flu-like syndrome. Increased susceptibility to sunburn (avoid UV).
Podofilox (Condylox)	0.5% gel or solution twice daily for 3 days, no therapy for 4 days; can use up to 4 such cycles	Local reactions—pain, burning, inflammation in 50%. Can ulcerate. Limit surface area treated as per label.
Sinecatechins (Veregen)	15% ointment. Apply 0.5 cm strand to each wart three times per day until healing but not more than 16 weeks.	Application site reactions, which may result in ulcerations, phimosis, meatal stenosis, superinfection.

NOTE: All dosage recommendations are for adults (unless otherwise indicated) & assume normal renal function.

TABLE 14A: SELECTED PHARMACOLOGIC FEATURES OF ANTIMICROBIAL AGENTS USED IN HIV-ASSOCIATED INFECTIONS IN ADULTS

For Cytochrome P450 interactions, see Table 14B. Table terminology key at bottom of each page. Additional footnotes at end of this table, page 183.

DRUG	REFERENCE DOSE/ROUTE	PREG RISK	FOOD EFFECT (PO)[1]	ORAL %AB	PEAK SERUM LEVEL (µg/mL)	PROTEIN BINDING (%)	VOL OF DISTRIB (Vd)	AVER SERUM T½, hrs[2]	BILE PEN (%)[3]	CSF/BLOOD (%)	CSF PEN[5]	AUC (µg*hr/mL)	Tmax (hr)
PENICILLINS: Natural													
Benz Pen G	1.2 million units IM	B			0.15 (SD)								
Penicillin G	2 million units IV	B			20 (SD)	65			500	5-10	Yes Pen-sens S. pneumo		
Penicillin V	500 mg po	B	Tab/soln no food	60-73	5-6 (SD)	65	0.35 L/kg	0.5					
PEN'ASE-RESISTANT PENICILLINS													
Cloxacillin[NUS]	500 mg	B	Cap no food	50	7.5-14 (SD)	95	0.1 L/kg	0.5					1-1.5
Dicloxacillin	500 mg	B	Cap no food	37	10-17 (SD)	98	0.1 L/kg	0.7	5-8				1-1.5
Nafcillin	500 mg	B			30 (SD)	90-94	27.1 L Vss	0.5-1	>100	9-20	Yes		
Oxacillin	500 mg	B			43 (SD)	90-94	0.4 L/kg	0.5-0.7	25	10-15	Yes	18.1	
AMINOPENICILLINS													
Amoxicillin	500 mg po	B	Cap/tab/susp ± food	80	5.5-7.5 (SD)	17	0.36 L/kg	1.2	100-3000	13-14	Yes (IV only)	22	1-2
Amoxicillin ER	775 mg	B	Tab + food		6.6 (SD)	20		1.2-1.5	100-3000			29.8	3.1
AM-CL	875/125 mg po	B	Cap/tab/susp ± food	80/30-98	11.6/2.2 (SD)	18/25		1.4/1.1	100-3000			AM: 26.8-CL: 5.1	
AM-CL-ER	2 tabs [2000/125 mg]	B	Tab + food		17/2.1 (SD)	18/25		1.3/1.0				AM: 71.6-CL: 5.3	AM: 1.5 CL: 1.03
Ampicillin	2 gm IV	B			100 (SD)	18-22	0.29 L/kg	1.2	100-3000	13-14	Yes	AM: 120-SB: 71	
AM-SB	3 gm IV	B			109-150/48-88 (SD)	28/38		1.2					
ANTIPSEUDOMONAL PENICILLINS													
PIP-TZ	3/375 gm IV	B			242/24 (SD)	16-48	PIP 0.24 L/kg	1.0	>100			PIP: 242-TZ: 25	
TC-CL	3.1 gm IV	B			330/8 (SD)	45/25	TC: 9.7 Vss	1.2/1.0				TC: 485-CL: 8.2	
CEPHALOSPORINS—1st Generation													
Cefadroxil	500 mg po	B	Cap/tab/susp ± food	90	16 (SD)	20	0.31 L/kg V/F	1.5	22			47.4	
Cefazolin	1 gm IV	B			188 (SD)	73-87	0.19 L/kg	1.9	29-300	1-4	No	236	
Cephalexin	500 mg po	B	Cap/tab/susp ±	90	18 (SD)	5-15	0.38 L/kg V/F	1.0	216			29	1

Preg Risk: FDA risk categories: **A** = no risk in adequate human studies. **B** = animal studies suggest no fetal risk, but no adequate human studies; OR adverse fetal effects in animals, but no adequate studies in humans. **C** = adverse fetal effects in animals, but no adequate human use despite potential risk. **D** = evidence of human fetal risk, but potential benefit may warrant use despite potential risk. **X** = evidence of human fetal risk that clearly exceeds potential benefits. **Food Effect (PO dosing): + food** = take with food, **no food** = take without food. **± food** = take with or without food. **Oral AB** = % absorbed. **Peak Serum Level: SD** = after single dose. **SS** = steady state after multiple doses; **Volume of Distribution (Vd): V/F** = Vd/oral bioavailability. **Vss/F** = Vd at steady state/oral bioavailability. **Vss** = Vd at steady state. **24hr** = AUC 0-24; **Tmax** = time to max plasma concentration. **AUC** = area under drug concentration curve; **CSF Penetration:** therapeutic efficacy comment based on dose, usual susceptibility of target organism & penetration into CSF.

TABLE 14A (2)

DRUG	REFERENCE DOSE/ROUTE	FOOD EFFECT (PO)[1]	ORAL %AB	PEAK SERUM LEVEL (μg/mL)	PROTEIN BINDING (%)	VOL OF DISTRIB (Vd)	AVER SERUM T½, hrs[2]	BILE PEN (%)[3]	CSF/ BLOOD (%)	CSF PEN[6]	AUC (μg*hr/mL)	Tmax (hr)
CEPHALOSPORINS—2nd Generation												
Cefaclor	500 mg po	Cap/susp ± food	93	13 (SD)	22-25	0.33 L/kg V/F	0.8	≥60			20.5	0.5-1.0
Cefaclor-ER	500 mg po	Tab + food		8.4 (SD)	22-25		0.8	≥60			18.1	2.5
Cefotetan	1 gm IV			158 (SD)	78-91	10.3 L	4.2	2-21			504	
Cefoxitin	1 gm IV			110 (SD)	65-79	16.1 L Vss	0.8	280	3	No		
Cefprozil	500 mg po	Tab/susp ± food	95	10.5 (SD)	36	0.23 L/kg Vss/F	1.5				25.7	
Cefuroxime	1.5 gm IV			100 (SD)	33-50	0.19 L/kg Vss	1.5	35-80	17-88	Marginal	150	
Cefuroxime axetil	250 mg tabs po	Susp ± food; Tab ± food	52	4.1 (SD)	50	0.66 L/kg V/F	1.5				12.9	2.5
CEPHALOSPORINS—3rd Generation												
Cefdinir	300 mg po	Cap/susp ± food	25	1.6 (SD)	60-70	0.35 L/kg V/F	1.7				7.1	2.9
Cefditoren pivoxil	400 mg po	Tab + food	16	4 (SD)	88	9.3 L Vss/F	1.6				20	1.5-3.0
Cefixime	400 mg po	Tab/susp ± food	50	3-5 (SD)	65	0.93 L/kg V/F	3.1	800			25.8	4
Cefotaxime	1 gm IV			100	30-51	0.28 L/kg	1.5	15-75	10	Yes	70	
Cefpodoxime proxetil	200 mg po	Tab + food Susp ± food	46	2.3 (SD)	40	0.7 L/kg V/F	2.3	115			14.5	2-3
Ceftazidime	1 gm IV			69 (SD)	<10	0.24 L/kg Vss	1.9	13-54	20-40	Yes	127	
Ceftibuten	400 mg po	Cap/susp no food	80	15 (SD)	65	0.21 L/kg V/F	2.4				73.7	
Ceftizoxime	1 gm IV			60 (SD)	30	0.34 L/kg	1.7	34-82	8-16	Yes	85	
Ceftriaxone	1 gm IV			150 (SD), 172-204 (SS)	85-95	5.8-13.5 L	8	200-500	8-16	Yes	1006	2.6
CEPHALOSPORIN—4th Generation and Anti-MRSA												
Cefepime	2 gm IV			164 (SD)	20	18 L Vss	2.0	10-20	10	Yes	284.8	
Ceftaroline	600 mg IV			21.3	20	20.3 Vss	2.7				56.3	
Ceftobiprole[A,15]	500 mg IV			33-34.2 (SD)	16	18 L Vss	2.9-3.3				116	
CARBAPENEMS												
Doripenem	500 mg IV			23	8.1	16.8 L Vss	1	117 (0-611)			36.3	
Ertapenem	1 gm IV			154	95	0.12 L/kg Vss	4	10			572.1	
Imipenem	500 mg IV			40	15-25	0.27 L/kg	1	minimal	8.5	+[6]	42.2	
Meropenem	1 gm IV			49	2	0.29 L/kg	1	3-300	Approx. 2	+	72.5	
MONOBACTAM												
Aztreonam	1 gm IV			90 (SD)	56	12.6 L Vss	2	115-405	3-52	±	271	

Preg Risk: FDA risk categories: **A** = no risk in adequate human studies. **B** = animal studies suggest no fetal risk, but no adequate studies in humans; potential benefit may warrant use despite potential risk. **C** = adverse fetal effects in animals, but no adequate studies in humans, potential benefit may warrant use despite potential risk. **D** = evidence of human risk, but potential benefit may warrant use despite potential risk. **X** = evidence of human risk that clearly exceeds potential benefits. **Food Effect (PO dosing): + food** = take with food. **± food** = take with or without food. **no food** = take without food. **Oral % AB** = % absorbed. **Peak Serum Level: SD** = after single dose. **SS** = steady state after multiple doses. **Volume of Distribution (Vd): V/F** = Vd/oral bioavailability. **Vss** = Vd at steady state. **Vss/F** = Vd at steady state/oral bioavailability. **CSF Penetration:** therapeutic efficacy comment based on dose, usual susceptibility of target organism & penetration into CSF. **AUC** = area under drug concentration curve. **24hr** = AUC 0-24; **Tmax** = time to max plasma concentration.

TABLE 14A (3)

DRUG	REFERENCE DOSE/ROUTE	PREG RISK	FOOD EFFECT (PO)[1]	ORAL %AB	PEAK SERUM LEVEL (μg/mL)	PROTEIN BINDING (%)	VOL OF DISTRIB (Vd)	AVER SERUM T½, hrs[2]	BILE PEN (%)[3]	CSF/ BLOOD (%)	CSF PEN[4]	AUC (μg·hr/mL)	Tmax (hr)
AMINOGLYCOSIDES													
Amikacin, gentamicin, kanamycin, tobramycin		D				0-10	0.26 L/kg	2.5	10-60	0-30	No. intrathecal dose: 5-10 mg		
Neomycin	po	D	Tab/soln ± food	<3	0								
FLUOROQUINOLONES[7]													
Ciprofloxacin	750 mg po q12h	C	± food	70	3.6 (SS)	20-40	2.4 L/kg	4	2800-4500			31.6 (24 hr)	1-2
	400 mg IV q12h	C	± food		4.6 (SS)	20-40		4	2800-4500	26	1 μg/mL: inadequate for Strep. sp. (QID 31;1131, 2000)	25.4 (24 hr)	
	500 mg ER po q24h	C	± food		1.6 (SS)	20-40		6.6				8 (24 hr)	1.5
	1000 mg ER po q24h	C	± food		3.1 (SS)	20-40		6.3				16 (24 hr)	2.0
Gemifloxacin	320 mg po q24h	C	Tab ± food	71	1.6 (SS)	55-73	2-12 L/kg Vss/F	7				9.9 (24 hr)	0.5-2.0
Levofloxacin	500 mg po/IV q24h	C	Tab ± food	99	5.7/6.4 (SS)	24-38	74-112 L Vss	7		30-50		PO:47.5, IV 54.6 (24 hr)	PO: 1.3
	750 mg po/IV q24h	C	Tab ± food / Oral soln no food	99	8.6/12.1 (SS)	24-38	244 L Vss	7				PO 90.7, IV 108 (24 hr)	PO: 1.6
Moxifloxacin	400 mg po/IV q24h	C	Tab ± food	89	4.2-4.6/4.5 (SS)	30-50	2.2 L/kg	10-14		>50	Yes (QID 49:1080, 2009)	PO 48, IV 38 (24 hr)	PO: 1-3
Ofloxacin	400 mg po/IV q12h	C	Tab ± food	98	4.6/6.2 (SS)	32	1-2.5 L/kg	7				PO 82.4, IV 87 (24 hr)	PO: 1-2
Prulifloxacin[AUS]	600 mg po		± food		1.6 (SD)	45	1231L	10.6-12.1		negligible	no	7.3	1
MACROLIDES, AZALIDES, LINCOSAMIDES, KETOLIDES													
Azithromycin	500 mg po	B	Tab/Susp ± food	37	0.4 (SD)	7-51	31.1 L/kg	68	High			4.3	2.5
	500 mg IV	B			3.6 (SD)	7-51	33.3 L/kg	12/68				9.6 (24 hr, pre SS)	
Azithromycin-ER	2 gm po	B	Susp no food	≈30	0.8 (SD)	7-50	31.1 L/kg	59	High			20	5.0
Clarithromycin	500 mg po q12h	C	Tab/Susp ± food	50	3-4 (SD)	65-70	4 L/kg	5-7	7000			20 (24 hr)	2.0-2.5
	1000 mg ER po q24h	C	Tab + food	≈50	2-3 (SS)	65-70		5-8					5-8

Preg Risk: FDA risk categories: A = no risk in adequate human studies. **B** = animal studies suggest no fetal risk, but no adequate human studies. **C** = adverse fetal effects in animals, but no adequate studies in humans; potential benefit may warrant use despite potential risk. **D** = evidence of human risk, but potential benefit may warrant use despite potential risk. **X** = evidence of human risk that clearly exceeds potential benefits. **Food Effect (PO dosing): + food** = take with food. **no food** = take without food: **± food** = take with or without food: **Oral % AB** = % absorbed: **Peak Serum Level: SD** = after single dose. **SS** = steady state after multiple doses. **Volume of Distribution (Vd): V/F** = Vd/oral bioavailability. **Vss** = Vd at steady state. **Vss/F** = Vd at steady state/oral bioavailability. **CSF Penetration:** therapeutic efficacy comment based on dose, usual susceptibility of target organism & penetration into CSF; **AUC** = area under drug concentration curve; **24hr** = AUC 0-24; **Tmax** = time to max plasma concentration.

TABLE 14A (4)

DRUG	REFERENCE DOSE/ROUTE	PREG RISK	FOOD EFFECT (PO)[1]	ORAL %AB	PEAK SERUM LEVEL (µg/mL)	PROTEIN BINDING (%)	VOL OF DISTRIB (Vd)	AVER SERUM T½, hrs[2]	BILE PEN (%)[3]	CSF/ BLOOD (%)	CSF/ PEN[a]	AUC (µg•hr/mL)[a]	Tmax (hr)
MACROLIDES, AZALIDES, LINCOSAMIDES, KETOLIDES *(continued)*													
Erythromycin Oral (various)	500 mg po	B	Tab/Susp no food DR Caps ± food	18-45	0.1-2 (SD)	70-74	0.6 L/kg	2-4		2-13	No		Delayed Rel: 3
Lacto/glucep	500 mg IV	B			3-4 (SD)	70-74		2-4					
Telithromycin	800 mg po q24h	C	Tab ± food	57	2.3 (SD)	60-70	2.9 L/kg	10	7			12.5 (24 hr)	1
Clindamycin	150 mg po / 900 mg IV	B / B	Cap ± food	90	2.5 (SD) / 14.1 (SS)	85-94 / 85-94	1.1 L/kg	2.4 / 2.4	250-300 / 250-300		No / No		0.75
MISCELLANEOUS ANTIBACTERIALS													
Chloramphenicol	1 gm po q6h	C	Cap ± food	High	18 (SS)	25-50	0.8 L/kg	4.1		45-89	Yes		
Colistin (Polymyxin E)	150 mg IV	C			5-7.5 (SD)	92	0.34 L/kg	2-3	0		No (AAC 53:4907, 2009)		
Daptomycin	4-6 mg/kg IV q24h	B			58-99 (SS)	92	0.1 L/kg Vss	8-9		0-8		494-632 (24 hr)	2
Doxycycline	100 mg po	B	Tab/cap/susp + food		1.5-2.1 (SD)	93	53-134 L Vss	18	200-3200		No (26%)	31.7	
Fosfomycin	3 gm po	-	Sachet ± food		26 (SD)	<10	136.1 L Vss/F	5.7				150	
Fusidic acid[AUS]	500 mg po	C	Tab ± food	91	30 (SD)	95-99	0.3 L/kg	5-15	100-200			315	2-4
Linezolid	600 mg po/IV q12h	C	Tab/susp ± food	100	15-20 (SS)	31	40-50 L Vss	5		60-70	Yes (AAC 50:3971, 2006)	PO: 276/IV 179 (24hr)	PO: 1.3
Metronidazole	500 mg po/IV q6h	B	ER tab no food, Tab/cap ± food	100	20-25 (SS)	20	0.6-0.85 L/kg	6-14	100	45-89		560 (24 hr)	Immed Rel: 1.6 ER: 6.8
Minocycline	200 mg po	D	Cap/tab ± food		2.0-3.5 (SD)	76	80-114 L Vss	16	200-3200		No	48.3	2.1
Polymyxin B	2 mg/kg IV	C			1-8 (SD)	78-92	0.07-0.2 L/kg	4.3-6			No		
Quinu-Dalfo	7.5 mg/kg IV q8h	B			3.2/8 (SS)	93	0.45/0.24 L/kg Vss	1.5				Quinu: 21.6 Dal: 31.8	
Rifampin	600 mg po	C	Cap no food	70-90	4-32 (SD)	80	0.65 L/kg Vss	2-5	10,000	7-56	Yes	58	1.5-2
Rifaximin	200 mg po	C	Tab ± food	<0.4	0.004-0.01 (SD)	67.5		2-5			No	0.008	1
Tetracycline	250 mg po	D	Cap no food		1.5-2.2 (SD)		1.3 L/kg	6-12	200-3200		No (7%)	30	2-4
Televancin	10 mg/kg q24h	C			108 (SS)	90	0.13 L/kg	8.1	Low		No	780 (24 hr)	

Preg. Risk: FDA risk categories: A = no risk in adequate human studies, **B** = animal studies suggest no fetal risk, but no adequate human studies, **C** = adverse fetal effects in animals, but no adequate human studies in humans; potential benefit may warrant use despite potential risk, **D** = evidence of human risk, but potential benefit may warrant use despite potential risk, **X** = evidence of human risk that clearly exceeds potential benefit. **Food Effect (PO dosing): + food** = take with food, **no food** = take with or without food, **± food** = take with or without food. **Oral % AB** = % absorbed. **Peak Serum Level: SD** = after single dose, **SS** = steady state after multiple doses. **Volume of Distribution (Vd): V/F** = Vd/oral bioavailability, **Vss** = Vd at steady state, **Vss/F** = Vd at steady state/oral bioavailability. **CSF Penetration:** therapeutic efficacy comment based on dose, usual susceptibility of target organism & penetration into CSF. **AUC** = area under drug concentration curve. **24hr** = AUC 0-24. **Tmax** = time to max plasma concentration.

TABLE 14A (5)

DRUG	REFERENCE DOSE/ROUTE	PREG RISK	FOOD EFFECT (PO)[1]	ORAL %AB	PEAK SERUM LEVEL (μg/mL)	PROTEIN BINDING (%)	VOL OF DISTRIB (Vd)	AVER SERUM T½, hrs[2]	BILE PEN (%)[3]	CSF/BLOOD (%)	CSF PEN[4]	AUC (μg*hr/mL)	Tmax (hr)
MISCELLANEOUS ANTIBACTERIALS *(continued)*													
Tigecycline	50 mg IV q12h				0.63 (SS)	71-89	7-9 L/kg	42	138		No	4.7 (24 hr)	
Trimethoprim (TMP)	100 mg po	C	Tab ± food	80	1 (SD)	44	100-120 V/F	8-15	100-200				1-4
TMP-SMX-DS	160/800 mg po q12h	C	Tab/susp ± food	85	1-2/40-60 (SS)	TMP: 44 SMX: 70	TMP: 100-120 L SMX: 18 L	TMP: 11 SMX: 9	40-70	50/40			TMP PO: 1-4 SMX IV: 1-4
	160/800 mg IV q8h	C			9/105 (SS)								
Vancomycin	1 gm IV q12h	C			20-50 (SS)	<10-55	0.7 L/kg	4-6		7-14			
ANTIFUNGALS													
Amphotericin B:													
Standard	0.4-0.7 mg/kg IV	B			0.5-3.5 (SS)	>90	4 L/kg	24		0		17.	
Lipid (ABLC)	5 mg/kg IV	B			1-2.5 (SS)		131 L/kg	173				14 (24 hr)	
Cholesteryl complex	4 mg/kg IV	B			2.9 (SS)		4.3 L/kg	39				36 (24 hr)	
Liposomal	5 mg/kg IV	B			83 (SS)		0.1-0.4 L/kg Vss	6.8 ± 2.1				555 (24 hr)	
Fluconazole	400 mg po/IV	D	Tab/susp ± food	90	6.7 (SD)	10	50 L V/F	20-50		50-94	Yes		PO: 1-2
	800 mg po/IV	D	Tab/susp ± food	90	Approx. 14 (SD)			20-50					
Itraconazole	200 mg po soln	C	Soln no food	Low	0.3-0.7 (SD)	99.8	796 L	35		0		29.3 (24 hr)	2.5 Hydroxy: 5.3
Ketoconazole	200 mg po	C	Tab ± food	75	1-4 (SD)	99	1.2 L/kg	6-9	ND	<10	No	12	1-2
Posaconazole	200 mg po	C	Susp + food		0.2-1.0 (SD)	98-99	1774 L	20-66			Yes (JAC 56:745, 2005)	15.1	3-5
Voriconazole	200 mg po q12h	C	Tab/susp no food	96	3 (SS)	58	4.6 L/kg Vss	6		22-100	Yes (CID 37:728, 2003)	39.8 (24 hr)	1-2
Anidulafungin	200 mg IV x 1, then 100 mg IV q24h	C			7.2 (SS)	>99	30-50 L	26.5			No	112 (24 hr)	
Caspofungin	70 mg IV x 1, then 50 mg IV qd	C			9.9 (SD)	97	9.7 L Vss	9-11			No	87.3 (24 hr)	
Flucytosine	2.5 gm po	C	Cap ± food	78-90	30-40 (SD)		0.6 L/kg	3-6			Yes		2
Micafungin	150 IV q24h	C			16.4 (SD)	>99	0.39 L/kg	15-17		60-100	No	167 (24 hr)	
ANTIMYCOBACTERIALS													
Bedaquiline	400 mg po qd	B	Tab + food	ND	3.3 (Wk 2)	>99	~60x total body water Vss	24-30	ND		ND	22 (24hr)	5
Capreomycin	15 mg/kg IM	C		ND	25-35 (SS)	ND	0.4 L/kg	2-5	ND	<10	No	ND	1-2
Cycloserine	250 mg po	C	Cap, no food	70-90	4-8 (SD)	<20	0.47 L/kg	10	ND	54-79	Yes	110	1-2
Ethambutol	25 mg/kg po	C	Tab + food	80	2-6 (SD)	10-30	6 L/kg Vss/F	4	ND	10-50		29.6	2-4

Preg Risk: FDA risk categories: **A** = no risk in adequate human studies. **B** = animal studies suggest no fetal risk, but no adequate human studies. **C** = adverse fetal effects in animals, but no adequate studies in humans; potential benefit may warrant use despite potential risk. **D** = evidence of human risk, but potential benefit may warrant use despite potential risk. **X** = evidence of human fetal risk that clearly exceeds potential benefits. **Food Effect (PO dosing): + food** = take with food. **no food** = take without food. **± food** = take with or without food. **Oral %AB** = % absorbed. **SD** = after single dose. **SS** = steady state after multiple doses. **Volume of Distribution (Vd): V/F** = Vd/oral bioavailability. **Vss/F** = Vd at steady state/oral bioavailability. **CSF Penetration:** therapeutic efficacy comment based on dose, usual susceptibility or target organism & penetration into CSF. **24hr** = AUC 0-24. **Tmax** = time to max plasma concentration.

TABLE 14A (6)

DRUG	REFERENCE DOSE/ROUTE	PREG RISK	FOOD EFFECT (PO)[1]	ORAL %AB	PEAK SERUM LEVEL (μg/mL)	PROTEIN BINDING (%)	VOL OF DISTRIB (Vd)	AVER SERUM T½, hrs[2]	BILE PEN (%)[3]	CSF/BLOOD (%)[f]	CSF PEN[g]	AUC (μg*hr/mL)[s]	Tmax (hr)
ANTIMYCOBACTERIALS *(continued)*													
Ethionamide	500 mg po	C	Tab ± food	90	2.2 (SD)	10-30	80 L	1.9	ND	≈100	Yes	10.3	1.5
Isoniazid	300 mg po	C	Tab/syrup no food	100	3-5 (SD)		0.6-1.2 L/kg	0.7-4	ND	Up to 90	Yes	20.1	1-2
Para-aminosalicylic acid (PAS)	4 gm po	C	Gran + food	ND	20 (SD)	50-73	0.9-1.4 L/kg (V/F)	0.75-1.0	ND	10-50	Marg	108	8
Pyrazinamide	20-25 mg/kg po	C	Tab ± food	95	30-50 (SD)	5-10		10-16		100	Yes	500	2
Rifabutin	300 mg po	B	Cap ± food	20	0.2-0.6 (SD)	85	9.3 L/kg (Vss)	32-67	300-500	30-70	ND	8.6	2.5-4.0
Rifampin	600 mg po	C	Cap no food	70-90	4-32 (SD)	80	0.65 L/kg Vss	2-5	10,000	7-56	Yes	58	1.5-2
Rifapentine	600 mg po q72h	C	Tab + food	ND	15 (SS)	98	70 L	13-14	ND	ND	ND	320 over 72hrs	4.8
Streptomycin	1 gm IV	D			25-50 (SD)	0-10	0.26 L/kg	2.5	10-60	0-30	No; Intrathecal: 5-10 mg		
ANTIPARASITICS													
Albendazole	400 mg po	C	Tab + food		0.5-1.6	70							Sulfoxide: 2-5
Artemether/ Lumefantrine	4 tabs po: 80/480 mg	C	Tab + food		Art: 9 (SS), D-Art: 1, Lum: 5.6-9 (not SS)			Art: 1.6, D-Art: 1.6, Lum: 101					Art: 1.5-2.0 Lum: 6-8
Atovaquone	750 mg po bid	C	Susp + food	47	24 (SD)	99.9	0.6 L/kg	67		<1	No	801 (750 mg x 1)	2-6
Dapsone	100 mg po q24h	C	Tab ± food	70-100	1.1 (SS)	70	1.5 L/kg	10-50					
Ivermectin	12 mg po	C	Tab no food		0.05-0.08 (SD)	70	9.9 L/kg						4
Mefloquine	1.25 gm po	C	Tab + food		0.5-1.2 (SD)	98	20 L/kg	13-24 days					17
Miltefosine	50 mg po tid	X	Cap + food		31 (SD)	95		7-31 (long); AAC 52:2855, 2008					
Nitazoxanide	500 mg po tab	B	Tab/susp + food		9-10 (SD)	99	1600-2000 L V/F					41.9 Tizoxanide	Tizoxanide: 1-4
Proguanil[e]	100 mg po	C	Tab ± food		No data	75	3 L/kg	96					
Pyrimethamine	25 mg po	C	Tab ± food	"High"	0.1-0.3 (SD)	87							2-6
Praziquantel	20 mg per kg po	B	Tab + food	80	0.2-2.0 (SD)		8000 L V/F	0.8-1.5				1.51	1-3
Tinidazole	2 gm po	B	Tab + food	48	48 (SD)	12	50 L	13				902	1.6

Preg Risk: FDA risk categories: A = no risk in adequate human studies. **B** = animal studies suggest no fetal risk, but no adequate human studies. **C** = adverse fetal effects in animals, but no adequate studies in humans; potential benefit may warrant use despite potential risk. **D** = evidence of human risk, but potential benefit may warrant use despite potential risk **X** = evidence of human risk that clearly exceeds potential benefits. **Food Effect (PO dosing): + food** = take with food. **no food** = take without food. **± food** = take with or without food. **Oral % AB** = % absorbed. **Peak Serum Level: SD** = after single dose. **SS** = after multiple doses. **Volume of Distribution (Vd): V/F** = Vd/oral bioavailability. **Vss** = Vd at steady state. **Vss/F** = Vd at steady state/oral bioavailability. **CSF Penetration:** therapeutic efficacy comment based on dose, usual susceptibility of target organism & penetration into CSF. **AUC** = area under drug concentration curve; **24hr** = AUC 0-24; **Tmax** = time to max plasma concentration.

TABLE 14A (7)

DRUG	REFERENCE DOSE/ROUTE	PREG RISK	FOOD EFFECT (PO)[1]	ORAL %AB	PEAK SERUM LEVEL (µg/mL)	PROTEIN BINDING (%)	VOL OF DISTRIB (Vd)	AVER SERUM T½ hrs[2]	BILE PEN (%)[3]	CSF/ BLOOD (%)	CSF PEN[4]	AUC (µg*hr/mL)	Tmax (hr)
ANTIVIRAL DRUGS—NOT HIV													
Acyclovir	400 mg po bid	B	Tab/cap/susp ± food	10-20	1.21 (SS)	9-33	0.7 L/kg	2.5-3.5				7.4 (24 hr)	
Adefovir	10 mg po	C	Tab ± food	59	0.02 (SD)	≤4	0.37 L/kg Vss	7.5				0.22	
Boceprevir	800 mg po q8h	B	Cap ± food		1.7 (SS)	75	772L (Vss/F)	3.4	ND	ND	ND	5.41 (8 hr)	1.75
Cidofovir w/Probenecid	5 mg/kg IV	C		100	19.6 (SD)	<6	0.41 L/kg (VSS)	2.2	ND	0	No	40.8	1.1
Entecavir	0.5 mg po q24h	C	Tab/soln no food		4.2 ng/mL (SS)	13	>0.6 L/kg V/F	128-149				0.14	0.5-1.5
Famciclovir	500 mg po	B	Tab ± food	77	3-4 (SD)	<20	1.1 L/kg*	2-3				8.9 Penciclovir	Penciclovir: 0.9
Foscarnet	60 mg/kg IV	C			155 (SD)	4	0.46 L/kg	<1	No			2195 µM*hr	
Ganciclovir	5 mg/kg IV	C			8.3 (SD)	1-2	0.7 L/kg Vss	3.5				24.5	
Oseltamivir	75 mg po bid	?	Cap/susp ± food	75	0.065/0.35§ (SS)	3	23-26 L/kg Vss*	1-3				5.4 (24 hr) Carboxylate	
Peramivir	600 mg IV	?			35-45 (SD)	<30	ND	7.7-20.8	ND	ND	ND	90-95	ND
Ribavirin	600 mg po	X	Tab/cap/soln + food	64	0.8 (SD)		2825 L/F	44				25.4	2
Rimantadine	100 mg po	C	Tab ± food		0.05-0.1 (SD)		17-19 L/kg	25				3.5	6
Telaprevir	750 mg po q8h	B	Tab+ food (high fat)		3.51 (SD)	59-76	252L (V/F)	4.0-4.7 (SD)	ND	ND	ND	22.3 (8 hr)	
Telbivudine	600 mg po q24h	B	Tab/soln ± food		3.7 (SD)	3.3	>0.6 L/kg V/F	40-49				26.1 (24 hr)	2
Valacyclovir	1000 mg po	B	Tab ± food	55	5.6 (SD)	13-18	0.7 L/kg	3				19.5 Acyclovir	
Valganciclovir	900 mg po q24h	C	Tab/soln + food	59	5.6 (SS)	1-2	0.7 L/kg	4				29.1 Ganciclovir	Ganciclovir: 1-3
ANTI RETROVIRAL DRUGS													
Abacavir (ABC)	600 mg po q24h	C	Tab/soln ± food	83	4.3 (SS)	50	0.86 L/kg	1.5	12-26	Low	No	12 (24 hr)	
Atazanavir (ATV)	400 mg po q24h	B	Cap + food	86	2.3 (SS)	86	88.3 L/F	7		Intermed	?	22.3 (24 hr)	2.5

Preg Risk: FDA risk categories: A = no risk in adequate human studies. **B** = animal studies suggest no fetal risk, but no adequate human studies. **C** = adverse fetal effects in animals, but no adequate studies in humans; potential benefit may warrant use despite potential risk. **D** = evidence of human risk, but potential benefit may warrant use despite potential risk. **X** = evidence of human risk that clearly exceeds potential benefits. **Food Effect (PO dosing): + food** = take with food. **no food** = take without food. **± food** = take with or without food. **Oral % AB** = % absorbed. **Peak Serum Level: SD** = after single dose. **SS** = steady state after multiple doses. **Volume of Distribution (Vd): V/F** = Vd/oral bioavailability. **Vss** = Vd at steady state. **Vss/F** = Vd at steady state/oral bioavailability. **CSF Penetration:** therapeutic efficacy comment based on dose, usual susceptibility of target organism & penetration into CSF. **24hr** = AUC 0-24. **Tmax** = time to max plasma concentration.

TABLE 14A (8)

DRUG	REFERENCE DOSE/ROUTE	PREG RISK	FOOD EFFECT (PO)¹	ORAL %AB	PEAK SERUM LEVEL (µg/mL)	PROTEIN BINDING (%)	VOL OF DISTRIB (Vd)	AVER SERUM T½, hrs¹	BILE PEN (%)³	CSF⁴/BLOOD (%)	CSF⁵ PEN⁶	AUC (µg·hr/mL)	Tmax (hr)
ANTI RETROVIRAL DRUGS *(continued)*													
Darunavir (DRV)	(600 mg + 100 mg RTV) bid	B	Tab + food	82	3.5 (SS)	95	2 L/kg	15		Intermed	?	116.8 (24 hr)	2.5-4.0
Delavirdine (DLV)	400 mg po tid	C	Tab ± food	85	19 ± 11(SS)	98		5.8	3		?	180 µM*hr	1
Didanosine (ddI)	400 mg EC¹⁰ po	B	Cap no food	30-40	?	<5	308-363 L	1.4	25-40	Intermed	?	2.6	2
Dolutegravir	50 mg po	B	± food		3.67 (SS)	>99	17.4 (V/F)	14				53.6	2-3
Efavirenz (EFV)	600 mg po q24h	D	Cap/tab no food	42	4.1 (SS)	99	252 L V/F	52-76	3			184 µM*hr (24 hr)	3-5
Elvitegravir (with cobicistat, TDF and FTC, as Stribild)	150 mg (EVG) 150 mg (Cobi) 200 mg (FTC) 300 mg (TDF)	B	Tab + Food	No data	EVG: 1.7 Cobi: 1.1	98-99 (EVG, cobi)		EVG: 12.9 Cobi: 3.5				EVG: 23 Cobi: 8.3	EVG: 4 Cobi: 3
Emtricitabine (FTC)	200 mg po q24h	B	Cap/soln ± food	93	1.8 (SS)	<4		10	39	Intermed	?	10 (24 hr)	1-2
Enfuvirtide (ENF)	90 mg sc bid	B		84	5 (SS)	92	5.5 L	4				97.4 (24 hr)	2.5-4.0
Etravirine (ETR)	200 mg po bid	B	Tab + food		0.3 (SS)	99.9		41	2			9 (24 hr)	2.5-4.0
Fosamprenavir (FPV)	(700 mg po + 100 mg RTV) bid	C	Boosted ped susp + food Adult susp no food Tab ± food	No data	6 (SS)	90		7.7	No data	Intermed	?	79.2 (24 hr)	2.5
Indinavir (IDV)	800 mg po tid	C	Boosted cap + food. Cap alone no food	65	9 (SS)	60	1.3 L/kg	1.2-2	18-22	High	Yes	92.1 µM*hr (24 hr)	0.8
Lamivudine (3TC)	300 mg po	C	Tab/soln ± food	86	2.6 (SS)	<36		5-7		Intermed	?	11	
Lopinavir/RTV (LPV/r)	400 mg po bid	C	Soln ± food	No data	9.6 (SS)	98-99		5-6 (LPV)		Intermed	?	186 LPV	LPV: 4
Maraviroc (MVC)	300 mg po bid	B	Tab ± food	33	0.3-0.9 (SS)	76	194 L	14-18		Intermed	No	3 (24 hr)	0.5-4.0
Nelfinavir (NFV)	1250 mg po bid	B	Tab/powd + food	20-80	3-4 (SS)	98	2-7 L/kg V/F	3.5-5		Low	No	53 (24 hr)	
Nevirapine (NVP)	200 mg po bid	C	Tab/susp ± food	>90	2 (SD)	60	1.2 L/kg Vss	25-30	4	High	Yes	110 (24 hr)	
Raltegravir (RAL)	400 mg po bid	C	Tab ± food	No data	5.4 (SS)	83	287 L Vss/F	9		Intermed	?	28.6 µM*hr (24 hr)	3
Rilpivirine	25 mg po	B	Tab + food		0.1-0.2 (SD)	99.7	152L	45-50	ND		-	2.4 (24 hr)	
Ritonavir (RTV)	600 mg po bid	B	Cap/soln + food	65	11.2 (SS)	98-99	0.41 L/kg V/F	3-5		Low	No		Soln: 2-4

Preg Risk: FDA risk categories: A = no risk in adequate human studies. **B** = animal studies suggest no fetal risk, but no adequate human studies, but no adequate studies in humans, potential benefit may warrant use despite potential risk. **D** = evidence of human risk, but potential benefit may warrant use despite risk. **X** = evidence of human risk that clearly exceeds potential benefits. **Food Effect (PO dosing):** **+ food** = take with food. **- food** = take without food. **± food** = take with or without food. **Oral %AB** = % absorbed. **Peak Serum Level: SD** = after single dose. **SS** = steady state, after multiple doses. **Volume of Distribution (Vd):** **V/F** = Vd/oral bioavailability. **Vss** = Vd at steady state. **Vss/F** = Vd at steady state/oral bioavailability. **CSF Penetration:** therapeutic efficacy comment based on dose, usual susceptibility of target organism & penetration into CSF. **AUC** = area under drug concentration curve; **24hr** = AUC 0-24; **Tmax** = time to max plasma concentration.

TABLE 14A (9)

ANTI RETROVIRAL DRUGS *(continued)*

DRUG	REFERENCE DOSE/ROUTE	PREG RISK	FOOD EFFECT (PO)[1]	ORAL %AB	PEAK SERUM LEVEL (µg/mL)	PROTEIN BINDING (%)	VOL OF DISTRIB (Vd)	AVER SERUM T½, hrs[2]	BILE PEN (%)[3]	CSF[f]/BLOOD (%)	CSF PEN[e]	AUC (µg*hr/mL)	Tmax (hr)
Saquinavir (SQV)	(1000 +100 RTV) mg po bid	B	Tab/cap + food	4	0.37 min (SS conc)	97	700 L Vss	1-2		Low	No	29.2 (24 hr)	
Stavudine (d4T)	40 mg po	C	Cap/soln ± food	86	0.54 (SS)	<5	46L	1	3-5	Low	No	2.6 (24 hr)	1
Tenofovir (TDF)	300 mg po	B	Tab ± food	25 fasted 39 w/food	0.3 (SD)	<1-7	1.3 L/kg Vss	17	>60	Low	No	2.3	1
Tipranavir (TPV)	(500 + 200 RTV) mg po bid	C	Cap/soln + food		47-57 (SS)	99.9	7.7-10 L	5.5-6		Low	No	1600 µM*hr (24 hr)	3
Zidovudine (ZDV)	300 mg po	C	Tab/cap/syrup ± food	60	1-2	<38	1.6 L/kg	0.5-3	11	High	Yes	2.1	0.5-1.5

FOOTNOTES

1. Refers to adult oral preparations unless otherwise noted.
2. Assumes CrCl >80 mL per min.
3. Peak concentration in bile/dose; concentration in serum x 100. If blank, no data.
4. CSF levels with inflammation.
5. Judgment based on drug dose & organism susceptibility. CSF concentration ideally ≥10 above MIC.
6. Concern over seizure potential; see Table 13, page 169.
7. Take all po FQs 2-4 hours before sucralfate or any multivalent cations: Ca++, Fe++, Zn++.
8. Given with atovaquone as Malarone for malaria prophylaxis.
9. Oseltamivir/oseltamivir carboxylate.
10. EC = enteric coated.

Preg Risk: FDA risk categories: A = no risk in adequate human studies. **B** = animal studies suggest no fetal risk, but no adequate human studies. **C** = adverse fetal effects in animals, but no adequate studies in humans, potential benefit may warrant use despite potential risk. **D** = evidence of human risk, but potential benefit may warrant use despite potential risk. **X** = evidence of human risk that clearly exceeds potential benefits. **Food: food** = take with food, **no food** = take without food, **± food** = take with or without food. **Oral % AB** = % absorbed. **Peak Serum Level: SD** = after single dose, **SS** = steady state after multiple doses; **Volume of Distribution (Vd):** V/F = Vd/bioavailability, **Vss/F** = Vd at steady state/bioavailability. **CSF Penetration:** therapeutic efficacy comment based on dose, usual susceptibility of target organism & penetration into CSF. **AUC** = area under drug concentration curve; **24hr** = AUC 0-24; **Tmax** = time to max plasma concentration.

TABLE 14B: CYTOCHROME P450 INTERACTIONS OF ANTIMICROBIALS

Cytochrome P450 isoenzyme terminology:
e.g., 3A4: 3 = family, A = subfamily, 4 = gene; **PGP** = P-glycoprotein; **UGT** = uridine diphosphate glucuronosyltransferase; **OATP** = organic anion transporter polypeptide; **OCT** = organic cation transporter; **BCRP** = breast cancer resistance protein

DRUG	Substrate	Inhibits	Induces
Antibacterials			
Azithromycin (all)	PGP	PGP (weak)	
Chloramphenicol		2C19, 3A4	
Ciprofloxacin (all)		1A2, 3A4 (minor)	
Clarithromycin (all)	3A4	3A4, PGP	
Erythromycin (all)	3A4, PGP	3A4, PGP	
Metronidazole		2C9	
Nafcillin			2C9 (?), 3A4
Quinu-Dalfo		3A4	
Rifampin	PGP		1A2, 2C9, 2C19, 2D6 (Weak), 3A4, PGP
Telithromycin		3A4, PGP	
TMP-SMX	SMX: 2C9 (major), 3A4	SMX: 2C9, TMP: 2C8	
Trimethoprim		2C8	
Antifungals			
Fluconazole (400 mg)	3A4 (minor), PGP	2C9, 2C19, 3A4, UGT	
Itraconazole	3A4, PGP	3A4, PGP	
Ketoconazole	3A4	3A4, PGP	
Posaconazole	PGP, UGT	3A4, PGP	
Terbinafine	2D6	2D6	
Voriconazole	2C9, 2C19, 3A4	2C9, 2C19 (major), 3A4	
Antimycobacterials (Also Rifampin, above)			
Bedaquiline	3A4		
Ethionamide	3A4 (?)		
Isoniazid	2E1	2C19, 3A4	
Rifabutin	3A4		3A4
Rifapentine	3A4	2C9, 3A4	
Dapsone	3A4		3A4, UGT

DRUG	Substrate	Inhibits	Induces
Antiparasitics			
Mefloquine	3A4, PGP	PGP	
Praziquantel	2C19, 3A4		
Proguanil	2C19 (conversion to cycloguanil)		
Tinidazole	3A4		
Antiretrovirals			
Atazanavir	3A4	1A2, 2C9, 3A4	
Cobicistat	3A4, 2D6	3A4, 2D6, PGP, BCRP, OATP1B1, OATP1B3	
Darunavir	3A4	3A4	
Delavirdine	2D6, 3A4	2C9, 2C19, 3A4	
Efavirenz	2B6, 3A4	2B6, 2C9, 2C19	2C19, 3A4
Etravirine	CYP3A, UGT	2C9, 2C19 (weak)	2C9
Fosamprenavir	2C9, 2C19, 3A4	2C19, 3A4	3A4
Indinavir	3A4, PGP	3A4, PGP	
Lopinavir	3A4	3A4	
Maraviroc	3A4, PGP		
Nelfinavir	2C19, 3A4, PGP	3A4, PGP	3A4
Nevirapine	2B6, 3A4		3A4
Raltegravir	UGT		
Ritonavir	2D6, 3A4, PGP	2B6, 2C9, 2C19, 2D6, 3A4, PGP	3A4, 1A2 (?), 2C9 (?), PGP (?)
Saquinavir	3A4, PGP	3A4, PGP	
Tipranavir	3A4, PGP	1A2, 2C9, 2C19, 2D6	3A4, PGP (weak)

Refs: Hansten PD, Horn JR. The top 100 drug interactions: a guide to patient management 2012; E. Freeland (WA): H&H Publications; 2010; and package inserts.

TABLE 15A: DOSAGE OF ANTIMICROBIAL DRUGS IN ADULT PATIENTS WITH RENAL IMPAIRMENT

- For listing of drugs with NO need for adjustment for renal failure, see *Table 17B.*
- Adjustments for renal failure are based on an estimate of creatinine clearance (CrCl) which reflects the glomerular filtration rate.
- **Different methods for calculating estimated CrCl are suggested for non-obese and obese patients.**
  - o Calculations for ideal body weight (IBW) in kg:
    - Men: 50 kg plus 2.3 kg/inch over 60 inches height.
    - Women: 45 kg plus 2.3 kg/inch over 60 inches height.
  - o Obese is defined as 20% over ideal body weight or body mass index (BMI) >30

- Calculations of estimated CrCl *(References, see (NEJM 354:2473, 2006 (non-obese), AJM 84:1053, 1988 (obese))*
  - o **Non-obese patient—**
    - Calculate ideal body weight (IBW) in kg (as above)
    - Use the following formula to determine estimated CrCl

$$\frac{(140 \text{ minus age})(\text{IBW in kg})}{72 \times \text{serum creatinine}} = \begin{array}{l} \text{CrCl in mL/min for men.} \\ \text{Multiply answer by 0.85} \\ \text{for women (estimated)} \end{array}$$

  - o **Obese patient—**
    - Weight ≥20% over IBW or BMI >30
    - Use the following formulas to determine estimated CrCl

$$\frac{(137 \text{ minus age}) \times [(0.285 \times \text{wt in kg}) + (12.1 \times \text{ht in meters}^2)]}{51 \times \text{serum creatinine}} = \text{CrCl (obese male)}$$

$$\frac{(146 \text{ minus age}) \times [(0.287 \times \text{wt in kg}) + (9.74 \times \text{ht in meters}^2)]}{60 \times \text{serum creatinine}} = \text{CrCl (obese female)}$$

- If estimated CrCl ≥90 mL/min, see *Tables 10A and 10D* for dosing.
- What weight should be used to calculate dosage on a mg/kg basis?
  - o If less than 20% over IBW, use the patient's actual weight for all drugs.
  - o **For obese patients** (≥20% over IBW or BMI >30).
    - **Aminoglycosides:** (IBW plus 0.4(actual weight minus IBW) = adjusted weight.
    - **Vancomycin:** actual body weight whether non-obese or obese.
    - **All other drugs:** insufficient data *(Pharmacotherapy 27:1081, 2007).*
- For slow or sustained extended daily dialysis **(SLEDD)** over 6-12 hours, adjust does as for CRRT. For details, see *CID 49:433, 2009; CCM 39:560, 2011.*
- General reference: Drug Prescribing in Renal Failure, 5th ed., Aronoff, et al. (eds.) *(Amer College Physicians, 2007 and drug package inserts).*

***Abbreviations:* HEMO** = hemodialysis; **CAPD** = chronic ambulatory peritoneal dialysis; **ESRD** = endstage renal disease; **NUS** = not available in the U.S.

TABLE 15A (2)

ANTIMICROBIAL	HALF-LIFE (NORMAL/ESRD) hr	DOSE FOR NORMAL RENAL FUNCTION	METHOD (see footer)	ADJUSTMENT FOR RENAL FAILURE — Estimated creatinine clearance (CrCl) mL/min >50-90	10-50	<10	HEMODIALYSIS, CAPD	COMMENTS & DOSAGE FOR CRRT
ANTIBACTERIAL ANTIBIOTICS								
Aminoglycoside Antibiotics: Traditional multiple daily doses—adjustment for renal disease								
Amikacin	1.4–2.3/17–150	7.5 mg/kg q12h or 15 mg/kg once daily (see below)	I	7.5 mg/kg q24h	30–70: 7.5 mg/kg q24h **Same dose for CRRT** 10–30: 7.5 mg/kg q48h	7.5 mg/kg q72h	HEMO: 7.5 mg/kg AD CAPD: 15–20 mg lost per L dialysate per day (see Comment)	**High flux hemodialysis** membranes lead to unpredictable aminoglycoside clearance; measure post-dialysis levels for efficacy and toxicity. With **CAPD**, pharmacokinetics highly variable—**check serum levels.** Usual method for CAPD: 2 liters of dialysis fluid placed qid or 8 liters per day (give 8/20 mg lost per L, i.e., 160 mg of amikacin supplement IV per day)
Gentamicin, Tobramycin (Monitor levels)	2-3/20-60	1.7 mg per kg q8h. Once daily dosing below	I	5-7 mg/kg once daily or 1.7-2.3 mg/kg q8h	1.7 mg/kg q12-48h **Same dose for CRRT** **See Comment for SLEDD dose**	1.7 mg/kg q48-72h	HEMO: 3 mg/kg AD. Monitor levels. CAPD: 3-4 mg lost per L dialysate per day	
Netilmicin	2-3/35-72	2 mg per kg q8h. Once daily dosing below	I	2 mg per kg q8h or 6.5 mg/kg once daily	2 mg/kg q12-24h **Same dose for CRRT**	2 mg/kg q48h	HEMO 3 mg/kg AD CAPD: 3-4 mg lost per L dialysate per day	Adjust dosing weight for obesity: [ideal body weight + 0.4 (actual body weight – ideal body weight)] (CID 25:112, 1997).
Streptomycin	2-3/30-80	15 mg per kg (max. of 1 gm) q24h. Once daily dosing below	I	15 mg/kg q24h	15 mg/kg q24-72h **Same dose for CRRT**	15 mg/kg q72-96h	HEMO: 7.5 mg/kg AD CAPD: 20-40 mg lost per L dialysate per day	Gent SLEDD dose in critically ill: 6 mg/kg IV q48h starting 30 min before start of SLEDD (daily SLEDD; q48h Gent) (AAC 54:3635, 2010).

ONCE-DAILY AMINOGLYCOSIDE THERAPY: ADJUSTMENT IN RENAL INSUFFICIENCY

Creatinine Clearance (mL per min.)	>80	60-80	40-60	20-30	10-20	<10-0
Drug		Dose q24h (mg per kg)		Dose q48h (mg per kg)	Dose q72h and AD	Dose q96h
Gentamicin/Tobramycin	5.1	4	3.5	4	3	2
Amikacin/kanamycin/streptomycin	15	12	7.5	7.5	8 q72h	8 q96h
Isepamicin	8	8		8		
Netilmicin	6.5	5	2.5	3	2.5	2

ANTIMICROBIAL	HALF-LIFE	DOSE FOR NORMAL RENAL FUNCTION	METHOD	>50-90	10-50	<10	HEMODIALYSIS, CAPD	COMMENTS & DOSAGE FOR CRRT
Carbapenem Antibiotics								
Doripenem	1/18	500 mg IV q8h	D&I	500 mg IV q8h	≥30 - ≤50: 250 mg IV q8h >10 - <30: 250 mg q12h	No data	No data	No data CRRT ref: AAC 55:1187, 2011.
Ertapenem	4/>4	1 gm q24h	D	1 gm q24h	0.5 gm q24h (CrCl <30)	0.5 gm q24h	HEMO: Dose as for CrCl <10. If dosed <6 hrs prior to HD, give 150 mg supplement AD	
Imipenem (see Comment)	1/4	0.5 gm q6h	D&I	250-500 mg q6-8h	250 mg q6-12h **Dose for CRRT: 0.5-1 gm bid** (AAC 49:2421, 2005)	125-250 mg q12h	HEMO: Dose AD CAPD: Dose for CrCl <10	↑ potential for seizures if recommended doses exceeded in pts with CrCl <20 mL per min. See pkg insert, esp. for pts <70 kg
Meropenem	1/6-8	1 gm q8h	D&I	1 gm q8h	1 gm q12h **Same dose for CRRT**	0.5 gm q24h	HEMO: Dose AD CAPD: Dose for CrCl <10	

Abbreviation Key: Adjustment Method: **D** = dose adjustment, **I** = interval adjustment; **CAPD** = continuous ambulatory peritoneal dialysis; **CRRT** = continuous renal replacement therapy; **HEMO** = hemodialysis; **AD** = after dialysis; "**Supplement**" or "**Extra**" is to replace drug lost during dialysis – additional drug beyond continuation of regimen for CrCl < 10 mL/min.

TABLE 15A (3)

ANTIMICROBIAL	HALF-LIFE (NORMAL/ ESRD) hr	DOSE FOR NORMAL RENAL FUNCTION	METHOD (see footer)	ADJUSTMENT FOR RENAL FAILURE Estimated creatinine clearance (CrCl) mL/min			HEMODIALYSIS, CAPD	COMMENTS & DOSAGE FOR CRRT
				>50-90	10-50	<10		
ANTIBACTERIAL ANTIBIOTICS (continued)								
Cephalosporin Antibiotics: DATA ON SELECTED PARENTERAL CEPHALOSPORINS								
Cefazolin	1.9/40-70	1-2 gm q8h	I	q8h	q12h Same dose for CRRT	q24-48h	HEMO: Extra 0.5-1 gm AD CAPD: 0.5 gm q12h	
Cefepime	2.2/18	2 gm q8h (max. dose)	D&I	2 gm q8h	2 gm q12-24h Same dose for CRRT	1 gm q24h	HEMO: Extra 1 gm AD CAPD: 1-2 gm q48h	
Cefotaxime, Cefizoxime	1.7/15-35	2 gm q8h	I	q8-12h	q12-24h Same dose for CRRT	q24h	HEMO: Extra 1 gm AD CAPD: 0.5-1 gm q24h	Active metabolite of cefotaxime in ESRD. ↓ dose further for hepatic & renal failure.
Cefotetan	3.5/13-25	1-2 gm q12h	D	100%	1-2 gm q24h Same dose for CRRT	1-2 gm q48h	HEMO: Extra 1 gm AD CAPD: 1 gm q24h	CRRT dose: 750 mg q12h
Cefoxitin	0.8/13-23	2 gm q8h	I	q8h	q8-12h Same dose for CRRT	q24-48h	HEMO: Extra 1 gm AD CAPD: 1 gm q24h	May falsely increase serum creatinine by interference with assay
Ceftaroline	1.6/–	600 mg IV q12h	D	600 mg q12h	30-50: 400 mg q12h 15-30: 300 mg q12h	< 15: 200 mg q12h	HEMO: Extra 1 gm AD CAPD: 200 mg q12h	1-hr infusion for all doses
Ceftazidime	1.2/13-25	2 gm q8h	I	q8-12h	Q12-24h Same dose for CRRT	q24-48h	HEMO: Extra 1 gm AD CAPD: 0.5 gm q24h	Since 1/2 dose is dialyzed, post-dialysis dose is max. of 3 gm.
Ceftobiprole	2.9-3.3/21	500 mg IV q8-12h	I	500 mg IV q8-12h	≥30 & ≤50: 500 mg q12h over 2 hrs ≥10 & <30: 250 mg q12h over 2 hrs	q8-12h	No data	
Cefuroxime sodium	1.2/17	0.75-1.5 gm q8h	I	q8h	q8-12h Same dose for CRRT	q24h	HEMO: Dose AD CAPD: Dose for CrCl <10	No data
Fluoroquinolone Antibiotics								
Ciprofloxacin	3-6/6-9	500-750 mg po (or 400 mg IV) q12h	D	100%	50-75% CRRT 400 mg IV q24h	50%	HEMO: 250 mg po or 200 mg IV q12h CAPD: 250 mg po or 200 mg IV q8h	
Gatifloxacin[NUS]	7-14/11-40	400 mg po/IV q24h	D	400 mg q24h	400 mg, then 200 mg q24h Same dose for CRRT	400 mg, then 200 mg q24h	HEMO: 200 mg q24h AD CAPD: 200 mg q24h	
Gemifloxacin	7/>7	320 mg po q24h	D	320 mg q24h	160 mg q24h	160 mg q24h	HEMO: 160 mg q24h AD CAPD: 160 mg q24h	
Levofloxacin	6-8/76	750 mg q24h IV, PO	D&I	750 mg q24h	20-49: 750 q48h	<20: 750 mg once, then 500 mg q48h	HEMO/CAPD: Dose for CrCl <20	CRRT 750 mg once, then 500 mg q48h; although not FDA-approved.
Ofloxacin	7/28-37	200-400 mg q12h	D	200-400 mg q12h	200-400 mg q24h Same dose for CRRT	200 mg q24h	HEMO: Dose for CrCl <10, AD CAPD: 300 mg q24h	

Abbreviation Key: Adjustment Method: **D** = dose adjustment; **I** = interval adjustment; **CAPD** = continuous ambulatory peritoneal dialysis; **CRRT** = continuous renal replacement therapy; **HEMO** = hemodialysis; **AD**: after dialysis; "**Supplement**" or "**Extra**" is to replace drug lost during dialysis – additional drug beyond continuation of regimen for CrCl < 10 mL/min.

TABLE 15A (4)

ANTIMICROBIAL	HALF-LIFE (NORMAL/ ESRD) hr	DOSE FOR NORMAL RENAL FUNCTION	METHOD (see footer)	ADJUSTMENT FOR RENAL FAILURE Estimated creatinine clearance (CrCl) mL/min			HEMODIALYSIS, CAPD	COMMENTS & DOSAGE FOR CRRT
				>50-90	10-50	<10		
ANTIBACTERIAL ANTIBIOTICS (continued)								
Macrolide Antibiotics								
Clarithromycin	5-7/22	500-1000 mg q12h	D	500 mg q12h	500 mg q12-24h	500 mg q24h	HEMO: Dose AD CAPD: None	CRRT as for CrCl 10-50
Erythromycin	1.4/5-6	250-500 mg q6h	D	100%	100%	50-75%	HEMO/CAPD/CRRT: None	Ototoxicity with high doses in ESRD
Miscellaneous Antibacterial Antibiotics								
Daptomycin	9.4/30	4-6 mg per kg per day	I	4-6 mg per kg per day	CrCl <30, 4-6 mg per kg q48h CRRT: 8 mg/kg q48h (CCM 39:19, 2011)	500 mg q24h	HEMO & CAPD: 6 mg per kg q48h (during or after q48h dialysis if possible). If next planned dialysis is 72 hrs away, give 9 mg/kg (AAC 57:864, 2013).	
Linezolid	5-6/6-8	600 mg po/IV q12h	None	600 mg q12h	600 mg q12h **Same dose for CRRT**	600 mg q12h AD	HEMO: As for CrCl <10 CAPD & CRRT: No dose adjustment	Accumulation of 2 metabolites— risk unknown (JAC 56:172, 2005)
Metronidazole	6-14/7-21	7.5 mg per kg q6h	D	100%	100% **Same dose for CRRT**	50%	HEMO: Dose as for CrCl <10 AD CAPD: Dose for CrCl <10	
Nitrofurantoin	0.5/1	50-100 mg	D	100%	Avoid	Avoid	Not applicable	
Sulfamethoxa-zole (SMX)	10/20-50	1 gm q8h	I	q12h	q18h Same dose for CAVH	q24h	HEMO: Extra 1 gm AD CAPD: 1 gm q24h	
Teicoplanin^NUS	45/62-230	6 mg per kg per day	I	q24h	q48h **Same dose for CRRT**	q72h	HEMO: Dose for CrCl <10 CAPD: Dose for CrCl <10	
Telithromycin	10/15	800 mg q24h	D	800 mg q24h	600 mg q24h (<30 mL per min.)	600 mg q24h	HEMO: 600 mg AD CAPD: No data	If CrCl <30, reduce dose to 600 mg once daily. If both liver and renal failure, dose is 400 mg once daily.
Telavancin	7-8/17.9	10 mg/kg q24h	D&I	10 mg/kg q24h	30-50: 7.5 mg/kg q24h <30: 10 mg/kg q48h	<30: 10 mg/kg q48h	HEMO: No data	No data
Temocillin		1-2 gm q12h	I	q12h	>30: q12h 10-30: q18h **Same dose for CRRT**	1 gm q48h	HEMO: 1 gm q48h AD CAPD: 1 gm q48h	
Trimethoprim (TMP)	11/20-49	100-200 mg q12h	I	q12h	>30: q12h 10-29: Reduce dose by 50%	q24h	HEMO: Dose AD CAPD: q24h	CRRT dose: q18h
Trimethoprim-sulfamethoxazole-DS (Doses based on TMP component)								
Treatment (based on TMP component)	As for TMP	5-20 mg/kg/day divided q6-12h	D	No dose adjustment	30-50: No dose adjustment 10-29: Reduce dose by 50%	Not recom-mended; but if used: 5-10 mg/kg q24h	Not recommended; but if used: 5-10 mg/kg q24h AD CRRT: 5-7.5 mg/kg q8h	

Abbreviation Key: Adjustment Method: **D** = dose adjustment, **I** = interval adjustment, **CAPD** = continuous ambulatory peritoneal dialysis; **CRRT** = continuous renal replacement therapy; **HEMO** = hemodialysis; **AD** = after dialysis; **"Supplement"** or **"Extra"** is to replace drug lost during dialysis – additional drug beyond continuation of regimen for CrCl < 10 mL/min.

TABLE 15A (5)

ANTIMICROBIAL	HALF-LIFE (NORMAL/ESRD) hr	DOSE FOR NORMAL RENAL FUNCTION	METHOD (see footer)	ADJUSTMENT FOR RENAL FAILURE Estimated creatinine clearance (CrCl), mL/min (Doses based on TMP component) (continued)			HEMODIALYSIS, CAPD	COMMENTS & DOSAGE FOR CRRT
				>50-90	10-50	<10		
ANTIBACTERIAL ANTIBIOTICS/Trimethoprim-sulfamethoxazole-DS								
TMP-SMX Prophylaxis	As for TMP	1 tab po q24h or 3 times per week	No change	100%	100%	100%		
Vancomycin[1]	6/200-250	1 gm q12h	D&I	15-30 mg/kg q12h	15 mg/kg q24-96h	7.5 mg/kg q2-3 days	HEMO: For trough conc of 15-20 μg/mL, give 15 mg/kg if next dialysis in 1 day; give 25 mg/kg if next dialysis in 2 days; give 35 mg/kg if next dialysis in 3 days (CID 53:124, 2011).	CAVH/CVVH 500 mg q24-48h. New hemodialysis membranes ↑ clear of vanco; **check levels**
Penicillins								
Amoxicillin	1/5-20	250-500 mg q8h	—	q8h	q8-12h	q24h	HEMO: Dose AD CAPD: 250 mg q12h	IV amoxicillin not available in the U.S. CRRT: dose for CrCl 10-50
Ampicillin	1/7-20	250 mg-2 gm q6h	—	q6h	q6-12h	q12-24h	HEMO: Dose AD CAPD: 250 mg q12h	
Amoxicillin/Clavulanate[2]	1.3 AM/1, 5-20/4	500/125 mg q8h (see Comments)	D&I	500/125 mg q8h	250-500 mg AM component q12h	250-500 mg AM component q24h	HEMO: As for CrCl <10; extra dose after dialysis	**If CrCl <30 per mL, do not use 875/125 or 1000/62.5 AM/CL**
Amoxicillin ext. rel. tabs	1.5/?	775 mg once daily	—	Once daily	CrCl <30: no data, avoid usage			
Ampicillin (AM)/Sulbactam(SB)	1 (AM)/1 (SB), 9 (AM)/10 (SB)	2 gm AM + 1 gm SB q6h	—	q6h	q8-12h	q24h	HEMO: Dose AD CAPD: 2 gm AM/1 gm SB q24h	CRRT dose: 1.5 AM/0.75 SB q12h
Aztreonam	2/6-8	2 gm q8h	D	100%	50-75% Same dose for CRRT	25%	HEMO: Extra 0.5 gm AD CAPD: Dose for CrCl <10	Technically is a β-lactam antibiotic.
Penicillin G	0.5/6-20	0.5-4 million U q4h	D	0.5-4 million U q4h	0.5-4 million U q8h Same dose for CRRT	0.5-4 million U q12h	HEMO: Dose AD CAPD: Dose for CrCl <10	1.7 mEq potassium per million units. ↑'s potential of seizure. 10 million units per day max dose in ESRD
Piperacillin	1/3-3.5-1	3-4 gm q4-6h	—	q4-6h	q6-8h Same dose for CRRT	q8h	HEMO: 2 gm q8h plus 1 gm extra AD CAPD: Dose for CrCl <10	1.9 mEq sodium per gm
Pip (Pi)/tazo(T)	0.71-1.2 (both)/2-6	3.375-4.5 gm q6-8h	D&I	100%	2.25 gm q6h <20: q8h Same dose for CRRT	2.25 gm q8h	HEMO: 2.25 gm q8h plus 1 gm extra AD CAPD: 4.5 gm q12h; CRRT: 2.25 gm q6h	
Ticarcillin	1.2/13	3 gm q4h	D&I	1-2 gm q4h	1-2 gm q8h Same dose for CRRT	1-2 gm q12h	HEMO: Extra 3.0 gm AD CAPD: Dose for CrCl <10	5.2 mEq sodium per gm
Ticarcillin/Clavulanate[2]	1.2/11-16	3.1 gm q4h	D&I	3.1 gm q4h	3.1 gm q8-12h Same dose for CRRT	2 gm q12h	HEMO: Extra 3.1 gm AD CAPD: 3.1 gm q12h	See footnote[2]
Tetracycline Antibiotics								
Tetracycline	6-10/57-108	250-500 mg qid	I	q8-12h	q12-24h Same dose for CRRT	q24h	HEMO/CAPD/CAVH: None	Avoid in ESRD

[1] If renal failure, use EMIT assay to measure levels; levels overestimated by RIA or fluorescent immunoassay.

[2] Clavulanate cleared by liver, not kidney. Her ce as dose of combination decreased, a deficiency of clavulanate may occur (JAMA 285:386, 2001).

Abbreviation Key: Adjustment Method: **D** = dose adjustment, **I** = interval adjustment; **CAPD** = continuous ambulatory peritoneal dialysis; **CRRT** = continuous renal replacement therapy; **HEMO** = hemodialysis; **AD** = after dialysis; "**Supplement**" or "**Extra**" is to replace drug lost during dialysis – additional drug beyond continuation of regimen for CrCl < 10 mL/min

TABLE 15A (6)

ANTIMICROBIAL	HALF-LIFE (NORMAL/ESRD) hr	DOSE FOR NORMAL RENAL FUNCTION	METHOD (see footer)	>50-90	10-50	<10	HEMODIALYSIS, CAPD	COMMENTS & DOSAGE FOR CRRT
ANTIFUNGAL ANTIBIOTICS								
Amphotericin B & Lipid-based ampho B	24h-15 days/unchanged	Non-lipid: 0.4–1 mg/kg/day; ABLC: 5 mg/kg/day; LAB: 3–5 mg/kg/day	I	q24h	Same dose for CRRT	q24h	HEMO/CAPD/CRRT: No dose adjustment	For ampho B, toxicity lessened by saline loading; risk amplified by concomitant cyclosporine A, aminoglycosides or pentamidine. CRRT: 200-400 mg q24h
Fluconazole	37/100	100–400 mg q24h	D	100%	50%	50%	HEMO: 100% of recommended dose AD; CAPD: Dose for CrCl <10	
Flucytosine	3-6/75-200	37.5 mg per kg q6h	I	q12h	q12-24h	q24h	HEMO: Dose AD; CAPD: 0.5-1 gm q24h	Goal is peak serum level >25 mcg per mL and <100 mcg per mL
Itraconazole, po soln	21/25	100–200 mg q12h	D	100%	100%	50%	HEMO/CAPD: oral solution: 100 mg q12-24h	
Itraconazole, IV	21/25	200 mg IV q12h	I	200 mg IV bid	Do not use IV titra if CrCl <30 due to accumulation of carrier cyclodextrin			
Terbinafine	36-200/?	250 mg po per day	–	q24h	Use has not been studied. Recommend avoidance of drug		Recommend avoidance of drug	
Voriconazole, IV	Non-linear kinetics	6 mg per kg IV q12h times 2, then 4 mg per kg q12h	–	No change	For CRRT: 4 mg/kg po q12h		If CrCl <50 mL per min, accum. of IV vehicle (cyclodextrin). Switch to po or DC	
ANTIPARASITIC ANTIBIOTICS								
Pentamidine	3-12/73-18	4 mg per kg per day	I	q24h	Same dose for CRRT	q24-36h	HEMO: 4 mg/kg q48h AD; CAPD: Dose for CrCl <10	
Quinine	5-16/5-16	650 mg q8h	I	q8h	q8-12h; Same dose for CRRT	650 mg q24h	HEMO: Dose AD; CAPD: Dose for CrCl <10	Marked tissue accumulation
ANTITUBERCULOUS ANTIBIOTICS (See http://11ntcc.ucsd.edu/TB)								
Amikacin/Streptomycin				No adjustment for mild-moderate renal impairment; **use with caution if severe renal impairment or ESRD**				
Bedaquiline	24-30	400 mg po qd x 2 wks, then 200 mg tiw x 22 wks						
Capreomycin		15 mg/kg q24h	I	15 mg/kg q24h; CRRT: 25 mg/kg q24h (max 2.5 gm q24h)		15 mg/kg AD 3x/wk	HEMO: 15 mg/kg AD 3x/wk	
Cycloserine		10-15 mg/kg/day in 2 div doses	I	10-15 mg/kg/day in 2 div doses	CrCl 10-20: 10-15 mg/kg q12-24h	10-15 mg/kg q24h	HEMO: 10-15 mg/kg AD 3x/wk	
Ethambutol	4/7-15	15-25 mg per kg q24h	I	15-25 mg/kg q24h	CrCl 30-50: 15-25 mg/kg q24-36h; For CrCl 10-20: 15-25 mg/kg q24-48h; Same dose for CRRT	15-25 mg/kg q48h	HEMO: 20 mg/kg 3x/wk AD; CAPD: 25 mg/kg q48h	If possible, do serum levels on dialysis pts.
Ethionamide	2/9	250-500 mg q12h	D	500 mg bid	500 mg bid	250 mg bid	HEMO/CAPD/CRRT: No dosage adjustment	

Abbreviation Key: Adjustment Method: **D** = dose adjustment, **I** = interval adjustment; **CAPD** = continuous ambulatory peritoneal dialysis; **CRRT** = continuous renal replacement therapy; **HEMO** = hemodialysis; **AD** = after dialysis; **"Supplement"** or **"Extra"** is to replace drug lost during dialysis – additional drug beyond continuation of regimen for CrCl < 10 mL/min.

TABLE 15A (7)

ANTIMICROBIAL	HALF-LIFE (NORMAL/ESRD) hr	DOSE FOR NORMAL RENAL FUNCTION	METHOD (see footer)	ADJUSTMENT FOR RENAL FAILURE Estimated creatinine clearance (CrCl), mL/min			HEMODIALYSIS, CAPD	COMMENTS & DOSAGE FOR CRRT
				>50-90	10-50	<10		
ANTITUBERCULOUS ANTIBIOTICS (Continued)								
Isoniazid	0.7-4/8-17	5 mg per kg per day (max. 300 mg)	D	100%	100%	100%	HEMO: Dose AD / CAPD: Dose for CrCl <10	
Pyrazinamide	9/26	25 mg per kg q24h (max. dose 2.5 gm q24h)	D	25 mg/kg q24h	CrCl 21-90: 25 mg/kg q24h For CrCl 10-20: 25 mg/kg q48h	12-25 mg per kg 3x/wk	HEMO: 25 mg/kg 3x/wk AD / CAPD: No reduction	Same dose for CRRT Same dose for CRRT Same dose for CRRT
Rifampin	1.5-5/1.8-11	600 mg per day	D	600 mg q24h	300-600 mg q24h	300-600 mg q24h	HEMO: No adjustment / CAPD: Dose for CrCl <10	Biologically active metabolite
ANTIVIRAL AGENTS For ANTIRETROVIRALS (See CID 40:1559, 2005)								
Acyclovir, IV	2-4/20	5-12.4 mg per kg q8h	D&I	100% q8h	100% q12-24h	50% q24h	HEMO: Dose AD / CAPD: Dose for CrCl <10	Rapid IV infusion can cause ↑ Cr. CRRT dose: 5-10 mg/kg q24h
Adefovir	7.5/15	10 mg po q24h	I	10 mg q24h	10 mg q48-72h[3]	10 mg q72h[3]	HEMO: 10 mg q week AD	CAPD: No data; CRRT: Dose?
Amantadine	12/500	100 mg bid	I	q12h	q24-48h	q 7 days	HEMO/CAPD: Dose for CrCl <10	CRRT: Dose for CrCl 10-50
Atripla	See each drug	200 mg emtricitabine + 300 mg tenofovir + 600 mg efavirenz	I	Do not use if CrCl <50				
Cidofovir: Complicated dosing—see package insert								
Induction	2.5/unknown	5 mg per kg once per wk for 2 wks.	–	5 mg per kg once per wk	Contraindicated in pts with CrCl ≤ 55 mL/min.			Major toxicity is renal. No efficacy, safety, or pharmacokinetic data in pts with moderate/severe renal disease.
Maintenance	2.5/unknown	5 mg per kg q2wks	–	5 mg per kg q2wks	Contraindicated in pts with CrCl ≤ 55 mL/min.			
Didanosine tablets[4]	0.6-1.6/4.5	125-200 mg q12h buffered tabs	D	125-200 mg q12h	200 mg q24h	<60 kg: 150 mg q24h >60 kg: 100 mg q24h	HEMO: Dose AD CAPD/CRRT: Dose for CrCl <10	Based on incomplete data. Data are estimates.
		400 mg q24h enteric-coated tabs	D	400 mg q24h	125-200 mg q24h	<60 kg: Do not use EC tabs >60 kg: 100 mg q24h	HEMO/CAPD: Dose for CrCl <10	**If <60 kg & CrCl <10 mL per min, do not use EC tabs**
Emtricitabine (CAPS)	10/>10	200 mg q24h	I	200 mg q24h	30-49: 200 mg q48h 10-29: 200 mg q72h	200 mg q96h	HEMO: Dose for CrCl <10	*See package insert for oral solution.*
Emtricitabine + Tenofovir	See each drug	200-300 mg q24h	I	No change	30-50: 1 tab q48h	CrCl <30: Do not use	HEMO: Dose for CrCl <10	
Entecavir	128-149/?	0.5 mg q24h	D	0.5 mg q24h	0.15-0.25 mg q24h	0.05 mg q24h	HEMO/CAPD: 0.05 mg q24h	Give after dialysis on dialysis days

3 Ref: *Transplantation* 80:1086, 2005
4 Ref: for NRTIs and NNRTIs: *Kidney International* 60:821, 2001

Abbreviation Key: Adjustment Method: **D** = dose adjustment, **I** = interval adjustment; **CAPD** = continuous ambulatory peritoneal dialysis; **CRRT** = continuous renal replacement therapy; **HEMO** = hemodialysis; **AD** = after dialysis; "**Supplement**" or "**Extra**" is to replace drug lost during dialysis – additional drug beyond continuation of regimen for CrCl < 10 mL/min.

TABLE 15A (8)

ANTIMICROBIAL	HALF-LIFE (NORMAL/ ESRD) hr	DOSE for NORMAL RENAL FUNCTION	METHOD (see footer)	ADJUSTMENT FOR RENAL FAILURE Estimated creatinine clearance (CrCl) mL/min >50-90	10-50	<10	HEMODIALYSIS, CAPD	COMMENTS & DOSAGE FOR CRRT
ANTIVIRAL AGENTS For ANTIRETROVIRALS (continued)								
Famciclovir	2.3-3/10-22	500 mg q8h	D&I	500 mg q8h	500 mg q12-24h	250 mg q24h	HEMO: Dose AD; CAPD: No data	CRRT: Not applicable

Foscarnet (CMV dosage):
Normal half-life (T½) 3 hrs with terminal T½ of 18-88 hrs. T½ very long with ESRD. Dosage adjustment based on est. CrCl divided by wt (kg)

CrCl (mL/min per kg body weight—only for Foscarnet)

	>1.4	>1-1.4	>0.8-1	>0.6-0.8	>0.5-0.6	>0.4-0.5	<0.4
IV: Induction: 60 mg/kg IV q8h x 2-3 wks	60	45 q8h	50 q12h	40 q12h	60 q24h	50 q24h	Do not use
Maintenance: 90-120 mg/kg/day IV	120 q24h	90 q24h	65 q24h	105 q48h	80 q48h	65 q48h	Do not use

Comments: See package insert for further details. HEMO: Dose AD; CAPD: No data

ANTIMICROBIAL	HALF-LIFE	DOSE NORMAL	METHOD	>50-90	10-50	<10	HEMODIALYSIS, CAPD	COMMENTS & DOSAGE FOR CRRT
Ganciclovir	3.6/30	IV: Induction 5 mg per kg q12h IV	D&I	70-90: 5 mg per kg q12h; 50-60: 2.5 mg/kg q12h	25-49: 2.5 mg per kg q24h; 10-24: 1.25 mg/kg q24h	1.25 mg per kg 3 times per wk	HEMO: Dose AD; CAPD: Dose for CrCl <10	Risk of side effects increased if concomitant CYP3A inhibitor
		Maintenance 5 mg per kg q24h IV	D&I	2.5-5.0 mg per kg q24h	0.6-1.25 mg per kg q24h	0.625 mg per kg 3 times per week	HEMO: 0.6 mg per kg AD; CAPD: Dose for CrCl <10	
	po:	1 gm tid po	D&I	0.5-1 gm tid	0.5-1 gm q24h	0.5 gm 3 times per week	HEMO: 0.5 gm AD	
Maraviroc	14-18/No data	300 mg bid	D&I	300 mg bid	300 mg po q24h	25-50 mg q24h	HEMO: Dose AD; CAPD: Dose for CrCl<10.	CRRT: 100 mg 1st day, then 50 mg/day.
Lamivudine	5-7/15-35	300 mg po q24h	D&I	300 mg po q24h	50-150 mg q24h	25-50 mg q24h	HEMO: Dose AD; CAPD: Dose for CrCl <10.	Dose for prophylaxis if CrCl <30: 75 mg once daily CRRT: 75 mg po bid
Oseltamivir, therapy	6-10/>20	75 mg po bid – treatment	I	75 mg q12h	30-50: 75 mg bid; <30: 75 mg once daily	No data	HEMO: 30 mg qd non-dialysis days; CAPD: 30 mg once per week	CRRT: http://www.cdc.gov/h1n1flu/eva/peramivir.htm
Peramivir		600 mg once daily	P&I	600 mg q24h	31-49: 150 mg q24h; 10-30: 100 mg q24h	100 mg (single dose) then 100 mg q24h	HEMO: 100 mg (single dose) then 100 mg 2 hrs AD (dialysis days only)	
Ribavirin	Use with caution in patients with creatinine clearance <50 mL per min.							
Rimantadine	13-65/Prolonged	100 mg bid po	I	100 mg bid	100 mg q24h-bid	100 mg q24h	HEMO/CAPD: No data	
Stavudine, po	1-1.4/5.5-8	30-40 mg q12h	D&I	100%	50% q12-24h	≥60 kg: 20 mg per day; <60 kg: 15 mg per day	HEMO: Dose as for CrCl <10 AD; CAPD: No data; CRRT: Full dose	Use with caution, little data
Stribild		1 tab daily		If CrCl < 70: contraindicated	If CrCl < 50: discontinue			
Telbivudine	40-49/No data	600 mg po daily	D&I	600 mg q24h	30-49: 600 mg q48h; <30: 600 mg q72h	600 mg q96h	HEMO: As for CrCl <10 AD	

* HEMO wt-based dose adjustments for children age >1 yr (dose after each HEMO): ≤15 kg: 7.5 mg; 16-23 kg: 10 mg; 24-40 kg: 15 mg; > 40 kg: 30 mg (CID 50:127, 2010).

Abbreviation Key: Adjustment Method: **D** = dose adjustment; **I** = interval adjustment; **CAPD** = continuous ambulatory peritoneal dialysis; **CRRT** = continuous renal replacement therapy; **"Supplement"** or **"Extra"** is to replace drug lost during dialysis – additional drug beyond continuation of regimen for CrCl < 10 mL/min.
HEMO = hemodialysis; **AD** = after dialysis;

TABLE 15A (9)

ANTIMICROBIAL	HALF-LIFE (NORMAL/ ESRD) hr	DOSE FOR NORMAL RENAL FUNCTION	METHOD (see footer)	ADJUSTMENT FOR RENAL FAILURE Estimated creatinine clearance (CrCl), mL/min			HEMODIALYSIS, CAPD	COMMENTS & DOSAGE FOR CRRT
				>50-90	10-50	<10		
ANTIVIRAL AGENTS For ANTIRETROVIRALS (continued)								
Tenofovir, po	17/?	300 mg q24h		300 mg q24h	**30-49:** 300 mg q48h **10-29:** 300 mg q72-96h	No data	HEMO: 300 mg q7d or after 12 hrs of HEMO.[6]	
Valacyclovir	2.5-3.3/14	1 gm q8h	D&I	1 gm q8h	1 gm q12-24h **Same dose for CRRT**	0.5 gm q24h	HEMO: Dose AD CAPD: Dose for CrCl <10	CAVH dose: As for CrCl 10-50
Valganciclovir	4/67	900 mg po bid	D&I	900 mg po bid	450 mg q24h to 450 mg every other day	DO NOT USE	See package insert	
Zalcitabine	2/>8	0.75 mg q8h	D&I	0.75 mg q8h	0.75 mg q12h **Same dose for CRRT**	0.75 mg q24h	HEMO: Dose AD CAPD: No data	CRRT dose: As for CrCl 10-50
Zidovudine	1.1-1.4/1.4-3	300 mg q12h	D&I	300 mg q12h	300 mg q12h **Same dose for CRRT**	100 mg q8h	HEMO: Dose for CrCl <10 AD CAPD: Dose for CrCl <10	

[6] Acute renal failure and Fanconi syndrome reported.

Abbreviation Key; Adjustment Method: **D** = dose adjustment, **I** = interval adjustment; **CAPD** = continuous ambulatory peritoneal dialysis; **CRRT** = continuous renal replacement therapy; **HEMO** = hemodialysis; **AD** = after dialysis; **"Supplement"** or **"Extra"** is to replace drug lost during dialysis – additional drug beyond continuation of regimen for CrCl < 10 mL/min.

194

TABLE 15B: NO DOSAGE ADJUSTMENT WITH RENAL INSUFFICIENCY

Antibacterials		Antifungals	Anti-TBc	Antivirals	
Azithromycin	Minocycline	Anidulafungin	Ethionamide	Abacavir	Lopinavir
Ceftriaxone	Moxifloxacin	Caspofungin	Isoniazid	Atazanavir	Nelfinavir
Chloramphenicol	Nafcillin	Itraconazole oral solution	Rifampin	Darunavir	Nevirapine
Ciprofloxacin XL	Polymyxin B	Ketoconazole	Rifabutin	Delavirdine	Raltegravir
Clindamycin	Pyrimethamine	Micafungin	Rifapentine	Efavirenz	Ribavirin
Doxycycline	Rifaximin	Voriconazole, **po only**		Enfuvirtide[1]	Saquinavir
Linezolid	Tigecycline			Fosamprenavir	Tipranavir
				Indinavir	

[1] Enfuvirtide: Not studied in patients with CrCl <35 mL/min. DO NOT USE

TABLE 15C: DOSAGE OF ANTIRETROVIRAL DRUGS IN PATIENTS WITH IMPAIRED HEPATIC FUNCTION
(See CID 40:174, 2005)
Dose reduction may be indicated in the presence of liver disease.

DRUG GENERIC (TRADE)	STANDARD DOSE	DOSING IF HEPATIC IMPAIRMENT CHILD-PUGH SCORE*	ADJUSTED DOSE	COMMENTS
Protease inhibitors				
Atazanavir (Reyataz)	300–400 mg po q24h	7–9 / >9	300 mg q24h / Do not use	No ritonavir boosting if hepatic impairment
Darunavir	600 mg po bid with ritonavir	Use with caution. No specific dose suggested		
Fosamprenavir (Lexiva)	1400 mg po q12h	5–9 / 10–15	700 mg q12h / 350 mg bid	
Indinavir (Crixivan)	800 mg po q8h	Mild to moderate hepatic insufficiency	600 mg q8h	
Lopinavir/ritonavir (Kaletra)	400 mg/ 100 mg po q12h	No dosage recommendations; use with caution if hepatic impairment		
Nelfinavir (Viracept)	1250 mg po q12h	No dosage recommendations; use with caution if hepatic impairment		
Ritonavir (Norvir)	600 mg po q12h	No dosage recommendations; use with caution if hepatic impairment		
Saquinavir (Invirase)	1000 mg po + 100 mg ritonavir bid	No dosage recommendations; use with caution if hepatic impairment		
Stribild	once daily	3 (Child-Pugh column)	Do not use	
Tipranavir	500 mg + 200 mg ritonavir po bid	5–9 / >9	No dosage adjustment / Do not use	
Fusion & Entry Inhibitors				
Enfuvirtide (Fuzeon)	90 mg subQ q12h	No dosage adjustment recommendations		
Maraviroc (Selzentry)	300 mg bid; *See page 35.*	No dosage recommendations; use caution if hepatic impairment		
Other Antiretrovirals				
Abacavir	600 mg po q24h	5-6 / >6	200 mg bid / Avoid	Use oral solution
Delavirdine	400 mg po tid	Metabolized in liver	No dosage adjustment data	
Efavirenz/Rilpivirine	600 mg po q24h	Metabolized in liver	No dosage adjustment data	
Etravirine	200 mg po bid	Up to 9 / >9	No dose adjustment / No data; **Caution**	
Nevirapine	200 mg po bid	Up to 6 / >6	**Caution** / Contraindicated	

*CALCULATION OF CHILD-PUGH SCORE—Classification below

CLINICAL FEATURE	SCORE GIVEN		
	1	2	3
Encephalopathy *(see below)***	None	Grade 1–2	Grade 3–4
Albumin	>3.5 gm/dl	2.8–3.5 gm/dl	<2.8 gm/dl
Total bilirubin	<2 mg/dl	2–3 mg/dl	>3 mg/dl
If taking indinavir or if Gilbert's syndrome	<4 mg/dl	4–7 mg/dl	>7 mg/dl
Prothrombin time or	<4	4–6	>6
INR	<1.7	1.7–2.3	>2.3

CLASSIFICATION

Score	Class
5–6	A
7–9	B
>9	C

**GRADE OF ENCEPHALOPATHY

Grade	Clinical Criteria
1	Mild confusion, anxiety, restlessness, fine tremor, slow coordination
2	Drowsiness, asterixis
3	Somnolent but arousable, marked confusion, speech incomprehensible, incontinent, hyperventilation
4	Coma, decerebrate posturing, flaccidity

TABLE 16A: DRUG/DRUG INTERACTIONS: ANTIRETROVIRAL DRUGS &
DRUGS USED IN TREATMENT OF HIV-ASSOCIATED INFECTIONS & MALIGNANCIES

Importance: ± = theory/anecdotal; + = of probable importance; + + = of definite importance
To check for interactions between more than 2 drugs, see: http://www.drugs.com/drug_interactions.html
and http://www.healthline.com/druginteractions

ANTI-INFECTIVE AGENT (A)	OTHER DRUG (B)	EFFECT	IMPORT
Abacavir	Methadone	↓ levels of B	++
Amantadine (Symmetrel)	Alcohol	↑ CNS effects	+
	Anticholinergic and anti-Parkinson agents (ex Artane, scopolamine)	↑ effect of B: dry mouth, ataxia, blurred vision, slurred speech, toxic psychosis	+
	Trimethoprim	↑ levels of A & B	+
	Digoxin	↑ levels of B	±
Aminoglycosides— parenteral (amikacin, gentamicin, kanamycin, netilmicin, sisomicin, streptomycin, tobramycin)	Amphotericin B	↑ nephrotoxicity	++
	Cis platinum (Platinol)	↑ nephro & ototoxicity	+
	Cyclosporine	↑ nephrotoxicity	+
	Neuromuscular blocking agents	↑ apnea or respiratory paralysis	+
	Loop diuretics (e.g., furosemide)	↑ ototoxicity	++
	NSAIDs	↑ nephrotoxicity	+
	Non-polarizing muscle relaxants	↑ apnea	+
	Radiographic contrast	↑ nephrotoxicity	+
	Vancomycin	↑ nephrotoxicity	+
Aminoglycosides— oral (kanamycin, neomycin)	Warfarin	↑ prothrombin time	+
Amphotericin B and ampho B lipid formulations	Antineoplastic drugs	↑ nephrotoxicity risk	+
	Digitalis	↑ toxicity of B if K⁺ ↓	+
	Nephrotoxic drugs: aminoglycosides, cidofovir, cyclosporine, foscarnet, pentamidine	↑ nephrotoxicity of A	++
Ampicillin, amoxicillin	Allopurinol	↑ frequency of rash	++
Artemether-lumefantrine	CYP3A inhibitors: amiodarone, atazanavir, itraconazole, ritonavir, voriconazole	↑ levels of A; ↑ QTc interval	++
	CYP2D6 substrates: flecainide, imipramine, amitriptyline	↑ levels of B; ↑ QTc interval	++
Atazanavir	See protease inhibitors and Table 16B		
Atovaquone	Rifampin (perhaps rifabutin)	↓ serum levels of A; ↑ levels of B	+
	Metoclopramide	↓ levels of A	+
	Tetracycline	↓ levels of A	++

Azole Antifungal Agents [**Flu** = fluconazole; **Itr** = itraconazole; **Ket** = ketoconazole; **Posa** = posaconazole **Vor** = voriconazole; **+** = occurs; **blank space** = either studied & no interaction OR no data found (may be in pharm. co. databases)]

Flu	Itr	Ket	Posa	Vor			
+	+				Amitriptyline	↑ levels of B	+
+	+	+		+	Calcium channel blockers	↑ levels of B	++
	+			+	Carbamazepine (vori contraindicated)	↓ levels of A	++
+	+	+	+	+	Cyclosporine	↑ levels of A; ↑ risk of nephrotoxicity	+
	+	+			Didanosine	↓ absorption of A	+
	+	+	+	+	Efavirenz	↓ levels of A, ↑ levels of B	++ (avoid)
+	+	+	+	+	H₂ blockers, antacids, sucralfate	↓ absorption of A	+
+	+	+	+	+	Hydantoins (phenytoin, Dilantin)	↑ levels of B, ↓ levels of A	++
+	+	+			Isoniazid	↓ levels of A	+
+	+	+	+	+	Lovastatin/simvastatin	Rhabdomyolysis reported; ↑ levels of B	++
			+	+	Methadone	↑ levels of B	+
+	+	+	+	+	Midazolam/triazolam, po	↑ levels of B	++
+	+			+	Warfarin	↑ effect of B	++
+	+				Oral hypoglycemics	↑ levels of B	++
			+	+	Pimozide	↑ levels of B—**avoid**	++
	+	+		+	Protease inhibitors	↑ levels of B	++
+	+	+	+	+	Proton pump inhibitors	↓ levels of A, ↑ levels of B	++
+	+	+	+	+	Rifampin/rifabutin (vori contraindicated)	↑ levels of B, ↓ serum levels of A	++
+	+				Rituximab	Inhibits action of B	++
			+	+	Sirolimus (vori and posa contraindicated)	↑ levels of B	++
+		+	+	+	Tacrolimus	↑ levels of B with toxicity	++
+		+			Theophyllines	↑ levels of B	+
		+			Trazodone	↑ levels of B	++
+					Zidovudine	↑ levels of B	+

TABLE 16A (2)

ANTI-INFECTIVE AGENT (A)	OTHER DRUG (B)	EFFECT	IMPORT
Bedaquiline	Rifampin	↓ levels of A	++
	Ketoconazole	↑ levels of A	
Caspofungin	Cyclosporine	↑ levels of A	++
	Tacrolimus	↓ levels of B	++
	Carbamazepine, dexamethasone, efavirenz, nevirapine, phenytoin, rifampin	↓ levels of A; ↑ dose of caspofungin to 70 mg/d	++
Chloramphenicol	Hydantoins	↑ toxicity of B, nystagmus, ataxia	++
	Iron salts, Vitamin B12	↓ response to B	++
	Protease inhibitors—HIV	↓ levels of A & B	++
Clindamycin (Cleocin)	Kaolin	↓ absorption of A	++
	Muscle relaxants, e.g., atracurium, baclofen, diazepam	↑ frequency/duration of respiratory paralysis	++
	St John's wort	↓ levels of A	++
Cobicistat	See *Stribild, below*		
Cycloserine	Ethanol	↑ frequency of seizures	+
	INH, ethionamide	↑ frequency of drowsiness/dizziness	+
Dapsone	Atazanavir	↑ levels of A - Avoid	++
	Didanosine	↓ absorption of A	+
	Oral contraceptives	↓ effectiveness of B	+
	Pyrimethamine	↑ in marrow toxicity	+
	Rifampin/Rifabutin	↓ serum levels of A	+
	Trimethoprim	↑ levels of A & B (methemoglobinemia)	+
	Zidovudine	May ↑ marrow toxicity	+
Daptomycin	HMG-CoA inhibitors (statins)	Consider DC statin while on dapto	++
Delavirdine (Rescriptor)	See *Non-nucleoside reverse transcriptase inhibitors (NNRTIs) and Table 16B*		
Didanosine (ddI) (Videx)	Allopurinol	↑ levels of A—**AVOID**	++
	Cisplatin, dapsone, INH, metronidazole, nitrofurantoin, stavudine, vincristine, zalcitabine	↑ risk of peripheral neuropathy	+
	Ethanol, lamivudine, pentamidine	↑ risk of pancreatitis	+
	Fluoroquinolones	↓ absorption 2° to chelation	+
	Drugs that need low pH for absorption: dapsone, indinavir, itra/ ketoconazole, pyrimethamine, rifampin, trimethoprim	↓ absorption	+
	Methadone	↓ levels of A	++
	Ribavirin	↑ levels ddI metabolite—**avoid**	++
	Tenofovir	↑ levels of A **(reduce dose of A)**	++
Doripenem	Probenecid	↑ levels of A	++
	Valproic acid	↓ levels of B	++
Doxycycline	Aluminum, bismuth, iron, Mg++	↓ absorption of A	+
	Barbiturates, hydantoins	↓ serum t/2 of A	+
	Carbamazepine (Tegretol)	↓ serum t/2 of A	+
	Digoxin	↑ serum levels of B	+
	Warfarin	↑ activity of B	++
Efavirenz (Sustiva)	See *non-nucleoside reverse transcriptase inhibitors (NNRTIs) and Table 16B*		
Elvitegravir	See *Stribild, below*		
Ertapenem (Invanz)	Probenecid	↑ levels of A	++
	Valproic acid	↓ levels of B	++
Ethambutol (Myambutol)	Aluminum salts (includes didanosine buffer)	↓ absorption of A & B	+
Etravirine	See *non-nucleoside reverse transcriptase inhibitors (NNRTIs) and Table 16B*		

Fluoroquinolones						(**Cipro** = ciprofloxacin; **Gati** = gatifloxacin; **Gemi** = gemifloxacin; **Levo** = levofloxacin; **Moxi** = moxifloxacin; **Oflox** = ofloxacin)		
Cipro	Gati	Gemi	Levo	Moxi	Oflox	NOTE: Blank space = *either studied and no interaction OR no data found*		
	+		+	+	+	**Antiarrhythmics (procainamide, amiodarone)**	↑ Q-T interval (torsade)	++
+	+		+	+	+	Insulin, oral hypoglycemics	↑ & ↓ blood sugar	++
+						Caffeine	↑ levels of B	+
+					+	Cimetidine	↑ levels of A	+
+					+	Cyclosporine	↑ levels of B	±
+	+		+	+	+	Didanosine	↓ absorption of A	++

TABLE 16A (3)

ANTI-INFECTIVE AGENT (A)	OTHER DRUG (B)	EFFECT	IMPORT

Fluoroquinolones *(continued)*

Cipro	Gati	Gemi	Levo	Moxi	Oflox	NOTE: Blank space = either studied and no interaction OR no data found		
+	+	+	+	+	+	**Cations: Al+++, Ca++, Fe++, Mg++, Zn++ (antacids, vitamins, dairy products), citrate/citric acid**	↓ absorption of A (some variability between drugs)	++
+						Methadone	↑ levels of B	++
+		+			+	**NSAIDs**	↑ risk CNS stimulation/seizures	++
+						Phenytoin	↑ or ↓ levels of B	+
+	+	+				Probenecid	↓ renal clearance of A	+
+						Rasagiline	↑ levels of B	++
				+		Rifampin	↓ levels of A (CID 45:1001, 2007)	++
+	+	+	+		+	**Sucralfate**	↓ **absorption of A**	++
+						Theophylline	↑ levels of B	++
+						Thyroid hormone	↓ levels of B	++
+						Tizanidine	↑ levels of B	++
+			+	+	+	Warfarin	↑ prothrombin time	+
Ganciclovir (Cytovene) & **Valganciclovir** (Valcyte)						Imipenem	↑ risk of seizures reported	+
						Probenecid	↑ levels of A	+
						Zidovudine	↓ levels of A, ↑ levels of B	+
Gentamicin						*See Aminoglycosides—parenteral*		
Imipenem & Meropenem						BCG	↓ effectiveness of B – avoid combination	++
						Divalproex	↓ levels of B	++
						Ganciclovir	↑ seizure risk	++
						Probenecid	↑ levels of A	++
						Valproic acid	↓ levels of B	++
Indinavir						*See protease inhibitors and Table 16B*		
Isoniazid						**Alcohol, rifampin**	↑ risk of hepatic injury	++
						Aluminum salts	↓ absorption (take fasting)	++
						Carbamazepine, phenytoin	↑ levels of B with nausea, vomiting, nystagmus, ataxia	++
						Itraconazole, ketoconazole	↓ levels of B	+
						Oral hypoglycemics	↓ effects of B	+
Lamivudine						Zalcitabine	Mutual interference—do not combine	++
Linezolid (Zyvox)						Adrenergic agents	Risk of hypertension	++
						Aged, fermented, pickled or smoked foods —↑ tyramine	Risk of hypertension	+
						Clarithromycin	↑ levels of A	++
						Rasagiline (MAO inhibitor)	Risk of serotonin syndrome	+
						Rifampin	↓ levels of A	++
						Serotonergic drugs (SSRIs)	Risk of serotonin syndrome	++
Lopinavir						*See protease inhibitors*		

Macrolides [**Ery** = erythromycin; **Azi** = azithromycin; **Clr** = clarithromycin; + = occurs; blank space = either studied and no interaction OR no data]

Ery	Azi	Clr			
+		+	Carbamazepine	↑ serum levels of B, nystagmus, nausea, vomiting, ataxia	++ (avoid w/ erythro)
+		+	Cimetidine, **ritonavir**	↑ levels of B	+
+		+	Clozapine	↑ serum levels of B, CNS toxicity	+
		+	**Colchicine**	↑ **levels of B (potent, fatal)**	++ (avoid)
+		+	Corticosteroids	↑ effects of B	+
+		+	Cyclosporine	↑ serum levels of B with toxicity	+
+	+	+	Digoxin, digitoxin	↑ serum levels of B (10% of cases)	+
		+	Efavirenz	↓ levels of A	++
+		+	Ergot alkaloids	↑ levels of B	++
		+	Linezolid	↑ levels of B	++
+		+	Lovastatin/simvastatin	↑ levels of B; rhabdomyolysis	++
+		+	Midazolam, triazolam	↑ levels of B, ↑ sedative effects	+
+		+	Phenytoin	↑ levels of B	+
+	+	+	Pimozide	**Q-T interval**	++
+		+	Rifampin, rifabutin	↑ levels of B	+
+		+	Tacrolimus	↑ levels of B	++
+		+	Theophylline	↑ serum levels of B with nausea, vomiting, seizures, apnea	++
+		+	Valproic acid	↑ levels of B	+
+		+	Warfarin	May ↑ prothrombin time	+
		+	Zidovudine	↓ levels of B	+

TABLE 16A (4)

ANTI-INFECTIVE AGENT (A)	OTHER DRUG (B)	EFFECT	IMPORT
Maraviroc	Clarithromycin	↑ serum levels of A	++
	Delavirdine	↑ levels of A	++
	Itraconazole/ketoconazole	↑ levels of A	++
	Nefazodone	↑ levels of A	++
	Protease Inhibitors (not tipranavir/ritonavir)	↑ levels of A	++
	Anticonvulsants: carbamazepine, phenobarbital, phenytoin	↓ levels of A	++
	Efavirenz	↓ levels of A	++
	Rifampin	↓ levels of A	++
Mefloquine	β-adrenergic blockers, calcium channel blockers, quinidine, quinine	↑ arrhythmias	+
	Divalproex, valproic acid	↓ level of B with seizures	++
	Halofantrine	Q-T prolongation	++ (avoid)
	Calcineurin inhibitors	Q-T prolongation (avoid)	++
Meropenem	See Imipenem		
Methenamine mandelate or hippurate	Acetazolamide, sodium bicarbonate, thiazide diuretics	↓ antibacterial effect 2° to ↑ urine pH	++
Metronidazole Tinidazole	Alcohol	Disulfiram-like reaction	+
	Cyclosporin	↑ levels of B	++
	Disulfiram (Antabuse)	Acute toxic psychosis	+
	Lithium	↑ levels of B	++
	Warfarin	↑ anticoagulant effect	++
	Phenobarbital, hydantoins	↑ levels of B	++
Micafungin	Nifedipine	↑ levels of B	+
	Sirolimus	↑ levels of B	+
Nafcillin	Warfarin	↑ Warfarin effect	++
Nelfinavir	See protease inhibitors and Table 16B		
Nevirapine (Viramune)	See non-nucleoside reverse transcriptase inhibitors (NNRTIs) and Table 16B		
Nitrofurantoin	Antacids	↓ absorption of A	+

Non-nucleoside reverse transcriptase inhibitors (NNRTIs): For interactions with protease inhibitors, see *Table 16B*.
Del = delavirdine; **Efa** = efavirenz; **Etr** = etravirine; **Nev** = nevirapine

Del	Efa	Etr	Nev	Co-administration contraindicated (See package insert):		
+		+		Anticonvulsants: carbamazepine, phenobarbital, phenytoin		++
+		+		Antimycobacterials: rifabutin, rifampin		++
+		+		Antipsychotics: pimozide		++
+	+	+		Benzodiazepines: alprazolam, midazolam, triazolam		++
+	+			Ergotamine		++
+	+	+		HMG-CoA inhibitors (statins): lovastatin, simvastatin, atorvastatin, pravastatin		++
+		+		St. John's wort		++
				Dose change needed:		
+				Amphetamines	↑ levels of B—**caution**	++
+	+		+	Antiarrhythmics: amiodarone, lidocaine, others	↓ or ↑ levels of B—**caution**	++
+	+	+	+	Anticonvulsants: carbamazepine, phenobarbital, phenytoin	↓ levels of A and/or B	++
+	+	+	+	Antifungals: itraconazole, ketoconazole, voriconazole, posaconazole	Potential ↓ levels of B, ↑ levels of A	++ (avoid)
+				Antirejection drugs: cyclosporine, rapamycin, sirolimus, tacrolimus	↑ levels of B	++
		+		Calcium channel blockers	↑ levels of B	++
+		+	+	Clarithromycin	↑ levels of B metabolite, ↑ levels of A	++
+		+		Cyclosporine	↑ levels of B	++
+		+		Dexamethasone	↓ levels of A	++
+	+	+		Sildenafil, vardenafil, tadalafil	↑ levels of B	++
+		+		Fentanyl, methadone	↑ levels of B	++
+				Gastric acid suppression: antacids, H-2 blockers, proton pump inhibitors	↓ levels of A	++
	+		+	Mefloquine	↓ levels of B	++
	+	+	+	Methadone, fentanyl	↓ levels of B	++
+	+	+	+	Oral contraceptives	↑ or ↓ levels of B	++
+	+	+	+	Protease inhibitors—see Table 16B		
+	+	+	+	Rifabutin, rifampin	↑ or ↓ levels of rifabutin; ↓ levels of A—**caution**	++
+	+	+	+	St. John's wort	↓ levels of B	++
+		+	+	Warfarin	↑ levels of B	++
Pentamidine, IV				Amphotericin B	↑ risk of nephrotoxicity	+
				Pancreatitis-assoc drugs, eg, alcohol, valproic acid	↑ risk of pancreatitis	+
Piperacillin				Cefoxitin	Antagonism vs pseudomonas	++
Pip-tazo				Methotrexate	↑ levels of B	++
Polymyxin B				Curare paralytics	Avoid: neuromuscular blockade	++

TABLE 16A (5)

ANTI-INFECTIVE AGENT (A)	OTHER DRUG (B)	EFFECT	IMPORT
Polymyxin E (Colistin)	Curare paralytics	Avoid: neuromuscular blockade	++
	Aminoglycosides, Ampho B, Vanco	↑ nephrotoxicity risk	++
Primaquine	Chloroquine, dapsone, INH, probenecid, quinine, sulfonamides, TMP/SMX, others	↑ risk of hemolysis in G6PD-deficient patients	++

Protease Inhibitors—Anti-HIV Drugs. *(Atazan* = atazanavir; **Darun** = darunavir; **Fosampren** = fosamprenavir; **Indin** = *indinavir;* **Lopin** = lopinavir; **Nelfin** = nelfinavir; **Saquin** = saquinavir; **Tipran** = tipranavir). For interactions with antiretrovirals, *see Table 16B* **Only a partial list—check package insert**

Also see http://aidsinfo.nih.gov
To check for interactions between more than 2 drugs, see: http://www.drugs.com/drug_interactions.html and http://www.healthline.com/druginteractions

Atazan	Darun	Fosampren	Indin	Lopin	Nelfin	Saquin	Tipran	OTHER DRUG (B)	EFFECT	IMPORT
							+	**Analgesics:** 1. Alfentanil, fentanyl, hydrocodone, tramadol	↑ levels of B	+
		+		+		+	+	2. Codeine, hydromorphone, morphine, methadone	↓ levels of B (JAIDS 41:563, 2006)	+
+	+	+	+	+	+		+	**Anti-arrhythmics: amiodarone, lidocaine, mexiletine, flecainide**	↑ levels of B; **do not co-administer or use caution (See package insert)**	++
		+	+	+	+			**Anticonvulsants: carbamazepine, clonazepam, phenobarbital**	↓ levels of A, ↑ levels of B	++
+		+	+					Antidepressants, all tricyclic	↑ levels of B	++
+	+						+	Antidepressants, all other	↑ levels of B; do not use pimozide	++
							+	Antidepressants: SSRIs	↓ levels of B - avoid	++
							+	Antihistamines	**Do not use**	++
+	+	+	+	+				**Benzodiazepines, e.g., diazepam, midazolam, triazolam**	↑ levels of B—do not use	++
								Boceprevir	↓ levels of B	++
+	+	+	+	+	+		+	Calcium channel blockers (all)	↑ levels of B	++
+			+	+		+	+	Clarithro, erythro	↑ levels of B if renal impairment	+
+		+		+	+			Contraceptives, oral	↓ levels of A & B	++
	+	+	+					Corticosteroids: prednisone, dexamethasone	↓ levels of A, ↑ levels of B	+
+		+	+	+	+		+	Cyclosporine	↑ levels of B, monitor levels	+
						+		Digoxin	↑ levels of B	++
+	+	+	+	+		+	+	Ergot derivatives	**levels of B—do not use**	++
		+	+	+		+		Erythromycin, clarithromycin	↑ levels of A & B	+
			+			+		Grapefruit juice (>200 mL/day)	↓ indinavir & ↑ saquinavir levels	+
+	+	+	+			+		H2 receptor antagonists	↓ levels of A	++
+	+	+	+	+	+	+	+	**HMG-CoA reductase inhibitors (statins): lovastatin, simvastatin**	↑ levels of B—do not use	++
+								Irinotecan	**levels of B—do not use**	++
	+	+	+	+	+	+	+	Ketoconazole, itraconazole, ? vori.	↓ levels of A, ↑ levels of B	+
+	+	+	+	+	+	+	+	Posaconazole	↓ levels of A, no effect on B	++
				+				Metronidazole	Poss. disulfiram reaction, alcohol	+
				+				Phenytoin (JAIDS 36:1034, 2004)	↓ levels of A & B	++
+	+	+	+	+	+	+	+	Pimozide	**levels of B—do not use**	++
+	+		+	+		+	+	Proton pump inhibitors	↓ levels of A	++
+	+	+	+	+	+	+	+	Rifampin, rifabutin	↓ levels of A, ↑ levels of B **(avoid)**	++ **(avoid)**
+	+	+	+	+	+	+	+	Sildenafil (Viagra), tadalafil, vardenafil	Varies, some ↑ & some ↓ levels of B	++
+	+	+	+	+	+	+	+	**St. John's wort**	↓ levels of A—do not use	++
+	+	+	+	+	+	+	+	**Sirolimus, tracrolimus**	↑ levels of B	++
+								Tenofovir	↓ levels of A—add ritonavir	++
	+		+					Theophylline	↓ levels of B	+
+		+		+				Warfarin	↓ levels of B	+

ANTI-INFECTIVE AGENT (A)	OTHER DRUG (B)	EFFECT	IMPORT
Pyrazinamide	INH, rifampin	May ↑ risk of hepatotoxicity	±
Pyrimethamine	Lorazepam	↑ risk of hepatotoxicity	+
	Sulfonamides, TMP/SMX	↑ risk of marrow suppression	+
	Zidovudine	↑ risk of marrow suppression	+
Quinine	Digoxin	↑ digoxin levels; ↑ toxicity	++
	Mefloquine	↑ arrhythmias	+
	Warfarin	↑ prothrombin time	++
Quinupristin-dalfopristin (Synercid)	Anti-HIV drugs: NNRTIs & PIs	↑ levels of B	++
	Antineoplastic: vincristine, docetaxel, paclitaxel	↑ levels of B	++
	Calcium channel blockers	↑ levels of B	++
	Carbamazepine	↑ levels of B	++
	Cyclosporine, tacrolimus	↑ levels of B	++

TABLE 16A (6)

ANTI-INFECTIVE AGENT (A)	OTHER DRUG (B)	EFFECT	IMPORT
Quinupristin-dalfopristin (Synercid) *(continued)*	Lidocaine	↑ levels of B	+ +
	Methylprednisolone	↑ levels of B	+ +
	Midazolam, diazepam	↑ levels of B	+ +
	Statins	↑ levels of B	+ +
Raltegravir	**Rifampin**	↓ levels of A	+ +
Ribavirin	Didanosine	↑ levels of B → toxicity—**avoid**	+ +
	Stavudine	↓ levels of B	+ +
	Zidovudine	↓ levels of B	+ +
Rifamycins (rifampin, rifabutin) Ref.: *ArIM* 162:985, 2002 The following is a partial list of drugs with rifampin-induced ↑ metabolism and hence lower than anticipated serum levels: ACE inhibitors, dapsone, diazepam, digoxin, diltiazem, doxycycline, fluconazole, fluvastatin, haloperidol, moxifloxacin, nifedipine, progestins, triazolam, tricyclics, voriconazole, zidovudine *(Clin Pharmacokinetic 42:819, 2003).*	Al OH, ketoconazole, PZA	↓ levels of A	+
	Atovaquone	↑ levels of A, ↓ levels of B	+
	Beta adrenergic blockers (metoprolol, propranolol)	↓ effect of B	+
	Caspofungin	↓ levels of B—increase dose	+ +
	Clarithromycin	↑ levels of A, ↓ levels of B	+ +
	Corticosteroids	↑ replacement requirement of B	+ +
	Cyclosporine	↓ effect of B	+ +
	Delavirdine	↑ levels of A, ↓ levels of B—avoid	+ +
	Digoxin	↓ levels of B	+ +
	Disopyramide	↓ levels of B	+ +
	Fluconazole	↑ levels of A	+
	Amprenavir, indinavir, nelfinavir, ritonavir	↑ levels of A (↓ dose of A), ↓ levels of B	+ +
	INH	Converts INH to toxic hydrazine	+ +
	Itraconazole, ketoconazole	↓ levels of B, ↑ levels of A	+ +
	Linezolid	↓ levels of B	+ +
	Methadone	↓ serum levels (withdrawal)	+
	Nevirapine	↓ levels of B—avoid	+ +
	Warfarin	Suboptimal anticoagulation	+ +
	Oral contraceptives	↓ effectiveness; spotting, pregnancy	+
	Phenytoin	↓ levels of B	+
	Protease inhibitors	↓ levels of A, ↑ levels of B—CAUTION	+ +
	Quinidine	↓ effect of B	+
	Raltegravir	↓ levels of B	+ +
	Sulfonylureas	↓ hypoglycemic effect	+
	Tacrolimus	**↓ levels of B**	+ +
	Theophylline	↑ levels of B	+
	TMP/SMX	↑ levels of A	+
	Tocainide	↓ effect of B	+
Rimantadine	*See Amantadine*		
Ritonavir	*See protease inhibitors and Table 16B*		
Saquinavir	*See protease inhibitors and Table 16B*		
Stavudine	Dapsone, INH	May ↑ risk of peripheral neuropathy	±
	Ribavirin	↓ levels of A—AVOID	+ +
	Zidovudine	Mutual interference—do not combine	+ +
Stribild (Elvitegravir & Cobicistat components) *(See Emtricitabine & Tenofovir for other components)*			
Elvitegravir	Antacids	↓ levels of A	+ +
Cobicistat	Antiarrhythmics & digoxin	↑ levels of B	+ +
Cobicistat	Clarithromycin, telithromycin	↑ levels of B	+ +
Cobicistat & Elvitegravir	Carbamazepine, phenobarbital, phenytoin	↓ levels of A – AVOID	+ +
Cobicistat	SSRIs, TCAs, trazodone, antidepressants	↓ levels of A – AVOID	+ +
Cobicistat	Itraconazole, ketoconazole, voriconazole	↑ levels of B	+ +
Cobicistat	Colchicine	↑ levels of B – lower dose	+ +
Elvitegravir & Cobicistat	Rifabutin, rifapentine	↓ levels of A – AVOID	+ +
Cobicistat	Beta blockers	↑ levels of B	+ +
Cobicistat	Calcium channel blockers	↑ levels of B	+ +
Cobicistat & Elvitegravir	Dexamethasone	↓ levels of A	+ +
Cobicistat	Bosentan	↑ levels of B	+ +
Cobicistat	HMG-CoA reductase inhibitor, sirolimus	↑ levels of B	+ +
Cobicistat	Cyclosporine, tacrolimus	↑ levels of B	+ +
Cobicistat	Neuroleptics	↑ levels of B	+ +
Cobicistat	PDE5 inhibitors, e.g., Sildenafil, vardenafil, tadalafil	↑ levels of B – AVOID	+ +
Cobicistat	Benzodiazepines	↑ levels of B	+ +
Cobicistat	Ergot derivatives	↑ levels of B – AVOID	+ +
Cobicistat	Cisapride	↑ levels of B – AVOID	+ +
Cobicistat & Elvitegravir	St. John's wort	↑ levels of B – AVOID	+ +

TABLE 16A (7)

ANTI-INFECTIVE AGENT (A)	OTHER DRUG (B)	EFFECT	IMPORT
Sulfonamides	Beta blockers	↑ levels of B	++
	Cyclosporine	↓ cyclosporine levels	+
	Methotrexate	↑ antifolate activity	+
	Warfarin	↑ prothrombin time; bleeding	+
	Phenobarbital, rifampin	↓ levels of A	+
	Phenytoin	↑ levels of B; nystagmus, ataxia	+
	Sulfonylureas	↑ hypoglycemic effect	+
Telithromycin (Ketek)	Carbamazine	↓ levels of A	++
	Digoxin	↑ levels of B—do digoxin levels	++
	Ergot alkaloids	**↑ levels of B—avoid**	++
	Itraconazole; ketoconazole	↑ levels of A; no dose change	+
	Metoprolol	↑ levels of B	++
	Midazolam	↑ levels of B	++
	Warfarin	↑ prothrombin time	+
	Phenobarbital, phenytoin	↓ levels of A	++
	Pimozide	**↑ levels of B; QT prolongation— AVOID**	++
	Rifampin	**↓ levels of A—avoid**	++
	Simvastatin & other "statins"	↑ levels of B (↑ risk of myopathy)	++
	Sotalol	↓ levels of B	++
	Theophylline	↑ levels of B	++
Tenofovir	Atazanavir	↓ levels of B—add ritonavir	++
	Didanosine (ddl)	**↑ levels of B (reduce dose)**	++
Terbinafine	Cimetidine	↑ levels of A	+
	Phenobarbital, rifampin	↓ levels of A	+
Tetracyclines	See Doxycycline, plus:		
	Atovaquone	↓ levels of B	+
	Digoxin	↑ toxicity of B (may persist several months—up to 10% pts)	++
	Methoxyflurane	↑ toxicity; polyuria, renal failure	+
	Sucralfate	↓ absorption of A (separate by ≥2 hrs)	+
Thiabendazole	Theophyllines	↑ serum theophylline, nausea	+
Tigecycline	Oral contraceptives	↓ levels of B	++
Tinidazole (Tindamax)	See Metronidazole—similar entity, expect similar interactions		
Tobramycin	See Aminoglycosides		
Trimethoprim	Amantadine, dapsone, digoxin, methotrexate, procainamide, zidovudine	↑ serum levels of B	++
	Potassium-sparing diuretics	↑ serum K⁺	++
	Repaglinide	↑ levels of B (hypoglycemia)	++
	Thiazide diuretics	↓ serum Na⁺	+
Trimethoprim-Sulfameth-oxazole	Ace inhibitors	↑ serum K+	++
	Amantadine	↑ levels of B (toxicity)	++
	Azathioprine	Reports of leukopenia	+
	Cyclosporine	↓ levels of B, ↑ serum creatinine	+
	Loperamide	↑ levels of B	+
	Methotrexate	Enhanced marrow suppression	++
	Oral contraceptives, pimozide, and 6-mercaptopurine	↓ effect of B	+
	Phenytoin	↑ levels of B	+
	Rifampin	↑ levels of B	+
	Warfarin	↑ activity of B	+
Valganciclovir (Valcyte)	See Ganciclovir		
Vancomycin	Aminoglycosides	↑ frequency of nephrotoxicity	++
Zalcitabine (ddC) (HIVID)	Valproic acid, pentamidine (IV), alcohol, lamivudine	↑ pancreatitis risk	+
	Cisplatin, INH, metronidazole, vincristine, nitrofurantoin, d4T, dapsone	↑ risk of peripheral neuropathy	+
Zidovudine (ZDV) (Retrovir)	Atovaquone, fluconazole, methadone	↑ levels of A	+
	Clarithromycin	↓ levels of A	±
	Indomethacin	↑ levels of ZDV toxic metabolite	+
	Nelfinavir	↓ levels of A	++
	Probenecid, TMP/SMX	↑ levels of A	+
	Rifampin/rifabutin	↓ levels of A	++
	Stavudine	**Interference—DO NOT COMBINE!**	++
	Valproic Acid	↑ levels of A	++

TABLE 16B: DRUG-DRUG INTERACTIONS BETWEEN NON-NUCLEOSIDE REVERSE TRANSCRIPTASE INHIBITORS (NNRTIs), PROTEASE INHIBITORS, CCR-5 ANTAGONIST.
(Adapted from Guidelines for the Use of Antiretroviral Agents in HIV-Infected Adults & Adolescents; see www.aidsinfo.nih.gov.)
For multiple drug-drug interactions, see http://www.drugs.com/drug_interactions.html

NAME (Abbreviation, Trade Name)	Atazanavir (ATV, Reyataz)	Darunavir (DRV, Prezista)	Fosamprenavir (FOS-APV, Lexiva)	Indinavir (IDV, Crixivan)	Lopinavir/Ritonavir (LP/R, Kaletra)	Nelfinavir (NFV, Viracept)	Saquinavir (SQV, Invirase)	Tipranavir (TPV)
Delavirdine (DLV, Rescriptor)	No data		**Co-administration not recommended**	IDV levels ↑ 40%. Dose: IDV 600 mg q8h; DLV standard	Expect LP levels to ↑. No dose data	NFV levels ↑ 2X. DLV levels ↓ 50%. Dose: No data	SQV levels ↑ 5X. Dose: SQV 800 mg q8h; DLV standard	No data
Efavirenz (EFV, Sustiva)	ATV AUC ↓ 74%. Dose: EFV standard. ATA/RTV 300/100 mg q24h with food	Standard doses of both drugs	FOS-APV levels ↓. Dose: EFV standard; FOS-APV 1400 mg + RTV 300 mg q24h or 700 mg FOS-APV + 100 mg RTV q12h	Levels: IDV ↓ 31%. Dose: IDV 1000 mg q8h. EFV standard	Level of LP ↓ 40%. Dose: LP/R 533/133 mg q12h, EFV standard	Standard doses	Level: SQV ↓ 62%. Dose: SQV 400 mg + RTV 400 mg q12h	No dose change necessary
Etravirine (ETR, Intelence)	↑ ATV & ↑ ETR levels.	Standard doses of both drugs	↑ levels of FOS-APV.	↓ level of IDV	↑ levels of ETR, **↓ levels of LP/R.**	↑ levels of NFV.	↓ ETR levels 33%; SQV/R no change. Standard dose of both drugs.	↓ levels of ETR, ↑ levels of TPV & RTV. **Avoid combination.**
Nevirapine (NVP, Viramune)	Avoid combination. ATZ increases NVP concentrations > 25%; NVP decreases ATZ AUC by 42%	Standard doses of both drugs	Use with caution. NVP AUC increased 14% (700/100 Fos/rit); NVP AUC inc 29% (Fos 1400 mg bid)	IDV levels ↓ 28%. Dose: IDV 1000 mg q8h or combine with RTV. NVP standard	LP levels ↓ 53%. Dose: LP/R 533/133 mg q12h; NVP standard	Standard doses	Dose: SQV + RTV 400/400 mg, both q12h	Standard doses

TABLE 17: ANTIMICROBICS IN PREGNANCY

Partial list with emphasis on anti-retrovirals and drugs used for opportunistic infections. For more complete list, see *Table 8, The Sanford Guide to Antimicrobial Therapy.*

Drug	FDA Pregnancy Categories*	Placental Transfer (%)	Breastfeeding	Adverse Effects: Fetus, Mother
Antibacterial Agents				
Clindamycin	B	6–46	OK	None
Fluoroquinolones	C	80–90	No	Potential arthropathy
Linezolid	C	ND	ND	
Macrolides:				
Azithromycin	B	ND	ND	None
Clarithromycin	C	ND	OK	Fetal toxicity in primates
Erythromycin	B	5–20	OK	None
Metronidazole	B	+	No	None: do not use in 1st trimester
Antifungal Agents:				
Amphotericin B	B	+	OK	None
Echinocandins:				
Anidulafungin	C			
Caspofungin:	C			
Micafungin	C			
Fluconazole, itraconazole	C	ND	ND	NHS
Flucytosine	C			
Posaconazole	C	ND	ND	
Voriconazole	D			**Risk of birth defects**
Antiparasitic Agents:				
Nitazoxanide	B	ND	ND	ND
Pentamidine	C	+	No	NHS
Pyrimethamine	C	+	No	None: do not use in 1st trimester
Sulfonamides	C	70–90	No	Potential kernicterus & hem-G6PD
Trimethoprim	C	30–100	OK	None
Antimycobacterial Agents:				
Dapsone	C	+	OK	Hem-G6PD
Ethambutol	ND	30	OK	None
Isoniazid	C	100	OK	None
Pyrazinamide	C	ND	OK	None
Rifabutin	B	ND	ND	–
Rifampin	C	33	OK	Postnatal bleeding in infant
Streptomycin	C	10–40	OK	Ototoxicity (16% deafness)
Thalidomide	**X**	Presumably	ND	**Major risk birth defects**
Antiviral Agents (Non- HIV Drugs):				
Acyclovir, valacyclovir	B	70	OK ?	None. No data with vala—administer with caution to breast feeding mother
Adefovir	C	ND	No	Not recommended in pregnancy
Cidofovir	C	ND	No	Not recommended in pregnancy
Entecavir	C	ND	ND	
Famcyclovir	B	ND	ND	
Ganciclovir, valganciclovir	C	No	No	Carcinogenic in animals, NHS
Interferons	C	ND	ND	
Ribavirin	**X**	ND	No	**Major risk of birth defects**
Antiretroviral Drugs:				
Nucleoside and nucleotide analogue reverse transcriptase inhibitors (NRTIs):				
Abacavir	C	> 80	No	Teratogen in rats at 35x human exposure
Didanosine	B	50	No	No evidence of teratogenicity
Emtricitabine	B	ND	No	No evidence of teratogenicity
Lamivudine	C	100	No	No evidence of teratogenicity
Stavudine	C	76	No	Tumors in rodents
Tenofovir	B	ND	No	
Zalcitabine	C	30-50	No	Tumors in rodents
Zidovudine	C	85	No	Tumors in rodents
Non-nucleoside reverse transcriptase inhibitors (NNRTIs):				
Delavirdine	C	ND	No	Teratogenic in rats; rodent tumors
Efavirenz	D	ND	No	**High risk of birth defects**
Etravirine	B	ND	No	
Nevirapine	C	100	No	Tumors in rodents
Rilpivirine	B	ND	No	No evidence of teratogenicity

TABLE 17 (2)

Drug	FDA Pregnancy Categories*	Placental Transfer (%)	Breastfeeding	Adverse Effects: Fetus, Mother
Protease Inhibitors (PIs):				
Fosamprenavir	C	ND	No	Tumors in rodents
Atazanavir	B	ND	No	Tumors in female mice
Darunavir	B	ND	No	Negative
Etravirine	B	ND	No	
Indinavir/	C	ND	No	Tumors in rodents
Lopinavir/ritonavir	C	ND	No	Tumors in rodents
Nelfinavir	B	ND	No	Tumors in rodents
Ritonavir	B	15-100	No	Tumors in rodents
Saquinavir	B	Minimal	No	No evidence of teratogenicity
Tipranavir	C	No		No evidence of teratogenicity
Fusion Inhibitors:				
Enfuvirtide	B	ND	No	No evidence of teratogenicity
Chemokine Receptor Antagonist:				
Maraviroc	B	ND	No	
Integrase Inhibitor:				
Dolutegravir	B	ND	No	
Raltegravir	C	ND	No	
Combinations:				
Stribild	B			

* **FDA Pregnancy Risk Categories:**

  A = Adequate studies in pregnant women, no risk

  B = Animal reproduction studies, no fetal risk; no controlled studies in pregnant women

  C = Animal reproduction studies have shown fetal adverse effect; no controlled studies in humans; potential benefit may warrant use despite potential risk

  D = Evidence of human fetal risk; potential benefit may warrant use despite potential risk

  X = Animal and human studies demonstrate fetal abnormalities; risks in pregnant women clearly exceed potential benefits

TABLE 18: SPECTRUM & TREATMENT OF HIV/AIDS-ASSOCIATED MALIGNANCIES
For current statistics, see *J Natl Cancer Inst* 163:753, 2011; *CID* 57:756, 2013; *JAMA* 305:1450, 2011.

I. **Spectrum of associated malignancies: AIDS-defining neoplasms**
  A. **Kaposi's sarcoma** & other KSHV/HHV8 related neoplasms:
    1. Primary body cavity lymphoma (primary effusion lymphoma)
    2. Multicentric Castleman disease
  B. **HIV-associated lymphoma**
    1. Primary CNS lymphoma (EBV)
    2. Non-Hodgkin's lymphoma (EBV)
    3. Body cavity lymphoma; primary effusion lymphoma (HHV8/EBV)
    4. Plasmablastic lymphoma of the oral cavity
  C. **Cervical carcinoma (human papillomavirus)**
  D. **Other neoplasms with increased incidence in AIDS patients**
    1. Anogenital neoplasia & squamous cell carcinoma of the anus (human papillomavirus)
    2. Basal cell carcinoma of the skin
    3. Hodgkin's disease
    4. Seminoma
    5. Pediatric leiomyosarcoma

II. **Kaposi's sarcoma (KS)—Epidemiology, pathophysiology & treatment**
  A. **Etiology & pathogenesis**
    1. Human herpesvirus type 8 (HHV8); also called Kaposi's sarcoma-associated herpesvirus (KSHV)
    2. HHV8/KSHV
      a. Viral DNA found in all KS tumors
      b. Infection precedes KS
      c. Seropositivity rate predicts KS rate
      d. Virus latent in most cells; lytic in <5% of cells
      e. Targets spindle cells
  B. **Diagnosis**
    1. Clinical appearance & then biopsy
    2. HHV8/KSHV serology; can now quantitate HHV8 in plasma by PCR
  C. **Treatment**
    1. **Immune reconstitution** (improvement) with effective antiretroviral therapy of HIV infection leads to:
      a. Reports of clearance of HHV8 from circulating cells; 60–80% response rate
      b. Protease inhibitors have anti-tumor activity in mice & patients: *Nature Med* 8:225, 2002
    2. **Suggest oncology consultation for best local and systemic therapy.**

III. **Primary body cavity lymphoma; primary effusion lymphoma**
  A. Etiology: HHV8/KSHV; some cells also positive for EBV
  B. Diagnosis: Biopsy of tumor masses in pleural space, pericardial space, intraabdominal cavity
  C. Treatment: Suggest oncology consult
  D. Concomitant ART prolongs survival *(CID 47:410, 418, 1209, 2008)*

IV. **Multicentric Castleman disease**
  A. Rare lymphoproliferative disorder
  B. Etiology: HHV8/KSHV
  C. Clinical: Fever, lymphadenopathy, splenomegaly
  D. Treatment: Very effective—Vinblastine or etoposide or rituximab

V. **HIV-associated lymphoma**
  A. **General**
    1. Compared to immunocompetent pts, present in advanced stage; median survival only 6 months
    2. HIV-associated non-Hodgkin's lymphomas virtually all of B-cell origin
    3. Viral association
      a. Systemic lymphomas—no viral association
      b. CNS lymphoma—EBV DNA present in 100% but predictive value low *(CID 38:1629, 2004)*
      c. Body-cavity lymphomas—HHV8 genome present in virtually all
    4. Prognosis improving coincident with effective antiretroviral therapy
  B. **Primary CNS lymphoma**
    1. Usually in patients with very low CD4 counts
    2. Detection of EBV DNA by PCR in CSF in >90% pts but predictive value low *(CID 38:1629, 2004)*
    3. Treatment
      a. Whole brain irradiation; prolongs survival 1–3 months; longer survival with concomitant ART
      b. Responses to combination of ZDV, ganciclovir, & IL-2 in a few patients *(CID 34:1660, 2002)*
  C. **Non-Hodgkin's lymphoma**
    1. **Continuous infusion EPOCH** (etoposide, prednisone, vincristine, cyclophosphamide, doxorubicin) leads to 92% probability of remission at 53 months *(Blood 101:4853, 2003)*. **No ART** during chemo—controversial

VI. **Cervical carcinoma**
  A. Epidemiology: More frequent, more severe in HIV patients
  B. Etiology: Human papilloma virus
  C. **Recommendations**
    1. Pap smears x 2 in year one & then annually if normal initially; every 3 yrs if CD4 >500/mm^3
    2. More frequent Pap smears if:
      a. Previous abnormal Pap smear
      b. History of papilloma (wart) virus infection
      c. Post-treatment for cervical intraepithelial neoplasia
      d. Symptomatic AIDS or CD4 count <200/mm^3
    3. If Pap smear abnormal, refer for colposcopy &/or biopsy
    4. If CD4 count >200 and under age 26, suggest human papilloma virus vaccine.

VII. **Anal neoplasia.** Prevalence of risk factors, *see NEJM 365:1576, 2011*
  A. Epidemiology
    1. HIV-infected immunodeficient patients at increased risk of human papillomavirus (HPV)-related anal neoplasia: 47% in one series of pts with anal warts *(CID 51:107, 2010)*
    2. ART may also slow progression *(CID 52:1174, 2011)*
  B. Recommendations for HIV-infected pts with history of anal intercourse
    1. Anal Pap smear
    2. Routine anoscopy with biopsy as indicated
    3. Wide surgical resection for established neoplasia

TABLE 19: RECOMMENDATIONS FOR ROUTINE IMMUNIZATION OF HIV+ CHILDREN (ASYMPTOMATIC & SYMPTOMATIC)

[Modified from USPHS/IDSA Guidelines *(MMWR 49:RR-9, Oct. 6, 2000; MMWR 51:32, 2002; AnIM 137, Nov. 5 [Suppl.]:468, 2002; MMWR 55: Q1, 2007); MMWR 60 (RR-2):1-60, 2011]*

Vaccine	Birth	1 mo.	2 mos.	4 mos.	6 mos.	12 mos.	15 mos.	18 mos.	24 mos.	4–6 yrs.	11–12 yrs.	14–16 yrs.
↓ Recommendations for these vaccines are the same as those for immunocompetent children ↓*												
Hepatitis B[1]	Hep B #1											
		Hep B #2			Hep B #3						Hep B	
Diphtheria & Tetanus toxoids, Pertussis[2]			DTaP	DTaP	DTaP		DTap			DTap	Tdap	
Hemophilus influenzae type b[3]			Hib	Hib	Hib	Hib					Hib	
Inactivated Polio[4]			IPV	IPV	IPV					IPV	IPV	
Hepatitis A[5]						Hep A series				Hep A series		
Meningo-coccal[10]									MPSV4	MPSV4	MCV4	MCV4
Human papilloma virus (HPV)[11]											HPV 3 doses	
↓ Recommendations for these vaccines differ from those for immunocompetent children ↓												
Pneumo-coccus[6]			PCV	PCV	PCV	PCV			PPV 23	PPV23 (age 5–7 yrs)		
Measles, Mumps, Rubella[7]	Do not give to severely immunosuppressed (Category 3) children				MMR					MMR	MMR	
Varicella[8]	Give only to asymptomatic non-immunosuppressed (Category 1) children. Contraindicated in all other HIV-infected children			Var	Var	Var	Var		Var			
Influenza[9]	A dose is recommended every year											

* For detailed recommendations for immunocompetent children see *MMWR 57:Q1-4, 2008.*

☐ Range of recommended ages for vaccination

▨ Vaccines to be given if previously recommended doses were missed or were given earlier than the recommended minimum age

This schedule indicates the recommended ages for routine administration of licensed childhood vaccines as of Jan. 1, 2006, for children aged birth–18 yrs. Additional vaccines might be licensed & recommended during the year. Licensed combination vaccines might be used whenever any components of the combination are indicated & the vaccine's other components are not contraindicated. Providers should consult the manufacturer's package inserts for detailed recommendations.

[1] **Hepatitis B vaccine (HepB).** *AT BIRTH:* All newborns should receive monovalent HepB soon after birth & before hospital discharge. **Infants born to mothers who are hepatitis B surface antigen (HBsAg)-positive** should receive HepB & 0.5 mL of hepatitis B immune globulin (HBIG) within 12 hrs of birth. **Infants born to mothers whose HBsAg status is unknown** should receive HepB within 12 hrs of birth. The mother should have blood drawn as soon as possible to determine her HBsAg status; if HBsAg-positive, the infant should receive HBIG as soon as possible (no later than age 1 wk). **For infants born to HBsAg-negative mothers,** the birth dose can be delayed in rare circumstances but only if a physician's order to withhold the vaccine & a copy of the mother's original HBsAg-negative laboratory report are documented in the infant's medical record. *FOLLOWING THE BIRTH DOSE:* The HepB series should be completed with either monovalent HepB or a combination vaccine containing HepB. The second dose should be administered at age 1–2 mos. The final dose should be administered at age ≥24 wks. Administering four doses of HepB is permissible (e.g., when combination vaccines are administered after the birth dose); however, if monovalent HepB is used, a dose at age 4 mos is not needed. **Infants born to HBsAg-positive mothers** should be tested for HBsAg & antibody to HBsAg after completion of the HepB series at age 9–18 mos (generally at the next well-child visit after completion of the vaccine series).

[2] **Diphtheria & tetanus toxoids & acellular pertussis vaccine (DTaP).** The fourth dose of DTaP may be administered as early as age 12 mos, provided 6 mos have elapsed since the third dose & the child is unlikely to return at age 15–18 mos. The final dose in the series should be administered at age ≥4 yrs. **Tetanus toxoid, reduced diphtheria toxoid, & acellular pertussis vaccine (Tdap adolescent preparation)** is recommended at age 11–12 yrs for those who have completed the recommended childhood DTP/DTaP vaccination series & have not received a tetanus & diphtheria toxoids (Td) booster dose. Adolescents aged 13–18 yrs who missed the age 11–12 yrs Td/Tdap booster dose should also receive a single dose of Tdap if they have completed the recommended childhood DTP/DTaP vaccination series. **Subsequent Td** boosters are recommended every 10 yrs.

TABLE 19 (2)

[3] **Three Hemophilus influenzae type b (Hib) conjugate vaccines** are licensed for infant use. If Hib conjugate vaccine (polyribosylribitol phosphate-meningococcal outer membrane protein [PRP-OMP]) (PedvaxHIB® or ComVax™ [Merck & Company, Inc., Whitehouse Station, NJ]) is administered at ages 2 & 4 mos, a dose at age 6 mos is not required. Because clinical studies among infants have demonstrated that using certain combination products might induce a lower immune response to the Hib vaccine component, DTaP/Hib combination products should not be used for primary immunization among infants at ages 2, 4, or 6 mos, unless approved by the FDA for these ages.

[4] An **all-inactivated poliovirus vaccine (IPV)** schedule is recommended for routine childhood polio vaccination in the U.S. All children should receive 4 doses of IPV at ages 2 mos, age 4 mos, ages 6–18 mos, & ages 4–6 yrs. Oral polio-virus vaccine should not be administered to HIV-infected persons or their household contacts.

[5] **Hepatitis A vaccine** (Hep A). HepA is recommended for all children at age 1 yr (i.e., 12–23 mos). The 2 doses in the series should be administered at least 6 mos apart. States, counties, & communities with existing HepA vaccination programs for children aged 2–18 yrs. are encouraged to maintain these programs. In these areas, new efforts focused on routine vaccination of children age 1 yr should enhance, not replace, ongoing programs directed at a broader population of children. HepA is also recommended for certain high-risk groups (see MMWR 1999;48 [No. RR-12]).

[6] **Heptavalent pneumococcal conjugate vaccine (PCV)** is recommended for all HIV-infected children aged 2–59 mos. Children aged ≥2 yrs. should also receive the **23-valent pneumococcal polysaccharide vaccine (PPV23);** a single revaccination with the 23-valent vaccine should be offered to children after 3–5 yrs. Refer to the Advisory Committee on Immunization Practices recommendations (see CDC. Preventing pneumococcal disease among infants & young children: recommendations of the Advisory Committee on Immunization Practices [ACIP], MMWR 49(RR-9):1–38, 2000) for dosing intervals for children starting the vaccination schedule after age 2 mos.

[7] **Measles, mumps, & rubella (MMR)** should not be administered to severely immunocompromised (Category 3) children. HIV-infected children without severe immunosuppression would routinely receive their 1st dose of MMR as soon as possible after reaching their 1st birthdays. Consideration should be given to administering the 2nd dose of MMR at 1 mo (i.e., a minimum of 28 days) after the 1st dose rather than waiting until school entry.

[8] **Varicella zoster virus vaccine** should be administered only to asymptomatic, non-immunosuppressed children. Eligible children should receive 2 doses of vaccine with a ≥3 mo interval between doses. The 1st dose can be administered at age 12 mos.

[9] **Inactivated split influenza virus vaccine** should be administered to all HIV-infected children aged ≥6 mos each year. For children aged 6 mos–<9 yrs who are receiving influenza vaccine for the first time, 2 doses administered 1 mo apart are recommended. For specific recommendations, see CDC. Prevention & control of influenza: recommendations of the Advisory Committee on Immunization Practices (ACIP), MMWR 51(RR-4):1–32, 2002.

[10] **Meningococcal vaccine (MCV4).** Meningococcal conjugate vaccine (MCV4) should be administered to all children at age 11–12 yrs as well as to unvaccinated adolescents at high school entry (age 15 yrs). Other adolescents who wish to decrease their risk for meningococcal disease may also be vaccinated. All college freshmen living in dormitories should also be vaccinated, preferably with MCV4, although **meningococcal polysaccharide vaccine (MPSV4)** is an acceptable alternative. Vaccination against invasive meningococcal disease is recommended for children & adolescents aged ≥2-10 yrs with terminal complement deficiencies or anatomic or functional asplenia & for certain other high risk groups (see MMWR 2005;54[No. RR-7]); use MPSV4 for children aged 2–10 yrs & MCV4 for older children, although MPSV4 is an acceptable alternative.

[11] **Human papillomavirus vaccine (HPV).** Minimum age 9 years. Administer the first dose of the HPV vaccine to females at age 11-12 years. Administer second dose 2 months after the first dose and the third dose 6 months after the first dose. Administer HPV vaccine series to females 13-18 years if not previously vaccinated.

For further information, see www.cdc.gov.

TABLE 20: IMMUNIZATION OF HIV+ ADULTS (ASYMPTOMATIC & SYMPTOMATIC)

General Principles/Guidelines:

- In HIV+ individuals, there are activated T-cells (CD25+) & quiescent T-cells (CD25-). Only activated T-cells produce virus & spread infection. In HIV+ adults, significant (2-36 fold) transient (≤6 wks) ↑ in plasma viral RNA after pneumo-coccal, influenza & tetanus immunization (NEJM 334:1222, 1996). A similar phenomenon occurs with acute infections, i.e., influenza. At present, there are no data suggesting that this is clinically relevant (AnIM 131:430, 1999; CID 28:548, 1999). Concurrently, antibody responses are ↓ in HIV+ individuals. Our recommendations are presented in the following table.

- **Administration of live attenuated vaccines is contraindicated in individuals with advanced HIV infection (AIDS) (MMR is an exception).**

- Immunization (when indicated) with killed whole cell vaccines &/or purified antigens should be done as soon as reasonable after HIV infection diagnosed, before CD4 cells ↓ further (JID 171:1217, 1995).

- Extended primary series &/or more frequent boosters often indicated.

- When specifically indicated, immune globulin (IG) & specific immune globulins can be administered.

- For general reference on licensed vaccine use in immunocompromised hosts, see Clin Microbiol Rev 11:1, 1998.

TABLE 20 (2)

RECOMMENDATIONS FOR ROUTINE IMMUNIZATION OF HIV+ ADULTS (United States)

*(From Update on Adult Immunization, Centers for Disease Control, MMWR 51:904, 2002; MMWR 54:Q1, 2006;
MMWR 55:Q1, 2006; Med Lett 9:75, 2011; AIM 156:214, 2012)*

VACCINE/TOXOID	STAGE OF HIV INFECTION		BOOSTER DOSE
	ASYMPTOMATIC HIV+*	SYMPTOMATIC (AIDS)*	
Td (tetanus/diphtheria), Tdap (tetanus/diphtheria/ pertussis)	Yes	Yes	10 yrs
Pneumococcal	Yes	Yes	6 yrs
Influenza	Yes	Yes	Annual
Hepatitis A	Yes	Yes	None
HBV (Hepatitis B)	(Yes)**	(Yes)**	None
eIPV (polio)	(Yes)**	(Yes)**	(None)
MMR (Measles, mumps, rubella)	Yes	(Yes)**	**
Meningococcal	Yes**	Yes**	None
HPV (Human papillomavirus)	Yes	Yes	3 doses total

Abbreviations: Td = tetanus & diphtheria toxoids, adsorbed (for adult use); **MMR** = measles, mumps & rubella vaccine; **HbCV** = Haemophilus influenzae type b conjugate vaccine; **Pneumococcal** = pneumococcal polysaccharide (23 component) vaccine; **HBV** = Hepatitis B vaccine; **eIPV** = enhanced-potency inactivated polio vaccine; **IDU** = injection drug user.
* Asymptomatic-CDC category A1, A2; Symptomatic-CDC A3, B1-3, C1-3
** *See Comments;* + = benefit > risk, 0 = benefit probably < risk. For further information, *see www.cdc.gov.*

COMMENTS ON "ROUTINE" VACCINES/TOXOIDS*

VACCINE/TOXOID	COMMENTS
Td	"Injection" drug users at ↑ risk of tetanus
HbCV	Is of unproven benefit & immune responses ↓; although the risk of H. influenzae type b disease is ↑ & adverse reactions are minimal, it is no longer recommended.
Pneumococcal	Risk of bacteremia is 9.4/1000/yr [as high as 9.4/1000/yr (*J Inf Dis* 162:1012, 1990)]. Revaccination 6 yrs after 1st dose is recommended. Benefit appears > risk. 7-valent pneumococcal conjugate vaccine protects HIV-infected adults from recurrent pneumococcal infection caused by vaccine serotype 6A (*NEJM* 362:812, 2010).
Hepatitis A	In the past several years hep A has ↑ in frequency in homosexual men in the U.S., Canada & Australia (*MMWR* 45:155, 1992). Outbreaks also reported in injection drug users (IDU) (*Am J Pub Health* 79:463, 1989). <10% U.S.-born young adults have antibody (*Mil Med* 157:579, 1992). 2 hep A vaccines, inactivated, are licensed in U.S. FDA-approved indications include: persons engaged in high-risk sexual activity (homosexually active men), IDU (*MMWR* 47:708, 1998; *MMWR* 48:RR-12, 1999).
Hepatitis B	If lifestyle or occupation was risk factor for HIV it is also a risk factor for hepatitis B. Series of 3 IM injections in deltoid, using 12-in needle (not into the buttocks), should be given. Test for antibody to HBs Ag 1-6 months after completing series. If anti-HBs is <10 milli-international units, revaccinate with 1 or more doses.
Influenza	Annual immunization with the current vaccine is recommended regardless of age. Benefit appears > risk (*AnIM* 131:430, 1999). Poor immune response in pts with CD4 count <200. Some recommend use of amantadine, rimantadine or neuraminidase inhibitors instead of immunization in this group (*CID* 28:548, 1999). Avoid live attenuated vaccine.
eIPV (enhanced-potency inactivated polio vaccine)	In adults ≥18 yrs, use only if specifically indicated: travel to developing countries (not Central or South America), prior to (~8 wks, time for initial 2 doses) household exposure to individuals given oral polio vaccine.
OPV (oral polio vaccine)	Contraindicated
Specific immunoglobulins: Hepatitis B (HBIG), human rabies (HRIG), tetanus (TIG), vaccinia (VIG), varicella zoster (VZIG)	Can be used for same indications, same dosage as in non-HIV infected individuals
MMR	Withhold MMR or other measles-containing vaccines from HIV-infected persons with severe immunosuppression (CD4 + T lymphocyte <200).
Meningococcal	*Medical indications:* adults with anatomic or functional asplenia or terminal complement component deficiencies. *Other indications:* 1styr college students living in dormitories; microbiologists who are routinely exposed to isolates of *Neisseria meningitidis;* military recruits; & persons who travel to or reside in countries in which meningococcal disease is hyperendemic or epidemic (e.g., the "meningitis belt" of sub-Saharan Africa during the dry season [Dec–June]), particularly if contact with local populations will be prolonged. Vaccination required by the government of Saudi Arabia for all travelers to Mecca during the annual Hajj. Meningococcal conjugate vaccine is preferred for adults meeting any of the above indications who are aged ≤55 yrs, although meningococcal polysaccharide vaccine MPSV4) is an acceptable alternative. Revaccination after 5 yrs might be indicated for adults (previously vaccinated with MPSV4 who remain at high risk for infection (e.g., persons residing in areas in which disease is epidemic). *See also Table 21B.*
Varicella zoster	Contraindicated in immunocompromised HIV+ patients: live virus vaccine.
Vaccinia (smallpox)	Contraindicated: live virus vaccine
Rotavirus	Contraindicated: live virus vaccine

* For further details, see *Topics in HIV Medicine* 14:154, 2007; *MMWR* 57:Q1, 2008; *MMWR* 57:53, 2009; *Med Lett* 9:75, 2011.

**TABLE 21A: MEASURES TO BE TAKEN BY PHYSICIANS IN PREPARING HIV+ PATIENTS
& INDIVIDUALS LIKELY TO HAVE "RISKY" BEHAVIOR FOR OVERSEAS TRAVEL*[1]**

The likelihood of developing an illness during a 3-wk vacation in a tropical area is about 50% (*J Travel Med 6:71, 1999*).

Since illnesses are likely to be more serious &/or become chronic in the HIV+ patient, there is advice to be given & measures to be taken to minimize risks. These include:

- If the traveler is likely to engage in risky behavior during travel, ascertain the HIV antibody status before travel, especially if travel is planned to a developing country. Condom use is an absolute requirement. No data exist regarding pre-exposure prophylaxis (PrEP). PrEP not currently recommended.

- If the traveler is known to be HIV+, take account of legal restrictions on travel for persons with HIV infection[2] (e.g., ability to transport ARV medications into the country). If traveler is on a ritonavir based regimen, make sure he/she is taking the newer Meltrex version (tablet) of the drug, not the liquid formulation (capsule), in order to avoid need for refrigeration. Assess the immune status (CD4 cell count) in infected persons.

- Review planned itinerary & activities in light of the patient's immune status & review the added risks for travel, especially to developing or tropical countries. In some instances, it may be prudent to recommend a change in itinerary or activities because of serious risks that cannot be eliminated or reduced.

- Recommend the following measures to reduce exposure to pathogens:
  - Assiduously avoid food & beverages that may be contaminated, especially raw or undercooked shellfish, fish, meat, or eggs; raw, unpeeled fruits & vegetables; tap water & ice; as well as unpasteurized milk & milk products (cheese).
  - Insist on eating only well-cooked foods & on drinking only very hot or bottled beverages.
  - Reduce contact with vectors, for example, by using insect repellent & avoiding outdoor exposure at dusk or other times & places of increased insect activity.
  - Frequent handwashing, ideally with alcohol based hand cleanser gels.

- Urge the patient to obtain prompt evaluation of symptoms of illness & early treatment of infection. Where possible, identify a physician knowledgeable about HIV infection at the destination prior to departure[3]. Arrange for continuation of medical management during travel (for example, prophylaxis for Pneumocystis jiroveci pneumonia).

- Use vaccine & prophylactic therapy as indicated by the planned itinerary & activities. Avoid live vaccines in pts with profound immunodeficiency not on ARV therapy. Assure most recent influenza vaccines have been administered, including H1N1 vaccine (regardless of time of year). Prescribe antimicrobial agents (with or without antimotility drugs) & counsel the patient on their use for early treatment of diarrheal disease.[4]

---

*   *Reproduced with permission from Wilson ME, von Reyn CF, Fineberg HV: Infections in HIV-infected travelers: risks & prevention (Table 2). AnIM 114:582, 1991. USPHS/IDSA Guidelines CID 21(Suppl. 1):520, 1999*

[1]   The most up-to-date source is: Health Information for the International Traveler, 1995. HHS Publication (CDC) No. 93-8280. Available from U.S. Government Printing Office, Washington, DC 20402. *See also www.travmed.com; www.fitfortravel.scot.nhs.uk.*
[2]   Duckett M., Orkin AJ: AIDS-related migration & travel policies & restrictions: a global survey. *AIDS 3: (Suppl. 1) S231-252, 1989.*
[3]   For a list of English-speaking doctors abroad & health information: International Association for Medical Assistance to Travelers (IAMAT), 417 Center St., Lewiston, NY 14092.
[4]   For suggestions regarding a medical kit & advice (for all travelers): Sanford JP: Self-help for the traveler who becomes ill. *Inf Dis Clin NA 6:405, 1992.*

TABLE 21B: IMMUNIZATION OF HIV+ ADULTS TRAVELING TO DEVELOPING COUNTRIES*

VACCINE/TOXOID	STAGE OF HIV INFECTION		COMMENTS
	ASYMPTOMATIC HIV+*	SYMPTOMATIC (AIDS)*	
"Routine" for All Developing Countries			
eIPV	Yes	Yes	See Table 19 & Table 20. OPV contraindicated
Hepatitis A	Yes	Yes	See Table 20 (2).
Typhoid Vi polysaccharide vaccine (Connaught)	Yes	Yes	Boosters recommended q2 yrs. Live attenuated (eg, Ty21a) oral typhoid vaccine contraindicated
Immune globulin (IG)	Yes	Yes	For 2–3 mos travel, 0.02 ml/kg IM single dose
"Special" Depending on Itinerary: Country & Activity			
Cholera (inactivated vaccine)	See Comments	See Comments	Vaccine does not prevent transmission, efficacy ~50%, risk to U.S. travelers very low. WHO does not recommend, but some countries require (check with Health Dept.). If required, have vaccination completed, signed, dated & validated to avoid risk of revaccination & quarantine.
Rabies (pre-exposure) (inactivated vaccine)	Yes, if indicated (Animal handlers, travelers spending 1 mo or more in country where rabies is a constant threat)	Yes, if indicated	Course: Three 1 mL of HDCV or RVA IM on days 0, 7, 28. Test serum for antibodies 2 wks after 3rd dose.
Meningococcal (polysaccharide vaccine) (Menomune) or polysaccharide-protein conjugate (Menactra)	Yes, if traveling to area where meningo-coccal disease is epidemic or endemic (sub Sahara Africa)		Note recent CDC advisory: 5 cases of Guillain-Barré syndrome reported after Menactra vaccination. Causal relationship NOT clear (www.phppo.cdc.gov)
Yellow Fever (live attenuated)	Yes (±); offer choice if potential exposure unavoidable	No (contraindicated)	
Japanese Encephalitis	Yes, if indicated: travel to Asia, in monsoon (summer) months, staying in rural areas		Requires 3 injections: day 0, 7, & 30. An abbreviated schedule at days 0, 7, 14 can be used but less effective.
Plague (inactivated)	Yes, if indicated: to areas of endemic plague, esp. if staying in rural areas, not in tourist hotels		
BCG (Bacillus Calmette-Guerin) vaccine	No	No	Live attenuated vaccine.

* All travelers should have current routine immunizations, *Table 20. See MMWR: January 15, 2010 / Vol. 59 / No. 1*
Asymptomatic-CDC category A1, A2; Symptomatic-CDC A3, B1-3, C1-3 *(Table 4A).*
For further information, *see www.travmed.com; www.fitfortravel.scot.nhs.uk.*

TABLE 22: STIMULATING RBCs, WBCs & PLATELETS IN HIV PATIENTS*

DRUG NAME, GENERIC (TRADE) COST	COMMENTS ON USE, ADVERSE EFFECTS
Erythropoietin (Epogen, Procrit) **Darbepoetin** (Aranesp, Nesp) = long-acting erythropoietin. **Peginesatide** (Omontys)

Meta-analysis of use in dialysis pts: increased risk of stroke, increased BP, vascular access thrombosis *(An Int Med 153:23, 2010).* | **FDA approved for Rx of anemia in HIV. FDA advisory warning:** ↑ risk of death, thromboembolic, and cardiovascular events. Monitor hemoglobin dose to maintain the hemoglobin level of ≤ 11 gm/dL. Antibody to erythropoietin can lead to red cell aplasia *(AJG 100:1415, 2005).* **Erythropoietin Dose:** 40,000–60,000 units subQ once weekly equal efficacy as 3x/wk. rx. *(AIDS Res Human Retroviruses 20:1037, 2004).* **Dose of darbepoetin:** 0.45 mcg/kg IV or subQ **q wk.** **Peginesatide Dose:** 0.04 mg/kg IV or sc once per month. |
Granulocyte-CSF or G-CSF, Filgrastim (Neupogen), Pegfilgrastim (Neulasta), **Granulocyte-monocyte CSF or GM-CSF**, Sargramostim (Leukine).	**G-CSF:** Standard dose 5 mcg/kg/day subQ; lower doses may work in HIV pts, i.e., 1 mcg/kg/day subQ until ANC >1000 cells/dl, then 1–2x/wk. No effect on HIV replication. Pegylated G-CSF—pegfilgrastim: 6 mg subQ once per chemotherapy cycle. **GM-CSF:** Dose 5 mcg/kg/day subQ → ↑ PMNs. Trend toward ↑ CD4 and slightly lower VL. Adverse effects: fever, myalgia, fatigue, malaise, headache, bone pain.
Intravenous immune serum globulin (IVIG) (Gamimune N, Gammar, & others). General dosage: (1) Adults: 200–400 mg/kg q21 days; (2) Children: 400 mg/kg/month	Few indications in the era of ART. For immune thrombocytopenia use IVIG if pt bleeding or for immediate invasive procedure; rapid but transient effects. Dose 1-2 gm/kg for 2-5 days. Rho (D) immune globulin more cost effective and may be more effective. *(See Immunol Allergy Clin N Am 28:851, 2008).*
Rho (D) Immune Globulin (Anti-Rh immunoglobulin), intravenous (human) (WinRho). 1500 intl units (equals 300 mcg)	Treatment for **HIV-induced ITP** in non-splenectomized Rh+ pts. Coats Rh+ RBC with antibody; competes with antibody-coated platelets for binding sites on splenic macrophages. Some RBC hemolysis. Effective AIDS pts. Dose: 25–50 mcg/kg x 7 days, then q3 wks. One small study of 9 patients found that rho immune globulin produced higher platelet counts and a longer duration of effect than IVIG *(Am J Hematol 82:335, 2007).*

* **NOTE:** Majority of hematologic problems resolve, or substantively improve, with control of HIV replication. In general, treat HIV first before using drugs outlined above.

TABLE 23: AIDS INFORMATION & REFERRAL SERVICES

- AIDS/HIV Clinical Trials conducted by National Institutes of Health & FDA-approved efficacy trials: 1-800-874-2572

- For a wide variety of AIDS/HIV information, resources, publications, call the National AIDS Clearinghouse: 1-800-458-5231

- To find out about AIDS resources in your area, call the National AIDS Hotline: 1-800-342-2437

- The AIDS/HIV Treatment Directory is published by the American Federation for AIDS Research (AmFAR) & is updated semi-annually; 733 Third Ave., 12th Floor, New York, NY 10017-3204. Telephone: 1-800-392-6327

- The HIV/AIDS Treatment Information Service (Public Health Coordinating Group): 1-800-HIV-0440

- Travel information for patients: www.travmed.com & www.fitfortravel.scot.nhs.uk

- The National Clinicians' Post-Exposure Prophylaxis Hotline, for the latest information on post-exposure protocols and preventative therapy: http://www.nccc.ucsf.edu/about_nccc/pepline/

- The Francis J. Curry National Tuberculosis Center, for information on educational programs and phone consultation (415-502-4700 or 877-390-NOTB(6682)) on prevention and management of tuberculosis: http://www.nationaltbcenter.edu/.

Helpful Websites for Information / Questions About HIV/AIDS:
CDC National Information Prevention Network: www.cdcnpin.org
AmFAR (American Foundation for AIDS Research): www.amfar.org
The HIV/AIDS Treatment Information Service (ATIS): www.hivatis.org
NATAP (National AIDS Treatment Advocacy Project) www.natap.org
San Francisco General Hospital: http://hivinsite.ucsf.edu
Stanford HIV Drug Resistance Database: http://hivdb.stanford.edu
University of Liverpool HIV Drug Interactions Assessment: www.hiv-druginteractions.org
Johns Hopkins AIDS Service: www.hopkins-aids.edu
WHO Treatment Guidelines: www.who.org
HHS HIV Treatment Guidelines: www.aidsinfo.nih.gov

TABLE 24: LIST OF GENERIC & COMMON TRADE NAMES

GENERIC NAME: TRADE NAMES	GENERIC NAME: TRADE NAMES	GENERIC NAME: TRADE NAMES
Abacavir: Ziagen	Efavirenz: Sustiva	Nitazoxanide: Alinia
Abacavir + Lamivudine: Epzicom	Efavirenz/Emtricitabine/Tenofovir: Atripla	Nitrofurantoin: Macrobid, Macrodantin
Abacavir + Lamivudine + Zidovudine: Trizivir	Elvitegravir + Cobicistat +	Nystatin: Mycostatin
Acyclovir: Zovirax	Emtricitabine + Tenofovir: Stribild	Ofloxacin: Floxin
Adefovir: Hepsera	Emtricitabine: Emtriva	Oseltamivir: Tamiflu
Albendazole: Albenza	Emtricitabine + tenofovir: Truvada	Oxacillin: Prostaphlin
Amantadine: Symmetrel	Emtricitabine + tenofovir + rilpivirine: Complera	Palivizumab: Synagis
Amikacin: Amikin	Enfuvirtide (T-20): Fuzeon	Paromomycin: Humatin
Amoxicillin: Amoxil, Polymox	Entecavir: Baraclude	Pentamidine: NebuPent, Pentam 300
Amoxicillin extended release: Moxatag	Ertapenem: Invanz	Piperacillin: Pipracil
Amox./clav.: Augmentin, Augmentin ES-600; Augmentin XR	Etravirine: Intelence	Piperacillin/tazobactam: Zosyn, Tazocin
Amphotericin B: Fungizone	Erythromycin(s): Ilotycin	Piperazine: Antepar
Ampho B-liposomal: AmBisome	*Ethyl succinate:* Pediamycin	Podophyllotoxin: Condylox
Ampho B-lipid complex: Abelcet	*Glucoheptonate:* Erythrocin	Polymyxin B: Poly-Rx
Ampicillin: Omnipen, Polycillin	*Estolate:* Ilosone	Posaconazole: Noxafil
Ampicillin/sulbactam: Unasyn	Erythro/sulfisoxazole: Pediazole	Praziquantel: Biltricide
Artemether-Lumefantrine: Coartem	Ethambutol: Myambutol	Primaquine: Primachine
Atazanavir: Reyataz	Ethionamide: Trecator	Proguanil: Paludrine
Atovaquone: Mepron	Famciclovir: Famvir	Pyrantel pamoate: Antiminth
Atovaquone + proguanil: Malarone	Fidaxomicin: Dificid	Pyrimethamine: Daraprim
Azithromycin: Zithromax	Fluconazole: Diflucan	Pyrimethamine/sulfadoxine: Fansidar
Azithromycin ER: Zmax	Flucytosine: Ancobon	Quinupristin/dalfopristin: Synercid
Aztreonam: Azactam, Cayston	Fosamprenavir: Lexiva	Raltegravir: Isentress
Bedaquiline: Sirturo	Foscarnet: Foscavir	Retapamulin: Altabax
Boceprevir: Victrelis	Fosfomycin: Monurol	Ribavirin: Virazole, Rebetol
Caspofungin: Cancidas	Fusidic acid: Taksta	Rifabutin: Mycobutin
Cefaclor: Ceclor, Ceclor CD	Ganciclovir: Cytovene	Rifampin: Rifadin, Rimactane
Cefadroxil: Duricef	Gatifloxacin: Tequin	Rifapentine: Priftin
Cefazolin: Ancef, Kefzol	Gemifloxacin: Factive	Rifaximin: Xifaxan
Cefdinir: Omnicef	Gentamicin: Garamycin	Rilpivirine: Edurant
Cefditoren pivoxil: Spectracef	Griseofulvin: Fulvicin	Rimantadine: Flumadine
Cefepime: Maxipime	Halofantrine: Halfan	Ritonavir: Norvir
Cefixime[NUS]: Suprax	Idoxuridine: Dendrid, Stoxil	Saquinavir: Invirase
Cefoperazone-sulbactam: Sulperazon[NUS]	INH + RIF: Rifamate	Spectinomycin: Trobicin
Cefotaxime: Claforan	INH + RIF + PZA: Rifater	Stavudine: Zerit
Cefotetan: Cefotan	Interferon alfa: Intron A	Stibogluconate: Pentostam
Cefoxitin: Mefoxin	Interferon, pegylated: PEG-Intron, Pegasys	Silver sulfadiazine: Silvadene
Cefpodoxime proxetil: Vantin	Interferon + ribavirin: Rebetron	Sulfamethoxazole: Gantanol
Cefprozil: Cefzil	Imipenem + cilastatin: Primaxin, Tienam	Sulfasalazine: Azulfidine
Ceftaroline: Teflaro	Imiquimod: Aldara	Sulfisoxazole: Gantrisin
Ceftazidime: Fortaz, Tazicef, Tazidime	Indinavir: Crixivan	Telaprevir: Incivek
Ceftibuten: Cedax	Itraconazole: Sporanox	Telavancin: Vibativ
Ceftizoxime: Cefizox	Iodoquinol: Yodoxin	Telbivudine: Tyzeka
Ceftobiprole: Zeftera	Ivermectin: Stromectol, Sklice	Telithromycin: Ketek
Ceftriaxone: Rocephin	Kanamycin: Kantrex	Temocillin: Negaban, Temopen
Cefuroxime: Zinacef, Ceftin	Ketoconazole: Nizoral	Tenofovir: Viread
Cephalexin: Keflex	Lamivudine: Epivir, Epivir-HBV	Terbinafine: Lamisil
Cephradine: Anspor, Velosef	Lamivudine + abacavir: Epzicom	Thalidomide: Thalomid
Chloroquine: Aralen	Levofloxacin: Levaquin	Thiabendazole: Mintezol
Cidofovir: Vistide	Linezolid: Zyvox	Ticarcillin: Ticar
Ciprofloxacin: Cipro, Cipro XR	Lomefloxacin: Maxaquin	Tigecycline: Tygacil
Clarithromycin: Biaxin, Biaxin XL	Lopinavir/ritonavir: Kaletra	Tinidazole: Tindamax
Clindamycin: Cleocin	Loracarbef: Lorabid	Tipranavir: Aptivus
Clofazimine: Lamprene	Mafenide: Sulfamylon	Tobramycin: Nebcin
Clotrimazole: Lotrimin, Mycelex	Maraviroc: Selzentry	Tretinoin: Retin A
Cloxacillin: Tegopen	Mebendazole: Vermox	Trifluridine: Viroptic
Colistimethate: Coly-Mycin M	Mefloquine: Lariam	Trimethoprim: Primsol
Cycloserine: Seromycin	Meropenem: Merrem	Trimethoprim/sulfamethoxazole: Bactrim, Septra
Daptomycin: Cubicin	Mesalamine: Asacol, Pentasa	Valacyclovir: Valtrex
Darunavir: Prezista	Methenamine: Hiprex, Mandelamine	Valganciclovir: Valcyte
Delavirdine: Rescriptor	Metronidazole: Flagyl	Vancomycin: Vancocin
Dicloxacillin: Dynapen	Micafungin: Mycamine	Voriconazole: Vfend
Didanosine: Videx	Minocycline: Minocin	Zalcitabine: HIVID
Diethylcarbamazine: Hetrazan	Moxifloxacin: Avelox	Zanamivir: Relenza
Diloxanide furoate: Furamide	Mupirocin: Bactroban	Zidovudine (ZDV): Retrovir
Doripenem: Doribax	Nafcillin: Unipen	Zidovudine + 3TC: Combivir
Doxycycline: Vibramycin	Nelfinavir: Viracept	Zidovudine + 3TC + abacavir: Trizivir
	Nevirapine: Viramune	

TABLE 24 (2)

LIST OF COMMON TRADE AND GENERIC NAMES

TRADE NAME: GENERIC NAME	TRADE NAME: GENERIC NAME	TRADE NAME: GENERIC NAME
Abelcet: Ampho B-lipid complex	Hepsera: Adefovir	Rifamate: INH + RIF
Albenza: Albendazole	Herplex: Idoxuridine	Rifater: INH + RIF + PZA
Aldara: Imiquimod	Hiprex: Methenamine hippurate	Rimactane: Rifampin
Alinia: Nitazoxanide	HIVID: Zalcitabine	Rocephin: Ceftriaxone
Altabax: Retapamulin	Humatin: Paromomycin	Selzentry: Maraviroc
AmBisome: Ampho B-liposomal	Ilosone: Erythromycin estolate	Septra: Trimethoprim/sulfa
Amikin: Amikacin	Ilotycin: Erythromycin	Seromycin: Cycloserine
Amoxil: Amoxicillin	Incivek: Telaprevir	Silvadene: Silver sulfadiazine
Ancef: Cefazolin	Intelence: Etravirine	Sirturo: Bedaquiline
Ancobon: Flucytosine	Intron A: Interferon alfa	Sklice: Ivermectin lotion
Anspor: Cephradine	Invanz: Ertapenem	Spectracef: Cefditoren pivoxil
Antepar: Piperazine	Invirase: Saquinavir	Sporanox: Itraconazole
Antiminth: Pyrantel pamoate	Isentress: Raltegravir	Stoxil: Idoxuridine
Aptivus: Tipranavir	Kantrex: Kanamycin	Stribild: Elvitegravir + Cobicistat +
Aralen: Chloroquine	Kaletra: Lopinavir/ritonavir	Emtricitabine + Tenofovir
Asacol: Mesalamine	Keflex: Cephalexin	Stromectol: Ivermectin
Atripla: Efavirenz/emtricitabine/tenofovir	Ketek: Telithromycin	Sulfamylon: Mafenide
Augmentin, Augmentin ES-600	Lamisil: Terbinafine	Sulperazon^NUS: Cefoperazone-
Augmentin XR: Amox./clav.	Lamprene: Clofazimine	sulbactam
Avelox: Moxifloxacin	Lariam: Mefloquine	Suprax: Cefixime^NUS
Azactam: Aztreonam	Levaquin: Levofloxacin	Sustiva: Efavirenz
Azulfidine: Sulfasalazine	Lexiva: Fosamprenavir	Symmetrel: Amantadine
Bactroban: Mupirocin	Lorabid: Loracarbef	Synagis: Palivizumab
Bactrim: Trimethoprim/sulfamethoxazole	Macrodantin, Macrobid: Nitrofurantoin	Synercid: Quinupristin/dalfopristin
Baraclude: Entecavir	Malarone: Atovaquone + proguanil	Taksta: Fusidic acid
Biaxin, Biaxin XL: Clarithromycin	Mandelamine: Methenamine mandel.	Tamiflu: Oseltamivir
Biltricide: Praziquantel	Maxaquin: Lomefloxacin	Tazicef: Ceftazidime
Cancidas: Caspofungin	Maxipime: Cefepime	Teflaro: Ceftaroline
Cayston: Aztreonam (inhaled)	Mefoxin: Cefoxitin	Tegopen: Cloxacillin
Ceclor, Ceclor CD: Cefaclor	Mepron: Atovaquone	Tequin: Gatifloxacin
Cedax: Ceftibuten	Merrem: Meropenem	Thalomid: Thalidomide
Cefizox: Ceftizoxime	Minocin: Minocycline	Ticar: Ticarcillin
Cefotan: Cefotetan	Mintezol: Thiabendazole	Tienam: Imipenem
Ceftin: Cefuroxime axetil	Monocid: Cefonicid	Timentin: Ticarcillin-clavulanic acid
Cefzil: Cefprozil	Monurol: Fosfomycin	Tinactin: Tolnaftate
Cipro, Cipro XR: Ciprofloxacin &	Moxatag: Amoxicillin extended release	Tindamax: Tinidazole
extended release	Myambutol: Ethambutol	Trecator SC: Ethionamide
Claforan: Cefotaxime	Mycamine: Micafungin	Trizivir: Abacavir + ZDV + 3TC
Coartem: Artemether-Lumefantrine	Mycobutin: Rifabutin	Trobicin: Spectinomycin
Coly-Mycin M: Colistimethate	Mycostatin: Nystatin	Truvada: Emtricitabine + tenofovir
Combivir: ZDV + 3TC	Nafcil: Nafcillin	Tygacil: Tigecycline
Complera: Emtricitabine + tenofovir +	Nebcin: Tobramycin	Tyzeka: Telbivudine
rilpivirine	NebuPent: Pentamidine	Unasyn: Ampicillin/sulbactam
Crixivan: Indinavir	Nizoral: Ketoconazole	Unipen: Nafcillin
Cubicin: Daptomycin	Norvir: Ritonavir	Valcyte: Valganciclovir
Cytovene: Ganciclovir	Noxafil: Posaconazole	Valtrex: Valacyclovir
Daraprim: Pyrimethamine	Omnicef: Cefdinir	Vancocin: Vancomycin
Dificid: Fidaxomicin	Omnipen: Ampicillin	Vantin: Cefpodoxime proxetil
Diflucan: Fluconazole	Pediamycin: Erythro. ethyl succinate	Velosef: Cephradine
Doribax: Doripenem	Pediazole: Erythro. ethyl succinate +	Vermox: Mebendazole
Duricef: Cefadroxil	sulfisoxazole	Vfend: Voriconazole
Dynapen: Dicloxacillin	Pegasys, PEG-Intron: Interferon,	Vibativ: Telavancin
Edurant: Rilpivirine	pegylated	Vibramycin: Doxycycline
Emtriva: Emtricitabine	Pentam 300: Pentamidine	Victrelis: Boceprevir
Epivir, Epivir-HBV: Lamivudine	Pentasa: Mesalamine	Videx: Didanosine
Epzicom: Lamivudine + abacavir	Pipracil: Piperacillin	Viracept: Nelfinavir
Factive: Gemifloxacin	Polycillin: Ampicillin	Viramune: Nevirapine
Famvir: Famciclovir	Polymox: Amoxicillin	Virazole: Ribavirin
Fansidar: Pyrimethamine + sulfadoxine	Poly-Rx: Polymyxin B	Viread: Tenofovir
Flagyl: Metronidazole	Prezista: Darunavir	Vistide: Cidofovir
Floxin: Ofloxacin	Priftin: Rifapentine	Xifaxan: Rifaximin
Flumadine: Rimantadine	Primaxin: Imipenem + cilastatin	Yodoxin: Iodoquinol
Foscavir: Foscarnet	Primsol: Trimethoprim	Zerit: Stavudine
Fortaz: Ceftazidime	Prostaphlin: Oxacillin	Zeftera: Ceftobiprole
Fulvicin: Griseofulvin	Rebetol: Ribavirin	Ziagen: Abacavir
Fungizone: Amphotericin B	Rebetron: Interferon + ribavirin	Zinacef: Cefuroxime
Furadantin: Nitrofurantoin	Relenza: Zanamivir	Zithromax: Azithromycin
Fuzeon: Enfuvirtide (T-20)	Rescriptor: Delavirdine	Zmax: Azithromycin ER
Gantanol: Sulfamethoxazole	Retin A: Tretinoin Retrovir:	Zovirax: Acyclovir
Gantrisin: Sulfisoxazole	Zidovudine (ZDV)	Zosyn: Piperacillin/tazobactam
Garamycin: Gentamicin	Reyataz: Atazanavir	Zyvox: Linezolid
Halfan: Halofantrine	Rifadin: Rifampin	

INDEX TO MAJOR ENTRIES